BARRON'S

AP®

ENGLISH LANGUAGE AND COMPOSITION

2ND EDITION

George Ehrenhaft, Ed.D.
Former Chairman, English Department
Mamaroneck High School
Mamaroneck, New York

BARRON'S

All inquiries should be addressed to:
Barron's Educational Series, Inc.
250 Wireless Boulevard
Hauppauge, New York 11788
www.barronseduc.com

ISBN-13: 978-0-7641-3690-0 (book only)
ISBN-10: 0-7641-3690-9 (book only)

ISBN-13: 978-0-7641-9330-9 (book with CD/ROM)
ISBN-10: 0-7641-9330-9 (book with CD/ROM)

Library of Congress Control Number: 2007027182

Library of Congress Cataloging-in-Publication Data
Ehrenhaft, George.
    AP English language and composition / George Ehrenhaft.—2nd ed.
        p. cm.
    Previous ed.: Barron's how to prepare for the AP advanced placement exam, 2004.
    Includes index.
    ISBN-13: 978-0-7641-3690-0 (alk. paper)
    ISBN-10: 0-7641-3690-9 (alk. paper)
    ISBN-13: 978-0-7641-9330-9 (book/CD-ROM package)
    ISBN-10: 0-7641-9330-9 (book/CD-ROM package)
    1. English philology—Examinations—Study guides. 2. Advanced placement programs (Education) I. Barron's Educational Series, Inc. II. Ehrenhaft, George. Barron's how to prepare for the AP advanced placement exam.
III. Title.

PE66.E38 2008
428.0076—dc22   2007027182

PRINTED IN THE UNITED STATES OF AMERICA

9 8 7 6

Contents

Acknowledgments

Grateful acknowledgment is made to the following sources for permission to include their materials in this book.

PAGE 16, F.M. Esfandiary, "The Mystical West Puzzles the Practical East," *New York Times Magazine*, February 6, 1967. © F.M. Esfandiary. Reprinted by permission.

PAGE 19, Brian P. Gill and Steven L. Schlossman, "My Dog Ate My Argument," *Los Angeles Times,* December 11, 2003.

PAGE 20, Tom Loveless, "Do Students Have Too Much Homework?" Brown Center on Education Policy, Brookings Institution, October 1, 2003.

PAGE 21, Etta Kralovec, *The End of Homework*, Beacon Press, Boston, © 2000. Reprinted by permission.

PAGE 22, Linda Sax *et al*, "The American Freshman: National Norms for Fall 2002," Higher Education Research Institute, UCLA, 2002.

PAGE 23, Brian Haley, "What is the Value of Homework?" July 6, 2006. *SearchWarp.com*.

PAGE 24, Gloria Chaika, "Help! Homework Is Wrecking My Home Life," *Education World*, 8 August 2000. © *EducationWorld.com*. Reprinted by permission.

PAGE 35, Joe B. Frantz, "The Frontier Tradition: An Invitation to Violence," *The History of Violence in America*, ed. Hugh Davis Graham and Ted Robert Gurr, Frederick A. Praeger, NY, pp. 127-128.

PAGE 41, M. Scott Momaday, *The Way to Rainy Mountain*, University of New Mexico Press, 1967.

PAGE 44, Richard Wright, *White Man, Listen!*, John Hawkins & Associates, New York, 1957.

PAGE 46, Daniel Goleman, "The Man Without Feelings," *Emotional Intelligence*, Bantam Books, New York, 1995, pp. 50-51.

PAGE 51, Ayn Rand, *For the New Intellectual*, New American Library, 1963. Printed in William J. Brandt, *The Rhetoric of Argumentation*, Bobbs Merrill, 1970.

PAGE 52, Adlai E. Stevenson, *Call to Greatness*, Atheneum, 1962. Printed in William J. Brandt, *The Rhetoric of Argumentation*, Bobbs Merrill, 1970.

PAGE 53, Katherine Hansen, "What Good is a College Education Anyway?" © Quintessential Careers, <*www.quintcareers.com*>. Reprinted with permission.

PAGE 54, Lori Kurtzman, "Remedial Classes Teach Freshmen What They Should Already Know," *The Cincinnati Enquirer*, posted online July 30, 2006.

PAGE 55, "Higher Education Means Lower Mortality Rates," Population Reference Bureau, Washington, D.C., 2005.

PAGE 56, "Creating Passionate Users," an online blog.

PAGE 57, Gregg Toppo and Anthony DeBarros, "Reality Weighs Down Dreams of College," *USA Today*, posted online February 2, 2005.

PAGE 58, Online blog, "Rob," "Declining College Standards," *Say Anything*, posted January 3, 2006.

PAGE 81, Edward Abbey, *Confessions of a Barbarian*, Little, Brown, 1994. Reprinted with permission.

PAGE 93, Richard Maxwell Brown, "Historical Patterns of Violence In America," *The History of Violence in America*, eds. Hugh Davis Graham and Ted Robert Gurr, Frederick A. Praeger, New York, 1969, pp. 66-67.

PAGE 110, Laura Eirmann, DVM, "The Facts About Euthanasia," Cornell University Pet Loss Hotline, *vet.cornell.edu*, November, 2004.

PAGE 194, Julie Hilden, "Does Celebrity Destroy Privacy?" *FindLaw* web site, accessed 6/28/06.

PAGE 195, Wendy McElroy, "Clinton and Privacy," Ludwig Von Mises Institute, Auburn, AL, posted September 14, 1998.

PAGE 196, Vincent M. deGrandpré, "Understanding the Market for Celebrity," Simpson Thacher and Bartlett, LLP, posted 15 September 2001, *<www.stb.com>*.

PAGE 197, "Average Circulation for Top 100 ABC Magazines," Magazine Publishers of America, © 2006.

PAGE 198, GNL, "For Today's Public Figures, Private Lives Really Matter, *www.Buzzle.com.,* . . . .??" Buzzle.Com, Inc., Costa Mesa, CA, November 30, 2004.

PAGE 199, "Invasion of Privacy," *First Amendment Handbook*, The Reporter's Committee for Freedom of the Press, Arlington, Virginia, 1992.

PAGE 217, Excerpt from *West With the Night* by Beryl Markam, © 1942, 1983 by Beryl Markham. Reprinted by permission of Northpoint Press, a division of Farrar, Straus, and Giroux, LLC.

PAGE 220, Henry Allen, "The Corps," *The Washington Post*, March 5, 1972. © *The Washington Post*. Reprinted by permission.

PAGE 224, Edward Said, "Reflections on Exile," *Granta*, 13 (Winter, 1984). © by Edward Said. Reprinted by permission of the Wylie Company.

PAGE 227, Deanna Paoli Gumina, *The Italians of San Francisco, 1850-1930*, Center for Migration Studies, 1978.

PAGE 234, Albert Einstein, *Out of My Later Years*, The Philosophical Library, Inc., 1950.

PAGE 236, "What Benefits Have Come From Medical Research Using Animals?" American Association for Laboratory Animal Science (AALAS), *<www.foundation.aalas.org>*.

PAGE 237, Claire Andre and Manuel Velasquez, "Of Cures and Creatures Great and Small," Issues in Ethics, v.1, No. 3, Spring, 1988, published by Markkula Center for Applied Ethics, Santa Clara University.

PAGE 238, "Numbers of Animals Used in Research in the United Kingdom," Home Office (2004), *Statistics of Scientific Procedures on Living Animals, Great Britain 2003.*

PAGE 239, Stuart Derbyshire, PhD., "Animal Experimentation," speech at Edinburgh Book Festival, 19 August 2002. By permission.

PAGE 240, "The Ethics of Research Involving Animals: A Guide to the Report," Nuffield Council on Bioethics, 25 May 2005. Reprinted by permission.

PAGE 241, Clare Haggarty, "Animals in Scientific Research: The Ethical Argument," National Anti-Vivisection Society, *<www.navs.org>*.

PAGE 260, Arnold Toynbee, *Civilization on Trial,* © 1958 by Oxford University Press, Inc. Used by permission of Oxford University Press.

PAGE 263, Aldous Huxley, *Music at Night and Other Essays,* Harper and Row, © 1931 by Aldous Huxley. Reprinted by permission.

PAGE 266, George Bernard Shaw, *Shaw on Music: A Selection from the Music Criticism of George Bernard Shaw,* 1927, ed. Eric Bentley, Anchor Books, Doubleday. Copyright The Society of Authors, London.

PAGE 269, Barbara W. Tuchman, *The Proud Tower,* MacMillan Company, New York, 1962, pp. 117-118. Reprinted by permission of Russell & Volkening as agents for the author. Copyright © 1966 by Barbara Tuchman. Copyright renewed 1994 by Dr. Lester Tuchman.

PAGE 274, Grayson Barber, "Would National ID Cards Increase Safety and Preserve Civil Liberties?" American Civil Liberties Union of New Jersey, *<www.aclu.org/safeand free>*.

PAGE 275, Alan Dershowitz, "Small Compromises," *Boston Review,* Dec 2002/Jan 2003, *<www.bostonreview.net>*.

PAGE 276, Amitai Etzioni, "You'll Love Those National ID Cards," *Christian Science Monitor,* January 14, 2002.

PAGE 277, "The Americans Oppressed Card," The Cobra's Lair, 2005. *<the cobraslair.com/images/ NATIONAL-ID-CARD-STREAM.gif>*

PAGE 278, Andrew Clement, et al., "National Identification Schemes: FAQ," Openflows Network, Ltd., 11/13/01. *<www.openflows.org>*.

PAGE 279, Jim Fussell, "Group Classification on National ID Cards as a Factor in Genocide and Ethnic Cleansing," published on the web site of Prevent Genocide International.

PAGE 280, Edward P. Gyokeres, "Camp Muckamungus," © by Edward P. Gyokeres, from *Operation Homecoming*, edited by Andrew Carroll. Used by permission of Random House, Inc. Originally published in *The New Yorker*.

PAGE 281, Maxwell Anderson, *Off Broadway*, William Sloane Associates, 1947.

PAGE 281, Susanne K. Langer, *Creation and Expression*, Scribner's, 1957.

PAGE 301, T.S. Eliot, "On Teaching the Appreciation of Poetry," *The Critic* XVIII, 1960, © the estate of T.S. Eliot, Harcourt, Brace, Jovanovich, and Faber and Faber, Ltd.

PAGE 309, *From The Island at the Center of the World: The Epic Story of Dutch Manhattan and the Forgotten Colony That Shaped America*, Russell Shorto, © 2004 by Russell Shorto. Used by permission of Doubleday, a division of Random House, Inc.

PAGE 315, Gary DeMar, "The Pledge of Allegiance Goes to Trial," American Vision Web site, <*www.americanvision.com*>.

PAGE 316, Austin Kline, "Defending 'Under God' in the Pledge of Allegiance," posted on the "About" web site, March 30, 2004, <*www.atheism.about.com*>.

PAGE 317, James Pinkerton, "On the God Issue, Let's Take the Pledge," *Los Angeles Times*, June 28, 2002.

PAGE 318, "Pledge Protection Act, H.R. 2028," Dr. Dave web site, Institute for Local Self-Reliance, <*http.www.newrules.org/*> .

PAGE 319, Jay Sekulow, "Keep the Pledge of Allegiance Intact," American Center for Law and Justice.

PAGE 320, Lindsey Elder, "Keep the Pledge in School," *The Daily Collegian—Online*," posted April 29, 2003.

PAGE 350, Excerpt from pp. 180-182 from *Stiffed: The Betrayal of the American Man*, Susan Faludi, © 1999 by Susan Faludi. Reprinted by permission of Harper Collins Publishers.

PAGE 357, Craig A. Depken, II, "Who Supports Internet Censorship?" *First Monday, Peer Reviewed Journal on the Net*, ,<*www.firstmonday.org*>, March 7, 2006.

PAGE 358, Richard J. Sagall, "Internet Censorship," *Pediatrics for Parents*, May, 1995, posted on *www.Looksmart.com*.

PAGE 359, Donna Rice Hughes, "Sexual Predators Online," posted on *www.protectkids.com*, 2001.

PAGE 360, Elena Kozakewich, "Adolescent Computer Use and Preferences for Leisure Time," posted on *www.students.haverford.edu.*, 2000.

PAGE 361, Wendy Kaminer, "Secret Censors," *Boston Globe*, March 13, 1997, p. 19, © Wendy Kaminer.

PAGE 362, Larry Magid, "Study Outlines Safety Tips for Kids," *San Jose Mercury News*, June 11, 2000.

CD-ROM #1

Frank Lloyd Wright, "*Modern Architecture*," (Kahn Lecture) Princeton University Press, 1931. Reprinted by permission of Princeton University Press.

John Irving, "My Dinner at the White House." Copyright © 1966 by Garp Enterprises, Ltd. Reprinted from *Trying to Save Piggy Snead*, Arcade Publishers, New York, pp. 150-152.

Bill Bryson, *A Short History of Nearly Everything*, Broadway Books, New York, 2003, pp.378-380.

Sarah Josepha Hale, letter to Abraham Lincoln, September 28, 1863, printed in *Women's Letters: America from the Revolutionary War to the Present*, eds. Lisa Grunwald and Stephen J. Adler, Dial Press, New York, 2005, pp. 303-304.

Don Heinzman, "Year-Round School Has Educational Advantages, *Hometown Source.com*, ECM Publishers, Inc.

Duke Helfand, "Year Round Discontent at Hollywood High," *Los Angeles Times*, November 20, 2000, Home Edition, Section A, p.1.

"The Problem," Center for Summer Learning, School of Professional Studies in Business and Education, Johns Hopkins University.

Graeme MacKay, MacKay Editorial Cartoons, *Hamilton Spectator*, Hamilton, Ontario, Canada, August 16, 2001.

Ann McGlynn, "Districts That School Year Round," *The School Administrator*, March 2002.

Christopher Newland, "Academics, the Year-Round Calendar, and the Color of the School Buses," *Offspring Magazine*, June 2000.

CD-ROM #2

Gloria Steinem, "Ruth's Song (Because She Could Not Sing It)," *Family Portraits*, ed. Carolyn Anthony, Doubleday, New York, 1989, pp. 253-254.

Christopher Hitchens, "For Patriot Dreams," *The Best American Essays 2002*, ed. Stephen Jay Gould, Houghton Mifflin, 2002, pp. 137-138. Originally published in *Vanity Fair*, December, 2001.

from *Henry Clay: Statesman for the Union* by Robert V. Remini, © 1991 by Robert V. Remini. Used by permission of W.W. Norton & Company, Inc.

Alonzo Delano, "Life on the Plains and Among the Diggings" in *Gold Rush: A Literary Exploration*, ed. Michael Kowalewski, Heyday Books, Berkeley, CA, pp. 93-94. © 1997 California Council for the Humanities.

"Boober," "A New Etiquette," <*www.mysocialnetwork.net*>, posted October 14, 2006.

Hans Geser, "Towards a Sociological Theory of the Mobile Phone," University of Zurich, May 2004, pp. 7-8.

"Cell Phones," Center on Media and Child Health, Children's Hospital, Boston, <*www.cmch.tv/monitors*>.

Robert Farmer, "Instant Messaging—Collaborator's Tool or Educator's Nightmare?" Mount St. Vincent University, Canada, 2003.

Excerpted from "Virtual Lives" by Anne Belden, an article printed on web site *Parenthood.com.*

Fahmida Y. Rashid, "The Wired Are a Rude Bunch," *Forbes.com,* July 28, 2005.

Introduction

In case you're not sure what the exam is all about, here it is in a nutshell: It's an exam that tests your understanding and appreciation of how writers use words to convey meaning and affect readers. To do that, the test gives you about 55 multiple-choice questions—sometimes more, sometimes fewer—based on a handful of non-fiction prose passages written in a variety of styles and representing a range of historical periods.

You'll also be asked to write three expository essays. One of the essays must analyze the rhetorical strategies used in a passage of nonfiction prose. Another question will ask you write a second analytical essay like the first one, *or* it will give you a short statement or passage with which you must agree, disagree, or qualify in some way.

The third essay, called a "synthesis" essay, requires an argument that supports your point of view on a given issue. To make your case, you must incorporate, or synthesize, material from several different sources that accompany the question.

The exam lasts three hours and fifteen minutes and consists of two sections. The short-answer section takes one hour and counts for 45 percent of the total score. The essay section, lasting two-and-a-quarter hours, comprises 55 percent of your grade.

Section I	Section II
Fifty to sixty multiple-choice questions based on your reading of four or five non-fiction passages about history, science, art, language, and many other topics (One hour)	• An essay that analyzes the style, rhetoric, and use of language in a selected prose passage • A second essay similar to the first one or an essay that argues for or against an opinion expressed in a statement or short passage • A synthesis essay that uses sources to support a point of view on a given issue (Two hours and 15 minutes)

Like all other AP exams, scores are reported on a scale of 1–5. In general, scores are interpreted to mean

5 Extremely well qualified
4 Well qualifed
3 Qualified
2 Possibly qualified
1 Not recommended for AP credit

A high score on this exam demonstrates a proficiency in English at least on a par with students who have successfully completed an introductory college level course in composition or rhetoric. Recognizing this, many colleges and universities may waive the freshman English requirement, give you academic credit for the required course, or permit you to take a more advanced course during your freshman year. Because each college and university has its own policies regarding the awarding of credit for a good score, be sure to check with the admissions office of the institution you hope to attend.

This book will familiarize you with the multiple-choice questions and give you practical help in essay writing. Various sections of the book offer a review of the grammar you need to know, an introduction to principles of rhetoric, practice in analyzing a variety of short passages, and basic information about using written and visual sources as evidence to support your position on a controversial issue. Use this book to prepare for the exam. Read each chapter. Take the practice tests and check your answers. Revel in the correct ones, but let the wrong ones steer you to chapters in the book that you should study.

Remember that preparation for the exam isn't instantaneous. For many students it's a gradual and often painstaking process of study, review, and more study. In other words, give yourself time. Take it slowly. If the exam is months away, it would be ideal for you to set aside, say, 30 minutes a day, to work your way through the pages of this book. Yes, 30 minutes takes a big bite out of a high school student's day, but to get ready for the AP exam, there's no substitute for the steady accumulation of knowledge over a period of time. If time is short between now and the exam, cramming may help you earn a good score, especially if you familiarize yourself with the test instructions and the format of the exam—but frankly, cramming is a less than perfect approach.

Regardless of how you go about preparing for the exam, however, I wish you luck. In May, when test day comes around, I'll be rooting for you.

George Ehrenhaft

A NOTE TO AP ENGLISH TEACHERS

Many AP teachers across the country find this book to be an invaluable resource. Questions and exercises throughout the book stimulate thinking and inspire students to write the kinds of essays required to do well on the AP exam. Some teachers use the book as an instant syllabus for their AP classes because it contains so much of what a high-level course in language and composition might offer, including:

- Reading passages that range from easy to hard
- Numerous exam questions, discussed and analyzed
- Essential rhetorical terms
- Sample student essays (with comments by AP readers)
- Annotated passages
- An analysis of the new AP synthesis essay question
- A full-length self-assessment exam
- Four complete practice exams
- Two additional exams on CD-ROM (*CD-ROM edition only*)
- Full explanations of all answers

As a veteran AP teacher, I'm aware of both the rewards and the hardships you face every day in the classroom. If anything, I hope this book will lighten your load and help you provide the best possible instruction for your students.

Overview of the Test

CHAPTER 1

- A preview of the test
- Types of short-answer questions
- Four ways to read the passages
- When to guess
- Analytical and synthesis essay questions: How they differ
- Using and citing sources
- How essays are scored
- What you can learn from past exams

The exam is basically a reading and writing test containing a number of prose passages to be read and analyzed. Merely understanding the words won't be quite enough. Instead, you must try to extract the full meaning of each text by identifying and explaining the author's composing techniques. To do that you'll need to know something about rhetoric, such as how an author's choice of details contributes to meaning and how form relates to content. You'll need to be acquainted with such concepts as *theme, tone, diction, syntax, allusion, imagery, paradox, irony, satire,* and a variety of other rhetorical devices that you've probably studied in English classes. High scores on the exam come to those who can skillfully dissect passages—students who know how to read passages and understand how their components work together to convey meaning and create an effect on a reader.

A recent addition to the test is the Synthesis Essay. The prompt for this essay will ask you to read several documents about a particular issue and then use material from the documents to write an essay that supports and develops your point of view on the issue. In other words, you will write an argument that draws on source material to prove the validity of your opinion.

STRUCTURE OF THE EXAM

The exam lasts three hours and fifteen minutes. During that time you'll be given both short-answer and essay questions. For the first 60 minutes you will read a handful of relatively short nonfiction passages and be asked roughly 10 multiple-choice questions about each one. During the remaining time you'll write three essays.

Typically, two of the essay questions pertain to the authors' use of rhetorical strategies in passages each about a page long. A third question consists of a statement, or prompt, on an issue of general concern in today's world. With the topic you'll receive five published sources related to the issue, each less than a page long. A sixth source will be an image—a photo, chart, map, cartoon, or other visual presentation also related to the issue. Your task is to write an essay that argues your position on the issue and incorporates at least three of the sources into your discussion.

The exam you take may not follow this precise structure, but any differences will be insignificant. The synthesis essay question, for example, may be given first instead of third.

OUTLINE OF THE EXAM
Total time: 3 hours and 15 minutes

Section I: 1 hour
50–60 multiple-choice questions about several nonfiction prose passages

45 percent of total score

Section II: 2 hours and 15 minutes
Three essays

Essay 1: an argument for or against an idea presented in a short passage incorporating provided published sources
Essay 2: an analysis of a prose passage
Essay 3: an analysis of another prose passage **or** an essay commenting on the validity of an opinion expressed in a statement or short passage

55 percent of total score

MULTIPLE-CHOICE QUESTIONS

Multiple-choice questions can pertain to almost anything that the authors have done to compose the passage. Thus, the list of what you need to know includes the functions of paragraphs and how paragraphs are used in developing ideas. You also must have a sense of sentences: how sentences function in a passage; how sentences of different lengths, structure, and type (simple, compound, complex, compound complex) relate to tone and meaning. You must be aware of the uses of subordination, coordination, periodic and loose sentences, and parenthetical ideas. You may also be asked about word order, tone, diction (word choice), transitions, repetition, parallelism, and use of alliteration, allusion, antithesis, apostrophe, and figurative language, including metaphors, allusions, similes, hyperbole, paradox, and irony. At least one of the passages will include footnotes or a bibliography, and some of the questions will ask you about the meaning, purpose, or effect of these citations.

Neither the passages on the test nor the accompanying questions are presented in order of difficulty. The sequence of questions usually coincides with the progress of each passage.

> **TIP**
>
> Ordinarily, it pays to answer each question as it comes, but if a question gives you trouble, skip it for the time being and return to it later with a fresh pair of eyes.

Typical Questions

Language

Questions about language may be worded as follows:

> The second paragraph of the passage contains all of the following EXCEPT
>
> (A) a simple sentence
> (B) a compound sentence
> (C) a complex sentence
> (D) a declarative sentence
> (E) an interrogative sentence

To answer this question you need to know sentence terminology and be able to identify sentence types. The review of sentence types later in this book will help you do just that.

Grammar

Another type of grammar question is apt to be phrased like this:

> Lines 12–18 contain which of the following?
>
> (A) Subordinate clauses
> (B) Hyperbole
> (C) A single periodic sentence
> (D) An allusion
> (E) Parallelism

Strictly speaking, only choices (A), (C), and (E) relate to grammar. The others are more rhetorical in nature. The nature of each choice, however, matters less than your ability to identify various examples of grammatical usage and rhetoric when you see them.

Typically, no more than two or three multiple-choice questions on the exam pertain to grammar. Most questions—other than a few comprehension questions—relate in some way to rhetoric.

Rhetoric

A question on rhetoric can be worded this way:

> The primary rhetorical function of lines 15–19 is to
>
> (A) provide a transition between paragraphs 1 and 2
> (B) reiterate the main idea of the passage
> (C) introduce an idea that will be discussed later in the passage
> (D) develop the controversial statement made in the first sentence of the passage
> (E) prove the validity of the statistics cited in the previous sentence

> Rhetoric is a catch-all term loosely referring to techniques and strategies used by an author in composing a particular passage.

Tone

Another question on rhetoric can be worded like this:

The speaker's tone in the last sentence of the passage can best be described as which of the following?

(A) hateful
(B) satirical
(C) pretentious
(D) resentful
(E) arrogant

Mood

A mood question can be worded like this:

The mood of the second paragraph of the passage is best described as

(A) anxious
(B) sentimental
(C) humorous
(D) suspenseful
(E) sarcastic

Footnotes

A documentation question on footnoting is likely to be worded this way:

The function of footnotes 2 and 4 is to tell readers that the quotations in lines 13–14 and 26–28

(A) come from the same source but were written by two different authors
(B) were both written in 2004
(C) are found in the same edition of the *Oxford Companion to American Literature*
(D) appear in books that are no longer in print
(E) reveal that the author quoted material from *The Modern Family* by Robert Winch

This question won't stump anyone acquainted with the conventions of footnoting. Although systems of documentation differ in their details, they all cite titles, authors, dates, and publishers. A complete footnote tells you where to find the cited quotation or information. It may also tell you, among other things, where the material originated, whether it was translated, and a great deal more. If you've ever labored on a research paper or project during your school career, you've probably written footnotes and prepared bibliographies, or lists of works cited. The AP exam won't give you esoteric or highly specialized footnotes or citations to interpret. Rather, it will serve up ordinary samples—those that a college freshman would be expected to know.

These questions represent a sample of the many types included in the exam. The following list will give you an idea of other kinds of questions that have recently appeared:

1. **Identify** the relationship of a sentence in the first paragraph to the passage as a whole.

2. **Name** the rhetorical strategy or device used in a particular section of the passage.

3. **Identify** the function of a sentence within a paragraph, or a paragraph within the whole.

4. **Choose** the best title or main topic of a passage.

5. **Compare** two segments of the passage for their theme, tone, style, sentence structure, diction, syntax, effect, or rhetorical purpose.

6. **Determine** how unity (or point of view, emphasis, contrast, or other feature) is achieved in all or part of the passage.

7. **Recognize** the overall genre of the passage.

8. **Identify** the author's implied or stated purpose, or the purpose of particular images, diction, organization, sentence structure, or other stylistic choice(s).

Many of the questions direct you to line numbers in the passage. To answer most of those questions you can find the place, read the specified lines, and respond. Some questions, however, require more than that. Some raise broad issues and can't be addressed without a fuller understanding of the context in which the lines appear. In such cases, you must read at least the two or three lines that precede the lines designated by the question and the two or three lines that follow.

For multiple-choice questions, AP test writers ordinarily choose passages written between the 17th and 21st centuries, although they might occasionally toss in a passage from ancient Greece or Rome. In each exam, they attempt to balance genre, time period, and individual style. Passages are nonfiction and are composed by essayists, historians, journalists, diarists, autobiographers, political writers, philosophers, and critics. You won't find simple passages that leave little room for interpretation, nor will you find passages that are so ornate or ambiguous that they invite numerous interpretations.

Authors and titles of the passages are not given, although the source of each passage is briefly identified: *"a nineteenth-century memoir," "a twentieth-century book," "a contemporary journalist's diary,"* and so on. Most students can readily read the passages and answer the questions, especially if they have a robust reading background, both in school and on their own. The kind of close textual analysis usually practiced in AP English classes will also serve you well.

READING TECHNIQUES

By this time in your school career you have taken numerous tests like the SATs or ACTs, for which you have read passages like those on the AP English exam and answered multiple-choice questions. No doubt you've developed certain techniques of test taking. You've probably also observed that there is no universal technique that serves everyone equally. What works for others may not work for you, and vice versa.

Nevertheless, it is helpful to be aware of which techniques lead you to do your best. As you prepare for the AP exam, consider trying each of the alternatives discussed below. If time permits, you might try each one in turn as you work your way through the exercises that follow or take the practice exams in the last section of this book. Gradually, you'll discover which technique—or combination of techniques—works best for you.

Read the Passage in Its Entirety

Read everything, including footnotes, from start to finish with pencil in hand. As you read, keep in mind that on this test you will be asked questions primarily about the language and rhetoric of the passage. (You may also get a small number of comprehension questions). While reading, underline any unusual turns of phrase. Make a note of particularly vivid images and of figures of speech. Try also to figure out the tone of the passage. Ask yourself, "What is the author trying to say about the subject?" Then mark any words, phrases, or ideas that clearly contribute to the tone. Finally, observe how the passage is organized. Is there a progression of ideas? What does each paragraph contribute to the main point of the passage? Then turn to the questions, referring to the passage as necessary to find or check your answers.

Skim the Passage

To get the general idea, read faster than you normally would. Try only to ascertain the general topic and the approach used by the author: Is the passage formal or informal? Personal or objective? Is it mainly a narrative? A description? An argument for or against some issue? The answers to these questions will be fairly apparent during a quick read-through. Make a mental note of any unusual words and phrases. Read intently enough to get an impression of the content and writing style of the passage, but don't dawdle. Then, as you answer the questions, refer to the passage.

Read Twice

Skim the passage for a general impression; then go back and read it more thoroughly, using your pencil to mark the passage and take notes. Two readings, one fast and one slow, allow you to pick out features of language and rhetoric that you might overlook during a single reading. Why? Because from the first reading you'll know what the passage is about, and during the second you'll be able to focus on the features that contribute to the overall meaning and effect of the passage. After the second reading proceed to the questions, referring to the passage to check your answers.

TEST STRATEGY

Whatever you do, don't even think of answering the questions without thoroughly reading the passage and footnotes, if any, from start to finish, including the blurb that tells you the origin of the passage.

Read Only the Questions

Do <u>not</u> look at the answer choices. Because it's virtually impossible to remember 10 or 12 questions about material you haven't read, go through the questions quickly—only to become acquainted with the kinds of information you are expected to draw out of the passage. Identify each question with a brief notation: "MI" (main idea), "T" (tone), "POV" (point of view), "SS" (sentence structure), and so on. (Or you can devise your own system.) When you know the questions beforehand, you can read the passage more purposefully, taking into account the matters raised by the questions.

Misguided students sometimes read one question first, then start scouring the passage in search of an answer. Then they move to the second question and repeat their search. Before they know it, time runs out, and they are far from finishing. Moreover, such a fragmented approach reduces the likelihood of grasping the overall point of the passage.

How to Increase Your Reading Power

To be a strong reader, you should develop the habit of dissecting passages piece by piece, line by line. Keep in mind that nothing in a well-written passage exists by accident. Good authors deliberately choose every syllable they write. Nothing is left to chance—not the words, the sentences, the punctuation, the footnotes, the order and content of paragraphs, nor the overall structure of their work. Every bit of their prose has a point and purpose behind it. (That, incidentally, is one of the great differences between good prose and bad prose. The good writer works very hard to find the best words to put in the best order.) Your job on the AP test is to analyze just what the author did.

> **TIP**
>
> Get in the habit of dissecting passages line by line.

The good news is that you can train yourself to read with greater awareness. By honing your reading skills, you'll find that the structure and composition of whatever you read becomes increasingly transparent. By regularly practicing the following steps, you will, in effect, be preparing yourself for the AP exam.

1. Condense the main idea of whatever you read into a pithy sentence or two. (An ambitious student might even jot down a brief outline.) If you can clearly and accurately identify the thesis, you've come a long way. Sometimes the thesis will be stated outright. In that case, underline or highlight it in some way. If it is only implied by the substance, however, put it into your own words. Writing it down on paper or on a computer screen is a sure sign that you are serious about finding the essence of a passage.

2. Look for clues to the author's attitude, purpose, and intent. Is the passage meant largely to entertain? To inform? To provoke controversy? To inspire or to enlighten the reader? Does the author have a bias, an ax to grind, an ulterior motive? It's hard to conceive of a piece of writing in which the author's attitude is totally hidden.

3. Analyze structure. Which ideas come first? Second? Third? Is there a reason for the sequence of ideas? How are ideas linked to each other? Does the end contain echoes of earlier ideas?

4. Examine how the author creates an effect on the reader. Study word choice, sentence structure and length, the order of ideas, figures of speech, the use of rhythm and sound. How does the author keep you interested? Is the writing formal or informal? Is the author friendly or stand-offish, enthusiastic or cool?

5. Think about the author's qualifications to write on a topic. Details usually reveal the authority of the writer. Writing by someone who doesn't know the topic intimately is apt to be top-heavy with generalities. Study the footnotes, if any. Do they refer to sources that are reliable and up-to-date?

6. Become an annotator. Mark up passages profusely, writing in margins and underlining noteworthy ideas and features.

What follows are two annotated passages. Although the notes are not exhaustive, they suggest what an alert reader might observe during a close reading of each passage.

Passage 1

Line

(5)

(10)

(15)

(20)

(25)

(30)

As soon as the Pigeons discover a sufficiency of food to entice them to alight, they fly around in circles, reviewing the countryside below. During these evolutions the dense mass which they form presents a beautiful spectacle, as it changes direction; turning from a glistening sheet of azure, as the backs of the birds come simultaneously into view, to a suddenly presented rich, deep purple. After that they pass lower, over the woods, and for a moment are lost among the foliage. Again they emerge and glide aloft. They may now alight, but the next moment take to wing as if suddenly alarmed, the flapping of their wings producing a noise like the roar of distant thunder, as they sweep through the forests to see if danger is near. However, hunger soon brings them to the ground. On alighting they industriously throw aside the withered leaves in quest of the fallen mast. The rear ranks continually rise, passing over the main body and alighting in front, and in such rapid succession that the whole flock seems still on the wing. The quantity of ground swept in this way is astonishing. So completely has it been cleared that the gleaner who might follow in the rear of the flock would find his labor completely lost. While feeding, their avidity is at times so great that, in attempting to swallow a large acorn or nut, they may be seen to gasp for a long while as if in the agonies of suffocation.

— From "Passenger Pigeon"
by John James Audubon

Annotations (margin notes):

- *Anthropomorphic view: (attributes human trait to birds' instinctive behavior)*
- *Suggests progressive change*
- *Sibilant sounds ("s," "sh," "z") suggest swoosh of birds' wings*
- *Visual images support "beautiful spectacle" (line 6)*
- *Passing in and out of view: evolutionary (line 4)*
- *Simple sentence structure contrasts with sentences 1 and 2 for variety and balance*
- *First half of passage concludes with sound imagery*
- *simile*
- *more anthropomorphism*
- *Turning point of passage Part 1: birds in air Part 2: birds on ground*
- *unusual term for "nuts/acorns on forest floor." (see line 30)*
- *Evolution of flock (line 4) evident here and throughout passage*
- *Observer's reaction . . . again*
- *defines "mast" (line 20) comparison "gasp" is "seen" instead of "heard" (?)*

Content of passage
1. Somewhat anthropomorphic description of birds' behavior
2. Observer's reaction

Overall purpose
To describe a natural phenomenon; written with sense of wonder and admiration
Tone: appreciative

Passage 2

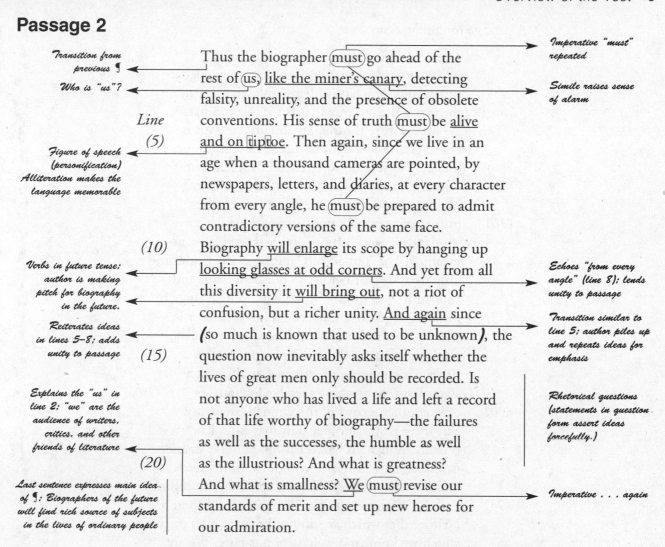

Transition from previous ¶

Thus the biographer (must) go ahead of the rest of (us), like the miner's canary, detecting falsity, unreality, and the presence of obsolete conventions. His sense of truth (must) be alive

Imperative "must" repeated

Who is "us"?

Simile raises sense of alarm

Line
(5)

Figure of speech (personification) Alliteration makes the language memorable

and on tiptoe. Then again, since we live in an age when a thousand cameras are pointed, by newspapers, letters, and diaries, at every character from every angle, he (must) be prepared to admit contradictory versions of the same face.

(10)

Biography will enlarge its scope by hanging up looking glasses at odd corners. And yet from all this diversity it will bring out, not a riot of confusion, but a richer unity. And again since

Verbs in future tense: author is making pitch for biography in the future.

Echoes "from every angle" (line 8); lends unity to passage

Reiterates ideas in lines 5–8; adds unity to passage

(15)

(so much is known that used to be unknown), the question now inevitably asks itself whether the lives of great men only should be recorded. Is

Transition similar to line 5: author piles up and repeats ideas for emphasis

Explains the "us" in line 2; "we" are the audience of writers, critics, and other friends of literature

not anyone who has lived a life and left a record of that life worthy of biography—the failures as well as the successes, the humble as well

(20)

as the illustrious? And what is greatness? And what is smallness? We (must) revise our

Rhetorical questions (statements in question form assert ideas forcefully.)

Last sentence expresses main idea of ¶: Biographers of the future will find rich source of subjects in the lives of ordinary people

standards of merit and set up new heroes for our admiration.

Imperative . . . again

—From *The Death of the Moth and Other Essays* by Virginia Woolf

Tone of passage: earnest, confident, authoritative, hopeful

Others may have made different, yet equally valid, comments about each of the passages. What matters is not that the words you use may differ from those of other readers but that they accurately convey the anatomy of the passages.

Now try your hand at annotating a sample passage written by John Livingston Lowes. Read the passage at least twice—first to see what the passage is about, and then, during the second reading, to jot down whatever you notice about its structure and composition. When you are done, write out a statement that summarizes the main idea of the passage and state your perception of the author's tone. Then compare your notes to those made by the author of this book (pp. 11–12). No doubt you will record ideas that he has missed and vice versa.

A passage for annotation:

There are two deep-seated idiosyncrasies
of human nature that bear on our acceptance
or rejection of what is offered us. We have, in
Line the first place, an innate bias for the familiar.
(5) Whatever we're thoroughly unfamiliar with is
apt to seem to us odd, or queer, or curious, or
bizarre. For it is no mere trick of speech, but
one of those appallingly veracious records of
human nature and experience in which the
(10) history of words abounds, through which
"outlandish" and "crude" attained their present
meaning. For "outlandish" meant in the beginning
only what doesn't belong to our own land, and
"uncouth" was simply "unknown." The change in
(15) meaning registers a universal trait. Whatever is
alien to our own ways—the costume, manners,
modes of speech of another race or of other
times—is strange; and "strange" itself, which
started out by meaning merely "foreign," is
(20) only another record of the same idiosyncrasy.
But there is still another trait that is no less
broadly human. Whatever is too familiar wearies
us. Incessant recurrence without variety breeds
tedium; the overiterated becomes the monotonous,
(25) and the monotonous irks and bores. And there we are.
Neither that which we do not know at all, nor that
which we know too well, is to our taste. We are
averse to shocks, and we go to sleep under narcotics.
Both the shock and the narcotic have, I grant, at
(30) times their fascination. But they are apt to be
forward, not permanent, sweet, not lasting.
The source of more or less abiding satisfaction
for most normal human beings lies in a happy
merging of the two—in the twofold delight in
(35) an old friend recognized as new, or a new friend
recognized as old. The experience and the
pleasure are universal. All the lovers who
have ever lived have made experiment of it;
a face that you have passed a hundred times,
(40) nor cared to see, remains the face you've
always known, but becomes all at once the
most beautiful and thrilling object in the world;
the person you've never known before, you find
all at once you've known from all eternity. Now
(45) art, like love, sends its roots deep into what we
are. And our most permanent aesthetic satisfaction
arises as a rule from things familiar enough to

give the pleasure of recognition, yet not so trite
as to rob us of the other pleasure of surprise.

(50)   We are keen for the new, but we insist that it
establish some connection with what is friendly
and our own; we want the old, but we want it
to seem somehow new. Things may recur as often
as they please, so long as they surprise us—like

(55)   the Ghost in Hamlet—each time they appear.

—From *Convention and Revolt in Poetry*

Here is the same passage annotated by the author:

Topic sentence of passage	There are <u>two</u> deep-seated idiosyncrasies of human nature that bear on our acceptance or rejection of what is offered us. We have, in → *Passage must cover <u>two</u> idiosyncrasies, or human traits*
Line	<u>the first place, an innate bias for the familiar.</u> → *Trait 1 (2nd trait in line 21)*
(5)	Whatever we're thoroughly unfamiliar with is

Author defines "bias for the familiar" (line 5) by explaining our aversion to the unfamiliar

apt to seem to us <u>odd</u>, or <u>queer</u>, or <u>curious</u>, or <u>bizarre</u>. For it is no mere trick of speech, but one of those appallingly veracious records of human nature and experience in which the

4 adjectives show subtle gradations of meaning

(10)   history of words abounds, through which "outlandish" and "crude" attained their present meaning. For "outlandish" meant in the beginning only what doesn't belong to our own land, and "uncouth" was simply "unknown." The change in

A digression into word origins. Purpose? — To show how deep-seated is our rejection of the unfamiliar (?)

(15)   meaning registers a universal trait. Whatever is alien to our own ways—the costume, manners, modes of speech of another race or of other times—is strange; and "strange" itself, which started out by meaning merely "foreign," is

Development of discussion of word origins. Several examples add up to convincing case.

(20)   only another record of the same idiosyncrasy. But there is <u>still another trait that is no less</u> → *2nd trait introduced*
<u>broadly human.</u> <u>Whatever is too familiar wearies</u> → *2nd trait defined*
us. Incessant recurrence without variety breeds

Development of 2nd trait

tedium; the overiterated becomes the monotonous, and the monotonous irks and bores. <u>And there we are</u>.

(25)   Neither that which we do not know at all, nor that

An interruption: gives the reader a chance to let ideas sink in.

An interim conclusion based on discussion in lines 1–25

which we know too well, is to our taste. We are averse to shocks, and we go to sleep under narcotics. Both the shock and the narcotic have, I grant, at

Author introduces another way to look at the issue

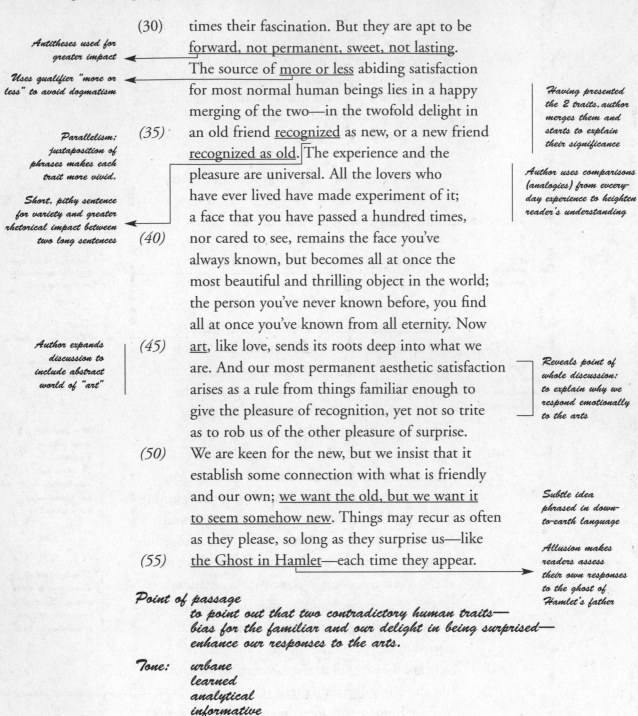

Antitheses used for greater impact

Uses qualifier "more or less" to avoid dogmatism

Parallelism: juxtaposition of phrases makes each trait more vivid.

Short, pithy sentence for variety and greater rhetorical impact between two long sentences

Author expands discussion to include abstract world of "art"

Having presented the 2 traits, author merges them and starts to explain their significance

Author uses comparisons (analogies) from every-day experience to heighten reader's understanding

Reveals point of whole discussion: to explain why we respond emotionally to the arts

Subtle idea phrased in down-to-earth language

Allusion makes readers assess their own responses to the ghost of Hamlet's father

(30) times their fascination. But they are apt to be forward, not permanent, sweet, not lasting. The source of more or less abiding satisfaction for most normal human beings lies in a happy merging of the two—in the twofold delight in

(35) an old friend recognized as new, or a new friend recognized as old. The experience and the pleasure are universal. All the lovers who have ever lived have made experiment of it; a face that you have passed a hundred times,

(40) nor cared to see, remains the face you've always known, but becomes all at once the most beautiful and thrilling object in the world; the person you've never known before, you find all at once you've known from all eternity. Now

(45) art, like love, sends its roots deep into what we are. And our most permanent aesthetic satisfaction arises as a rule from things familiar enough to give the pleasure of recognition, yet not so trite as to rob us of the other pleasure of surprise.

(50) We are keen for the new, but we insist that it establish some connection with what is friendly and our own; we want the old, but we want it to seem somehow new. Things may recur as often as they please, so long as they surprise us—like

(55) the Ghost in Hamlet—each time they appear.

Point of passage
to point out that two contradictory human traits—bias for the familiar and our delight in being surprised—enhance our responses to the arts.

Tone: *urbane*
learned
analytical
informative

Under the pressure of time on the AP exam, you can't do a complete annotation as illustrated above. However, if you get into the habit of writing comments, underlining, and generally scrawling notes all over the things you read, it's likely that you'll sail through the passages on the exam. Like most other skills, proficiency in annotation diminishes if you stop practicing—so keep at it because it's easy to slip out of the groove if you stop for any length of time.

Answering the Questions

The multiple-choice questions on the exam have been carefully written to separate well-qualified students from those who are less qualified. To earn a "5" you must answer most of the questions correctly. To earn a grade of "3" on the whole exam, you need to get about 50 or 60 percent of the short-answer questions right—provided that your essays are generally acceptable.

In the scoring, wrong answers count against your score to compensate for random guessing. Therefore, don't guess unless you can eliminate one or more of the five choices. Here's the rationale:

Each question is worth one point. For each correct answer, one point will be added to your raw score. For every wrong answer, however, a quarter of a point will be deducted. An item left blank will neither add to nor take away from your score. So, if you don't have a clue about how to answer a question, leave it blank.

Suppose that on four of the roughly 50 questions you can eliminate one wrong answer and guess four times. If you guess right just once, you will have earned a point and lost three-quarters of a point, a net gain of one quarter. If you leave all four blank, you will gain nothing. This method is risky because you could make four incorrect guesses, but the chances of an incorrect answer every time are only 1 in 4.

When a question gives you trouble, and you can't decide among three choices, conventional wisdom says you should go with your first impulse. You may be right. Testing experts and psychologists agree there's a better than average chance of success if you trust your intuition. There are no guarantees, however. Because the mind works in so many ways, relying on your initial choice may not always work for you.

> **TIP**
>
> Questions are not arranged in order of difficulty as they are on some standardized tests. Usually, they follow the progress of the passage, but not always.

> **TEST STRATEGY**
>
> If you can confidently eliminate one of the five choices, it pays to guess. You have a 1 in 4 chance to get it right.

ESSAY QUESTIONS

After an hour of answering multiple-choice questions, you'll have 2 hours and 15 minutes to write three essays:

- A **synthesis essay** in which you use sources to argue your point of view on a given issue.
- **One analytical essay** that examines, interprets, and explains the meaning and structure of prose passage.
- **Another essay** similar to the second one **or** an essay that supports, refutes, or qualifies an opinion expressed in a statement or brief passage.

The suggested writing time for each essay is 40 minutes. For the synthesis essay, you are given an extra 15 minutes to read the sources.

Questions from Previous AP Exams

To give you a more concrete idea of the essays you are expected to write on the exam, here are essay topics that students were given during each of the last few years.

2004

1. Analyze how the rhetorical strategies used by the 18th-century author Lord Chesterfield in a letter to his son reveal the writer's values.

2. After reading a passage from a book by Richard Rodriguez, analyze how the author uses contrasts between Mexico and California to explore and convey his conflicting feelings.

2005

1. Select what you think is the most compelling observation made by George F. Kennan, an expert in foreign affairs, about America's foreign policy during the period following World War II. Then write an essay commenting on the validity of the observation today.

2. Write an essay that analyzes how a mock press release printed in *The Onion*, a popular satirical publication, pokes fun at the marketing techniques used by producers to sell their goods to consumers.

2006

1. In an essay analyze how Jennifer Price, the author of an essay titled "The Plastic Pink Flamingo: A Natural History," crafts her text to reveal her view of United States culture.

2. After reading a passage from an essay by the 19th-century author William Hazlitt, write an essay analyzing the rhetorical strategies Hazlitt used to develop his point of view about money.

2007

1. After reading six sources on the effects of extensive advertising on society, write an essay that presents the benefits derived from voluminous advertising or an essay that discusses the overall negative effects of widespread advertising. In your essay, synthesize at least three of the given sources to support your position.

   (*Note that on the 2007 exam, the assignment for the synthesis essay was given first—before the other two essay questions.*)

2. Read a passage by Scott Russell Sanders that discusses an idea proposed by the Indian writer Salman Rushdie, who believes that a life lived in more than one location offers a person a new and imaginative relationship with the world, while staying put deprives one of many enriching opportunities and adventures. Then write an essay that analyzes the strategies Sanders uses to express his point of view.

3. Write an essay that takes a position on the following ethical question: Should incentives be offered for acts of charity? For example, is it ethical for teachers to offer extra points to students who contribute money, food, or clothing to help victims of a natural disaster? To support your position, use evidence from your reading, observation, and/or experience.

SAMPLE SYNTHESIS QUESTION FROM THE COLLEGE BOARD

In 2005, while spreading the word about the new synthesis question, the College Board provided the following example:

Introduction

Television has been influential in United States presidential elections since the 1960's. But just what is this influence, and how has it affected who is elected? Has it made elections fairer and more accessible, or has it moved candidates from pursuing issues to pursuing images?

Assignment

Read the following sources (including any introductory information) carefully. **Then, in an essay that synthesizes at least three of the sources for support, take a position that defends, challenges, or qualifies the claim that television has had a positive impact on presidential elections.**

Six sources, labeled A to F, accompanied the question. Most were commentaries by scholars, journalists, and political scientists who articulated their views about the impact of television on presidential elections. The visual source was a chart that showed Television Ratings for Presidential Debates: 1960–1966.

Sample Analytical Essay Question

Question 1

(Suggested time—40 minutes)

Read the following passage, written in 1967 and published in the Sunday magazine of the *New York Times*. Then write an essay in which you analyze how the structure of the passage and the use of language help convey the writer's views.

Americans and Western Europeans, in their sensitivity to lingering problems around them, tend to make science and progress their scapegoats. There is a belief that progress has precipitated widespread unhappiness, anxieties, and other social and emotional problems. Science is viewed as a cold mechanical discipline having nothing to do with human warmth and the human spirit.

But to many of us from the nonscientific East, science does not have such repugnant associations. We are not afraid of it, nor are we disappointed by it. We know all too painfully that our social and emotional problems festered long before the age of technology. To us, science is warm and reassuring. It promises hope. It is helping us at long last gain some control over our persecutory environments, alleviating age-old problems—not only physical but also, and especially, problems of the spirit.

Shiraz, for example, a city in southern Iran, has long been renowned for its rose gardens and nightingales; its poets, Sadi and Hafiz; and its mystical, ascetic philosophy, Sufism. Much poetry has been written in glorification of the spiritual attributes of this oasis city. And to be sure, Shiraz is a green, picturesque town, with a quaint bazaar and refreshing gardens. But in this "romantic" city thousands of emotionally disturbed and mentally retarded men, women, and children were, until recently, kept in chains in stifling prison cells and lunatic asylums.

Every now and again, some were dragged, screaming and pleading, to a courtyard and flogged for not behaving "normally." But for the most part, they were made to sit against damp walls, their hands and feet locked in chains, and thus immobilized, without even a modicum of affection from their helpless families and friends, they sat for weeks and months and years—often all their lives. Pictures of these wretched men, women, and children can still be seen in this "city of poetry," this "city with a spiritual way of life."

It was only recently that a wealthy young Shirazi who, against the admonitions of his family, had studied psychology at the University of Teheran and foreign universities, returned to Shiraz and after considerable struggle with city officials succeeded in opening a psychiatric clinic, the first in those regions. After still more struggle, he arranged to have the emotionally disturbed and the mentally retarded transferred from prison to their homes, to hospitals, and to his clinic, where he and his staff now attend them.

Line
(5)

(10)

(15)

(20)

(25)

(30)

(35)

They are fortunate. All over Asia and other backward areas, emotionally disturbed men and women are still incarcerated in these medieval dungeons called lunatic asylums. The cruel rejection and punishment are
(40) intended to teach them a lesson or help exorcise evil spirits.

The West, still bogged down in its ridiculous romanticism, would like to believe that emotional disturbances, dope addiction, delinquency are all modern problems brought on by technological progress, and that backward societies are too spiritual and beautiful to need the ministrations of
(45) science. But while the West can perhaps afford to think this way, the people of backward lands cannot. . . .

. . .The obstacles are awesome, the inertia too entrenched, the people's suffering too anguished, their impatience too eruptive. Moreover, the total cultural reorganizations such as Asia and Africa are undergoing inevitably
(50) engender their own temporary dislocations and confusions. But their goals, the direction, remain constant. We are on the move, however awkwardly at first, to a saner, better world.

How to answer this question:

Go back to the original question, which asks you to analyze two aspects of the passage: 1) its structure, or organization, and 2) its language. The first aspect is fairly specific. As you read the passage, you need to observe what the author discusses first, second, third, and so on. Your essay must explain not only the order of ideas but the reasons the author may have chosen that order.

The second part of the question is more general. It invites you to analyze the use of language, which may include the author's choice of words (diction), syntax (word order), figures of speech, sentence structure, rhythm, sound, tone, or any other characteristics of style and rhetoric you choose.

Although the question directs you to write about two different aspects of the passage, the essay itself should be unified. That is, a good essay should not consist of, say, two disparate paragraphs, one exclusively devoted to structure and another to language. Rather, the essay should include material that shows the interrelationship of structure and language in the passage. This might be covered in a separate paragraph, or it could be woven into the overall fabric of the essay.

Before you begin to write, read the passage at least *twice:* once for an overview and once to begin your analysis. You may notice early on that the opening paragraph contains generalizations about Westerners' concepts of science and progress. Then the author contrasts the Western view of science and progress with the Eastern view. Immediately, you see that the author, by using the first person pronoun (as in "many of us") will be speaking from the perspective of an Easterner. Consequently, his discussion of Eastern views is apt to come across as more well-informed, more authoritative, perhaps more personal.

To support his position, the author gives an extended example—the city of Shiraz—to illustrate just how different the East is from the West. The description and vivid images of Shiraz memorably convey the idea that the "spiritual way of life" has a side to it that Westerners don't know about. This is the heart of the passage. The use of quotation marks around "romantic" and "city of poetry" is meant to point out the discrepancy between the idealized and real versions of Shiraz.

TIP

Read the passage at least twice.

As the passage draws to a close, the author reiterates the initial contrast between West and East, with the emphasis on the East. The last paragraph offers a generalized statement about conditions in Asia and Africa, reminding the reader of the contrast made at the beginning of the passage.

Sample Synthesis Essay Question

Time—

15 minutes for reading the question and sources
40 minutes for writing an essay

Instructions: The following essay topic is accompanied by six sources.

Respond to the question below in a well-written, coherent essay that draws on ideas and information found in **at least three** of the sources. Don't simply summarize or paraphrase the sources. Instead, **focus the essay on your point of view**, and use the sources to support or bolster your argument.

Topic: Homework has always been part of going to school. In recent years, however, the media have run numerous stories about a trend to increase the homework assigned to students from kindergarten to 12th grade. Critics claim that heavy loads of homework ultimately do more harm than good, not only to children but also to their families.

Your task: Read the following sources carefully. **Then, in an essay that synthesizes at least three of the sources, take a position that supports, denies, or modifies the claim that large amounts of homework have more negative effects than positive ones.**

In your essay, you may refer to the sources simply as Source A, Source B, etc., or by the authors listed below.

Source A (Gill and Schossman)

Source B (Loveless)

Source C (Kralovic and Buell)

Source D (Chart)

Source E (Haley)

Source F (Chaika)

SOURCE A

Brian P. Gill and Steven L. Schlossman, "My Dog Ate My Argument," Op/Ed page of the *Los Angeles Times*, December 11, 2003.

The following passage is an excerpt from an opinion article written by a social scientist at the RAND Corporation and a history professor at Carnegie Mellon University.

In our view, homework is the prime window into the school for parents to see, understand and connect with the academic mission of the teachers. It is the primary arena in which children, parents and schools interact on a daily basis. Yet it gets less systematic thought and attention than any other key component of education. Other than the admonition that kids should do more of it, we pay almost no attention to how to improve its design and content. Nor do we do much to prepare teachers to use and evaluate homework, to hold administrators accountable for monitoring the homework load or to cultivate parents' collaboration. Homework remains an orphan child of the educational excellence movement.

The debate over homework must be redirected. Moral exhortation—accusing our kids and parents of being lazy, comparing them unfavorably with their counterparts in Japan (as in the 1980s) or Russia (as in the 1950s)—just doesn't seem to have much effect in changing long-term homework trends.

After half a century of failure to increase student buy-in, it's time to rethink how to make homework a more valued part of the pedagogic process. In addition to promoting academic achievement, homework can inculcate habits of self-discipline and independent study and can help inform parents about the educational agenda of their school. We must find ways to make homework an interesting and challenging educational experience for students, instead of the uniform, seat-bound, memorization-focused solo exercise it has been. Otherwise, all our talk about high standards and improving student achievement will run up against the same roadblock that has stymied the pursuit of educational excellence in the past.

SOURCE B

Tom Loveless, "Do Students Have Too Much Homework?" A report for the Brown Center on Education Policy at the Brookings Institution, Washington, D.C., 2003.

The following passage is excerpted from a report on American education.

. . . The most reliable data support the following conclusions: 1) the typical student, even in high school, does not spend more than an hour per day on homework, 2) the homework load has not changed much since the 1980s, 3) the students whose homework has increased in the past decade are those who previously had no homework and now have a small amount, 4) most parents feel the homework load is about right and, of those who would like to change it, more parents would rather see homework increased than decreased.

Why is it important to get the homework story right? Mainly because it is positively associated with student learning. Research shows that the relationship of homework with student achievement is positive for both middle and high school students and neutral for elementary school students. The research does not prove causality, an ever-present difficulty with research on many educational practices. High-achieving students in high school, for example, may do more homework because they enjoy studying. They take tough classes that require a lot of work. That does not necessarily mean that homework is boosting their achievement. Low-achieving students in elementary school, on the other hand, may do more homework because they are struggling to catch up. The homework is not causing their learning problems.

Despite these limitations, the evidence is convincing enough to provide sober guidance on the current controversy. Excessive homework is not a common problem. The critics of homework need to produce some very powerful evidence before policymakers start mandating reductions in homework or even banning it altogether. To date, the evidence put forth by homework critics has been weak.

SOURCE C

From Etta Kralovec and John Buell, *The End of Homework: How Homework Disrupts Families and Overburdens Children*, Beacon Press, Boston, 2000, pp. 32–33

"The Case of Daniel"

Most of us do not live our lives according to research findings; rather, we struggle with questions about homework at our kitchen table. For the sake of argument, though, let's take the research findings in their most positive light and assume that, yes, homework does boost school achievement for high school students. Then, let's turn to an actual case, a story that will probably sound familiar to anyone with children.

Daniel is a sixteen-year-old junior in high school. A typical boy with boundless energy and an unfailing enthusiasm for life, he is an astute observer of human nature, a budding photographer, and an amateur naturalist. He could easily occupy all his free time with reading, exploring tidal flats, and playing with his friends. A member of the soccer and tennis teams, he uses sports to burn off his unused energy after a day of sitting at school desks.

Daniel does satisfactory work in school, primarily as a consequence of a strong dose of parental and peer pressure. Nonetheless, he hates math, and always has. Daniel leaves for school every morning at 6:45 and returns home after sports practice, at around 6:00 in the evening. He usually has between two and three hours of homework each night, much of it Algebra II. By the end of the evening, Daniel tends to feel rather low. His inability to complete his math homework causes him to feel stupid. His frustration at not being able to pursue his own interests leaves him hating the "learning" part of school even as he thrives on the sports and social scenes there.

Daniel wants to go to college, but his grades are only so-so. His parents now push a little harder for him to pull up his B- grade average. But Daniel wants to use his evenings to take a photography class at the local university, because he can't fit photography into his college prep program at school. He also wants to join a search-and-rescue team. He loves adventure and helping people and thinks it would be "cool" to assist in rescuing stranded climbers in the nearby national park. Daniel doesn't have time to engage in these activities, however, because his weekends are consumed by homework and sports. Daniel's grandfather lives nearby and is getting older; he and Daniel were very close when Daniel was younger, but now they rarely see each other. Daniel just doesn't have the time.

SOURCE D

Prepared by Linda Sax, J.A. Lindholm, A.W. Astin, W.S. Korn, and K.M. Mahoney, this chart was published in "The American Freshman: National Norms for Fall 2002," Higher Education Research Institute, UCLA, 2002.

Students spending more than five hours per week on activities in their last year of high school (percentage)

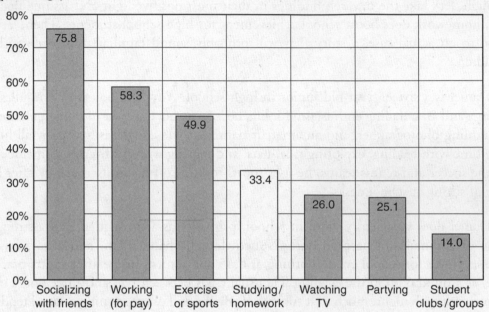

SOURCE E

Brian Haley, "What Is the Value of Homework?" July 6, 2006. SearchWarp.com. Accessed August 2, 2006. <*http://www.searchwarp.com/*>

The passage that follows is adapted from an article published by a web site that promotes the writing of authors in many disciplines, including education.

Assigning homework serves various educational needs. It serves as an intellectual discipline, establishes study habits, eases time constraints on the amount of curricular material that can be covered in class, and supplements and reinforces work done in school. In addition, it fosters student initiative, independence, and responsibility, and brings home and school closer together.

Homework is the time students spend outside the classroom in assigned activities to practice, reinforce, or apply newly-acquired skills and knowledge and to learn necessary skills of independent study.

Practice assignments reinforce newly acquired skills. For example, students who have just learned a new method of solving a mathematical problem should be given sample problems to complete on their own. Preparation assignments help students get ready for activities that will occur in the classroom. Students may, for example, be required to do background research on a topic to be discussed later in class. Extension assignments are frequently long-term continuing projects that parallel classwork. Students must apply previous learning to complete these assignments, which include science fair projects and term papers.

Like mowing the lawn or taking out the garbage, homework seems to be a fact of life. . . . But the value of homework extends beyond school. We know that good assignments, completed successfully, can help children develop wholesome habits and attitudes. . . . It can teach children to work independently, encourage self-discipline and responsibility (assignments provide some youngsters with their first chance to manage time and meet deadlines), and encourage a love of learning. . . . Homework can help parents learn about their children's education and communicate both with their children and the schools.

Research in the last decade has begun to focus on the relationship between homework and student achievement and has greatly strengthened the case for homework. Although there are mixed findings about whether homework actually increases students' academic achievement, many teachers and parents agree that homework develops students' initiative and responsibility and fulfills the expectations of students, parents, and the public. Studies generally have found homework assignments to be most helpful if they are carefully planned by the teachers and have direct meaning to students.

SOURCE F

Gloria Chaika, "Help! Homework Is Wrecking My Home Life," *Education World*, August 8, 2000.

The following passage is from an article for school administrators published in an online educational journal.

"Teachers should devote energy to creating homework that is stimulating and provocative rather than banal," Howard Gardner, the John H. and Elisabeth A. Hobbs Professor in Cognition and Education at the Harvard Graduate School of Education and the creator of the theory of multiple intelligences, told Education World. "And parents or mentors should go shoulder-to-shoulder with youngsters, helping to motivate them, thinking of ways in which to help them without giving the answer, and being aware of the child's special gifts and weaknesses."

It sounds great, "but you need parent input for kids to perform, and with the increase in single-parent families, there's no one at home to help," veteran fifth-grade teacher Loretta Highfield told Education World.

"It isn't that the kids don't want to do homework; the majority of my students don't have the skills to go home and do it independently," added Highfield, a teacher at Florida Avenue Elementary in Slidell, Louisiana. "Even young students are not getting the help at home that they used to."

The same seems to hold true for older children. "I have students who have been thrown out of the house or have a financial situation brought on by an ill parent," Northshore High School (Slidell, Louisiana) teacher Kathleen Modenbach told Education World. "There are others whose after-school jobs pay for car insurance and clothes or whose involvement in extra-curricular activities, private lessons, or sports leaves little time for homework."

"For some students, a lot of homework can seem irrelevant," Modenbach added. "High school students become expert at evaluating the validity of assignments and assigning priorities to them. Kids who wouldn't dream of cheating on a test or copying a research paper think nothing of copying homework. I find students will do homework when it must be done to pass the class. Anything else is a waste of time and feeds into the vicious circle of beating the homework system."

Therefore, as kids deal with assigned homework in their own ways—or grow increasingly frazzled—their too-busy parents are uncertain what to do. Some, wanting their children to be academically competitive, demand extra homework, while others wonder just how much is too much.

Answering the Synthesis Question

Homework. Now, there's a topic that you must know something about. Being a seasoned doer of homework, you're probably bursting with ideas on the pros and cons of the stuff and could probably argue brilliantly against homework, make a passionate case in its favor, or come down somewhere between the two poles. Regardless of where you stand, you're not apt find yourself short of ideas on the issue. In fact, you may be overloaded and find yourself sifting out only the best arguments among many to include in an essay on the subject.

But beware. This essay assignment is not intended simply to give you a chance to vent about homework. Although your biases will no doubt shape your argument, you cannot rely solely on your personal experience and observations. This, after all, is what the AP people call a **"synthesis essay,"** a label that you've got to take seriously.

What it means is that you are being asked to write an essay based not solely on your personal opinion but to some exent on your interpretation of at least three of the sources. You can use them as evidence to support your point of view, or you can comment on them in other ways. For example, you can criticize them for inaccuracies or reject them as dead-wrong observations of the homework scene. You can quote from them directly, use indirect quotations, paraphrase ideas, or put ideas into your own words. But remember this: However you incorporate the sources, you must say where the material came from. That is, you must cite each source you use, as though your were writing a term paper for a class.

> **TEST TIP**
>
> Cite three sources; there's no extra credit for more.

CITE SOURCES

Stylistically, it may serve you well to use phrases like *"According to Source B, . . ."* or *"In Loveless' opinion . . .", or "A survey of high school students (Source D) shows that . . . ,"* etc. Or you can simply cite your sources with parenthetical references—(*Source A, Source B*)—in your text. Another approach is to name the author or even the title of the sources, but spelling out lengthy titles uses up precious time. AP essay readers will look for citations and will penalize essays that contain fewer than three. At the same time, you won't earn extra credit for citing more than three.

Whether or not you agree with the premise that "large amounts of homework have more negative effects than positive ones," your task is to write an argument that defends your point of view. Because a researched argument is meant to sway readers whose views may be contrary to yours, you need to gather compelling evidence in support of your position.

Let's say that you think homework is generally good for you and the more you get, the better. Right off the bat, then, you have a main idea, or thesis, for your essay. But even if you know immediately where you stand on the issue, take the time to read all the sources carefully, underscoring or circling those ideas you might consider mentioning in your essay. It's good to read the material with which you don't agree, too, because in making your case, you can bolster your argument by refuting and revealing the weaknesses in what you'd expect your opponent to say.

> **TEST TIP**
>
> Be sure to read all the sources carefully.

SUPPORT YOUR POSITION

In building a convincing case, it often pays to gather at least three compelling reasons to support your position. Although AP students ought not be constrained by the familiar "five-paragraph" essay, you won't go wrong following its structure: an introduction, three paragraphs of development, and a conclusion. Why *three* paragraphs of development? Mainly because *three* is a number that works. If you can come up with three different arguments, you appear to speak with the voice of authority. One paragraph is too simple. Two is better but still shallow. Three is thoughtful. It suggests depth and insight. Psychologically, three also creates a sense of wholeness for the reader, like the beginning, middle, and end of a story. (Incidentally, it's no accident that the number three recurs in all literature, from *Goldilocks and the Three Bears* to *The Bible*.)

In writing this synthesis essay you needn't depend totally on the sources. In fact, AP readers are likely to look kindly on your own original ideas, provided they are relevant to the issue, clearly expressed, and well-developed. The sources, however, contain ample arguments for and against large amounts of homework. On the positive side, you might pick out such ideas as:

- Homework permits parents to participate with teachers in the education of their children (Source A).
- "[T]he relationship of homework with student achievement is positive for both middle and high school students" (Source B).
- Homework helps high school seniors balance their lives between work and recreation (Source D).
- Homework fosters the development of individual initiative and effective study habits (Source A).
- Homework provides opportunities for low-achieving students to catch up (Source B).
- Homework leads to a lifelong love of learning (Source F).

Or, if you have an unfavorable view of homework, the following ideas can be used to bolster your argument:

- Much homework is poorly designed and pointless (Source A).
- Large amounts of homework can keep a student from pursuing worthwhile personal interests (Source C).
- Homework assigned during vacations is counterproductive; it turns kids away from the joys of learning and deprives them of reading for pleasure (Source E).
- More homework does not necessarily lead to better grades (Source E).

DETERMINE ORDER

Once you've collected your ideas for or against the issue, stop for a moment to figure out which idea to put first, which to put second, and so on. Order is important. The best order is the clearest order, the arrangement that readers can follow with the least effort. No plan is superior to another, provided you have a valid reason for using it. The plan least likely to succeed is the aimless one, the one in which you state and develop ideas in random order as they happened to come to mind. It's better by far to rank your ideas in order of importance by deciding which provides the strongest support for your thesis. Although your best argument may be listed first in your notes, save it for last on the essay. Giving it away at the start is self-defeating because everything that follows will be anticlimactic. An excellent way to plot three good ideas is to lead with your second best, save your best for the end, and sandwich your least powerful idea between the others. This structure recognizes that the end and the beginning of an essay are its most critical parts. A good opening draws the reader in and creates an all-important first impression, but a memorable ending, coming last, is what readers have fresh in their minds when they assign you a grade. But, as always, don't just follow these guidelines slavishly. If you can justify another organization, by all means use it.

TEST TIP

Work *toward* your best point, not away from it.

Be confident that AP exam readers won't judge your essay based on the opinion you express. Even if they disagree with you, they are obliged to ignore their own biases and grade you according to the criteria of good writing. They may consider your view off by a mile, but if you write a cogent, forceful essay that smoothly integrates the sources and demonstrates mastery of argumentation, your essay will receive a high score.

REMINDER

No matter how skillfully written, your essay will be penalized for faulty reasoning and misinformation.

How Essays Are Scored

When it comes time to make judgments about writing, the word *effectively* comes up repeatedly. It's a popular word because it's easy to use and hard to define. It means so much, and yet so little. You probably know effective writing when you see it, but what the AP folks have in mind is the thoughtful organization of ideas, appropriate word choice, proper syntax, varied sentence structure, a mature style of writing, sensible paragraphing, coherent development, and correct mechanics (grammar, spelling, and punctuation).

AP readers don't sit there with a checklist to see whether your essay meets all these criteria, however. Rather, they read it *holistically*, meaning that they read it quickly for an overall impression of your writing and then assign your essay a grade from 1 (low) to 9 (high). Readers are trained to look for clearly organized, well-developed, and forceful responses that reveal a depth of understanding and insight.

Frankly, the 40 minutes suggested for each essay is not a great deal of time to read the question, plan what you will say, write a few hundred words, edit and proofread your draft, and submit a finished piece of work. In effect, you must condense into a short time what would normally take far longer. A saving grace, however, is that the AP test readers don't expect three polished pieces of immortal prose, but just three competently written essays.

TIP

AP readers don't expect three polished pieces of immortal prose, just three good essays.

A WORD ABOUT WORD COUNT

Are 250 words enough? Yes, but the number of words in your essays is up to you. To AP essay readers, length takes a back seat to answering the question and covering the subject. A single paragraph most likely won't allow you to fully develop ideas. Multiparagraph essays allow you to be expansive, to use a variety of details to support your main idea, and to show that you have what it takes to cover a complex subject clearly and logically. Keep in mind that the number of words is less crucial than what the words say.

Each year in early June, more than a thousand college and high-school teachers get together to read and evaluate the essays written by students like you from across the country and overseas. Readers are chosen for their ability to make sound judgments about student writing and are trained to use a common set of scoring standards.

HOW ESSAYS ARE READ AND GRADED

As part of their training, AP readers are given guidelines that have the ring of common sense and stress the need for fairness. They are told:

1. To read each essay once.

2. To read quickly and to assign a grade immediately.

3. To read mainly for what has been done well.

4. To take everything into account, including organization, word choice, the mechanics of writing, and so on.

5. To ignore poor handwriting as much as possible.

6. Not to penalize a well-developed but unfinished essay.

7. Not to use length as a criterion of evaluation.

8. To keep in mind that any essay that contains even a marginal response to the question should be judged according to the logic of the argument developed by the writer.

9. To remember that each essay is a first draft written under pressure in about 40 minutes by a 17- or 18-year-old.

Each essay is scored on a scale of 0 (low) to 9 (high) and is read by two different readers. If the scores assigned by the two readers differ by more than one grade, a third reader evaluates the essay.

A **9** ESSAY

Essays deserving a score of 9 demonstrate the writer's exceptional control of effective writing techniques. They are clear, interesting, and correct. They analyze rhetorical strategies with insight and precision. They refer frequently to the text, directly or indirectly, and succinctly describe how such matters as tone, irony, diction, and use of examples contribute to the structure and meaning of a passage.

Synthesis essays present a persuasive argument cogently and convincingly, synthesizing source material seamlessly in their discussion of the issue.

If the essay contains an occasional flaw in analysis, prose style, or mechanics, the errors are inconsequential.

AN **8** ESSAY

Essays earning an 8 are extremely well-written and demonstrate considerable mastery of written English. They meet all the criteria for essays earning a 9, but fall just slightly short of distinction.

A **7** ESSAY

Essays scored 7 competently analyze rhetorical strategies. They often use specific examples from the text and discuss, directly or indirectly, such matters as tone, irony, diction, and use of examples. They are reasonably well-developed and coherent. A few errors in word choice or sentence structure may exist, but no error is egregious enough to interfere with the clear expression of the writer's ideas.

A synthesis essay earning a score of 7 effectively supports the writer's position and appropriately incorporates at least three sources into the discussion of the issue. The overall argument may be less developed or less precise than arguments presented in essays that earn an 8 or a 9.

A **6** ESSAY

Essays earning a 6 are generally the same as those receiving a 7 except that the prose style may be less mature, or lapses in diction, syntax or clarity may be more serious.

A **5** ESSAY

Essays given a grade of 5 adequately answer the question but may lack full development. Ideas may be presented clearly but remain unsupported. The essay may be well organized and convey the writer's ideas, but lapses in diction or syntax weaken the impact of the essay and suggest that the writer is not fully in control of effective writing techniques.

The position taken in the synthesis essay is supported by incorporating and citing at least three sources, but the arguments and the use of citations is somewhat limited, inconsistent, or questionable.

A **4** ESSAY

An essay earning a 4 responds inadequately to the question. It may miss the point of the question or analyze secondary stylistic or rhetorical strategies. It may be superficial, or its ideas may be developed incoherently—jumping from topic to topic. Although the point of the essay may be clear, the prose is immature, showing the writer's lack of control over organization, word choice, or syntax.

A synthesis essay deserving a score of 4 makes a relatively weak or incomplete argument related to the topic. It may use too few sources or misapply or misrepresent material from the sources.

A **3** ESSAY

Essays deserving a score of 3 are similar to essays scored 4 except the analysis is even less astute or is seriously flawed. The prose demonstrates that the writer has difficulty controlling organization, choosing the correct words, or using standard English syntax to convey ideas.

In citing sources in the synthesis essay, the writer demonstrates a weak understanding of the meaning or function of sources.

A **2** ESSAY

An essay earning a score of 2 demonstrates the writer's inability to analyze the passage. It may wander off the topic or substitute a simpler task than that assigned by the question. The prose often reveals weaknesses in organizing material, in expressing ideas clearly, and in writing grammatically.

A score of 2 on the synthesis essay suggests that the writer has failed to address the issue, has improperly used or cited sources, or has responded to the issue largely by summarizing material in the sources.

A **1** ESSAY

An essay deserving a 1 may be similar to an essay scored 2, but the ideas are more simplistic and the expression flawed, perhaps bordering on the incomprehensible.

In the synthesis essay, the writer has neglected to cite or even to allude to any sources.

A **0** ESSAY

A 0 score indicates a blank paper, an essay not on the assigned topic, or a piece of writing that merely paraphrases the prompt.

You've no doubt noticed that the foregoing descriptions lack precision. It's no secret that grading essays is far from an exact science. But the readers are expected to be fair and to focus their attention on an essay's strengths rather than its weaknesses.

Diagnostic Test

- Taking a full-length AP exam
- Finding the *best* answers
- Checking your answers
- How to score your own essays
- What the numbers tell you
- Calculating your AP test score

Introduction

This self-assessment test is similar in length and format to the AP exam. Use it to determine your readiness to take the actual exam, administered in May of each year.

Take the test as though it were the real thing. Set aside three hours and 15 minutes at a time when you are wide awake and your mind is fresh. Remove all distractions, sharpen your pencil, read the directions, and go to work.

Allow yourself one hour to answer the multiple-choice questions. Use the answer sheet provided. At the end of the hour take a five-minute break and then tackle the essay questions. Write your essays on standard 8½" × 11" composition paper, the approximate size of an official AP essay response sheet. Allow yourself 40 minutes each for Essays 1 and 2. For Essay 3, allot 15 minutes to read the sources and 40 minutes to write the essay.

When you have finished, check your answers with the Answer Key on page 59. Then read the Answer Explanations. Spend some time analyzing your wrong answers. Try to identify the reason you missed each question: Did you misinterpret the question? Was your choice too specific or too general? Did you misread the passage? Did you base your answer on the wrong material in the passage? Did you jump to a conclusion that led you astray? Knowing why you stumbled can help you avoid similar errors on future tests.

At the same time, don't ignore the items you got right. You may discover a helpful pointer or two.

Although it is hard to evaluate your own essays, don't shy away from trying. Let the essays cool off for a while—maybe even for a day or two—and then, insofar as possible, reread them with an open mind and a fresh pair of eyes. Rate your essays using the Self-Scoring Guide on pages 69–70.

Finally, using data from the Answer Key and the Self-Scoring Guide, calculate the grade you earned on this test.

Diagnostic Test
ANSWER SHEET

Multiple-Choice Questions Time—1 hour

1. Ⓐ Ⓑ Ⓒ Ⓓ Ⓔ
2. Ⓐ Ⓑ Ⓒ Ⓓ Ⓔ
3. Ⓐ Ⓑ Ⓒ Ⓓ Ⓔ
4. Ⓐ Ⓑ Ⓒ Ⓓ Ⓔ
5. Ⓐ Ⓑ Ⓒ Ⓓ Ⓔ
6. Ⓐ Ⓑ Ⓒ Ⓓ Ⓔ
7. Ⓐ Ⓑ Ⓒ Ⓓ Ⓔ
8. Ⓐ Ⓑ Ⓒ Ⓓ Ⓔ
9. Ⓐ Ⓑ Ⓒ Ⓓ Ⓔ
10. Ⓐ Ⓑ Ⓒ Ⓓ Ⓔ
11. Ⓐ Ⓑ Ⓒ Ⓓ Ⓔ
12. Ⓐ Ⓑ Ⓒ Ⓓ Ⓔ
13. Ⓐ Ⓑ Ⓒ Ⓓ Ⓔ
14. Ⓐ Ⓑ Ⓒ Ⓓ Ⓔ
15. Ⓐ Ⓑ Ⓒ Ⓓ Ⓔ
16. Ⓐ Ⓑ Ⓒ Ⓓ Ⓔ
17. Ⓐ Ⓑ Ⓒ Ⓓ Ⓔ
18. Ⓐ Ⓑ Ⓒ Ⓓ Ⓔ
19. Ⓐ Ⓑ Ⓒ Ⓓ Ⓔ
20. Ⓐ Ⓑ Ⓒ Ⓓ Ⓔ

21. Ⓐ Ⓑ Ⓒ Ⓓ Ⓔ
22. Ⓐ Ⓑ Ⓒ Ⓓ Ⓔ
23. Ⓐ Ⓑ Ⓒ Ⓓ Ⓔ
24. Ⓐ Ⓑ Ⓒ Ⓓ Ⓔ
25. Ⓐ Ⓑ Ⓒ Ⓓ Ⓔ
26. Ⓐ Ⓑ Ⓒ Ⓓ Ⓔ
27. Ⓐ Ⓑ Ⓒ Ⓓ Ⓔ
28. Ⓐ Ⓑ Ⓒ Ⓓ Ⓔ
29. Ⓐ Ⓑ Ⓒ Ⓓ Ⓔ
30. Ⓐ Ⓑ Ⓒ Ⓓ Ⓔ
31. Ⓐ Ⓑ Ⓒ Ⓓ Ⓔ
32. Ⓐ Ⓑ Ⓒ Ⓓ Ⓔ
33. Ⓐ Ⓑ Ⓒ Ⓓ Ⓔ
34. Ⓐ Ⓑ Ⓒ Ⓓ Ⓔ
35. Ⓐ Ⓑ Ⓒ Ⓓ Ⓔ
36. Ⓐ Ⓑ Ⓒ Ⓓ Ⓔ
37. Ⓐ Ⓑ Ⓒ Ⓓ Ⓔ
38. Ⓐ Ⓑ Ⓒ Ⓓ Ⓔ
39. Ⓐ Ⓑ Ⓒ Ⓓ Ⓔ
40. Ⓐ Ⓑ Ⓒ Ⓓ Ⓔ

41. Ⓐ Ⓑ Ⓒ Ⓓ Ⓔ
42. Ⓐ Ⓑ Ⓒ Ⓓ Ⓔ
43. Ⓐ Ⓑ Ⓒ Ⓓ Ⓔ
44. Ⓐ Ⓑ Ⓒ Ⓓ Ⓔ
45. Ⓐ Ⓑ Ⓒ Ⓓ Ⓔ
46. Ⓐ Ⓑ Ⓒ Ⓓ Ⓔ
47. Ⓐ Ⓑ Ⓒ Ⓓ Ⓔ
48. Ⓐ Ⓑ Ⓒ Ⓓ Ⓔ
49. Ⓐ Ⓑ Ⓒ Ⓓ Ⓔ
50. Ⓐ Ⓑ Ⓒ Ⓓ Ⓔ
51. Ⓐ Ⓑ Ⓒ Ⓓ Ⓔ
52. Ⓐ Ⓑ Ⓒ Ⓓ Ⓔ
53. Ⓐ Ⓑ Ⓒ Ⓓ Ⓔ
54. Ⓐ Ⓑ Ⓒ Ⓓ Ⓔ
55. Ⓐ Ⓑ Ⓒ Ⓓ Ⓔ

SELF ASSESSMENT

SECTION 1
Total time—1 hour

Questions 1–12. Carefully read the following passage and answer the accompanying questions. *The passage is an excerpt from a essay that appeared in a 20th-century book on violence in America.*

On September 26, 1872, three mounted men rode up to the gate of the Kansas City Fair, which was enjoying a huge crowd of perhaps 10,000 people. The bandits shot at the ticket seller, hit a small girl in the leg, and made
Line off for the woods with something less than a thousand dollars. It was high-
(5) handed, and it endangered the lives of a whole host of holiday-minded people for comparatively little reward.

What makes the robbery and the violence notable is not the crime itself but the way it was reported in the Kansas City *Times* by one John N. Edwards. In his front-page story he branded the robbery "so diabolically
(10) daring and so utterly in contempt of fear that we are bound to admire it and revere its perpetrators."

Two days later the outlaws were being compared by the *Times* with knights of King Arthur's Round Table:

"It was as though three bandits had come to us from storied Odenwald,
(15) with the halo of medieval chivalry upon their garments and shown us how the things were done that poets sing of. Nowhere else in the United States or in the civilized world, probably, could this thing have been done."

Quite likely this deed was perpetrated by the James brothers: Jesse and Frank, and a confederate. The details really do not matter. What pertains is
(20) the attitude of the innocent toward the uncertainly identified guilty. The act had been perpetrated by violent, lawless men. If the *Times* is any indication, a respectable section of people approved of their action. No one, of course, thought to ask the little girl with the shattered leg how she felt about such courage. Nearly 17 months later, Edwards was quoted in the St.
(25) Louis *Dispatch* as preferring the Western highwayman to the Eastern, for "he has more qualities that attract admiration and win respect . . . . This comes from locality . . . which breeds strong, hardy men—men who risk much, who have friends in high places, and who go riding over the land, taking all chances that come in the way." The purpose here is not to bela-
(30) bor one reasonably anonymous newspaperman of nearly a century ago, but merely to point up a fact—and a problem—of the American frontier.

The frontier placed a premium on independent action and individual reliance. The whole history of the American frontier is a narrative of taking what was there to be taken. The timid never gathered riches, the polite
(35) nearly never. The men who first carved the wilderness into land claims and town lots were the men who moved in the face of dangers, gathering as they progressed. The emphasis naturally came to be placed on gathering and not on procedures. Great tales of gigantic attainments abound in this frontier

story; equally adventurous tales of creative plundering mark the march
(40) from Jamestown to the Pacific. It was a period peopled by giants, towers of
audacity with insatiable appetites. The heroes are not the men of moderate
attitudes, not the town planners and commercial builders, not the farmers
nor the ministers nor the teachers. The heroes of the period, handed along
to us with all the luster of a golden baton, are the mighty runners from Mt.
(45) Olympus who ran without looking back, without concern about social values or anywhere they might be going except onward.

We revere these heroes because they were men of vast imagination and
daring. We have also inherited their blindness and their excesses.

1. It can be inferred that the speaker knows the facts about the incident in
   Kansas City on September 26, 1872 because he

   (A) was an eyewitness to the events described.
   (B) happened to be a visitor to the fair.
   (C) interviewed the ticket seller.
   (D) read about it in a newspaper.
   (E) was related to the girl who got shot.

2. In which of the following ways does the sentence that starts "It was
   highhanded . . ." (line 5) differ from the other sentences in the paragraph?

   I. It is a compound sentence.
   II. It expresses the opinion of the speaker.
   III. It employs alliterative language.

   (A) I only
   (B) III only
   (C) I and II only
   (D) II and III only
   (E) I, II, and III

3. In line 8 "the way it was reported" refers to

   (A) the appearance of the story on the front page.
   (B) John N. Edwards' qualifications to write the story.
   (C) the reporter's praise of the bandits.
   (D) the flowery language used by the reporter.
   (E) the matter-of-fact tone in which the story was written.

4. In lines 8–17, the speaker's attitude toward John N. Edwards and his
   newspaper can best be described as one of

   (A) outright scorn.
   (B) profound disillusion.
   (C) extreme hatred.
   (D) honest skepticism.
   (E) exaggerated uneasiness.

5. Which of the following rhetorical devices is most in evidence in lines 12–17?

   (A) An inspiring myth
   (B) An extended analogy
   (C) A parable
   (D) A caricature
   (E) An annotation

6. Which of the following best describes the rhetorical effect of the sentence beginning "Quite likely . . ." (line 18)?

   (A) To restate the main idea of the passage
   (B) To reinforce a theory stated earlier in the passage
   (C) To shift the focus of the passage to an entirely new topic
   (D) To emphasize the foolishness of the preceding quotation
   (E) To endorse the position taken by the Kansas City newspaper

7. The phrase "such courage" (line 24) can best be described as an example of

   (A) a subtle use of irony
   (B) a metaphorical allusion
   (C) a witty analogy
   (D) a paradox
   (E) an oxymoron

8. In the context of the passage, the word "innocent" (line 20) can be interpreted to mean all of the following EXCEPT

   (A) gullible people.
   (B) those who cannot make up their minds.
   (C) individuals who don't know right from wrong.
   (D) uncritical readers.
   (E) simple-minded people.

9. The quotation from the St. Louis newspaper (lines 26–29) serves the author's purposes in which of the following ways?

   (A) It makes a case for more accuracy in newspaper writing.
   (B) It makes clear the author's intention to destroy Edwards' career as a reporter.
   (C) It further illustrates the thinking of many Americans.
   (D) It reinforces the author's view expressed earlier that the bandits were "violent" and "lawless."
   (E) It provides a generalization on which the author will comment in the next paragraph.

10. The author mentions "creative plundering" (line 39) as an example of which of the following?

    (A) Dividing up land for private property
    (B) Earning fortunes on the frontier
    (C) Ignoring dangers to life and limb
    (D) "independent action and individual reliance" (lines 32–33)
    (E) "taking what there was to be taken" (lines 33–34)

11. The conclusions drawn in the last paragraph (lines 47–48) contribute to the unity of the passage in which of the following ways?

    (A) They reiterate a similar idea stated early in the passage.
    (B) They justify the lawlessness that dominated the frontier.
    (C) They indicate the similarity between frontier people and the knights of King Arthur.
    (D) They explain why the bandits in Kansas City were admired instead of condemned.
    (E) They mock the values of the frontier just as the author has mocked John N. Edwards.

12. As described in the passage, the bandits, the Knights of the Round Table, and the people of the frontier all share which of the following?

    (A) A concern for upholding their reputations
    (B) An intense commitment to strive for their goals
    (C) Uncertainty about their position in society
    (D) A sentimental attachment to the past
    (E) A reckless disregard of the truth

Questions 13–23. Carefully read the following passage and answer the accompanying questions. *This passage is a speech delivered in 1873 by the renowned social reformer and advocate for women's suffrage, Susan B. Anthony.*

Friends and fellow citizens:

I stand before you tonight under indictment for the alleged crime of having voted in the last presidential election, without having a lawful right to
Line vote. It shall be my work this evening to prove to you that in thus voting,
(5)   I not only committed no crime, but, instead, simply exercised my *citizen's rights*, guaranteed to me and all United States citizens by the National Constitution, beyond the power of any State to deny . . . . The preamble of the Federal Constitution says:

"We, the people of the United States, in order to form a more perfect
(10)   union, establish justice, insure *domestic* tranquillity, provide for the common defense, promote the general welfare, and secure the blessings of liberty to ourselves and our posterity, do ordain and establish this Constitution for the United States of America."

It was we, the people; not we, the white male citizens; nor yet we, the
(15)   male citizens; but we, the whole people, who formed the Union. And we formed it, not to give the blessings of liberty, but to secure them; not the half of ourselves and the half of our posterity, but to the whole people— women as well as men. And it is downright mockery to talk to women of their enjoyment of the blessings of liberty while they are denied the use of
(20)   the only means of securing them provided by this democratic-republican government—the ballot.

For any state to make sex a qualification that must ever result in the dis-
enfranchisement of one entire half of the people is to pass a bill of attainder,[1] or an *ex post facto* law,[2] and is therefore a violation of the supreme law
(25) of the land. By it the blessings of liberty are forever withheld from women
and their female posterity. To them this government has no just powers
derived from the consent of the governed. To them this government is not
a democracy. It is not a republic. It is an odious aristocracy; a hateful oligarchy[3] of sex; the most hateful aristocracy ever established on the face of
(30) the globe; an oligarchy of wealth, where the rich govern the poor. An oligarchy of learning, where the educated govern the ignorant, or even an oligarchy of race, where the Saxon rules the African, might be endured; but
this oligarchy of sex, which makes father, brothers, husbands, sons, the oli-
garchs over the mother and sisters, the wife and daughters of every house-
(35) hold—which ordains all men sovereign, all women subjects, carries
dissension, discord and rebellion into every home of the nation.

Webster, Worcester and Bouvier all define a citizen to be a person in the
United States, entitled to vote and to hold office. The only question left to
be settled now is: Are women persons? And I hardly believe any of our
(40) opponents will have the hardihood to say they are not. Being persons, then,
women are citizens; and no State has a right to make any law, or to enforce
an old law, that shall abridge their privileges or immunities. Hence, every
discrimination against women in the constitutions and laws of the several
States is today null and void, precisely as in every one against negroes.

---

[1] *An act that takes away one's civil rights.*
[2] *A law that imposes punishment for an act not punishable when it was committed.*
[3] *The exercise of power in the hands of a privileged few.*

13. The opening sentence of the passage (lines 2–4) performs which of the
following rhetorical functions?

   I. It states the main idea of the passage.
   II. It provides a reason for delivering the speech.
   III. It reveals the speaker's mood.

   (A) I only
   (B) III only
   (C) I and II only
   (D) II and III only
   (E) I, II, and III

14. Which of the following phrases does the author use to support her claim
that she is innocent of committing a crime?

   (A) "under indictment" (line 2)
   (B) "the last presidential election" (line 3)
   (C) "exercised my *citizen's rights*" (lines 5–6)
   (D) "form a more perfect union" (lines 9–10)
   (E) "establish justice" (line 10)

15. The primary rhetorical purpose of quoting the Federal Constitution can best be described as

    (A) an emotional appeal.
    (B) evidence to support an earlier assertion.
    (C) a use of elegant words to earn the good will of the audience.
    (D) up-to-date background information.
    (E) an opportunity to weigh both sides of the argument.

16. In the preamble (lines 9–13), which of the following words is parallel in function to "establish" (line 10)?

    (A) "union" (line 10)
    (B) *domestic* (line 10)
    (C) "promote" (line 11)
    (D) "general" (line 11)
    (E) "ordain" (line 12)

17. Throughout the second paragraph (lines 14–21), the rhetorical strategy most in evidence is

    (A) antithesis
    (B) abstract allusion
    (C) sentimentality
    (D) euphemism
    (E) extended metaphor

18. The phrase "downright mockery" (line 18) is reinforced by the author's later reference to

    (A) "this democratic-republican government" (lines 20–21)
    (B) "*ex post facto* law" (line 24)
    (C) "supreme law of the land" (lines 24–25)
    (D) "blessings of liberty are forever withheld" (line 25)
    (E) "female posterity" (line 26)

19. Lines 22–25 contain which of the following?

    (A) Two independent clauses
    (B) A single periodic sentence
    (C) An analogy
    (D) Understatement
    (E) A rhetorical question

20. By comparing an "oligarchy of sex" (lines 28–29) with an "oligarchy of race" (lines 31–32) the speaker primarily means to suggest that

    (A) racial discrimination is tolerable; sexual discrimination isn't
    (B) racism needs to be abolished
    (C) America has a long tradition of discriminatory practices against minorities
    (D) our country's democracy is being torn apart
    (E) equality in America is a myth, not a reality

21. The point of view expressed in "It is an odious . . .the poor" (lines 28–30) is that of

    (A) the framers of the Constitution
    (B) political scientists
    (C) citizens who exercise their right to vote
    (D) all present-day and future women
    (E) the author

22. The organization of the last paragraph (lines 37–44) can best be described as a

    (A) question followed by several possible answers.
    (B) series of premises leading to a logical conclusion.
    (C) generalization supported by illustrative details.
    (D) hypothesis proven by factual data.
    (E) sequence of truths from which it may be possible to draw an inference.

23. The tone of the passage as a whole can best be described as

    (A) proud and idealistic.
    (B) petty and inflexible.
    (C) pompous but generally cautious.
    (D) embarrassed but self-righteous.
    (E) angry and resentful.

Questions 24–34. Carefully read the following passage and answer the accompanying questions. *This passage is taken from a 20th-century book on the history and culture of the Kiowa Indians.*

> Yellowstone, it seemed to me, was the top of the world, a region of deep lakes and dark timber, canyons and waterfalls. But, beautiful as it is, one might have the sense of confinement there. The skyline in all directions is
> *Line* close at hand, the high wall of the woods and deep cleavages of shade. There
> *(5)* is a perfect freedom in the mountains, but it belongs to the eagle and the elk, the badger and the bear. The Kiowas reckoned their stature by the distance they could see, and they were bent and blind in the wilderness.
>
> Descending eastward, the highland meadows are a stairway to the plain. In July the inland slope of the Rockies is luxuriant with flax and buckwheat,
> *(10)* stonecrop and larkspur. The earth unfolds and the limit of the land recedes. Clusters of trees, and animals grazing far in the distance, cause the vision to reach away and wonder to build upon the mind. The sun follows a longer course in the day, and the sky is immense beyond all comparison. The great billowing clouds that sail upon it are shadows that move upon the grain like
> *(15)* water, dividing light. Farther down, in the land of the Crows and Blackfeet, the plain is yellow. Sweet clover takes hold of the hills and bends upon itself to cover and seal the soil. There the Kiowas paused on the way; they had come to the place where they must change their lives. The sun is at home on the plains. Precisely there does it have the certain character of a god.
> *(20)* When the Kiowas came to the land of the Crows, they could see the dark lees of the hills at dawn across the Bighorn River, the profusion of light on

the grain shelves, the oldest deity ranging after the solstices. Not yet would they veer southward to the caldron of the land that lay below; they must wean their blood from the northern winter and hold the mountains a while *(25)* longer in their view. . . .

A dark mist lay over the Black Hills, and the land was like iron. At the top of a ridge I caught sight of Devil's Tower upthrust against the gray sky as if in the birth of time the core of the earth had broken through its crust and the motion of the world was begun.

24. The diction and content of the passage suggest that the speaker is most likely

    (A) a tourist on an Indian reservation.
    (B) a botanist studying plant life in Yellowstone.
    (C) a Native American visiting the land of his ancestors.
    (D) a student of Indian customs and traditions.
    (E) a historian returning to a familiar place.

25. The main rhetorical function of the last sentence in paragraph 1 (lines 6–7) is

    (A) to provide a transition to the next paragraph.
    (B) to support the main idea of the passage.
    (C) to introduce a contradiction that needs to be explained later.
    (D) to illustrate an idea presented earlier in the paragraph.
    (E) to present a thesis that will be developed later in the passage.

26. In line 8, "Descending" modifies

    (A) "highland" (line 8).
    (B) "meadows" (line 8).
    (C) "stairway" (line 8).
    (D) "plain" (line 8).
    (E) "slope" (line 9).

27. Which of the following best describes the rhetorical function of the first sentence of the second paragraph (line 8)?

    (A) It shifts the focus of the passage.
    (B) It reiterates the main idea of the preceding paragraph.
    (C) It conveys the speaker's feelings about being in the wilderness.
    (D) It dismisses the first paragraph as unimportant to the development of the thesis.
    (E) It emphasizes the speaker's profound understanding of his subject.

28. Lines 12–15 contain which of the following rhetorical devices?

    (A) Onomatopoeia and hyperbole
    (B) Personification and euphemism
    (C) Paradox and ambiguity
    (D) Synecdoche and rhyme
    (E) Metaphor and simile

29. The principal contrast employed by the author of the passage is between

    (A) Kiowas and Crows.
    (B) winter and summer.
    (C) light plains and dark mountains.
    (D) the past and the present.
    (E) near and far.

30. The speaker's tone throughout the passage is best described as

    (A) earnest and profound.
    (B) reverent and poetic.
    (C) sensible and scholarly.
    (D) exotic and sentimental.
    (E) sober and philosophical.

31. The sentences in lines 18–22 contain all of the following EXCEPT

    (A) elaborate personification
    (B) parallel syntax
    (C) a subordinate clause
    (D) direct comparison
    (E) a balance of overstatement and understatement

32. In context, the phrase "wean their blood" (line 24) is referred to elsewhere as

    (A) "reckoned their stature" (line 6)
    (B) "bent and blind in the wilderness" (line 7)
    (C) "wonder to build upon the mind" (line 12)
    (D) "paused on their way" (line 17)
    (E) "change their lives" (line 18)

33. The rhetorical style of the passage is best described as

    (A) wordy and pedantic.
    (B) ornate and flowery.
    (C) graphic and graceful.
    (D) terse and didactic.
    (E) severe and classic.

34. The last paragraph (lines 26–29) contributes to the overall unity of the passage in which of the following ways?

    I. It echoes the sense of darkness that dominated the first paragraph.
    II. It describes the land in ways that recall earlier descriptions.
    III. It brings the speaker's perspective back into the narrative.

    (A) II only
    (B) III only
    (C) I and II only
    (D) I and III only
    (E) I, II, and III

Questions 35–45. Carefully read the following passage and answer the accompanying questions. *This passage is an excerpt from a book about the world's black people written in the mid-20th century.*

Let's imagine a mammoth flying saucer from Mars landing, say, in a peasant Swiss village and debouching swarms of fierce-looking men whose skins are blue and whose red eyes flash lightning bolts that deal instant death.

Line The inhabitants are all the more terrified because the arrival of these men
(5) had been predicted. The religious myths of the Western world—the Second Coming of Christ, the Last Judgment, etc., have conditioned Europeans for just such an improbable event. Hence, those Swiss natives will feel that resistance is useless for a while. As long as the blue strangers are casually kind, they are obeyed and served. They become the Fathers of the people.
(10) Is this a fragment of paperback science fiction? No. It's more prosaic than that. The image I've sketched above is the manner, by and large, in which white Europe overran Asia and Africa.

But why did Europe do this? Did it only want gold, power, women, raw materials? It was more complicated than that. The fifteenth-, sixteenth-, and
(15) seventeenth-century neurotic European, sick of his thwarted instincts, restless, filled with self-disgust, was looking for not only spices and gold and slaves when he set out; he was looking for an Arcadia, a Land's End, a Shangri-la, a world peopled by shadow men, a world that would permit free play for his repressed instincts. Stripped of tradition, these misfits, adventur-
(20) ers, indentured servants, convicts and freebooters were the most advanced individualists of their time. Rendered socially superfluous by the stifling weight of the Church and nobility, buttressed by the influence of the ideas of Hume and Descartes, they had been brutally molded toward attitudes of emotional independence and could doff the cloying ties of custom, tradition,
(25) and family. The Asian-African native, anchored in family-dependence systems of life, could not imagine why or how these men had left their homelands, could not conceive of the cold, arid emotions sustaining them. . . .

Living in a waking dream, generations of emotionally impoverished colonial European whites wallowed in the quick gratification of greed, reveled in
(30) the cheap superiority of racial domination, slaked their sensual thirst in illicit sexuality, draining off the dammed-up libido[1] that European morality had condemned, amassing through trade a vast reservoir of economic fat, thereby establishing vast accumulations of capital which spurred the industrialization of the West. Asia and Africa thus became a neurotic habit that
(35) Europeans could forgo only at the cost of a powerful psychic wound, for this emotionally crippled Europe had, through the centuries, grown used to leaning upon this black crutch. But what of the impact of those white faces upon the personalities of the native? Steeped in dependence systems of family life and anchored in ancestor-worshiping religions, the native was prone
(40) to identify those powerful white faces falling athwart his existence with the potency of his dead father who has sustained him in the past. Temporarily accepting the invasion, he transferred his loyalties to those white faces, but, because of the psychological, racial, and economic luxury which those faces derived from their denomination, the native was kept at bay.

---

[1] *sexual drive*

35. The subject of the passage is introduced in the first paragraph by means of

    (A) an exposé
    (B) an allusion
    (C) a parable
    (D) an exposition
    (E) a fable

36. In context, the word "Fathers" (line 9) is best interpreted as having which of the following meanings?

    (A) Role-models
    (B) Ruthless tyrants
    (C) Priests
    (D) Masters
    (E) Representatives

37. Which of the following words is grammatically and thematically parallel to "restless" (lines 15–16)?

    (A) "neurotic" (line 15)
    (B) "sick" (line 15)
    (C) "thwarted" (line 15)
    (D) "self-disgust" (line 16)
    (E) "looking" (line 17)

38. The speaker mentions Arcadia, Land's End, Shangri-la (lines 17–18) as examples of which of the following?

    (A) Destinations for wealthy European travelers of the 15th–17th centuries.
    (B) Places where slaves, spices, and gold, could be traded for goods to take back to Europe.
    (C) Utopian societies where people could be free and happy.
    (D) Lost civilizations that disappeared centuries ago.
    (E) Exotic places that attracted explorers and adventurers.

39. The phrase "advanced individualists" (lines 20–21) is best described as an example of

    (A) irony
    (B) hyperbole
    (C) an oxymoron
    (D) understatement
    (E) parody

40. The characteristics of the colonial European described in the clause beginning on line 23 ("they had been. . .") is referred to elsewhere in all of the following phrases EXCEPT

    (A) "filled with self-disgust" (line 16).
    (B) "socially superfluous" (line 21).
    (C) "Stripped of tradition" (line 19).
    (D) "cold, arid emotions" (line 27).
    (E) "emotionally impoverished" (line 28).

41. Which rhetorical device is most evident in line 30: "slaked their sensual thirst in illicit sexuality"?

    (A) onomatopoeia
    (B) a metaphor
    (C) assonance
    (D) allegory
    (E) alliteration

42. Which of the following best describes the prevailing tone of the passage?

    (A) Objective and impartial
    (B) Irate and contentious
    (C) Pedantic and nitpicking
    (D) Restrained and thoughtful
    (E) Moralistic and circumspect

43. Throughout the passage, the speaker contrasts the European colonists and the Asian-African natives on the basis of

    (A) their economic wealth.
    (B) the strength of their belief in God.
    (C) their attitude toward family life.
    (D) their desire to own property.
    (E) their attachment to the land.

44. The speaker's repeated use of questions (lines 10, 13–14, and 37–38) serves which of the following rhetorical purposes?

    (A) To raise issues that would not otherwise be raised
    (B) To discuss the issue from a new, totally different, point of view
    (C) To provide a quick transition from one topic to a different but related one
    (D) To anticipate objections that readers may have in mind
    (E) To establish the speaker as an authority on the subject

45. Throughout the passage, which of the following rhetorical strategies is most in evidence?

    (A) Specific examples and anecdotes to illustrate the main idea
    (B) The testimony of experts on the subject of European colonialism
    (C) Well-reasoned logical argumentation in support of a thesis
    (D) The use of highly-charged, emotional language to create an effect
    (E) The testing of a hypothesis using observation and the massing of data

Questions 46–55. Carefully read the following passage and answer the accompanying questions. This passage is taken from a book written in the late 20th century.

Gary infuriated his fiancée, Ellen, because even though he was intelligent, thoughtful, and a successful surgeon, Gary was emotionally flat, completely unresponsive to any and all shows of feeling. While Gary could speak
Line brilliantly of science and art, when it came to his feelings—even for Ellen—
(5) he fell silent. Try as she might to elicit some passion from him, Gary was impassive, oblivious. "I don't naturally express my feelings," Gary told the

therapist he saw at Ellen's insistence. When it came to emotional life, he added, "I don't know what to talk about; I have no strong feelings, either positive or negative."

(10)   Ellen was not alone in being frustrated by Gary's aloofness; as he confided to his therapist, he was unable to speak openly about his feelings with anyone in his life. The reason: He did not know what he felt in the first place. So far as he could tell he had no angers, no sadness, no joys.[1]

As his own therapist observes, this emotional blankness makes Gary and
(15)   others like him colorless, bland: "They bore everybody. That's why their wives send them into treatment." Gary's emotional flatness exemplifies what psychiatrists call *alexithymia*, from the Greek *a* for "lack," *lexis* for "word," and *thymos* for "emotion." Such people lack words for their feelings. Indeed, they seem to lack feelings altogether, although this may actually be because of their
(20)   inability to *express* emotion rather than from an absence of emotion altogether. Such people were first noticed by psychoanalysts puzzled by a class of patients who were untreatable by that method because they reported no feelings, no fantasies, and colorless dreams—in short, no inner emotional life to talk about at all.[2] The clinical features that mark alexithymics include having
(25)   difficulty describing feelings—their own or anyone else's—and a sharply limited emotional vocabulary.[3] What's more, they have trouble discriminating among emotions as well as between emotions and bodily sensation, so that they might tell of having butterflies in the stomach, palpitations, sweating, and dizziness—but they would not know they are feeling anxious.

(30)   "They give the impression of being different, alien beings, having come from an entirely different world, living in the midst of a society which is dominated by feelings," is the description given by Dr. Peter Sifneos, the Harvard psychiatrist who in 1972 coined the term *alexithymia*.[4] Alexithymics rarely cry, for example, but if they do their tears are copious.
(35)   Still, they are bewildered if asked what the tears are all about. One patient with alexithymia was so upset after seeing a movie about a woman with eight children who was dying of cancer that she cried herself to sleep. When her therapist suggested that perhaps she was upset because the movie reminded her of her own mother, who was in actuality dying of cancer, the
(40)   woman sat motionless, bewildered, and silent. When her therapist then asked her how she felt at that moment, she said she felt "awful," but couldn't clarify her feelings beyond that. And, she added, from time to time she found herself crying, but never knew exactly what she was crying about.[5]

---

[1] *Larry Cahill et al., "Beta-adrenergic activations and memory for emotional events,"* Nature *(Oct. 20, 1994).*

[2] *Psychoanalytic theory and brain maturation: the most detailed discussion of the early years and the emotional consequences of brain development is by Allan Schore,* Affect Regulation and the Origin of Self *(Hillsdale, NJ: Lawrence Erlbaum Associates, 1994).*

[3] *Dangerous, even if you don't know what it is; Joseph LeDoux, quoted in "How Scary Things Got That Way,"* Science *(Nov. 6, 1992), p. 887.*

[4] *Much of this speculation about the fine-tuning of emotional response by the neocortex comes from Ned Kalin, M.D., Departments of Psychology and Psychiatry, University of Wisconsin, prepared for the MacArthur Affective Neuroscience Meeting, Nov., 1992.*

[5] *See Ned Kalin, Departments of Psychology and Psychiatry, University of Wisconsin, "Aspects of Emotion Conserved Across Species," an unpublished manuscript presented at the MacArthur Affective Neuroscience Meeting, Nov., 1992; and Alan Schore,* Affect Regulation and the Origin of Self *(Hillsdale, NJ: Lawrence Erlbaum Associates, 1994).*

46. Which of the following best states the main subject of the passage?

    (A) The difficulties of treating alexithymia
    (B) Research in alexithymia
    (C) Symptoms of alexithymia
    (D) A puzzling psychological disorder of modern times
    (E) The causes of alexithymia

47. Which of the following best explains the function of the passage's first sentence?

    (A) It introduces a conflict to be resolved by the end of the passage.
    (B) It defines the limits of the discussion that follows.
    (C) It establishes the author as an expert on the subject of the passage.
    (D) It makes a claim that the author will try to prove in the remainder of the passage.
    (E) It describes a situation that illustrates the central concern of the passage.

48. The structure of the footnoted paragraph (lines 10–13) can best be described as

    (A) a statement describing a situation followed by an explanation of its cause.
    (B) movement from particular details to generalizations.
    (C) a series of controversial ideas unrelated to the preceding paragraph.
    (D) the introduction and definition of an abstract psychological term.
    (E) the presentation of a hypothesis that will be proved later in the passage.

49. Which of the following best explains why the word *express* in line 20 is italicized?

    (A) To differentiate between the expression of emotion and the feeling of emotion.
    (B) To emphasize that in order to talk about emotions you must feel them.
    (C) To indicate that those suffering from alexithymia never have emotions to express.
    (D) To alert the reader that the word is being used ironically.
    (E) To suggest that the author has borrowed the word from one of the passage's footnoted sources.

50. In context, the word "colorless" (line 23) is best interpreted to mean

    (A) humdrum and routine.
    (B) silent but full of action.
    (C) vague but creative.
    (D) crazy but meaningful.
    (E) gray and impressionistic.

51. The primary purpose of footnote 3 (line 26) is to inform readers that

    (A) Joseph LeDoux's main academic interest is "emotional vocabulary."
    (B) Joseph LeDoux wrote an article published in a science periodical.
    (C) Joseph LeDoux is the author of a book named *Science*.
    (D) the footnoted material has been adapted from words written by Joseph LeDoux.
    (E) lines 24–26 were originally published in an article entitled "How Scary Things Got That Way."

52. The author includes footnote 4 (line 33) in the text of the passage mainly to

    (A) inform readers where the term *alexithymia* originated.
    (B) specify where the quotation in lines 30–32 can be found in print.
    (C) establish the academic credentials of an authority on the subject of emotional responses.
    (D) suggest that several researchers have contributed to an understanding of emotional responses.
    (E) indicate that alexithymia came into existence in 1972.

53. Which of the following is an inference that can be drawn based on information in footnote 5 (line 43)?

    (A) An article by Ned Kalin was published after November, 1992.
    (B) The University of Wisconsin sponsored a meeting on affective neuroscience.
    (C) Both Ned Kalin and Alan Schore have written about alexithymia.
    (D) "Aspects of Emotion Conserved Across Species" was published in New Jersey.
    (E) In his book, Alan Schore cited words spoken by Ned Kalin at the meeting on affective neuroscience.

54. The development of the passage can best be described as

    (A) a discussion of physical symptoms related to a psychological problem.
    (B) the explanation of a psychological condition illustrated by specific cases.
    (C) an argument for employing therapy in order to overcome a psychological disorder.
    (D) the outline of a procedure for treating a 20th-century mental disease.
    (E) an analysis of consequences stemming from a widespread mental deficiency.

55. The attitude of the author toward people suffering from alexithymia is primarily one of

    (A) indifference.
    (B) awe.
    (C) puzzlement.
    (D) compassion.
    (E) respect.

SECTION 2

Essay Questions
Total time—2 hours and 15 minutes

Write your essays on standard 8½" by 11" composition paper.
(*At the AP exam, you'll be given a bound booklet containing 12 lined pages.*)

Essay Question 1
(Suggested time—40 minutes)

The passage below, adapted from an essay written in 1920 by A.A. Milne, is a mock-serious reflection on the passing of summer. Read it carefully. Then, in a well-written essay, analyze how the rhetorical strategies that Milne uses reveal the speaker's personality and values.

Line

(5)

(10)

(15)

(20)

(25)

(30)

Last night the waiter put the celery on with the cheese, and I knew that summer was indeed dead. Other signs of autumn there may be—the reddening of the leaf, the chill in the early-morning air, the misty evenings—but none of these comes home to me so truly. There may be cool mornings in July; in a year of drought the leaves may change before their time; it is only with the first celery that summer is over. . . .

There is a crispness about celery that is the essence of October. It is as fresh and clean as a rainy day after a spell of heat. It crackles pleasantly in the mouth. Moreover, it is excellent, I am told, for the complexion. One is always hearing of things which are good for the complexion, but there is no doubt that celery stands high on the list. After the burns and freckles of summer one is in need of something. How good that celery should be there at one's elbow. . . .

"Season of mists and mellow fruitfulness," said Keats, not actually picking out celery in so many words, but plainly including it in the general blessings of autumn. Yet, what an opportunity he missed by not concentrating on that precious root. Apples, grapes, and nuts he mentions specially—how poor a selection! For apples and grapes are not typical of any month, so ubiquitous are they, while as for nuts, have we not a national song which asserts distinctly, "Here we go gathering nuts in May"? Season of mists and mellow celery, then let it be. A pat of butter underneath the bough, a wedge of cheese, a loaf of bread and—Thou.

How delicate are the tender shoots that unfold layer by layer. Of what a whiteness is the last baby one of all, of what a sweetness his flavor. It is well that this should be the last rite of the meal so that we may go straight on to the business of the pipe. Celery demands a pipe rather than a cigar, and it can be eaten better in an inn or a London tavern than in the home.

Yes, and it should be eaten alone, for it is the only food which one really wants to hear oneself eat. Besides, in company one may have to consider the wants of others. Celery is not a thing to share with any man. Alone in your country inn you may call for celery; but if you are wise you will see

that no other traveler wanders into the room. Take warning from one who has learnt a lesson. One day I lunched alone at an inn, finishing with cheese and celery. Another traveler came in and lunched too. We did not speak—
(35) I was busy with my celery. From the other end of the table he reached across for the cheese. That was all right! It was the public cheese. But he also reached across for the celery—my private celery for which I owed. Foolishly—you know how one does—I had left the sweetest and crispest shoots till the last, tantalizing myself pleasantly with the thought of them.
(40) Horror! To see them snatched from me by a stranger. He realized later what he had done and apologized, but of what good is an apology under such circumstances? Yet at least the tragedy was not without its value. Now one remembers to lock the door.

I can face the winter with calm. I suppose I had forgotten what it was
(45) really like. I had been thinking of the winter as a horrid, wet, dreary time fit only for professional football. Now I can see other things—crisp and sparkling days, long pleasant evenings, cheery fires. Good work shall be done this winter. Life shall be lived well, The end of the summer is not the end of the world. Here's to October—and, waiter, some more celery.

Essay Question 2
(Suggested time—40 minutes)

The two passages below comment on the state of American society during the early 1960s. Read the passages carefully. Then, in a well-organized essay, analyze the specific stylistic and rhetorical differences between the two passages, paying particular attention to how the two authors present themselves to the reader.

Passage A

When a man, a business corporation, or an entire society is approaching bankruptcy, there are two courses that those involved can follow: they can evade the reality of their situation and act on a frantic, blind, rage-of-the-
Line moment expediency—not daring to look ahead, wishing no one would
(5) name the truth, yet desperately hoping that something will save them somehow—or they can identify with the situation, check their premises, discover their hidden assets, and start rebuilding.

America, at present, is following the first course. The grayness, the stale cynicism, the noncommittal cautiousness, the guilty evasiveness of our
(10) public voices suggest the attitude of the courtiers in the story "The Emperor's New Clothes" who have professed admiration for the Emperor's nonexistent garments, having accepted the assertion that anyone who failed to perceive them was morally depraved at heart.

Let me be the child in the story and declare that the Emperor is naked—
(15) or that America is culturally bankrupt.

PASSAGE B

Great movements and forces, springing from deep wells, have converged at this midcentury point, and I suspect we have barely begun to comprehend what has happened and why. In the foreground is the mortal contest with
Line   world communism, which is apparent, if the means of dealing with it are not
(5)   always apparent. But in the background are the opaque, moving forms and shadows of a world revolution, of which communism is more the scavenger than the inspiration; a world in transition from an age with which we are familiar to an age shrouded in mist. We Americans have to deal with both the foreground and the background of this troubled, anxious age.

(10)   It is easy to state our ends, our goals, but it is hard to fit them to our means. Every day, for example, politicians, of which there are plenty, swear eternal devotion to the ends of peace and security. They always remind me of the elder Holmes' apostrophe to a katydid: "Thou say'st an undisputed thing in such a solemn way." And every day statesmen, of which there are a few, must
(15)   struggle with limited means to achieve these unlimited ends, both in fact and in understanding. For the nation's purposes always exceed its means, and it is finding a balance between means and the ends that is the heart of foreign policy and that makes it such a speculative, uncertain business.

Essay Question 3
Time—
15 minutes to read the question and sources
40 minutes to write the essay

Instructions: The following essay topic is accompanied by six sources.

Respond to the question below in a well-written, coherent essay that draws on ideas and information found in **at least three** of the sources. Don't simply summarize or paraphrase the sources. Instead, **focus the essay on your point of view**, and use the sources to support or bolster your argument.

Topic: Because an educated population enjoys a level of prosperity, culture, and well-being unavailable to those with few educational opportunities, some people argue that all students, regardless of their ability to pay, should go to college—or at least be pushed hard in that direction—after graduating from high school.

Your task: Read the following sources carefully. Then, in an essay that synthesizes at least three of the sources, take a position that supports, challenges, or modifies the claim that all students should attend college.

In your essay, you may refer to the sources simply as Source A, Source B, etc., or by the key words in parentheses below.

Source A (Hansen)

Source B (Kurtzman)

Source C (Mortality Rates)

Source D (Photo with caption)

Source E (Toppo and DeBarros)

Source F (Rob)

SOURCE A

Katherine Hansen, "What Good is a College Education Anyway?" Quintessential Careers <*www.quintcareers.com.*> Accessed, August 7, 2006.

The following comes from an article describing the value of a college education.

. . . If you doubt that knowledge is power, consider the societies that have denied education to selected segments of the population. The Taliban in Afghanistan keeps women from having any power by outlawing their education, much as antebellum American society kept slaves from possessing power by denying them schooling.

[C]ollege education is a legacy for your children. The idea of having children may be as remote to you as the international space station, but trust us, your college education will benefit your children—and not just so you can impress them with how well you play "Who Wants to be a Millionaire."

Research shows that children of college-educated parents are healthier, perform better academically, and are more likely to attend college themselves than children of those with lower educational attainment.

Your education builds a foundation for your children—for our nation's children, and for the children of our global community—which leads to the last point: Education is the cornerstone of public progress.

Education is the essence of the democratic ideals that elevated the United States from a backward land of rebellious colonists to the greatest, most spirited, powerful and successful nation in the world.

And we are the greatest nation. America leads the world in educational attainment, and with one exception, we lead in per-capita income. Speaking at a symposium on American values, Anne L. Heald[1] said there is "an extraordinary consensus that the preparation of young people for work is one of the singular most important things a society can do to improve its ability to prosper in a new international economy."

Similarly, Federal Reserve Board Chairman Alan Greenspan said recently, "We must ensure that our whole population receives an education that will allow full and continuing participation in this dynamic period of American economic history." What Greenspan is saying is that, without college, you may be left out. And the relationship between a college education and success will become more and more significant in our information-driven global economy. Higher education will be increasingly important for landing high-paying jobs.

Technology and the information age are not the only reasons to be well educated; the trend is toward multiple jobs and even multiple careers, and higher education prepares you to make the transition to new fields.

So what more could you ask of your investment in higher education than prosperity, quality of life, the knowledge that bolsters social change, a legacy for your children, and the means to ensure the continuing success of the American dream?

---

[1]*Administrator of Center for Learning and Competitiveness, University of Maryland*

SOURCE B

Lori Kurtzman, "Remedial Classes Teach Freshmen What They Already Know," *Cincinnati Enquirer*, July 30, 2006.

The following passage is an excerpt from a feature story about the problems of remedial college students.

It's not always easy to pinpoint why students, fresh out of high school, need to enroll in remedial "catch-up" courses when they get to college. What's clear, however, is that many of them do.

Of the thousands of freshmen entering Ohio colleges and universities this fall, it's a safe bet that more than one-third won't be completely ready for the next level of their education. In the most recent figures available (2003), 41 percent of newly minted Ohio high school graduates who went to Ohio public colleges enrolled in remedial math or reading courses during their freshman year. . . .

The experiences of local graduates show that even the best area high schools—those rated "excellent" by the state—are graduating students who need extra help once they get to college. . . .

. . .So why be concerned over some students playing a little bit of catch-up? Education experts say this isn't just about a student taking a few extra classes. Remediation, which often affects minorities from poor families in low-income public districts, has an impact that stretches from families to schools to taxpayers.

Remedial needs strain the student, who might pay hundreds or thousands of dollars for classes that don't count toward a degree.

. . .They strain colleges, too, which devote instructors, classrooms and supplies to classes that ideally wouldn't be necessary.

And they strain the state—in essence, taxpayers—to the tune of about $30 million a year in remedial costs. . . .

But perhaps the greatest problem is what so often happens to students who require remediation: They struggle. They fail. They drop out. They lose the earning power of a college degree. The state tracked a group of students for six years and found that among the remedial students, only 15 percent earned a bachelor's degree in that time; nearly three times as many nonremedial students received their degrees. . . .

The growing need for college remedial classes hasn't gone unnoticed by high schools, colleges, or the state. Governor Bob Taft, in his final State of the State speech in January, proposed better preparing high school graduates by toughening the core high school curriculum with additional math, science and foreign language requirements.

"For too many, a high school diploma is not a passport to success, but rather a broken promise," he said.

SOURCE C

Anonymous, "Higher Education Means Lower Mortality Rates," published online at *www.etcs.ipfw.edu*, June 28, 2006.

The following is the complete text of a note appended to an article entitled "Is a College Education Worth It?"

When asked to list the benefits of a college education, most people name higher incomes and a rich intellectual life. Now it is clear that better health should be added to the list.

Mortality rates for Americans ages 25 to 64 who have attended college are less than half the rates for those who stopped education after completing high school. In 1999, the most recent year for which final mortality rates have been published, there were 219 deaths per 100,000 people per year for those with 13 or more years of education, compared with 474 per 100,000 for those with 12 years, and 585 per 100,000 for those with fewer than 12 years of education. These differences are somewhat greater for men than for women.

The mortality advantage for Americans with higher education has been growing in recent decades, according to several studies that used census and survey data. And there is an added advantage for educated people in rates of illness and disability, so that those with some college education enjoy extra years of healthy life. Two factors that partly explain the education advantage are lifestyle (educated people are less likely to smoke or engage in other risky behaviors) and health insurance (people with more education tend to have better coverage than those with less education).

SOURCE D

The following illustration and its caption come from the blog "Creating Passionate Users" and was submitted as a response to the question, "Does college matter?"

Does college matter?

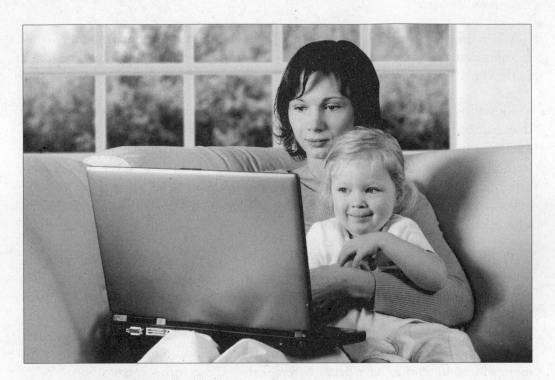

". . . and then you'll go to college for five years getting an outrageously expensive four-year degree (it'll take decades to pay off your student loans) in a subject which you don't even like but that everyone says is best for your future, learning things that become obsolete in 24 months, and then you'll discover that the so-called "great career opportunities" have been outsourced or automated, or that the world has changed in ways nobody could have predicted and you'll work part-time at Starbucks for the medical plan before you realize that you should have. . . ."

SOURCE E

Gregg Toppo and Anthony DeBarros, "Reality Weighs Down Dreams of College," *USA Today*, posted online, February 2, 2005.

What follows is part of an article analyzing the trend toward increased college enrollment.

Adults increasingly are urging young people to go to college—even students who a generation ago might have expected to work in blue-collar jobs their entire lives. And teens are taking the message to heart: From 1990 to 2002, the percentage of 10th-graders aspiring to college rose 21 percentage points, to 80%.

But new research also reveals a huge gap between aspirations and reality, especially for poor and minority students. For them, high school dropout rates remain high and college graduation rates low.

. . . Recent studies also show that many low-income and minority students who aspire to college are poorly served by their schools and their families, arriving at college unprepared and forcing colleges and universities to spend an estimated $1 billion a year on remediation.

"There is a real gap between the aspirations teenagers have and the realities of what happens to them," says Christopher Swanson of the Urban Institute, a think tank in Washington, D.C. "Teenagers grow up hearing these 'college for all' expectations, and they internalize this. While rhetorically it makes sense, in reality all students are not going to go to college."

". . . We're not being honest with a lot of kids today," says Thomas Toch, author of *High Schools on a Human Scale* and co-founder of Education Sector, another Washington think tank.

"We're telling kids that they can do it, when we're not giving them the academic tools to be successful. We're not giving them an education that will truly prepare them to be successful in college."

A *USA Today* analysis of two Department of Education surveys shows how quickly aspirations have risen. In 1990, 59% of 10th-graders with educational aspirations expected to get a four-year college degree or higher; by 2002, nearly 80% said the same.

"The word's out there," says Tom Mortenson of the Pell Institute for the Study of Opportunity in Higher Education. "The people doing the best in this kind of economy have college educations."

Nudged by economic trends showing manufacturing, farming and other blue-collar jobs disappearing or being shipped overseas, public schools are telling students—even low-income and underperforming students—that they need college degrees.

SOURCE F

"Rob," Declining College Standards, "Say Anything," an online blog, posted, January 3, 2006.

In the following passage, a blogger identified as "Rob" makes observations about what it means to go to college.

I can't speak for other places in this country, but my experience in my community during my post high-school days (which weren't just a few years ago) was one where college was "just something you do" after high school. Kids who didn't plan to go to college were considered "lazy" or "unambitious," while those who did go to college usually didn't even know what they wanted to do with their careers. I often wondered if a lot of the kids who decided to hold off on college weren't making the wiser decision. After all, drifting through a couple of years of classes with no real career direction was a good way to waste ten thousand dollars or so.

But not a lot of kids do this, mostly because I think kids go off to college seeking the "college experience" rather than a real education for a specific career. They go off looking for the frat parties, sporting events, campus life and activism, all of which is commonly associated with higher education. What many of them don't understand is that while all that stuff has its place it doesn't exactly translate into a lot of intellectual capital for the business market. I don't know how many acquaintances of mine have graduated from college with a "business" or "criminal justice" degree and absolutely no idea how to get a job with it. Most of them end up starting on the bottom rung of some company, about where they would have started without a degree, only now with a degree and thousands of dollars of debt.

The quality of education kids receive has really gone downhill, too, but again that might have something to do with all-around lowering of academic standards. Anyway, one need look no further than the sort of classes college kids take (A class in Prank/Social Activism is the most ridiculous one I've seen of late) to see that this is true.

But don't get me wrong. I'm not saying that college is a bad idea. I just think that too many students and parents go into it with their eyes shut. Rather than focusing on the "college experience," more of these people need to focus on what skills higher education will give them for the job market.

ANSWER KEY FOR SELF-ASSESSMENT

Answers to Multiple-Choice Questions

1. D	12. B	23. E	34. D	45. D
2. E	13. D	24. C	35. C	46. C
3. C	14. C	25. D	36. E	47. E
4. A	15. B	26. B	37. B	48. A
5. B	16. C	27. A	38. C	49. A
6. D	17. A	28. E	39. A	50. A
7. A	18. D	29. C	40. A	51. D
8. B	19. C	30. B	41. E	52. D
9. C	20. A	31. E	42. B	53. C
10. D	21. D	32. E	43. C	54. B
11. D	22. B	33. C	44. C	55. D

Summary of Answers in Section 1 (Multiple-Choice)

Number of correct answers   _____

Number of incorrect answers   _____

Number of questions not answered _____

(Use this information when you calculate your score on this exam. See page 71)

Answer Explanations

Section 1 Multiple-Choice Questions

Passage 1: Richard Maxwell Brown, "Historical Patterns of Violence In America."

1. **(D)** Much of the passage is devoted to the newspaper coverage of the event, especially the work of John N. Edwards, a "reasonably anonymous newspaper-man of nearly a century ago" (line 30). Because the incident took place long ago, the speaker's probable source of information is old newspapers. (A), (B), and (C) are wrong choices because the robbery probably occurred before the speaker was born. (E) is not mentioned or implied in the passage.

2. **(E)** All the characteristics listed set the sentence apart from the others.

3. **(C)** The speaker is referring to the sentiment expressed by the reporter in lines 9–11. Eliminate (A) as an answer because the speaker has no argument with the placement of the story, only with its contents. (B) is incorrect because the speaker has no reason to question Edwards' qualifications to report on the incident. (D) may be referring to quoted material that appeared in the newspaper two days later, but in line 8 he means the report written immediately after the crime. (E) does not accurately describe the tone of the story.

4. **(A)** The speaker finds it hard to believe and accept reportage that praises "violent, lawless men" who "endangered the lives" of innocent people.

5. **(B)** The lines compare the bandits to medieval knights. (A) comes close to a correct answer, but in the context, the reference to King Arthur's knights is not meant to be inspiring. (C) may be a tempting answer because a parable is a kind of story, but its purpose—to reveal moral or spiritual truths—does not apply here. (D) is not a bad choice, but a caricature points out grotesque likenesses, not complimentary ones. (E) refers to notes made while analyzing or explaining a written work, and so does not apply here.

6. **(D)** The sentence in question is written like an offhand remark that stands in contrast to the overblown passage that compares the bandits to the legendary Knights of the Round Table. (A) is incorrect because the main idea of the passage has not yet been stated or established. (B) is wrong because no particular theory has been stated earlier. (C) is a promising answer, but the discussion of the newpaper's coverage of the event continues into the next paragraph. (E) is contrary to fact; the speaker is criticizing the newspaper's position.

7. **(A)** The phrase is used ironically. In lines 14–17, the bandits are compared to noble and courageous knights. Here the author pokes fun at the comparison with a wry comment on the "courage" it took to shoot a little girl. (B) is incorrect because the phrase is not a figure of speech referring metaphorically to a particular place, person, or thing. The other choices don't apply. (C) is a humorous comparison of two unlike things, (D) a self-contradictory statement that is nevertheless valid, and (E) is a term consisting of contradictory elements that create a paradoxical effect.

8. **(B)** In the context "innocent" refers to those who embrace, or at least unquestioningly accept, the newspaper's glorification of the bandits. Because people who are undecided fall into a different category, (B) is the correct answer.

9. **(C)** The quotation exemplifies a mentality prevalent in parts of America—a way of thinking that, as the author goes on to explain, originated on the frontier. (A) is irrelevant in the context. (B) is not accurate because the author specifically denies in lines 29–30 that he is out to "belabor one reasonably anonymous newspaperman"—i.e., Edwards. (D) does not apply in the context. (E) has some merit because the author discusses frontier mentality in the next paragraph, but in the context (E) does not accurately describe the author's purpose.

10. **(D)** Lines 32–46 develop the paragraph's first sentence, the topic sentence, which introduces the phrase "independent action and individual reliance." One of the examples offered to illustrate this kind of activity is "creative plundering." The other choices are also examples of "independent action and individual reliance," some more specific than others.

11. **(D)** The conclusions reveal the ambiguity of the entire passage. At first, the author objects to the glorification of the bandits. Then, he acknowledges the impulse—inherited from the frontier—to admire men of "imagination and daring." In the end, though, he regards the legacy of the frontier a "problem" (line 31) that has left us with a kind of "blindness" (line 48). (A) and (B) are irrelevant to the conclusions in the last paragraph. (C) misses the point. Where similarities exist, they describe frontier people such as those who came to

admire the bandits. (E) inaccurately describes the author's attitude toward both the frontier and Mr. Edwards.

12. **(B)** All three groups are marked by their drive to carry out their goals: the bandits aimed to rob and hurt others, the knights strove to be chivalrous, and the frontier people did all they could to thrive in a rugged and often hostile environment. (A) has no validity because they didn't care what others thought. What counted was self-satisfaction. (C) was of little or no concern to any of the groups, although one might argue that knights probably devoted considerable effort to improve their standing in King Arthur's court. Neither (D) nor (E) is discussed in the passage.

Passage 2: Speech by Susan B. Anthony

13. **(D)** The opening creates the context for the speech—the speaker's indictment for an alleged crime. In just a few words, the speaker also reveals her anger and indignity. The sentence does not state the main idea, which comes just afterward.

14. **(C)** In the speaker's view, the act of voting is not a crime. Rather it is only an "alleged crime" and a right guaranteed to her by the Constitution. (A) cannot be the answer because the term "under indictment," in and of itself, doesn't suggest innocence or guilt. The same holds for the other incorrect choices. A sense of a wrongful accusation is not associated with any of them.

15. **(B)** Just prior to the quotation, the speaker claims that voting is a right guaranteed by the Federal Constitution. To prove her point, she quotes the preamble. (A) is a possible answer because the Constitution is an inspiring document to which Americans are emotionally attached, but it doesn't accurately describe the purpose of quoting the preamble in the passage. (C), (D), and (E) do not explain the purpose of the quotation.

16. **(C)** For sentence elements to be parallel, they must be grammatical equivalents. The word *establish* appears in a series of phrases, each using the infinitive form of a verb: *to form, to insure, to provide,* etc. None of the other choices except (E) is a verb, but *ordain* is used not in its infinitive form but as a verb in the present tense.

17. **(A)** An antithesis sets up an opposition or contrast of ideas. This paragraph is dominated by contrasts between conditions as they exist and conditions as they should be, according to the Constitution. (B) is a tempting answer because the paragraph alludes to the language of the Constitution, but by no means are the allusions abstract. (C) does not apply. If anything, the paragraph is written in a direct, down-to-earth manner. (D) is not in the speaker's repertoire. Just the opposite; she describes the unjust treatment of women in vivid terms. (E) is not present in the paragraph.

18. **(D)** The author used the phrase "downright mockery" to describe the empty promise of the blessings of liberty for women. The idea is echoed by the sentence that begins in line 25.

19. **(C)** The author uses an analogy to compare two things: using gender to determine eligibility to vote, and passing a bill of attainder. Both actions violate the law by depriving people of their civil rights. (A) is incorrect. A sentence containing two independent clauses needs two separate subjects. This sentence has just one, the infinitive phrase *to make sex a qualification*. (B) is wrong because the main thought of periodic sentences is completed only at the end of the sentence. Neither (D) nor (E) appear in the sentence.

20. **(A)** The message contained in the whole sentence that begins in line 28 is that the oligarchy of race "might be endured," while the oligarchy of sex has dire consequences. (B) is just the opposite of what the speaker is saying. (C) and (E) are vaguely implied, but those ideas do not reflect the speaker's main purpose. (D) refers only to what may happen if the oligarchy of sex is permitted to continue.

21. **(D)** The ideas in the sentence are attributed to "women and their female posterity" (lines 25–26). As the passage says, *To them*, the government is an "odious aristocracy," etc. Everyone named in choices (A), (B), and (C) might agree with the sentiment expressed in lines 28–30, but they play no role in the passage. (E) certainly has merit as the answer because the author speaks the words, but she attribute the ideas to "women and their female posterity" (lines 25–26).

22. **(B)** Using logic, the author lists several truths from which she has drawn the only possible conclusion: that laws disenfranchising women are "null and void." (A) is valid only to the extent that the author includes a question (line 39), but asking whether women are "persons" is but one step in the development of the paragraph. (C) and (D) are not applicable. (E) comes close to describing how the final paragraph is developed, but the author's inference, or conclusion, is clearly spelled out in the last sentence of the passage.

23. **(E)** The passage is full of strong language that reflects the speaker's bitterness about women being deprived of their rights. (A) is not accurate because the speaker is far from idealistic. She doesn't dream of a better tomorrow, she demands it based on what the Constitution says. (B) ignores the fact that the speaker is concerned about big issues, not petty ones. (C) cannot characterize a speech that includes a number of bold statements, including the accusation that the government is the "most hateful aristocracy . . . on the face of the globe." (D) may be half right, for the speaker is justifiably self-righteous, but she is not at all embarrassed by her strong convictions.

Passage 3: From N. Scott Momaday, *The Way to Rainy Mountain*

24. **(C)** The speaker's obvious reverence for the land implies that he has strong ties to Yellowstone. To him, it is almost sacred. (A) indicates that the speaker is a casual visitor, which he most certainly is not, considering his feeling for the place. (B) overlooks the fact that the speaker hardly mentions plant life in his description of the land and nature. (D) is incorrect because the passage contains no evidence to support it. (E) cannot be correct. The awe that the speaker feels about the scenery suggests that he has come to Yellowstone for the first time.

25. **(D)** The sentence shows the effect of the "sense of confinement" mentioned earlier in the paragraph. (A) is not the answer because the discussion of the Kiowas is not immediately picked up in paragraph 2. (B) is incorrect because the sentence merely adds detail to the portrait of the Kiowas. (C) is wrong because the sentence fails to contradict other material in the paragraph. (E) cannot be the answer because the notion of the Kiowas' freedom/confinement is dropped after the first paragraph.

26. **(B)** "Descending" is a verbal that functions like an adjective. It describes (i.e., modifies) the noun "meadows," the subject of the sentence.

27. **(A)** The sentence takes the reader from the high country down the "stairway to the plain." Choices (B) and (C) do not apply. (D) is incorrect because the author needs the first paragraph to tell the full story of the Kiowas' migration southward from the mountains to the plains. (E) is partly correct because the speaker has observed the terrain very closely. But it is not his main intent to show off his knowledge.

28. **(E)** The lines contain examples of metaphor—"clouds . . . are shadows," and of simile—"move upon the grain like water." To eliminate the wrong choices, you must be familiar with the definitions of several rhetorical terms, all defined in the Glossary, page 375.

29. **(C)** In the passage, the mountainous Yellowstone area is characterized by darkness, as in "dark timber" (line 2) and "deep cleavages of shade" (line 4), while the sun-filled plains are "yellow" (line 16) and marked by a "profusion of light" (line 21).

30. **(B)** The passage is filled with poetic images and reflects the speaker's sense of wonder and pleasure over the changing beauty of the land across which the Kiowas once passed. (A) may be partly correct; the speaker is earnest but not noticeably profound. (C) is not correct; the passage is not at all scholarly but rather impressionistic. In (D) *exotic* does not accurately describe either the land or the speaker's state of mind. (E) is not a good choice because the passage is not philosophical. Rather, much of it is down to earth—literally.

31. **(E)** Choices (A) and (D) are found in the extended comparison between the sun and a god, including the phrase "the oldest deity." (B) is exemplified by the series of phrases beginning with "dark lees . . . ." (C) is present in the clause that begins "When the Kiowas . . . ."

32. **(E)** The phrase refers to the Kiowas' need to accustom themselves to their new surroundings. Choice (D) comes close to the correct answer, but it fails to suggest the reason for the Kiowas' break in their southward journey.

33. **(C)** The language is fluent, rhythmic, and poetic. The speaker portrays the land in vivid images. No adjective in the four other choices accurately describes the style of the passage.

34. **(D)** The last paragraph, like the first, is filled with images of darkness. In both paragraphs, too, the speaker puts himself into the narrative: "it seemed to me" in the first paragraph and "I caught sight" in the last. What differs between the two paragraphs is the style of description. In the first, the speaker tells what he sees and how he reacted to it. In the other, the speaker's impression of the landscape is literally earth-shattering.

Passage 4: From Richard Wright, *White Man, Listen!*

35. **(C)** The imaginative account of Martians conquering a Swiss village is a parable—a short, fictitious story that illustrates a moral attitude or religious principle. In this case, the story represents European seizures of Asian and African communities. None of the other choices apply: (A) is a factual revelation of something discreditable. (B) is a reference to a familiar person, place, or thing. (D) explains the background or situation in a story or play. (E) is a tale that uses animals to point out a moral or truth.

36. **(E)** According to line 9, the invaders are "obeyed and served," a description that implies that "Fathers" is another name for "Masters." (A), (C), and (E) are inappropriate in the context of the passage. (B) is a possibility, although the passage says that the strangers, unlike tyrants, are "casually kind" (line 9)—at least for a while.

37. **(B)** The adjective "restless" comes after "European," the noun it modifies. "Sick" is parallel to "restless" because it is an adjective that both modifies and comes after the very same noun. Also, because both adjectives have unfavorable connotations, they are linked thematically.

38. **(C)** Arcadia, Land's End, and Shangri-la are not real places but metaphors for idealized places inhabited by "shadow men" (line 18)—that is, men who would allow Europeans to come and do whatever they wished.

39. **(A)** Ordinarily the phrase might have a positive connotation. In this context, however, the phrase is ironic because the speaker's point is that the colonists behaved like destructive barbarians. (B) may seem like a possible answer because some of the passage may seem exaggerated, but in this context, irony is more powerful than hyperbole. One could argue for (C) as the answer because in the context the phrase seems contrary to truth. But an oxymoron must itself contain contradictory terms. (D) is wrong because there is nothing understated in the passage. (E) cannot be correct because there is no suggestion of ridicule in the phrase.

40. **(A)** Except for (A), each choice reiterates a quality of the colonial European individualist not bound by emotional ties to custom, tradition, the church, or the family.

41. **(E)** Alliteration is the repetition of initial consonant sounds. Note the prevalence of the *s* sound in the words in question. (A) applies to words that imitate sounds. (B) is a figurative comparison without using *like* or *as*. (C) is the repetition of vowel sounds without the repetition of consonants. (D) is a type of story in which people, things, and actions represent an idea or generalization about life.

42. **(B)** The speaker vigorously condemns Europeans who cruelly exploited others for material gain. None of the other choices apply.

43. **(C)** The most obvious contrast is the two groups' loyalty to family life. The speaker says of the colonists that they had cast off the "ties . . . of family" (lines 24–25). The natives, on the other hand, were "[s]teeped in dependence systems of family life" (lines 38–39). None of the other choices have a significant role in the passage.

44. **(C)** Questions like those used in the passage are a rhetorical device that allows the speaker to add new ideas to a discussion, move a discussion along quickly, or to rapidly change the subject. They also serve to involve the reader because the questions serve as a kind of conversation between the author and reader. None of the other choices apply.

45. **(D)** From the opening scenario in which "fierce-looking men whose skins are blue and whose red eyes flash lightning bolts" (lines 2–3) to the image of an "emotionally crippled Europe . . . leaning upon this black crutch" (lines 34–37), powerful, almost inflammatory language dominates the passage. All the other choices describe a more sedate and conventional passage.

Passage 5: From Daniel Goleman, "The Man Without Feelings," *Emotional Intelligence*

46. **(C)** The passage concentrates on the typical symptoms of alexithymia. All the other choices are mentioned only in passing.

47. **(E)** The opening sentence introduces a person with a problem: an inability to express emotion. That is the main concern of the passage. (A) alludes to a conflict—the anger that Ellen felt toward Gary—but the passage discusses neither how, or whether, the conflict was resolved. (B) , (C), and (D) list functions of some introductory sentences, but not this one.

48. **(A)** The paragraph states the effect of Gary's behavior on Ellen, then explains the cause of her frustration. (B) is a poor choice, for the paragraph moves in the opposite direction—from the general to the specific. (C) represents a misreading of the paragraph. If anything, lines 11–13 continue to develop ideas presented earlier. (D) is wrong. Although "frustrated" is a psychological term, it is hardly abstract, and it is not defined in the rest of the paragraph. (E) does not apply. No hypothesis is presented in the paragraph.

49. **(A)** In context, the phrase "to express" is meant to contrast with the phrase "to lack feelings" (line 19). In other words, the inability to *express* emotion does not mean the inability to *feel* emotion.

50. **(A)** In the context, the phrase "colorless dreams" is paired with "no feelings, no fantasies," suggesting that the dreams are dull. This interpretation is supported by the author's use of the same word, "colorless," in line 15 as a synonym for dull and boring.

51. **(D)** Because the footnoted lines of the passage are presented without quotation marks, they have been paraphrased or otherwise adapted by the author of the passage. (A) draws an inference unjustified by either the footnote or anything else in the passage. (B) is incorrect because the footnote says that LeDoux is quoted in the article, not that he wrote it. (C) *Science* is the name of a periodical, as indicated by the volume number following the title. (E) is incorrect because the lines, based on an idea expressed by LeDoux, were composed by the author of this passage.

52. **(D)** Unlike most footnotes, this one does not pertain directly to the text of the passage. Rather, it serves as a supplement, suggesting that the field of emotional response has long been of interest to researchers. (A) is stated in the text of the passage (lines 33–34), making a footnote superfluous. (B) is not a likely answer because the footnote does not say where Dr. Sifneos' words can be found. (C) The "authority," Ned Kalin, has impressive credentials, but that is incidental to the purpose of the footnote. (E) is faulty conjecture. Although alexithymia was named in 1972, it cannot be assumed to have suddenly made its appearance in that year.

53. **(C)** The two works cited in footnote 5 pertain to aspects of alexithymia. (A) is incorrect because the footnote fails to say whether the manuscript had been published. (B) is possible but the meeting place is not mentioned. (D) is incorrect because that information is not given. (E) is a possibility, but the footnote doesn't contain that information.

54. **(B)** The passage explains alexithymia and provides two illustrative case studies, one at the beginning and the other at the end. (A) is partly right; the passage mentions physical symptoms but not extensively. (C) may be a tempting choice because therapists do treat alexithymics. The passage doesn't take a position on the use of therapists, however. (D) is incorrect because no procedure is discussed in the passage. (E) has some validity, although the passage never mentions the incidence of alexithymia.

55. **(D)** The author doesn't come right out and say how he feels about alexithymics. Yet, he stresses their anguish throughout the passage, suggesting that he is sympathetic to their plight. (A) reflects an inaccurate reading of the passage. (B), (C), and (E) may be somewhat valid, but they do not describe the author's primary attitude toward alexithymics.

Answers to Essay Questions

For an overview of how essays are graded, turn to "How Essays Are Scored," pages 27–30.

Although answers to essay questions will vary greatly, the following descriptions suggest a possible approach to each question and contain ideas that could be used in responding to the question.

Essay Question 1, based on
"A Word for Autumn" by A.A. Milne

Most readers are likely to find Milne's essay a piece of fluff—witty, lighthearted, urbane—not to be taken seriously. Some, however, may legitimately see a more solemn purpose behind Milne's musings on celery. Both responses are valid, provided that readers can support their views with evidence from the passage.

Those in the first group might immediately point out that assigning significance of any kind to something as inconsequential as celery is just plain silly. Yes, silly it is, and that is just the point. Milne is out to entertain his readers by playing with a ridiculous idea, exaggerating the importance of celery beyond all reason: Celery marks the change of seasons, it enhances the complexion, it is an excellent end to a meal and is a prelude to smoking a pipe rather than a cigar.

What sort of person would actually put such ideas on paper? Well, the sort that is the speaker in the passage. Presumably, he is a man of independent means who dines out a lot and takes himself to be a gentleman. He is cultured enough to quote Keats, but he seems to take no interest in the affairs of the world. His main concerns are being comfortable, feeling good, enjoying the benefits of his station in life, and enjoying "crisp and sparkling days, long pleasant evenings, cheery fires." Then he adds, toward the end of the passage, "Life shall be lived well."

Other readers, reading between the lines, may see the essay as a piece of social criticism. A case can be made that the speaker represents an egocentric, hedonistic, empty-headed class of people, whose existence serves no useful purpose. Milne uses celery as a symbol to represent the trivialities that dominate the speaker's life. Not only is the man out of touch with the real world but he contributes nothing to it. That Milne chose celery as the speaker's concern merely emphasizes the speaker's shallowness. The anecdote about lunch at the inn reinforces the point. "Horror!" says the speaker about having his celery snatched, an event he also terms a "tragedy," as though the stranger had done something truly horrendous. Although Milne chose celery as the subject, anything of equal insignificance could have served his purpose.

Essay Question 2, based on passages
by Ayn Rand and Adlai Stevenson

Your task is simply to answer the question, "What does the style and rhetoric of each passage tell you about the person who wrote it?"

The author of the first passage comes across as someone who speaks with authority. To put it bluntly, the author, Ayn Rand, presents herself as a know-it-all, a forceful critic who confidently declares that she knows exactly what is wrong with America and is anything but timid about asserting her views. "America, at present, is following the first course," she says, referring to the course that is epitomized by the foolish, "morally depraved" courtiers in "The Emperor's New Clothes." The analogy is apt, for the widely known tale is a universally accepted allusion to stupidity and self-delusion. Then, assuming the mantle of the uncorrupted child in the story, the author declares "that America is culturally bankrupt."

Rand establishes the voice of a prophet early in the passage. In the first sentence she asserts that "there are two courses"—and *only* two—for a society to follow when it is approaching bankruptcy. (Whether she means a literal or figurative bankruptcy remains unclear until the end of the passage.) The first course is described with emotionally loaded language—"frantic, blind, rage-of-the-moment expediency," as if to say that no right-thinking person could subscribe to such a course. The second, by contrast, is laid out in 1-2-3 order with clipped phrases: "identify with the situation, check their premises, discover their hidden assets, and start rebuilding" (lines 6–7)—steps that are serious and precise and stand in stark contrast to the current wimpiness of an America "not daring to look ahead, wishing no one would name the truth, yet desperately hoping that something will save them somehow" (lines 4–6).

While Rand concludes that America is a defective country in need of major repair, the author of the second passage, Adlai E. Stevenson, takes a more circumspect view. Unlike Rand, Stevenson disclaims the role of expert by insisting on the complexity of the problems and conceding that neither he nor anyone else has any clear-cut solutions. He acknowledges that the country is troubled and anxious. But rather than identify causes and offer simple formulaic solutions, as Rand does, Stevenson tries to describe the forces at play in America. He cannot precisely pinpoint them, however. Having sprung mysteriously—and metaphorically—from "deep wells" (line 1), they defy definition. The author calls them "opaque, moving forms and shadows" (lines 5–6), and—carrying the metaphor still further—says that our vision of the future is "shrouded in mist." In brief, his approach, unlike Rand's, is tentative, exploratory, and suggestive.

The phrase "We Americans" (line 8) stands for the author's attempt to maintain a dialogue-like relationship with the audience. A brief anecdote, in which politicians are compared to insects, is bound to appeal to readers (politicians are always easy to ridicule). The personal, colloquial language—"They always remind me of . . ."—makes the author sound like a friendly uncle rather than an intellect, yet his allusion to the discrepancy between ends and means is the product of considerable cerebral activity. The author describes the business of foreign policy as "speculative, uncertain." Considering the style and rhetoric of the passage, he might have well been describing his own approach to the subject of the passage.

Essay Question 3, based on the topic:
"College for All"

As an AP student on the verge of college, you're likely to hold some strong views on the issue of college for all. Your opinions can serve as the core of your essay, but the sources offer a number of ideas on both sides of the question that you may not have considered before.

If you argued in favor of college for all, these are some of the points you might have made:

- Education is the key to progress and prosperity. (Source A)
- Education is the essence of democracy; it gives everyone an equal chance to succeed.
- Investment in education has long-lasting personal and financial benefits. (Source A)
- College graduates lead healthier lives and live longer than non-graduates. (Source C)
- College graduates lead rich intellectual lives. (Source C)
- A college degree is necessary for jobs that formerly required less education. (Source E)

If you argued that not everyone should go to college, you might have used some of these ideas to support your claim:

- Many students are not academically prepared for college work. (Source B)
- The cost of remedial work for unprepared students strains resources. (Source B)
- The drop-out rate for remedial students is very high. (Source B)
- Pressure to attend college forces students deep into debt when they graduate. (Source D)
- For many students college is a waste of time and money. (Source F)
- Students with unreal aspirations are doomed to be disappointed and disillusioned by the reality of college. (Source E)

Self-Scoring Guide for Diagnostic Test

After referring to "How Essays Are Scored" on pages 27–30, use this guide to help you evaluate each essay. Do your best to evaluate your performance in each category by using the criteria spelled out below. Because it is hard to achieve objectivity when assessing your own writing, you may improve the validity of your score by having a trusted and well-informed friend or experienced teacher read and rate your essay.

On the following Rating Chart, enter a number (from 1 to 6) that you think represents your level of performance in each category (A–F).

Category A: OVERALL PURPOSE/MAIN IDEA

6 extremely well-defined and insightful

5 clearly defined and generally insightful

4 mostly clear

3 somewhat clear but occasionally confusing

2 generally unclear and confusing

1 virtually incomprehensible

Category B: HANDLING OF THE PROMPT

6 self-evident or extremely clear throughout

5 mostly clear

4 somewhat clear

3 somewhat unclear

2 generally unclear or ambiguous

1 confusing or nonexistent

Category C: ORGANIZATION AND DEVELOPMENT

6 insightfully organized; fully developed with excellent supporting evidence

5 reasonably well organized; developed with appropriate supporting material

4 appropriately organized; developed with some relevant material

3 inadequately organized; weak development

2 poorly organized; little or no development

1 no discernible organization; no relevant development

Category D: SENTENCE STRUCTURE

6 varied and engaging

5 sufficiently varied to create interest

4 some variety

3 little variety; minor sentence errors

2 frequent sentence errors that interfere with meaning

1 serious sentence errors that obscure meaning

Category E: USE OF LANGUAGE

6 precise and effective word choice

5 competent word choice

4 conventional word choice; mostly correct

3 some errors in diction or idiom

2 frequent errors in diction or idiom

1 meaning obscured by word choice

Category F: GRAMMAR AND USAGE

6 error-free or virtually error-free

5 occasional minor errors

4 basically correct but with several minor errors

3 meaning somewhat obscured by errors

2 meaning frequently obscured by errors

1 meaning blocked by several major errors

RATING CHART

Rate your essay:	Essay 1	Essay 2	Essay 3
Overall Purpose/Main Idea	_____	_____	_____
Handling of the Prompt	_____	_____	_____
Organization and Development	_____	_____	_____
Sentence Structure	_____	_____	_____
Use of Language	_____	_____	_____
Grammar and Usage	_____	_____	_____
Composite Scores (Sum of each column)	_____	_____	_____

By using the following scale, in which composite scores are converted to the nine-point AP rating scale, you may determine the final score for each essay:

Composite Score	AP Essay Score
33–36	9
29–32	8
25–28	7
21–24	6
18–20	5
15–17	4
10–14	3
7–9	2
6 or below	1

AP Essay Scores Essay 1 _____ Essay 2 _____ Essay 3 _____

TEST SCORE WORKSHEET

The scores you have earned on the multiple-choice and essay sections of the exam may now be converted to the AP five-point scale by performing the following calculations:

I. Determine your score for Section I (Multiple Choice)

Step A: Number of correct answers _____.

Step B: Number of wrong answers _____ (Note: Do not count unanswered questions.)

Step C: Multiply the number of wrong answers by .250 and enter the figure here _____ .

Step D: Subtract the figure in Step C from the figure in Step A _____ .

Step E: Multiply the figure in Step D by 1.2500 to find your Multiple-Choice Score _____ (If less than zero, enter zero.)

II. Determine your score for Section II (Essays)

Step A: Enter your score for Essay 1 (out of 9) _____

Step B: Enter your score for Essay 2 (out of 9) _____

Step C: Enter your score for Essay 3 (out of 9) _____

Step D: Add the figures in Steps A, B, and C _____

Step E: Multiply the figure in Step D by 3.0556 _____. (Do not round.) This is your Essay Score.

III. Determine Your Total Score

Add the scores for I and II to find your composite score _____ .

To convert your composite score to the AP five-point scale, use the chart below. The range of scores only approximates what you would earn on the actual test because the exact figures may vary from test to test. Be aware, therefore, that your score on this test, as well as on other tests in this book, may differ slightly from your score on an actual AP exam.

Composite Score	AP Grade
108–150	5
93–107	4
72–92	3
43–71	2
0–42	1

AP essays are ordinarily judged in relation to other essays written on the same topic at the same time. Therefore, the scores you assign yourself for these essays may not be the same as the scores you would earn on an actual exam.

Mastering
Multiple-Choice Questions

CHAPTER 3

- Six routes to correct answers
- What you need to know about:
  grammar
  rhetoric
  sentences
- Word choice and details of diction
- Understanding footnotes
- Passages and sample questions for practice

With the Diagnostic Test behind you, you've tasted the types of questions that will be coming your way on the AP exam. Whether you breezed through the Diagnostic Test or struggled with every question, it's worth your while to look at the following tried-and-true techniques for answering multiple-choice questions:

Untold numbers of students have relied on the following half dozen rules of thumb. You should, too.

SIX RULES OF THUMB

1. Read each question slowly and carefully. To be sure you understand what a question asks, put it into your own words. Then re-read the question to be sure you haven't misread it.

2. Read the five choices slowly and carefully. Remember that you must select the *best* choice, which could mean that one or more of the incorrect choices may be partially valid. With a stroke of your pencil or an "X" in the margin, eliminate all the choices that are obviously wrong. Then concentrate on the others. Examine each remaining choice for irrelevancies, for absolute words such as *always* and *never*, and for meanings that merely approximate what the passage says. If a question refers you to a specific line or lines in the passage, re-read not only those lines but the two or three lines that come both before

and after the designated lines. Knowing the context in which the lines appear can lead you to the correct answer.

3. After you've make your choice, scan the passage for evidence to support your decision. Just before filling the space on your answer sheet, be sure the question number is correct, and re-read the question to check whether you've interpreted every word correctly.

4. If you're stumped by a question, put a "?" in the margin and come back to it later. Return visits often provide a new perspective that helps you find the answer. Also mark any questions about which you have any doubts.

5. It's generally to your advantage to guess at the answer if you can eliminate at least one of the choices. Otherwise, leave it blank.

6. If time remains after you've filled in all the blanks, review your answers, especially those, if any, that gave you trouble. Oh, yes, one more thing: Ridiculous as it may sound, make sure you've put your answers in the right places. Don't blacken a space for question 12 in a space for question 11, etc. (Please don't snicker; it's been done, and not just once.)

These six guidelines deserve to be practiced over and over again while taking model exams. They can take you only so far toward earning a top score on the AP exam, however. What will take you the rest of the way is your knowledge of language and rhetoric.

LANGUAGE AND RHETORIC

All the question-answering techniques in the world won't do you much good without knowledge of the subject matter covered by the exam. Moreover, a book like this can't tell you everything you need to know or should have remembered from years of English classes. But it can hit some of the highlights. That is, it can call your attention to matters regularly included in past AP exams. That's what the following pages aim to do.

English Grammar Questions

Three or four multiple-choice grammar questions customarily turn up on the test. Typically, they ask how a certain grammatical structure, such as a series of compound sentences or a list of adjectives, has been used in a passage to convey meaning or create certain effects.

For example, the following paragraph by the American author Washington Irving is tailor-made for a question about sentence structure—particularly the use of parallelism.

Her mighty lakes, like oceans of liquid silver; her mountains, with their bright aerial tints; her valleys, teeming with wild fertility; her tremendous cataracts, thundering in their solitudes; her boundless plains, waving with spontaneous verdure; her broad deep rivers, rolling in the solemn silence to the ocean; her trackless forests, where vegetation puts forth all its magnificence; her skies, kindling with the magic of summer clouds and glorious sunshine;—no, never need an American look beyond his own country for the sublime and beautiful of natural scenery.

Notice that the paragraph—except for the clause after the dash—consists of a single sentence composed of a series of nouns and modifiers, most followed by a participle phrase. The effect of this pattern is cumulative. It creates an image of the vastness of America, an idea aided not only by the piling up of visual images but by the repeated used of adjectives such as "tremendous," "boundless," and "broad."

Another type of grammar question asks about the function of certain words. You may, for example, find a question that expects you to know about modifiers, as in

In line 34, the word "moral" modifies

(A) crowd
(B) demands
(C) persuasion
(D) leadership
(E) rectitude

Sometimes questions dealing with other matters list grammatical terms among the choices, as in

In the opening sentence of the passage, the author employs all of the following EXCEPT

(A) an analogy
(B) irony
(C) a coordinate clause
(D) conjunctions
(E) parallel structure

> A full treatment of English grammar lies beyond the scope of this volume. So, if your grammar skills are rusty, spend time with a grammar book. Bookstore shelves are loaded with them, or borrow one from the library or your English teacher.
>
> Also, review the material in this chapter for a discussion of standard English usage and some related practice exercises.

Thus, it's important for you to know about types of sentences (*simple, compound, complex;* also *periodic* and *loose* sentences), the parts of speech (*noun, pronoun, verb, adjective, adverb, conjunction, preposition, exclamation*), and parts of sentences (*subject, predicate, object, clauses*).

TEST TIP

To do well, you should be familiar with common everyday grammatical terms and concepts.

Comprehension Questions

Answering questions about an author's rhetorical strategies requires you to know what the passage says. It would be pointless to ask about why the author used a particular sentence structure if you had no clue about the purpose and meaning of the passage. Therefore, the exam often includes comprehension questions. Sometimes a question asks about the meaning of the passage as a whole. Other questions pinpoint particular words in context, and still others may ask about the meaning or significance of certain details. Such questions require you to read closely, of course, but they also serve as a springboard to answering the majority of the questions, which have to do with rhetoric.

Questions About Rhetoric

Questions about rhetoric test your understanding of such concepts as tone, diction, syntax, imagery, irony, figures of speech, theme, point of view, and many other rhetorical concepts. Also, you'll most certainly have a chance to demonstrate your awareness of how certain kinds of sentences reveal an author's intent and convey meaning.

Rhetoric is a broad term. Having come this far in your education, you are already acquainted with many of its varieties. Everything you have ever written or read—from a movie review to a college application—is subject to analysis in rhetorical terms.

In fact, virtually all writing has a rhetorical purpose. If authors aim to describe a place, person, or object, they try to recreate the look, the sound, the smell, the taste, and the feel of things. If their aim is to tell a story, they try to communicate an event or a sequence of events by selecting and arranging particulars, usually in the order they occurred. An author with a point to make takes a position and offers reasons to support it. Whatever the mode, the author's choice of words, syntax (order of words and phrases), sentence sound and structure, the sequence of ideas, the selection of details—all these elements and more are meant to serve the purpose of the whole.

The purpose is often more complex than simply conveying an experience or telling a story. Authors may, for example, want to stimulate certain responses in their readers, who may react to a vivid re-creation of an experience as though they themselves had the experience: they may laugh out loud, become tense or frightened, weep, grow angry. A biographer may want to communicate the facts of his subject's life. A. Scott Berg, for instance, wrote a prize-winning biography of Charles Lindbergh. In doing so, Berg established a tone that revealed his own thoughts about Lindbergh. In laying out the facts about Lindbergh, he also meant to convince the reader that Lindbergh was both an admirable and a reprehensible figure. He wants us to admire and despise the man at the same time, just as he, the biographer, does.

Of course, a writer's attitude toward the subject is not necessarily identical with the response of the reader. An advertising copywriter for Nike may be totally indifferent to the shoes he crows about, but since his job is to make readers feel a certain way, he purposefully uses words to produce a particular response—namely, to turn readers into consumers of Nike products.

TONE

In the multiple-choice section of the exam, you will certainly need to deal with tone. One of the most common questions asks you to identify the tone of a passage, a sentence, or even a single word or phrase. To answer the question you will need a sense of the narrator's or speaker's attitude toward the subject of the passage. This may differ from the author's attitude, of course. An author may portray a scoundrel in a favorable way, but that doesn't necessarily mean the author has a soft spot in his heart for scoundrels.

Because an author's tone may be complex or may shift part way through a passage or poem, it can be described in innumerable ways, often by one or more adjectives. For example,

Negative

bitter	flippant	petty
condescending	indignant	sarcastic
contemptuous	irreverent	satiric
disdainful	mocking	scornful
disgusted	patronizing	teasing
facetious	pedantic	threatening

Positive

benevolent	effusive	laudatory
compassionate	elegiac	learned
determined	enthusiastic	supportive
ecstatic	hopeful	sympathetic

Neutral

bantering	didactic	objective
colloquial	factual	restrained
confident	informal	scholarly
detached		

Words themselves and the manner in which they are expressed work together to establish the tone. Consider the simple question, "Who are you?" Depending on the tone in which the words are expressed, the question may be funny, sassy, inquisitive, challenging. Because the inflection of the speaker's voice is not available to writers, they must rely more on diction—the writer's choice of words, including figures of speech—to establish a tone. The differences between "Shut your mouth," "Please keep still," and "Would you be kind enough not to talk now?" are apparent. In a general sense the three sentences mean the same thing. The tone in each, however, could hardly differ more, because the words chosen to convey the meaning evoke very different feelings.

While the form of sentences significantly influences tone, other rhetorical elements also play a major part, especially diction, metaphors, and other figures of speech such as symbols and allusions. One way an author reveals tone is by the form of sentences.

> **TIP**
>
> In essence, tone is the psychological quality of the words.

EXCLAMATORY SENTENCES

An exclamatory sentence expresses a wish, a desire, a command—and is often, but not always, indicated with an exclamation point:

> Heads up!
>
> May the Force be with you!
>
> Have a nice day!

Such sentences can express various gradations of begging, beseeching, praying, imploring, apologizing, requesting, advising, commanding, persuading, and so on. "Let the word go forth," intoned John F. Kennedy in his inauguration address, "that the torch has been passed to a new generation . . . ." Kennedy's inspirational tone is initiated by the use of the imperative verb *let*. The highsounding verb *go forth* and the metaphorical use of *torch* also contribute a sense of mission to the mood of the occasion.

INTERROGATIVE SENTENCES

An *interrogative* sentence also offers a writer a variety of tones. Questions are usually asked in order to obtain information: "When is the next train to Mount Kisco?" But the tone of a question can also be:

> A CHALLENGE: Who are you calling a nerd, Mac?
> A DENIAL: Do you actually think that I'm capable of such a thing?
> DISBELIEF: Can you believe the nerve of that driver?
> HESITATION: Do you really think I should step off the edge of the cliff?

and so on.

On the AP exam, the questions you may find within passages are most likely to be rhetorical questions—questions whose answers are implied by the question itself. Used in argumentation, a rhetorical question calls attention to an obvious proposition—or it can be used to make an argument more dramatic and convincing. The author of the following uses a series of questions and answers, structured somewhat like a dialogue:

> When our ancestors condemned a woman for one crime, they considered that by this single judgment she was convicted of many transgressions. How so? Judged unchaste, she was also deemed guilty of poisoning. Why? Because, having sold her body to the basest passion, she had to live in fear of many persons. Who are these? Her husband, her parents, and the others . . . .

DECLARATIVE SENTENCES

A *declarative* sentence, the most common form of sentence, makes a factual statement. Unlike exclamatory and interrogative sentences, the declarative sentence does not blatantly reveal its tone. Much of the time, the tone of a declarative sentence is neutral. It merely states information in a matter-of-fact way:

> In 1897, Columbia University moved from 49th Street and Madison Avenue, where it had stood for 40 years, to its present location on Morningside Heights at 116th Street and Broadway.

While this matter-of-fact tone is prevalent in scientific and other informational prose, declarative sentences can also be highly charged with emotion:

> People who knew the American novelist Thomas Wolfe recall that he habitually roamed down the long aisles of the library stacks, grabbing one book after the other from the shelves and devouring its contents as if he were a starving man suddenly let loose in an immense storehouse of food. He wrote with abandon, turning out incredible quantities of manuscript, filling whole packing cases with the product of his frenzied pen.

On the surface, this may seem like a factual description of Thomas Wolfe. The writer is informing us that Wolfe read many books and wrote prodigiously. But the words create a portrait of an awe-inspiring, larger-than-life figure. The simile, "as if he were a starving man suddenly let loose in an immense storehouse of food," while possibly overstating Wolfe's behavior in the library, does not exaggerate the passion Wolfe evidently felt for reading books.

Sentence Length

Sentences can vary in length between one word ("Walk!") and hundreds, even thousands, of words. Usually, the complexity of an idea determines sentence length, but not always. Profound ideas can also be expressed in very few words: "I think, therefore I am."

On the AP exam you could be asked why an author may have chosen to write very long sentences or why the author put a short sentence in a particular place or wrote a whole string of very short sentences. In general, long sentences allow authors to differentiate important ideas from less important ideas. Material in subordinate clauses, appositives, or any other secondary sentence element receives less emphasis than an idea expressed in the main clause. On the other hand, when an author uses several brief sentences in a row, no one sentence stands out. All are equally emphatic, and a thoughtful author most likely has a rhetorical reason for structuring a passage that way.

Short sentences are easier to grasp. A short sentence makes its point quickly and often with considerable force, as in this sample passage about authors and critics:

> A person who pries into the private lives of others, with no other motive but to discover their faults and tell the world about them, deserves a name that can't be published here, just like a reviewer who reads books with an eye toward destroying the reputation of the author. Both are odious vermin.

The blunt closing sentence produces a mild jolt, especially because it sits next to a windy 50-word sentence. The effect is intentional.

Sentence Structure

Experienced writers know how sentence parts should be arranged to convey meaning and affect a reader's response to the sentence. Of the three main sections of a sentence—the beginning, the middle, and the end—the end is the best place for emphasizing an idea. Why? Because the reader comes to a very brief stop at the end of a sentence—brief, but still long enough for the last idea to sink in.

This principle underlies the use of so-called *periodic* sentences—sentences that save the most important idea for the end. Compare these two sentences:

1. A harmful economic system develops when a worker cannot get a job that pays a enough to support a family

2. When a worker cannot get a job that pays enough to support a family, a harmful economic system develops.

Both sentences state their point clearly, but if the writer wanted to stress that certain conditions lead to a destructive economic system, the second sentence does it more emphatically. In sentence 1, the main point is stated first but is then pushed into the background by the example of the underpaid worker.

What distinguishes a periodic sentence from its opposite, the *loose* sentence, is that its thought is not completed until the end. In a way, the reader is held in suspense. The loose sentence, in contrast, gives away its "secret" at the start. It follows the most common structure of English sentences: subject-verb, as in *Kevin called*, or subject-verb-object: *He used a cell phone.*

As you probably know, every sentence has a main clause consisting of at least a subject and a verb. That's all a *simple* sentence needs to be complete—a subject and a verb. Even if many modifiers and objects are added, it still remains a *simple* sentence.

For example, both of the following sentences, despite the disparity in their length, are *simple* sentences:

> Berkeley admitted Sarah.

> Situated on the eastern side of San Francisco Bay, Berkeley, the University of California's flagship institution, admitted Sarah as a freshman in the class of 2008, to the delight not only of Sarah herself but to the satisfaction of her family, teachers, and friends.

Leaving aside the wordiness and wisdom of including so much miscellaneous information in the second sentence, you still find a simple declarative sentence—*Berkeley admitted Sarah*—lurking within its jumble of modifiers, participles, prepositional phrases, and appositives.

To turn a *simple* sentence into a *compound* sentence, add a conjunction, a word like *and* or *but,* as in

> Berkeley admitted Sarah and she was delighted.

You can infer from this example that a *compound* sentence is made up of at least two simple sentences joined by a conjunction. What is rhetorically noteworthy about a compound sentence is that the author gives more or less equal emphasis to the information in each of the clauses. Clauses of equal rank and structure are called *coordinate clauses* and are joined by *coordinating conjunctions* (*and, but, or, nor, yet, so*) and sometimes by a semicolon with connective words like *however, moreover, nevertheless, otherwise, therefore, consequently,* and others. In this case, whether logical or not, Sarah's acceptance has been given equal importance to her reaction to the news.

If the author's intent, however, is to emphasize Sarah's state of mind, the sentence might best be turned into a *complex* sentence—that is, a sentence that contains both a subordinate and a main clause:

> *Because Berkeley admitted her,* Sarah was delighted. (Subordinate clause italicized)

Here, the cause-and-effect relationship between the two ideas is made clearer. The addition of a subordinating conjunction *because* gives prominence to the information in the main, or independent, clause. (Other widely used subordinating conjunctions include *although, before, even though, while, unless, if,* and *when.*)

The Sound of Sentences

Some AP exam questions may well ask you to consider the sounds found in a passage. For one, you should recognize **onomatopoeia**—words that imitate the sound they describe. Is there a more expressive word than *moan,* for example, to make the sound of . . . well, a moan? Similarly, *murmur* resembles the sound of a murmur. And other words, too—*boom, buzz, clang, crack,* and so on—all echo their sense.

You should also be attuned to **alliteration,** the repetition of initial sounds in words and syllables, as in *Peter Piper picked a peck of pickled peppers.* Sometimes such repetition is for ornament, but authors sometimes use it for emphasis as in such words as *flim-flam* and phrases such as *fickle fortune* and *bed and breakfast.* (*Turn to the Glossary, p. 375, for definitions of other terms related to sound:* assonance, *conso-nance, and* rhyme.)

Unlike rhythm in music, the **rhythm** of prose is more subtle. Rhythmic sentences don't have a foot-tapping beat, but they often possess a graceful combination of sounds, accents, phrases, and pauses. Authors intentionally use rhythm to arouse emotions. In fact, rhythm can have at least as much power as well-chosen words to create an emotional effect. A passage that is meant to create a sense of peace and calm demands a slow, even rhythm, as in this sample of prose from the pen of the American naturalist/writer Edward Abbey. Describing early morning in the desert, he writes:

> The sun is not yet in sight but signs of the advent are plain to see. Lavender clouds sail like a fleet of ships across the pale green dawn; each cloud, planed flat on the wind, has a base of fiery gold. Southeast, twenty miles by line of sight, stand the peaks of the Sierra La Sal, twelve to thirteen thousand feet above sea level, all covered with snow and rosy in the morning sunlight. The air is dry and clear as well as cold; the last fogbanks left over from last night's storm are scudding away like ghosts, fading into nothing before the wind and the sunrise.

In an entirely different mood, Abbey writes on the topic "Transcendence":

> It is this which haunts me night and day. The desire to transcend my own limits, to exceed myself, to become more than I am. How? I don't know. To transcend this job, this work, this place, this kind of life—for the sake of something superlative, supreme, exalting. But where? Again, how? Don't know. It will come of itself . . . like lightning, like rain, like God's gift of grace, in its own good time. (If it comes at all.)

In this passage, the inner turmoil Abbey feels about himself is revealed in the short, choppy phrases, the combination of questions and fragmentary sentences, and the clipped rhythm of his thoughts.

A typical question on the exam may ask about the effects of rhythm in a passage. Perhaps the author intentionally used it to arouse emotions.

Diction

Diction, or word choice, is one of the elements of style that gives each person's writing a quality that is is uniquely his or her own. Diction determines whether an author has succeeded in communicating a particular message to a particular audience. In the following passage, from an article titled "Fenimore Cooper's Literary Offenses," Mark Twain comments on the diction of a well-regarded American writer.

TIP

In large measure diction creates tone.

> Cooper's word sense was singularly dull. When a person has a poor ear for music, he will flat and sharp right along without knowing it. He keeps near the tune, but it is not the tune. When a person has a poor ear for words, the result is a literary flatting and sharping; you perceive what he is intending to say, but

you also perceive that he doesn't say it. This is Cooper. He was not a word musician. His ear was satisfied with the *approximate* word. I will furnish some circumstantial evidence in support of this charge. My instances are gathered from half a dozen pages of the tale called *Deerslayer.* He used "verbal" for "oral"; "precision" for "facility"; "phenomena" for "marvels"; "necessary" for "predetermined"; "unsophisticated" for "primitive"; "preparation" for "expectancy"; "rebuked" for "subdued"; "dependent on" for "resulting from"; "fact" for "condition"; . . . "brevity" for "celerity"; "distrusted" for "suspicious"; "mental imbecility" for "imbecility"; "eyes" for "sight"; "counteracting" for "opposing"; . . . . There have been daring people in the world who claimed that Cooper could write English, but they're all dead now.

Apparently, Cooper's diction left much to be desired. In Twain's view, Cooper was insensitive to the connotation of many, many words. He may well have known the definitions of words, but he had a so-called tin ear when it came to understanding the words in context. He seems deaf to the feelings that words represent, and, therefore, chose his words badly.

Authors usually can select from several possibilities words that are best suited to their purposes. For instance:

insult/slur, spit/expectorate, complain/gripe, excellent/superior, eat/stuff one's face

The words in each pair mean more or less the same thing, but none is a perfect synonym for another. Some are plain, others are fancy. Some are clinical, euphemistic, or slang; each has a distinct connotation.

Connotation

Words derive their connotation from two sources: people's common experience and an individual's personal experience. Words represent not only ideas, events, and objects, but also the feelings we attach to ideas, events, and objects. Thus, the word *rat* represents a certain kind of rodent—among other things. That is its *denotative* meaning. But a rat also evokes in us feelings of fear and disgust—its *connotation.* What is true of *rat* is also true of countless other words: *mother, home, candy, money, grease, America, dog,* and so on. They all evoke feelings and ideas.

Connotations may change over time, and our personal experience often adds connotative value to words that may at first mean nothing beyond their definition. Scientific words that at one time merely named physical phenomena or technical achievements—*cloning, abortion, www.com*—have since acquired rich connotative meanings.

Really good descriptive writing often gets its power from the author's choice of connotative words. The more closely you read a passage, the more you may enjoy it. Notice how the following passage employs connotation to create a graphic impression of a very agreeable place:

There couldn't be a more idyllic spot in May than Albion, on the Mendocino coast. The land, strung between redwood groves and sea, is lush with flowers. Summer crowds are weeks away, and it's still possible to find a quiet beach or stroll the cliffs above the ocean without seeing another soul. Four miles from the coastal highway, the road narrows, loses its paving, and curves into the woods. A graveled driveway winds to a graceful country house close to a pond and surrounded by park-like grounds. A trellis of interlocking timbers draped with vines leads to the front door of the house. A Chinese lantern hangs overhead. From high on a post a clay mask stares at passersby. Pieces of driftwood lie on a wooden bench weathered to a silver-grey. Attention has been paid to make visitors feel welcome.

In familiar but carefully chosen words the author of the passage has tried to convey how pleased he was to be there—a feeling he wants his readers to share. References to things that most people enjoy and value—redwood groves, flowers, a quiet beach, a country house—create a sense of peace and pleasure.

Metaphorical Language

Because figures of speech often reveal an author's tone, be prepared to deal with questions that refer to the most common figures of speech found in non-fiction prose:

- Metaphor
- Simile
- Allusion
- Analogy
- Metonymy
- Synecdoche

As a group, these figures of speech constitute what might be called generally metaphorical language.

> **TIP**
>
> Metaphorical language functions as a means of making comparisons.

When an author can't find the exact words to describe a feeling or to capture experiences that seem almost inexpressible, a metaphor may come to the rescue: "She has a voice of gold," says the music critic, using a metaphor to express not only the beauty of her voice but also its value. Indeed, in a particular context the metaphor could mean that the singer makes big money with her voice. Figures of speech are economical. They condense a lot of thought and feeling into a few words. Ernie Pyle, a famous World War II war correspondent, reported his stories as though they were being told by the average GI lying in a foxhole. He said, "I write from a worm's eye point of view." The idea gives a fresh slant to an old expression and cogently fixes Pyle's position on the battlefield.

Because metaphorical language evokes mental images, it has a good deal to do with the emotional content of a piece of writing. If an author relies on trite, second-hand expressions to convey an idea, using such metaphors as *walking on air* or *life in the fast lane,* you can fairly well conclude that the author may have nothing new or surprising to say. On the other hand, a passage full of fresh metaphorical language may give readers rich new insights and understandings.

> **TIP**
>
> In short, figures of speech have the power to make something clearer or more vivid, or to turn a vague impression into something concrete.

Allusion

An allusion—an implied or direct reference to something in history or culture—is, like a richly connotative word, a means to suggest far more than it says. An allusion of a single word or phrase can expand the reader's understanding more completely than a long, discursive comparison. You may know Robert Frost's poem "Out, Out . . . ," a narrative poem that recounts a farmyard accident that takes the life of a young boy. A theme of the poem, the uncertainty and unpredictability of life, is alluded to in the title, which you may know comes from Macbeth's soliloquy upon hearing of his wife's death: "Out, out, brief candle./Life's but a walking shadow, . . ." Macbeth's speech is a reflection on both the tragedy of a premature death and the impermanence of life. While readers unfamiliar with *Macbeth* may read "Out, Out . . . " with insight and pleasure, understanding the allusion to Shakespeare's play enriches the experience.

Metaphorical language that seems inappropriate to the general tone and purpose of the passage will grate on readers and weaken the overall effect that the author has in mind. It also suggests that the author lacks a clear sense of purpose or just doesn't know how to achieve a particular purpose. Take, for example, this attempt to describe how memories of childhood fade with the passing of time:

> As you grow older, your memory of childhood is obliterated like Hiroshima after the bomb.

Isn't it obvious that the author missed the point? After all, memories fade slowly, not cataclysmically. Whatever tone the author may have intended is lost in the incongruity of the simile. A more appropriate way to capture the idea that memories erode gradually might be:

> As you grow older, memories of childhood vanish like sand dunes at the edge of the sea.

Of course, there may be another possibility. Perhaps the author purposely wrote an incongruous metaphor for a particular purpose. To heighten interest, authors often try to surprise their readers. They introduce an inappropriate or contradictory metaphor, for instance, for the sake of contrast. They invent a figure of speech with a connotation that is off kilter in order to create a kind of tension or to make an ironic or amusing comment.

During the Spanish Civil War, Ernest Hemingway, writing a dispatch from the front lines, said of the enemy planes, "If their orders are to strafe the road on their way home, you will get it [be wounded or killed]. Otherwise, when they are finished with their jobs on a particular objective, they go off like bank clerks, flying home." The comparison of deadly fighters and bank clerks may seem frivolous, but it does make the point effectively. Both are eager to scurry away from their jobs as quickly as possible. Moreover, by contrasting bank clerks—generally harmless, well-meaning functionaries—with ruthless fighters, Hemingway heightens the viciousness of the enemy aircraft strafing the people on the road.

Analogy

Another form of comparison is the *analogy,* usually defined in words like these: *A comparison of two objects or situations that have several common characteristics.* An extended analogy, showing parallels between two unlike things, can simplify a complicated idea and leave a powerful impression on a reader. Consider the tone established in the following excerpt from a speech by President Woodrow Wilson:

> I had a couple of friends who were in the habit of losing their tempers, and when they lost their tempers they were in the habit of using very unparliamentary language. Some of their friends induced them to make a

TIP

Good writers choose metaphors carefully

promise that they never would swear inside the town limits. When the impulse next came upon them, they took a street car to go out of town to swear, and by the time they got out of town they did not want to swear . . . . Now, illustrating the great by the small, that is true of the passions of nations.

Wilson used this analogy in support of his position that a country must not jump into a war in the heat of passion. By using colloquial words (e.g., "a couple of friends") and telling a personal anecdote, Wilson established a folksy tone. The analogy, which would be accessible to every listener, draws on everyday experience, and makes good common sense. Wilson, in effect, has taken on the persona of one of the guys. Neither moralistic nor panicky, he creates the image of a fellow whose judgment the country can trust in a crisis.

Metonymy

An author's use of metonymy and synecdoche also contributes to the establishment of tone. Unlike metaphors, which make comparisons, these two figures of speech make substitutions—usually something abstract for something concrete (or vice versa), a container for the thing contained (or vice versa), a part for the whole, a cause for the effect, and so on.

In the statement, "Marv has a good head," the word *head* has been substituted for *brain* (the container for the thing contained). But *head* also means "IQ" or "intelligence"—both abstract concepts that are made more tangible by the use of *head*. To some degree, metonymy can simplify an idea—unlike a metaphor, which tends to complicate a thought—particularly when a concrete substitution is made for an abstraction, as in "Your hands made you rich," in which the word *hands* means occupation, trade, or line of work.

TIP

In general, metonymy tends to bring a kind of vitality to a phrase or idea.

Synecdoche

Synecdoche is a type of metonymy, in which a part is substituted for the whole, or vice versa. Any time you use the word *sail* for ship ("A fleet of a hundred sails"), or call a truck an *eighteen-wheeler*, you are using synecdoche. When Hamlet is about to remove the body of Polonius from Gertrude's bedchamber, he says, "I'll lug the guts into the neighbor room." His synecdoche *guts* clearly stands for corpse, but its connotation also suggests the disdain that Hamlet felt for Polonius. Indeed, both metonymy and synecdoche can be rich with implied meaning.

As you consider the metaphorical language in passages on the AP exam, keep in mind the passages' purpose and tone. Ask yourself whether each figure of speech is appropriate, and how it contributes to or detracts from the reader's response.

Footnotes

Three or four questions on the exam ask you to interpret information found in the footnotes and/or a bibliography that accompanies one of the passages. Footnoting is basically a shorthand method for giving readers detailed information about where the author found specific material used in the passage. A bibliography is more general. It lists the works the author cited or consulted while doing research. Not every system presents information in exactly the same format, but they all give readers essentially the same information.

For example, here are **standard forms for citing books**:

> Author's Name, *Title of Book* (Place of Publication: Publisher, Year), Page Number
>
> Michael André Bernstein, *Conspirators* (New York: Picador, 2004), p. 223

The same form is used for **a book with two or more authors**. The authors' names are listed in the same order as on the book's title page:

> Richard Polay and Mark Restaino, *Wines of the World* (Sacramento: Prima, 2000), p. 76

If a book has four or more authors, however, only the first author is named. The co-authors are listed as "*et al*," meaning *and others*.

> Dick Burns, *et al, Old Kew Gardens: A History* (New York: Metro Avenue Press, 2006).

In a **book with an editor but no author**, the name of the editor is listed first and is followed by *(ed.)* as in

> Matthew Speier (ed.), *Fighting for Peace* (Vancouver: Alt Green Press, 2006).

In a **book with an editor and an author**, the author's name is listed first, as in

> Miles Hochman, *Soap*, Ed. Robert Moseman (Ossining, NY, 1990), p. 50

Some books—as well as shorter works—are published without saying who wrote it. Such a work is cited this way:

> *Atlas of the World's Biggest Harbors* (New York: Allison Press 2004).

Sometimes a corporation or organization takes credit for writing a work, as in

> League of Veterans, *The March of Patriots* (Gettysburg, PA, 1985).

For a work published in an anthology or other book:

> Author's Name, "Title of Article," *Title of Book*, Name of Editor (Place of Publication: Publisher, Year), Page Number
>
> Lucinda Goo, "Spectral Realities," *Nineteenth Century Plein Air Painting*, ed. P.J. Steadman (White Plains, NY: Windmill Books, 2003), p. 333.

A passage may use material from a book's introduction, preface, forward, or an afterword written by someone other than the author of the book:

> Kenneth Iverson, preface to *Safe No More* by Walter Lipow (New York: Victory Press, 2003), p. xi.

For material that comes from a multi-volume work, the number of the volume must be included, as in

> Edward Gilbert, *The Rise and Fall of Ancient Rome* (Chicago: Lakeshore Press, 2006), Vol. 3, p. 332.

Writers sometime refer to material they found printed in a second-hand source. Say, for example, that Book A contains an excerpt from Book B, and a writer quotes part of the excerpt in a passage. Because the writer didn't get the material directly from Book B, a footnote must cite both Book A and Book B. The excerpt is listed first, its source second.

> Margorie Mottus, *The Cliff Walker*, as published in Rudolph Schmidt, *Dangerous Pursuits* (New York: Beverly Publishers, 1999), p. 56.

For articles printed in magazines, newspapers, and other periodicals:

> Author's Name, "Title of Article," Title of Periodical, Volume Number and/or (Date), Page Number

> Lilah Collins, "The Fairyland Myth," *The Montclarion*, (June 5, 2006), p. 60.

If you run into a footnote that seems incomplete—the author's name may be omitted, for example—the writer of the passage may have cited the name in the text, and there is no need to repeat it in a footnote. Likewise, you may occasionally run into a footnote consisting only of the author's last name and a page number, as in

> Altick, p. 35.

An abbreviated note often signifies that information about Altick's work was given earlier in the article or chapter. Therefore, it's pointless to repeat it. If, however, the writer of the passage has used more than one of Altick's works, the footnote needs to specify which title is now being referred to, as in

> Altick, *Preface to Critical Reading*, p.43

Occasionally, you may encounter a footnote containing multiple titles. This tells you that the writer of the passage probably found two or more sources containing similar, if not identical, material:

> Michael DiGennaro, "Teaching Wharton's *The Age of Innocence*," *Modern Literary Studies*, Vol 16, (2006), p. 455.

> Joseph Downey, "Wharton's Age of Anxiety," *Guide to Literary Theory*, 14 November 2002, Columbia University, accessed 18 March 2006 *<http://apps.columbia.edu/resource/library/5589 >*

Documentation of scholarly journals, such as those named in the previous footnote, usually include a volume number and/or issue number. Page numbers may also be cumulative, so that the first issue in a calendar year may contain pages 1–200, the next issue starts on page 201, etc.

ELECTRONIC SOURCES

Contemporary passages often cite electronic sources—emails, films, CD-ROMs, DVDs, and especially the Internet. Because web sites don't always publish complete information about themselves, citations will vary, but you're apt to find at least a few of the following:

- Name of web site
- Name of author and/or editor
- Title of article
- Title of online publication
- Institution/organization sponsoring site
- The date material was posted on the web/date of revisions
- Date that the author of the passage accessed the material
- URL, often printed between two carets < >

Example:

"Find the Right College for You," CollegeBoard.com, posted March, 2006; accessed 28 March 2007, <http://apps.collegeboard.com/search/index/jsp>

TECHNIQUES FOR TACKLING READING PASSAGES

Passage 1

Questions 1–8

Read the following passage carefully before you answer the questions.

This passage comes from the autobiography of Edward Bok, an American journalist. In 1870, at age seven, Bok emigrated to the U.S. from Holland. He and his family settled in Brooklyn. This excerpt recounts boyhood experiences.

The elder Bok did not find his "lines cast in pleasant places" in the United States. He found himself, professionally, unable to adjust the methods of his own land and of a lifetime to those of a new country. As a result
Line the fortunes of the transplanted family did not flourish, and Edward soon
(5) saw his mother physically failing under burdens to which her nature was not accustomed nor her hands trained. Then he and his brother decided to relieve their mother in the housework by rising early in the morning, building the fire, preparing breakfast, and washing the dishes before they went to school. After school they gave up their play hours, and swept and
(10) scrubbed, and helped their mother to prepare the evening meal and wash the dishes afterward. It was a curious coincidence that it should fall upon Edward thus to get a first-hand knowledge of woman's housework which was to stand him in such practical stead in later years.

It was not easy for the parents to see their boys thus forced to do work
(15) which only a short while before had been done by servants. And the capstone of humiliation seemed to be when Edward and his brother, after having for several mornings found no kindling wood or coal to build a fire,
decided to go out evenings with a basket and pick up what would they
could find in neighboring lots, and the bits of coal spilled from the coal-bin
(20) of the grocery store, or left on the curbs before houses where coal had been
delivered. The mother remonstrated with the boys, although in her heart
she knew that the necessity was upon them. But Edward had been started
upon his Americanization career, and answered: "This is America, where
one can do anything if it is honest. So long as we don't steal wood or coal,
(25) why shouldn't we get it?" And, turning away, the saddened mother said
nothing.

But while doing these homely chores was very effective in relieving the
untrained and tired mother, it added little to the family income. Edward
looked about and decided that the time had come for him, young as he was,
(30) to begin some sort of wage-earning. But how and where? The answer he
found one afternoon when he was standing before the shop-window of a
baker in the neighborhood. The owner of the bakery, who had just placed
in the window a series of trays filled with buns, tarts, and pies, came outside to look at the display. He found the hungry boy wistfully regarding the
(35) tempting-looking wares.

"Look pretty good, don't they?" asked the baker.

"They would," answered the Dutch boy with his national passion for
cleanliness, "if your window were clean."

"That's so, too," mused the baker. "Perhaps you'll clean it."

(40) "I will," was the laconic reply. And Edward Bok, there and then, got his
first job. He went in, found a step-ladder, and put so much Dutch energy
into the cleaning of the large shop-window that the baker immediately
arranged with him to clean it every Tuesday and Friday afternoon after
school. The salary was to be fifty cents per week!

1. The events described in the passage are narrated by

   (A) one of Edward's parents
   (B) Edward himself
   (C) Edward's brother
   (D) a participant in the events
   (E) an outside observer

Explanation:

Questions that ask you to identify or characterize the speaker in a passage appear regularly on the AP exam. To determine the identity of the speaker in any passage, look
first for pronoun usage. A passage written in the first person—that is, using "*I*" or
"*we*"—clearly indicates that the speaker is writing from his or her own point of view.
(Note that the speaker may or may not be not be the same person as the author;
authors sometimes invent speakers whose words are used in the passage.)

In this case, the author has chosen a narrator who speaks with the voice of someone who knows all the details but plays no part in the events—in other words, an omniscient observer. When you consider that the passage is autobiographical, Bok has made an unusual choice: By using the third person ("*he*") he writes as though Edward were someone other than himself.

Choice (E) is the best answer.

2. Which of the following phrases does the author use to illustrate that the elder Bok failed to find his "lines cast in pleasant places" (line 1)?

   (A) "professionally, unable to adjust" (line 2)
   (B) "transplanted family" (line 4)
   (C) "physically failing" (line 5)
   (D) "her nature was not accustomed" (lines 5–6)
   (E) " capstone of humiliation" (lines 15–16)

Explanation:

Because the phrase "lines cast in pleasant places" is a quotation, it is safe to assume that it refers to something that was said or something that occurred earlier in the story. It might have been used, for example, when the family arrived in America and Mr. Bok optimistically began searching for a job. Regardless of its precise context, the opening sentence of the passage implies that Mr. Bok experienced some sort of disappointment. Two reasons are given to explain the cause: 1) the family's fortunes "did not flourish," and 2) Mr. Bok's old-world professional methods were incompatible with his new environment.

   (A) therefore, is the best answer.
   (B) is not related to Mr. Bok's discontent.
   (C) and (D) refer only to Mrs. Bok.
   (E) relates to both of Edward's parents, not only to Mr. Bok.

3. Which of the following best describes the rhetorical function of the last sentence of the first paragraph (lines 11–13)?

   (A) It changes the tone of the passage from serious to lighthearted.
   (B) It contrasts the personalities of Edward and his brother.
   (C) It explains the general significance of the details contained in the paragraph.
   (D) It describes the state of the family's poverty.
   (E) It hints at a dilemma that will become important later in the story.

Explanation:

To answer a question about the *rhetorical function* of a sentence, you must try to define what that sentence contributes to the passage. Also ask what it adds to the meaning of the passage and whether it affects the author's tone. Does it help to develop the purpose of the passage, or does the sentence help the author achieve a particular effect? In short, you must analyze the role that the sentence plays in the passage.

Much of the first paragraph details the chores performed by Edward and his brother. The last sentence draws a conclusion about the boys' efforts, saying, in effect, that Edward's work was preparing him for the future.

(A) is incorrect because the tone of the passage remains consistent.

(B) doesn't apply because we don't learn much about the brother except that he worked alongside Edward.

(D) should be rejected because the sentence has no relevance to the poverty of the family.

(E) may be a tempting answer because of the phrase "later years," but the sentence contains no hint of a dilemma.

(C) is the best answer.

4. In line 14, "work" refers to which of the following?

    I. fixing breakfast before school (line 8)
    II. washing the dinner dishes (lines 10–11)
    III. picking up bits of spilled coal (lines 18–20)

(A) I only
(B) III only
(C) I and III only
(D) I and II only
(E) I, II, and III

Explanation:

Before answering this question you should read the entire sentence in which the word "work" appears. Note that the work in question had once been done by servants—presumably the servants who worked for the family back in Holland. Nothing in the passage, however, suggests that the servants went out looking for coal. Note also that the sentence contains the phrase "thus forced," indicating that *work* refers to something stated earlier in the passage. Because the boys' decision to go out looking for pieces of coal comes later (lines 18–20), the *work* alluded to does not include item III.

5. In context, the expression "necessity was upon them" (line 22) is best interpreted as having which of the following meanings?

(A) It didn't matter
(B) Things would never be the same
(C) The time had come to meet the challenge
(D) It was all in a day's work
(E) It could not be helped

Explanation:

Mrs. Bok found it difficult to permit her sons to scour the neighborhood for scraps of wood and coal, but circumstances prevented her from doing anything about it.

Only (E) expresses the idea that she had no choice but to accept the boys' decision.

6. Edward can best be described as a person who

    (A) is determined to go into business for himself
    (B) has made up his mind not to follow in his father's footsteps
    (C) believes that honesty is the best policy
    (D) is quick to seize opportunities that come his way
    (E) can be counted on to keep his word

Explanation:

Much of the passage is devoted to a description of Edward's energy and initiative. Whether he is out scrounging for bits of coal and wood or talking his way into a part-time job as a window washer, he uses his quick mind to get ahead.

(A) cannot be the correct answer. Even though Edward seems to be very ambitious, the passage does not contain enough information to support it.

(B) is not mentioned in the passage.

(C) is probably true, but Edward's honesty is not emphasized in the passage.

(D) accurately describes one of Edward's most important traits.

(E) may also be valid, but Edward's integrity is not discussed.

7. Which of the following themes best serves to unify the passage?

    (A) the rundown neighborhood in which the Boks lived
    (B) a passion for cleanliness
    (C) a closely-knit family
    (D) the difficulty of assimilating into American life
    (E) the generation gap between the Bok parents and children

Explanation:

(A) is not a valid choice because the passage does not describe the neighborhood.

(C) is implied, but is not significant enough to contribute to the unity of the passage.

(D) and (E) are not discussed in the passage.

(B) is the best choice. Edward's "passion for cleanliness" is suggested by his after-school sweeping and scrubbing of the house (lines 9–10), by the fact that his knowledge of housework will "stand him in such practical stead in later years" (line 13), and by his acquisition of a job as the bakery's window cleaner.

8. The style of the passage as a whole can best be characterized as

    (A) descriptive and informal
    (B) abstract and profound
    (C) plain and analytical
    (D) subtle and inspirational
    (E) symbolic and sentimental

Explanation:

Each choice consists of two adjectives. For a choice to be correct, both adjectives must accurately describe the style of the passage.

(B) is an unlikely choice because the passage is full of concrete detail. Nor does it contains profound thoughts and ideas.

(C), (D), and (E) all contain adjectives that characterize the passage: plain, inspirational, and sentimental. But the other adjective in each pair does not apply.

(A) is the best choice, for the author takes pains to describe the plight of the Bok family and what Edward and his brother do to help. The last section of the passage describes what Edward does and says while looking for a job. The story is told in a friendly, casual manner. Note, for example, that several sentences start with "But" and "And"—just one characteristic of informal, conversational prose.

Passage 2

Questions 9–17

Read the following passage carefully before you answer the questions.

This passage, written in the 1960s, is from an anthology on the history of violence in America.

Unquestionably the longest and most remorseless war in American history was the one between whites and Indians that began in Tidewater, Virginia, in 1607 and continued with only temporary truces for nearly 300
Line years down to the final massacre at Wounded Knee, South Dakota in 1890.
(5) The implacable hostility that came to rule white-Indian relations was by no means inevitable. The small Indian population that existed in the continental United States allowed plenty of room for expansion of white settlement. The economic resources of the white settlers were such that the Indians could have been easily and fairly reimbursed for the land needed for occu-
(10) pation by the whites. In fact, a model of peaceful white-Indian relations was developed in 17th-century New England by John Eliot, Roger Williams, and other Puritan statesmen. The same was true in 18th-century Pennsylvania, where William Penn's humane and equitable policy toward the Indians brought that colony decades of white-Indian amity.[1] Racial
(15) prejudice and greed in the mass of New England whites finally reaped the whirlwind in King Phillip's War of 1675–76, which shattered the peaceful New England model.[2] Much later the same sort of thing happened in Pennsylvania in 1763 when Pontiac's Rebellion (preceded by increasing tensions) ended the era of amicable white-Indian relations in the Keystone
(20) colony.

Other Indian wars proliferated during the 17th and 18th centuries, nor did the pace of the conflict slacken in the 19th century. It is possible that no other factor has exercised a more brutalizing influence on the American character than the Indian wars. The struggles with the Indians have some-
(25) times been represented as being "just" wars in the interest of promoting superior Western civilization at the expense of the crude stone-age culture of the Indians. The recent ethnohistorical approach to the interpretation of white-Indian relations has given us a more balanced understanding of the relative merits of white and Indian civilizations. The norms of Indian
(30) warfare were, however, at a more barbaric level than those of Western Europe. Among the Indians of Eastern America torture was an accepted

and customary part of warmaking.[3] In their violent encounters with Indians, the white settlers brought themselves down to the barbaric level of Indian warfare. Scalping was adopted by white men,[4] and down to the very
(35) last battle at Wounded Knee, lifting the hair of an Indian opponent was the usual practice among experienced white fighters. Broken treaties, unkept promises, and the slaughter of defenseless women and children, along with the un-European atrocity of taking scalps, continues to characterize the white American's mode of dealing with the Indians. The effect on our
(40) national character has not been a healthy one; it has done much to shape our proclivity to violence.

---

[1] *Douglas E. Leach,* The Northern Colonial Frontier, 1607–1763 *(New York et al.: Holt, Rinehart & Winston, [1966]). See also Alden T. Vaughan,* New England Frontier: Puritans and Indians, 1620–1675 *(Boston and Toronto: Little, Brown [1965]).*

[2] *Douglas E. Leach,* Flintlocks and Tomahawk: New England in King Phillip's War *(New York: W. W. Norton paperback, 1966).*

[3] *Leach,* Northern Colonial Frontier, *pp. 12–13.*

[4] *Leach,* Northern Colonial Frontier, *p. 112. William T. Hagan,* American Indians *(Chicago: University of Chicago Press, 1961) is a general history in which the major Indian wars are duly treated.*

9. Which of the following best states the main subject of the passage?

(A) A tragedy that should never have happened
(B) Problems of colonial America
(C) The long-term effects of conflict between whites and Indians
(D) The history of violence in America
(E) Consequences of racial prejudice and greed

Explanation:

To find the main subject you must read the whole passage, then step back from its many details in order to determine what the author is really saying. Because this particular passage tells of horrific events in American history, you might be distracted from its true subject. Don't let that happen to you. Instead, look for general statements that capture the essence of the passage.

(A) is a reasonable inference to draw from the passage, but the passage contains little evidence to support it as the primary subject.

(B), (D), and (E) are broad subjects, far too general to be the subject of a short passage.

(C) is the best answer. In one way or other, the author reiterates the idea that Americans tend toward violence, a characteristic with roots in the long history of white-Indian conflict. See lines 22–24 and 39–41.

10. In which of the following did the author most likely stretch the truth for the purpose of creating a rhetorical effect?

(A) "Unquestionably the longest and most remorseless war in American history" (lines 1–2)
(B) "hostility . . .was by no means inevitable" (lines 5–6)
(C) "William Penn's humane and equitable policy . . .brought . . . decades of white-Indian amity" (lines 13–15)
(D) "The norms of Indian warfare were . . . at a more barbaric level than those of Western Europe" (lines 29–31)
(E) "The effect on our national character has not been a healthy one" (lines 39–40)

Explanation:

Authors use rhetorical effects for numerous reasons: to emphasize ideas, to provoke thought, to arouse readers' emotions, etc. Your task now is to decide which of the choices contains *hyperbole*—an overstatement or exaggeration used to create an effect.

All the choices with the exception of (C) contain provocative ideas. But the one that exaggerates the truth more than any other is (A), a statement containing such extreme words as "*Unquestionably*," "*longest*," and "*most remorseless*"—words that are meant to surprise, if not shock, the reader. Appearing at the start of the passage, those words serve the author's purpose—to capture the reader's attention. Once you've read the sentence, it is hard to resist reading the next one, and perhaps the next one after that, in order to understand what lies behind the author's remarkable assertion.

11. Which of the following is an accurate reading of footnote 1 (line 14)?

(A) In his book *The Northern Colonial Frontier, 1607–1763*, Douglas E. Leach cites the work of Alden T. Vaughan.
(B) A passage by Vaughan is quoted in Leach's book.
(C) Leach's book discusses some of the same matters discussed in Vaughan's book.
(D) Holt, Rinehart and Winston are the editors of Leach's book.
(E) *The Northern Colonial Frontier, 1607–1763* deals with the history of New York and other states.

Explanation:

This question is strictly about footnotes and can be answered even if you haven't read a word of the passage. Familiarity with details of documentation will lead you to the correct answer (*See pages 86–88*). Footnote 1 cites two different books. Your job is to explain why.

(A) is wrong because the footnote gives no indication that one author quoted another. Had Leach quoted Vaughan, part of the footnote would read "cited by Leach," or something to that effect.

(B) is the same as (A).

(C) accurately explains the reason that both titles appear in the same footnote. It is the correct answer.

(D) Holt, Rinehart and Winston are the publishers of the book, not its editors. In footnotes editors are always identified by "*eds.*" or a similar notation.

(E) New York is the place of publication and is unrelated to the book's contents.

12. The primary function of lines 6–14 is to support which of the following ideas?

    (A) That the war between whites and Indians lasted longer than any other
    (B) That the white-Indian hostility was resolved at Wounded Knee
    (C) That conflict between whites and Indians could have been avoided
    (D) That whites and Indians should share the blame equally for years of conflict
    (E) That whites and Indians fought constantly from 1607 to 1890

Explanation:

Each sentence from line 6 to 14 develops the statement in lines 5–6 that hostility between whites and Indians "was by no means inevitable." Putting it another way, the author asserts that white-Indian relations didn't have to be hostile, and devotes lines 6–14 to explain why.

(C) is the only choice that correctly identifies the idea supported by lines 6–14.

13. Taken altogether, the footnotes in this passage suggest that

    (A) historians should rely only on recent works
    (B) the author wants his work to seem scholarly
    (C) for historical background information, the author depended heavily on the work of others
    (D) the author wrote this passage to appeal to an audience of historians
    (E) almost nothing was published about antagonism between whites and Indians prior to the 1960s

Explanation:

Authors generally use footnotes for no other reason than to give credit to others for ideas and quotations. It's possible of course to guess that an author has other motives, too, such as to flatter a colleague who has written on the same subject. But the footnotes themselves reveal nothing about an author's hidden agenda.

For that reason, eliminate (B) and (D).

(A) seems like a valid point but the footnotes fail to suggest that historians ought to rely solely on recent works. Recent books may contain the latest information and up-to-date interpretations of history, but they're not necessarily more relevant or more informative than works of the past.

(E) is almost absurd. To be sure, the works cited all come from the 1960s (when the passage was written), but it is unreasonable to assume that three hundred years of white-Indian conflict had been ignored until then.

(C) is the best answer. The passage contains many of the author's own opinions, but for background, the author went to the works of others.

14. The organization of the passage can best be described as

   (A) an interpretation of the past supported by published documentation
   (B) a chronological account of a historical situation and its influence today
   (C) the presentation of a problem and several possible solutions
   (D) an examination of historical events from two different perspectives
   (E) the refutation of a thesis using evidence arranged chronologically

Explanation:

The passage opens with a generalization about the extended war between whites and Indians. Employing a chronological approach, the passage then lists several events in the centuries-long struggle. Emphasizing the brutality used by both sides, the author argues that this history of bloodshed and violence has left an unhealthy mark on the American character.

(A) has some merit because the passage is an interpretation of a certain historical condition. The second part of the description disqualifies it as the answer, however, because the author supports his views not with published documentation but with his own opinions.

(C) is only partly accurate. The passage discusses a long-standing problem but offers no solutions.

Neither (D) nor (E) comes close to describing the passage accurately.

(B) is the best answer.

15. Footnote 4 (line 34) has been included in the passage to tell readers that the information in lines 32–34

   (A) was revealed for the first time in 1961
   (B) appears in an article entitled *American Indians* written by William T. Hagan
   (C) was found by a researcher at the University of Chicago
   (D) describes a practice that probably began between 1607 and 1763
   (E) came from the paperback edition of a book written by Douglas E. Leach

Explanation:

To answer this question, you must read not only footnote 4 but others, too, because one of the works listed in footnote 4—a book by Leach—is also cited in footnotes 1 and 3.

(A) cannot be confirmed by the footnotes. It's true that a book published in 1961 discusses the footnoted information but there's no way to tell whether it originated in Hagan's book.

(B) is incorrect because book titles are italicized and the names of articles appear inside quotation marks.

(C) is nonsense. Although the University of Chicago Press published Hagan's book, it's impossible to tell from the footnote where the research was done.

(D) According to the footnote, the information came from Leach's book, *The Northern Colonial Frontier, 1607–1763*. Although one can't be absolutely sure, whites probably began taking scalps at some point during those 150 years. (D) is the best answer.

(E) represents a misreading of the footnotes. The only paperback cited is another title by Leach, in footnote 2.

16. According to the speaker, white settlers engaged in all of the following practices EXCEPT

    (A) paying Indians for the use of their land for settlement
    (B) treating native Americans humanely
    (C) failing to abide by treaties and bargains
    (D) taking the lives of innocent people
    (E) believing that whites were superior to Indians

Explanation:

To answer this question you must search the passage for references to each of the choices. The one you don't find is the correct answer.

(A) is the correct answer. It names a practice avoided by white settlers. In fact, the author makes the point (lines 8–10) that the whites could have reimbursed the Indians for their land but didn't.

(B) is discussed in lines 10–14.

(C) and (D) are mentioned in the last paragraph, lines 36–38.

(E) is dealt with by the sentence beginning "The struggles with" (line 24).

17. The speaker's tone at the end of the passage (lines 39–41) can best be described as

    (A) agitated
    (B) remorseful
    (C) pessimistic
    (D) fussy
    (E) devastated

Explanation:

Whenever you see the word *tone* on the AP exam, think of the speaker's attitude or state of mind. Ask yourself: "What is going on in the speaker's head and heart as he writes the passage?"

When the speaker, at the end of this passage reflects on the national character of Americans, the tone is dark, disapproving, almost sad. The choice that best captures that feeling is (C).

Passage 3

Questions 18–28

Read the following passage carefully before you answer the questions.

This passage is an excerpt from a book written early in the twentieth century.

"Do you wiz zo haut can be?"

That was what the guide asked, when we were looking up at the bronze horses on the Arch of Peace. It meant, *Do you wish to go up there?* I give it
Line as a specimen of guide-English. These are the people that make life a bur-
(5) den to the tourist. Their tongues are never still. They talk forever and forever, and that is the kind of billingsgate[1] they use. Inspiration itself could
hardly comprehend them. If they would only show you a masterpiece of
art, or a venerable tomb, or a prison-house, or a battlefield, hallowed by
touching memories, or historical reminiscences, or grand traditions, and
(10) then step aside and hold still for ten minutes and let you think, it would
not be so bad. But they interrupt every dream, every pleasant train of
thought, with their tiresome cackling. Sometimes when I have been standing before some cherished old idol of mine that I remembered years and
years ago in pictures in the geography at school, I have thought I would give
(15) a whole world if the human parrot at my side would suddenly perish where
he stood and leave me gaze, and ponder, and worship.

No, we did not "wiz zo haut can be." We wished to go to La Scala, the
largest theater in the world, I think they call it. We did so. It was a large
place. Seven separate and distinct masses of humanity—six great circles and
(20) a monster parquette.[2]

We wished to go to the Ambrosian Library, and we did that also. We saw a
manuscript of Virgil, with annotations in the handwriting of Petrarch, the
gentleman who loved another man's Laura, and lavished upon her all
through life a love which was clear waste of the raw material. It was sound
(25) sentiment, but bad judgment. It brought both parties fame, and created a
fountain of commiseration for them in sentimental breasts that is running
yet. But who says a word in behalf of poor Mr. Laura? (I do not know his
other name.) Who glorifies him? Who bedews him with tears? Who writes
poetry about him? Nobody. How do you suppose *he* liked the state of
(30) things that has given the world so much pleasure? How did he enjoy having another man following his wife everywhere and making her name a
familiar word in every garlic-exterminating mouth in Italy with his sonnets
to her preempted eyebrows? *They* got fame and sympathy—he got neither.
This is a peculiarly felicitous instance of what is called poetical justice. It is
(35) all very fine; but it does not chime with my notions of right. It is too one-
sided—too ungenerous. Let the world go on fretting about Laura and
Petrarch if it will; but as for me, my tears and lamentations shall be lavished
upon the unsung defendant.

---

[1]*coarse or offensive language*
[2]*the lowest floor of a theater; the orchestra section*

18. The opening sentence of the first main paragraph (lines 2–3) contains all of the following EXCEPT

    (A) a proper noun
    (B) a personal pronoun
    (C) a dependent clause
    (D) prepositional phrases
    (E) parallelism

Explanation:

This is one of the few grammar questions you'll find on the AP exam. To answer the question you need to know about sentence structure and be familiar with basic grammatical terminology.

Examine the sentence in the passage. Look for the features listed in the five choices. The one feature that doesn't appear is the correct answer. (NOTE: The exam usually contains two or three questions that ask you to identify the **exception**, or to name which of several choices apply—as in Question 19.)

(A) is not a good choice because the *Arch of Peace* is a proper noun.

(B) is incorrect because *we* is a personal pronoun.

(C) is not the correct choice because the sentence contains a subordinate clause (*when we were looking*).

(D) is wrong because the sentence contains two prepositional phrases: *at the bronze horses* and *on the Arch of Peace*.

(E) is the best answer, determined by the process of elimination.

19. In line 12, the word "cackling" derives its effect from

    I. its use as a description of human speech
    II. its position as the last word in the sentence
    III. the sound of the word

    (A) I only
    (B) I and II only
    (C) I and III only
    (D) II and III only
    (E) I, II, and III

Explanation:

The question implies that readers will find the word "cackling" unusual in some way. Your job is to determine why.

It goes without saying that chickens, turkeys, and other fowl are known to cackle—not humans. Therefore, Roman numeral I is a good choice. What about the position of "cackling" in the sentence? Beginnings and endings are often places of prominence in a sentence. Knowing that, writers make an impact on a reader by saving a catchy or unusual word for the end. Roman numeral II, therefore, is also a valid answer.

As for Roman numeral III, you must ask yourself whether the sound of the word "cackling" has a particular force. It probably does because it is somewhat onomatopoeic—that is, it sounds like the action it describes. Because all three descriptions fit, (E) is the best answer to this question.

20. The guide's question (line 1) is written in nonsensical language because the narrator

    (A) disapproves of guides who talk too much
    (B) does not speak Italian
    (C) cannot understand what the guide is saying
    (D) would rather be at home where English is spoken
    (E) would prefer that the guide keep his mouth shut

Explanation:

Look for the answer to this question in lines 2–16, which provide a context for the statement and also reveal the narrator's state of mind.

Several of the choices seem to be potential answers because they accurately describe the narrator's opinions. But don't be misled. These so-called distractors are meant to draw unwary students away from the question being asked.

(A) is a tempting answer because the narrator disapproves of guides whose "tongues are never still." But remember that the question is about those opening words, and there is no clear link between the nonsense syllables that the narrator hears and the amount of talking done by the guide.

(B) may seem valid because it's quite possible that the narrator doesn't speak Italian. But that fact is not related to the opening words, which are meant to represent the sounds that the narrator hears.

(D) may also be true, but the narrator's longing for home is not evident anywhere in the passage.

(E) resembles (A). It may accurately convey the narrator's feelings but is unrelated to the use of nonsensical language.

That leaves Choice C. Because the narrator cannot understand the guide's words, he mocks them. Indeed, later he adds, "Inspiration itself could hardly comprehend them" (lines 6–7). (C) is the best answer.

21. The sights listed in lines 7–8 are things and places that

    (A) tourists favor
    (B) Italy has in great abundance
    (C) inspire dreams
    (D) demand visitors respect
    (E) provoke emotions

Explanation:

The answer to the question is found in the overall context and tone of the passage.

(B) should be eliminated because the passage contains no evidence that Italy is abundantly endowed with masterpieces of art, venerable tombs, and so forth. (Italy, in fact, has plenty of art and tombs, but the passage doesn't imply that.)

(C), (D), and (E) are all partly true, but not all the places listed inspire dreams, demand respect, or provoke emotions. Some do, some don't.

(A), being the most inclusive choice, is the best answer.

22. The tone in the clause "and we did that also" (line 21) suggests that the narrator

    (A) relishes seeing all the sights
    (B) is tired of traveling in Italy
    (C) remembers seeing a photo of the Ambrosian Library in a geography schoolbook
    (D) is an indifferent tourist
    (E) dutifully follows the guide from place to place

Explanation:

To answer this question, you must know the definition of tone—the author's attitude toward his subject. If you re-read the previous paragraph (lines 17–20), you'll find that the narrator could hardly care less about the opera house and the library—at least until he lays eyes on the Virgil manuscript.

(A) is highly unlikely, considering the totality of the narrator's account of his time in Italy.

(B) may be valid to a point, although the narrator never states outright that he'd like to go home.

(C) has no basis in fact.

(D) the correct answer, is evident in the narrator's account of La Scala and of his visit to the Ambrosian Library.

(E) seems reasonable except that the narrator twice says, "we wished to go . . .," implying an act of volition that is contrary to following the guide around from place to place.

23. Upon seeing Petrarch's handwriting on the Virgil manuscript (line 22), the narrator

    (A) reflects on the nature of the love between Petrarch and Laura
    (B) understands why tourists are drawn to the Ambrosian Library
    (C) realizes that he's in the presence of a rare literary masterpiece
    (D) wonders why Petrarch got away with defacing the manuscript
    (E) imagines the consequences of Petrarch's love for Laura

Explanation:

In the last paragraph of the passage, the narrator focuses not on the Virgil manuscript *per se* but on Petrarch's annotations. Petrarch's handwritten notes inspire the narrator to reflect on Petrarch's relationship with Laura. Rather than sentimentalize Petrarch's love, the narrator thinks about "Mr. Laura," the "wronged" husband. In that sense, Choice (E) most accurately describes the narrator's response to the Virgil manuscript.

24. In line 24, "a clear waste of raw material" is best interpreted to mean that

    (A) Petrarch's love of Laura was unrequited
    (B) Petrarch should have loved another woman
    (C) Petrarch's sonnets were of poor quality
    (D) Petrarch's annotations on Virgil's manuscript were pointless
    (E) Too many tears have been spilled over the sad story of Petrarch and Laura

Explanation:

Questions that ask you to interpret the meaning of a sample of figurative language are popular on AP exams.

The metaphor "clear waste of raw material" refers to "a love" that evidently was unhappy, making Choice (A) the best answer. If you piece together the story from hints in the passage, it seems that Petrarch loved Laura, who was married to another man. His love lasted a long time ("lavished upon her all through life"), and brought the pair not only fame but sympathy ("created a fountain of commiseration"). Hindsight suggests that Petrarch might have been better off loving another woman—Choice (B)—but then his famous love sonnets might never have been written. Neither (C) nor (D) are not supported by material in the passage. (E) is suggested by lines 36–37 ("Let the world go on fretting . . ."), but there is no obvious connection to the phrase "a clear waste of raw material."

25. In which of the following sentences does the narrator use hyperbole to convey the intensity of his feelings?

    (A) Line 4: "These are the people . . ."
    (B) Line 12: "Sometimes when I . . ."
    (C) Line 17: "We wished to go . . ."
    (D) Line 27: "But who says a word . . ."
    (E) Lines 34–35: "It is all very fine . . ."

Explanation:

To find the answer to this question you must recognize *hyperbole,* or overstatement.

Read all the sentences indicated by Choices (A)–(E). Look for an exaggeration meant to achieve a rhetorical effect.

(B) contains such an overstatement: "I would give the whole world if the human parrot at my side would suddenly perish . . . ." The "whole world" is a lot to give to be rid of the guide. Moreover, the author's wish that the guide "would suddenly perish" is an extreme measure that overstates his desire to be rid of the man.

26. Which of the following best describes the narrator's overall tone?

   (A) admiring and respectful
   (B) hostile and condescending
   (C) contemptuous and hateful
   (D) satirical and ironic
   (E) moralistic and solemn

Explanation:

For a choice to be correct, *both* the adjectives listed must accurately describe the narrator's tone.

In (A) neither adjective seems to apply.

(B) contains one appropriate adjective, *condescending*. From the outset, the narrator assumes an air of superiority toward the tour guide. But he is never *hostile*.

(C) overstates the narrator's attitude. While his words border on the *contemptuous*, they don't cross the line into hatefulness.

(E) is wrong because the passage is full of humor.

(D) is the best answer. Throughout the passage the narrator pokes fun not only at the hapless guide but to his own situation as a tourist in Italy. What's more, in sympathizing with Laura's husband,"Mr. Laura," the narrator's tongue is lodged firmly in his cheek. In other words, the passage reeks of irony.

27. The structure of the sentences in lines 27–29 does all of the following EXCEPT

   (A) create suspense
   (B) express a mock indignation
   (C) provoke amusement
   (D) vary the rhythm of the prose
   (E) add a touch of playfulness

Explanation:

This question asks you to determine the effect of a series of short questions all answered by a single word—"Nobody." The writing in the passage is informal, its tone more lighthearted than ponderous. A series of terse questions can suggest anger, but the subject matter (the long-ignored husband of the famous Laura) is far from somber. Thus, Choices (B), (C), and (E) accurately describe the passage. Choice (D) is also valid because the rest of the passage is made up predominantly of longer, complex, and compound sentences. Only Choice (A) does not apply.

Mastering Essay Questions

CHAPTER 4

- Reaching your goal: 3 essays in 135 minutes
- Two analytical essays: what AP readers look for
- Choosing and narrowing a topic
- Arranging ideas purposefully
- A writing style that works
- Polishing your essays for a top score
- Sample questions and student responses

Just as you don't learn to play the piano, twirl a baton, or dance hip-hop by reading books on music, baton-twirling, or dancing, you're not likely to become a better writer of essays by reading about essay writing. The best this book can do is to lay out some basic principles of essay writing for you to contemplate and incorporate into the writing you do every day. The more experience you have, the more control you'll have, and the better you'll perform not only on the AP exam, but also in future college courses and whatever work you do afterwards.

Our language contains many adjectives that describe good writing: *eloquent, well-written, lively, stylish, polished, descriptive, honed, vivid, engaging,* and countless others. On the AP exam you're instructed to write "well-organized" or "carefully reasoned" or "effective" essays—directions that mean, in effect, that your writing should be:

1. **Clear**, or easy to follow, because your ideas need to be clear to you before you can make them clear to others.

2. **Interesting**, or expressed in economical, entertaining language, because readers are put off by dull and lifeless prose.

3. **Correct**, because you and your work will inevitably be judged according to how well you demonstrate the conventions of writing.

If your ideas are expressed clearly, interestingly, and correctly, there is no reason that you can't expect to write three winning essays on the exam.

STEPS FOR WRITING THE PERFECT ESSAY

You won't have time to invent an essay-writing process during the exam. So, it pays to have a process in mind ahead of time, one that helps you to work rapidly and efficiently. Try to map out ahead of time the steps to take during each stage of the writing process. The plan that follows is a place to start. Use it while writing a few practice essays, but alter it in any way that helps you produce the best essays you can.

First Stage: PREWRITING

Prewriting consists of the planning that needs to be done before you actually start writing an essay:

- Reading and analyzing the question, or prompt
- Choosing a main idea, or thesis for your essay
- Gathering and arranging supporting ideas

Second Stage: COMPOSING

- Introducing the thesis
- Developing paragraphs
- Choosing the best words for expressing your ideas
- Structuring sentences for variety and coherence
- Writing a conclusion

Third Stage: EDITING and PROOFREADING

- Editing for clarity and coherence
- Editing to create interest
- Checking for standard usage and mechanical errors, including spelling, punctuation, and capitalization

How long does each stage last?

The truth is that the three stages overlap and blend. Writers compose, revise, and proofread simultaneously. They jot down sentences during pre-writing, and even late in the process may weave new ideas into their text. In fact, no stage really ends until the final period of the last sentence is put in place—or until the AP proctor calls "Time!"

No book can tell you how to divide up the 40 minutes recommended for each essay. What works for you may be different from what works for others. But most students get good results by devoting at least half the time—20 minutes—to composing and no more than 10 minutes each to prewriting and editing/proofreading.

How to prepare

During the weeks before the exam, or even sooner, write an essay a day for several days in a row, until you get the feel of 40 minutes' writing time. Pace yourself and keep track of how much time you spend thinking about the topic, how many minutes you devote to composing the essay, and how long it takes you to proofread and edit.

TIP

Once you've developed a pattern that works, stick to it, and practice, practice, practice until it becomes second nature.

To make every second count, don't waste time inventing titles for your essays (no titles are needed on the exam). Don't count words, and don't expect to re-copy your first drafts. Because AP readers understand that the essays are first drafts, feel free to cross out, insert words using carets (^), and move blocks of text with neatly drawn arrows. If necessary, number the sentences to make their sequence clear. You won't be penalized for sloppy looking essays. Just be sure they're legible.

> **TIP**
>
> Don't waste time inventing titles; you don't need them.

POINTERS FOR WRITING ANALYTICAL ESSAYS

One, or sometimes two, of the three essays on the exam are analytical. That is, you must read passages and **analyze** them. (A question sometimes contains two short passages to be analyzed and compared.) The author, date, and context of the passage are often identified.

Analytical essay questions most often instruct you to write about the "rhetorical strategies" used by the author to convey meaning, achieve a purpose, or create an effect. Regardless of how the question is worded, however, you are expected to dissect the passage, breaking it down into its component parts in order to explain how the author put it together.

> **HIGHLIGHT**
>
> Most analytical essays examine the purpose, content, structure, and rhetoric of a passage.

Sometimes, you may be asked to read a short statement or a passage and analyze its validity. In such cases, you will be asked to write an essay which supports the sentiment expressed, refutes the author's view, or comes down somewhere between the two extremes. To support your point of view, you are free to use evidence drawn from your reading, observations, studies, and personal experience.

> ### A Message From the Author
>
> The next pages are full of pointers for writing analytical essays. But many of the guidelines also apply to writing the third essay, the synthesis essay.
>
> *(For details on writing the synthesis essay, turn to page 176.)*

Reading and Analyzing the Topic

At the risk of stating the obvious, your preparations for writing an analytical essay should begin by reading the question, or prompt, very carefully. Read it twice or three times, underlining significant ideas and words until you know *exactly* what you are being asked to write about.

> Here is a recent AP analytical essay question. As you read it, underline the words that tell you precisely what to do:

Read carefully the following autobiographical narrative by Gary Soto. Then, in a well-written essay, analyze some of the ways in which Soto recreates the experience of his guilty six-year-old self. You might consider such devices as contrast, repetition, pacing, diction, and imagery.

You're on the right track if you underlined <u>analyze</u>, the key word in the instructions. It means that your job is to disassemble the passage, looking at how the author recreated the experience of his childhood guilt.

The question also says that you "*might consider* such devices as contrast, repetition, pacing, diction, and imagery." The phrase *might consider* turns the instruction from a requirement into a suggestion that you may accept or reject. In fact, AP readers look kindly on essays containing a spark of originality.

Practice in Reading and Analyzing Questions

Read the following pair of AP questions carefully. Underline the key words that define the task to be performed. Then, write your interpretation of the task in the blank spaces provided.

Question A   Carefully read the following excerpt from an essay by the columnist Charles Donahue entitled "People With Noses in the Air." Then write an essay in which you define the Donahue's attitude toward snobs and analyze the rhetorical strategies the writer uses to communicate that attitude.

Required task:_____

_____

_____

Explanation:

Question A doesn't include the word *tone* but instead refers to the author's attitude toward a subject, which amounts to pretty much the same thing. (Incidentally, in AP lingo, the term *rhetorical stance* is sometimes used in place of *tone*.) In this instance, Donahue may employ a sarcastic tone to ridicule snobbish behavior, or he may convey resentment or envy or disbelief or any number of other feelings about snobs.

An essay responding to the question must contain at least two things: 1) a definition of Donahue's attitude toward snobs, and 2) a discussion of how Donahue communicated that attitude—that is, what rhetorical methods he used to achieve his goal.

The essay might discuss these two concerns separately, or it might deal with both issues simultaneously. However the material is organized, though, it must address both concerns.

Question B   Carefully read the following passage from ____(Title)____ written by _____(Author)_____. Then write an essay on the given passage analyzing the rhetorical strategies the author used to achieve her purpose.

Required task:_____

_____

_____

Explanation:

This question gives you the chance to write about virtually any rhetorical technique that you can find in the passage. On one hand, that's easy because the choice is completely yours. On the other hand, it's tough because you must search the passage for rhetorical techniques that help to shape the purpose of the passage. Because you happen to locate a metaphor doesn't necessarily make figurative language significant to the passage. To be important, the metaphor must somehow contribute to the overall impact that the passage leaves on its readers. In other words, this open-ended question forces you to scrutinize the passage with great care in order to locate rhetorical devices that help the author to achieve her goal.

Reading the Passage

Reading a passage that you must analyze in an essay differs little from reading a passage in order to answer multiple-choice questions. If anything, the approach is somewhat simpler because you need not zero in on every tiny detail but only on the rhetorical strategies, if any, specified by the question.

If a question instructs you to discuss figurative language, search the passage for metaphors, symbols, analogies, samples of irony and imagery, and so forth. If you're told to analyze diction, look for words and phrases that serve as clues to the author's background, personality, and especially the author's tone and purpose.

Read the passage at least twice—first for an overview of its point and purpose and then to track down examples of rhetorical devices. Mark up the page with underscoring, asterisks, circles, arrows, or whatever helps you highlight those parts of the passage that could be used in writing a response to the question. Scribble notes in the margin. Jot down thoughts and ideas that occur to you as you read. Your notes may well serve as an outline of an essay.

Regardless of the question, an understanding the content of the passage is crucial. That means reading *every word*, not just enough of it to give you a vague sense of the passage's main idea. By the time you've finished reading you ought to be able complete the following statement in 10 or fewer well-chosen words:

This passage is about _____.

Everything you discuss in your essay must be tied to your understanding of the passage's content. It won't be enough simply to identify figures of speech, to say the tone is nostalgic, or that the writing style is sophisticated. What counts is your analysis of the author's rhetorical choices—or how the purpose of the passage was achieved.

> **TIP**
>
> Depend on the question itself to tell you what to search for while reading the passage.

Planning Your Essay

PREPARING AN OUTLINE

Spend a few minutes outlining your essay before writing your opening sentence. You don't need a formal outline, but just a list of ideas arranged in the order that you'll use them in your essay. It speaks well of you as a writer when you present ideas in a well-thought-out sequence instead of spilling them onto the page in the order they happened to pop into your head. Since time is short on the AP exam, your outline may consist of no more than scrawled words or phrases that tell you what each paragraph will be about.

> **TIP**
>
> In general, an essay outlined in advance is likely to be clearer and more coherent than one thrown together willy-nilly.

After reading the following passage, Bridget B, a high school senior, prepared an outline for an essay that analyzed the author's use of rhetorical devices.

PASSAGE

This passage by Laura Eirmann appeared on the web site of the Cornell University Pet Loss Hotline.

When an owner and veterinarian decide that a pet is suffering or unlikely to make a recovery, euthanasia offers a way to end a pet's pain. The decision is difficult for both the owner and the veterinarian, but we should recog-
Line nize that sometimes this is the kindest thing we can do in the final stage of
(5)   a pet's life.

Understanding how the procedure is performed may help an owner in this decision. It may also help an owner decide whether they wish to be present during the euthanasia. Initially, a pet is made as comfortable as possible. Some veterinarians will perform the procedure in a pet's home. If the animal
(10)   is brought to the hospital, veterinarians often choose a quiet room where the pet will feel at ease. Sometimes a mild sedative or tranquilizer is first given if the animal appears anxious or painful. Frequently an indwelling catheter is placed in the pet's vein to ensure that the euthanasia solution is delivered quickly. The euthanasia solution is usually a barbiturate—the same class of
(15)   drugs used for general anesthesia. At a much higher dose, this solution pro-
vides not only the same effects as general anesthesia (loss of consciousness, loss of pain sensation), but suppresses the cardiovascular and respiratory systems. As the solution is injected, the animal loses consciousness and within minutes the heart and lungs stop functioning. Since the pet is not
(20)   conscious, they do not feel anything. Most times, the animal passes away so smoothly, that it is difficult to tell until the veterinarian listens for absence of a heartbeat. The eyes remain open in most cases. Sometimes, the last few breaths are what's termed "agonal," meaning involuntary muscle contractions, but again, the pet is not aware at this point. After the animal dies,
(25)   there is complete muscle relaxation, often accompanied by urination and defecation. This is completely normal and is something an owner should expect. In addition, after death, chemicals normally stored in nerve endings are released causing occasional muscle twitching in the early post-mortem period. Many owners who choose to stay with their pets are surprised how
(30)   quickly and easily the pet is put to rest.

The decision to stay or not stay with a pet is a very personal one. Some owners feel they could comfort their pet in its final minutes. Others feel their emotional upset would only upset their pet. Those who choose not to stay may wish to view the pet's body after the procedure is complete.
(35)   Euthanasia is emotional for veterinarians as well. Sometimes, the veterinar-
ian has known the pet for a long time or has tried very hard to make the animal well again. James Herriot stated the view of most veterinarians in *All Things Wise and Wonderful:* "Like all vets I hated doing this, painless though it was, but to me there has always been a comfort in the knowledge
(40)   that the last thing these helpless animals knew was the sound of a friendly voice and the touch of a gentle hand."

After reading the passage carefully, Bridget jotted down her impressions of the passage and its author:

1. The author of the passage is a veterinarian.

2. The passage was written for an audience of pet owners.

3. The passage reflects the writer's concern for the well-being of animals.

4. The writer is trying to help pet owners make decisions about taking the life of their terminally ill pets.

5. The writer describes the process of pet euthanasia unemotionally.

Using these thoughts as a springboard, Bridget prepared an outline for an essay on the author's rhetorical strategies.

(For the record, Bridget's outline below is far more detailed than an outline hurriedly written during an AP test.)

Point of passage: to help pet owners deal with euthanasia

Main idea: Author's tone, point of view and diction comfort pet owners, put them at ease about making a difficult decision.

1. **Tone**: *Uses compassionate tone*
   Avoids harsh words-e.g. kill, destroy, put to death, deathly ill.
   Uses euphemisms and soft words: "euthanasia," (line 2) "end a pet's pain," (2) "put to rest," (30) final stage of . . . life" (4-5)

2. **Point of view**: *Author identifies with pet owner, maybe to help relieve owner's guilt about killing a pet.*
   (Implication: We're in this together, so don't blame yourself.)
   - - difficult decision for both owner and vet (3)
   - - emotional for vets (35)
   - - - quote by J. Herriot (38-41)

3. **Dicton** *(word choice)*
   Plenty of repetition of words with connotations that stress painlessness, ease, and speed of the euthanasia "procedure"
   Painless: "Pet is made . . . comfortable" (8)
   *   Quiet room where pet feels "at ease" (10-11)*
   *   "sedative," "tranquillizer," "same as general anesthesia," "loss of pain," etc.*
   Ease of process: "animal passes away so smoothly" (20-21)
   Speed of process: "solution delivererd quickly" (13-14)
   *   Owner's surprise at "how quickly and easily the pet is put to rest" (29-30)*

Possible conclusion: Author covers process thoroughly from start to finish; thoroughness shows respect for pet owner, causing pet owner to feel confident in the vet.

As you prepare for the AP exam, get into the habit of writing outlines. If you're not accustomed to outlining before you write, it may take a while to get into the groove. But once in, the rewards may be astounding.

TIP

Get into the habit of writing outlines.

CHOOSING A MAIN IDEA

The purpose, or point, of any essay is its **main idea**, also called its **thesis**. Essays may be written with beautiful words, contain profound thoughts, and make readers laugh or weep. But without a main idea, an essay remains just words in search of a meaning, causing readers to scratch their heads and ask, "Huh? What's the point?"

Open-ended essay questions on general topics invite you to range far and wide in search of a main idea. Not on the AP exam, however. Because the analytical essay questions ask you to perform a specific writing task, devising a main idea is reasonably simple: Just identify the relationship between the rhetorical strategies used in a passage and the point or purpose of the passage. In fact, a main idea may include the actual words or a paraphrase of the question itself. For example:

> Laura Eirmann, the author of the passage, makes use of such rhetorical devices as a sympathetic tone, a friendly point of view, and a soothing choice of words to achieve her purpose.

This opening sentence won't win a prize for originality but it gets the job done. It shows that the writer understands the question and it suggests that the essay to follow will contain a three-part analysis of Eirmann's writing style.

It's not essential, nor is it particularly desirable to state the main idea at the essay's outset. In fact, it's often preferable to lead up to your main idea with a general discussion of the context in which the passage was written. For instance,

> Pet owners, experiencing great anxiety when their pets develop incurable illnesses, often face the terrible decision of whether to let their pets suffer until they die or to "put them to sleep." Knowing that pet owners agonize over what to do, Laura Eirmann carefully constructed an essay intended to help pet owners make an informed, guilt-free decision about euthanizing their pets. *To make readers feel comfortable, Eirmann uses a sympathetic tone, a friendly point of view, and a soothing choice of words.*

Still another approach is to save the thesis statement for your conclusion. Instead of giving away your main idea at the start, let it emerge naturally and inevitably from evidence presented in all the prior paragraphs.

Arranging Ideas

The words you've underlined while reading a passage, the thoughts you've written in the margins, the items listed in your outline—these are the raw materials of your essay. Before you begin composing, select the details that will best support your main idea. Discard the others, or better, hold them in reserve—to be used in case one of your selections turns out to be a dud.

Then, arrange those materials. Decide what comes first, second, and third. The best order is the clearest order, the one your reader can follow with the least effort. But, just as a highway map may show several routes from one place to another, there is no single way to get from the beginning to the end of an essay.

> **TIP**
>
> The best order is the clearest order.

No plan is superior to another provided there's a valid reason for using it. The plan that fails is the aimless one, the one in which ideas are presented solely according to when they occurred to you. To guard against aimlessness, rank the ideas in your outline in order of importance. Then work toward your best point, not away from it. Giving away your *pièce de resistance* at the start is self-defeating. Therefore, if you've identified, say, three good rhetorical strategies, save the best one for the end of the essay. Start with your second best, and sandwich your least favorite between the other two. A solid opening draws readers into the essay and creates that all-important first impression, but a memorable ending is even more important. Coming last, it is what readers have fresh in their minds when they assign the essay a grade.

The Formula

The five-paragraph essay formula is a fundamental, all-purpose plan for arranging ideas into clear, easy-to-follow order. It's a technique you can rely on any time you need to set ideas in order. Its greatest virtue is clarity. Each part has its place and purpose.

THE FORMULA	
Introduction	Point 1
Body	Point 2
Conclusion	Point 3

You needn't follow the formula slavishly. In fact, professionally written essays rarely adhere to this five-paragraph arrangement. Yet, many essay writers, even those who take a circuitous path between the beginning and end, use some version of it.

A WORD OF CAUTION

The five-paragraph essay is taught so widely in schools that it has almost become a cliché. AP readers will recognize it instantly and may grade it accordingly. The highest scores are usually reserved for essays that demonstrate a particularly strong command of essay-writing techniques. Essays that rely on an obvious organizational formula may not reach that lofty level.

Writing Style in Analytical Essays

Choose your words carefully, of course, and try to adopt a plain, natural style. Don't drag out your SAT vocabulary in an attempt to snow your readers. AP readers are not world-class intellectuals who scoff at all but the most sophisticated prose. They're just teachers with plenty of experience evaluating students' writing. They won't be impressed by formal, pompous, or elegant writing. Think of them as everyday folks who appreciate straight, plain, everyday language. You have a natural voice. Use it.

Analytical essays are likely to be more formal than informal. It's inappropriate to be casual when you are analyzing a text, providing quotes, paraphrasing others' words, using the terminology of literary criticism and scholarship. At the same time, though, don't be stuffy or pompous. AP essay readers are old hands at spotting pretense in students' writing.

TIP

Don't be pretentious. Use your natural voice.

Just let your genuine voice ring out, although the way you speak is not necessarily the way you should write. Spoken language is often vague, clumsy, repetitive, confused, wordy. Adopt a writing style not unlike the everyday speech of someone who speaks grammatical English, free of pop expressions and clichés. Think of it as the kind of mature speech expected of you in serious conversation, say, during a college interview. Or maybe even the way this paragraph sounds. You could do a lot worse!

Use plain and precise language. Fortunately, English is loaded with simple words that can express the most profound ideas. A sign that says STOP! conveys its message more clearly than CEASE AND DESIST. When a dentist pokes at your teeth, it *hurts*, even if dentists call it "experiencing discomfort." Simple doesn't necessarily mean short, however. It's true that plain words tend to be the short ones, but not always. The word *fid* is short, but it's not plain unless you are a sailor, in which case you'd know that a fid supports the mast on a boat. On the other hand, *spontaneously* is five syllables long. Yet it is a plain and simple word because of its frequent use.

Simple ideas dressed up in ornate words not only obscure meaning but make writers sound phony, as in:

Fancy: The epistle states that politicians have a proclivity toward prevarication.
Plain: The letter says that politicians often lie.

Ernest Hemingway called a writer's greatest gift a "built-in, shock-proof crap detector." Hemingway's own detector worked well. He produced about the leanest, plainest writing in the English language—not that you should try to emulate Hemingway. (That's already been done by countless imitators.) But an efficient "crap detector" of your own will encourage you to choose words only because they express exactly what you mean.

Euphemisms

Of course, there are occasions when the plainest words won't do. When you wish to soften or mitigate painful, unsavory, or objectionable truths, our language offers innumerable euphemisms. For example, there are scores of euphemisms for the verb "to die" (*pass away, pass on, be deceased, rest, expire, meet one's maker*, and so on), for "bathroom" (*restroom, ladies'/men's room, W.C., lounge*), and for "drunk," "vomiting," and everything else that might upset a prissy sensibility. Pussyfooting with words has its place. We do it all the time, but in your AP essays resort to euphemisms only when you have a valid reason for doing so.

TIP

Steer clear of language and abbreviations customarily used in text messages and blogs.

Don't interpret this admonition to use plain words as *carte blanche* to use current, everyday slang or street talk in your AP essays. Spoken language, which brims with colorful words and expressions like *chill, pig out, dissed*, and *bummed* has its place, but its place is not in your AP essay unless you definitely need such lingo to create an effect that you can't produce another way. If you insist on writing like a blogger, that's fine, but don't use quotation marks to call attention to the fact that you can't think of standard or more original words. If, to make a point, you overload your essay with digital slang, be sure to demonstrate your mastery of standard English in at least part of the piece. After all, an AP student must be able to write good, standard prose.

PUTTING YOURSELF IN THE ESSAY

In formal essays, custom requires you to remove yourself from stage center and focus on the subject matter. In AP essays, however references to yourself are perfectly acceptable, as in "*I think* that the author's use of hyperbole . . . , etc." Using *I* is often preferable to using the more impersonal *one*, as in "When *one* is writing an AP essay, *one* sometimes writes funny," or *you*, as in "Sometimes *you* feel like a dope," or by avoiding pronouns altogether. But an essay that expresses the writer's personal views will sound most natural when cast in first-person singular.

TIP

In AP essays, references to yourself are perfectly okay.

VARYING SENTENCES

When writing your essay, try to use a variety of sentences to show your awareness that the type, structure, and length of sentences help authors convey meaning and create effects on readers. It's easy to fall into a rut by using the same sentence structure over and over and over. But if you are aiming for a high AP score, vary your sentences. For one thing, variety adds life to your prose.

English sentences, as you probably know, are structured in three ways: ***simple, compound, and complex***.

SIMPLE: Metaphors are great.

The sentence is *simple* because it contains one grammatical subject (*Metaphors*) and one verb (*are*). It also states a single main idea.

COMPOUND: Grammar is difficult, but it helps you write well.

The sentence is *compound* because it is made up of two simple sentences joined by a coordinating conjunction (*but*). Other coordinating conjunctions used in compound sentences are *and, yet, or, for, nor*, and *so*, as in:

Grammar is difficult, *and* it drives many people up the wall.
Samantha studied hard, *for* she wanted an 5 on the AP exam.

Notice that the structure of each of these compound sentences gives roughly equal emphasis to its two main ideas.

COMPLEX: Although he's taking four AP courses, Mark won't study.

The sentence is *complex* because it is made up two parts—a simple sentence (*Mark won't study*) and a dependent clause (*Although he's taking four AP courses*). Because the clause begins with a subordinating conjunction (*Although*), it is called a *subordinate clause*. Subordinate clauses contain ideas related to the complete sentence (called the *independent* or *main* clause), but they are usually less important. Other common subordinating conjunctions include *because, after, before, though, unless, until, whenever*, and *while*.

Not every simple, compound, and complex sentence is structured in the way just described. In fact, variations abound because English is a remarkably flexible language that can be shaped in countless ways, as you'll see below.

Most simple sentences start with the grammatical subject followed by the verb:

Cats (subject) *fall* (verb) asleep in about three seconds.
They (subject) *sleep* (verb) best after eating and cleaning themselves.
I (subject) *wish* (verb) to be a cat in my next life.

A string of sentences with this subject-verb pattern resembles the prose in a grade-school primer—a style that just won't do on an AP essay. To be sure that you write in a more mature and engaging way, analyze one of your recent essays. Do several sentences begin with grammatical subjects? If so, try shifting the subject elsewhere. Try leading off with a prepositional phrase, or with an adverb, adjective, or some other grammatical unit.

The following pairs of sentences show how a subject can be shifted from its customary position:

Before the shift: Ms. Bennett is one of the most popular teachers in the school.
After the shift: In this school Ms. Bennett is one of the most popular teachers.

After a prepositional phrase was added, the subject (*Ms. Bennett*) has been moved further along in the sentence.

Before: She taught the novel *Beloved* to our AP English class with enthusiasm.
After: Enthusiastically, she taught the novel *Beloved* to our AP English class.

Obviously, the revised sentence begins with an adverb.

Before: Students were less excited about the book than she was.
After: Yet, students were less excited about the book than she was.

Well, here the subject (*students*) is stated after an opening connective.

Before: I loved the book, although it turned out to be an intolerable drag for most of my classmates.
After: Although the book turned out to be an intolerable drag for most of my classmates, I loved it.

After introducing the sentence with a dependent clause, the writer names the subject, *I*, and then adds the rest of the sentence.

Before: Bennett pushed the class to find symbolic meaning in various scenes to make the book more meaningful.
After: To make the book more meaningful, Ms. Bennett pushed the class to find symbolic meaning is various scenes.

To revise this sentence the writer begins with a verbal, in this case "to make," the infinitive form of the verb. (Verbals look and feel much like verbs but serve a different function. Verbals, though, come from verbs. Hence, their name and their resemblance.)

Before: I read the book in two days, hoping that it would never end.
After: Hoping that it would never end, I read the book in two days.

Aiming to diversify sentence openings, the writer starts this sentence with another kind of verbal, known as a *participle*. The *-ing* ending often indicates that a word is a participle.

> *Before*: I was awed by the tenacity of the characters and absorbed by every soul-stirring syllable of the story.
>
> *After*: Awed by the tenacity of the characters, I was absorbed by every soul-stirring syllable of the story.

Determined to try something different, the writer begins the sentence with an adjective that happens to sound like a verb because of its *-ed* ending.

Still another variation to try now and then is the sentence constructed from matched ideas set in juxtaposition. President Kennedy used such a sentence to memorable effect in his inaugural speech:

> "Ask not what your country can do for you, ask what you can do for your country."

The power of such sentences lies in the balance of parallel clauses. Each clause could stand alone, but together they express the idea more vigorously. Another example:

> It wasn't that the spirit of the pioneers caught my imagination, it was my imagination that caught the pioneer spirit.

Emphasis can also come from a reversal of customary word order. Out of context, a sentence in which the predicate precedes the subject may seem awkward. But in the right spot, an inverted sentence can leave an indelible mark. "Dull the book is not" packs more wallop than "The book is not dull" or "The book is exciting." In the right context, "Perilous was the climb to the top of the cliff" sounds more ominous than, "The climb to the top of the cliff was perilous." Inverted sentences should be used sparingly, however. More than once in an essay diminishes the vigor of each occurrence and may sound silly.

No rule of thumb says that a certain percentage of sentences in an essay ought to be different from the usual subject-verb structure. It really depends on the purpose and style of the essay. But if you find yourself repeating the same sentence pattern, restructure some of your sentences. Your readers are bound to reward you for the effort.

SENTENCE TYPES

Our language offers a rich menu of sentence types. Declarative sentences predominate in most essay writing. (Just to refresh your memory, a *declarative* sentence, such as the one you are now reading, simply makes a statement.) But other types of sentences can create all sorts of fascinating effects. Take interrogative sentences, for example. (Do you remember that *interrogative* sentences ask questions?) An interrogative sentence appropriately placed in an essay consisting of declarative sentences can change the pace and rhythm of the prose, underscore an idea, and promote the reader's involvement.

Don't forget about imperative sentences (keep in mind that *imperative* sentences make requests or give commands) and exclamatory sentences (What strong emotion an *exclamatory* sentence can express!).

Furthermore, you can write sentences interrupted at some point by a dash—although some editors and teachers claim that it's not proper to do so in formal prose. Direct and indirect quotations are useful, and on occasion you can drive home a point with a single emphatic word. Excellent!

There's peril, however, in scrambling sentence types for no other reason than to scramble sentence types, for you may end up with a mess on your hands. Be guided by what expresses your ideas most clearly and seems varied enough to interest your readers.

REPETITION OF IDEAS

Repetition can be annoying, but, adroitly used, it adds clout to an idea. When your sweetheart says, "I love you. I love you very much," the repetition intensifies the sentiment. If a coach admonishes his team, "OK, guys, knock it off. I said knock it off," you know he really means it.

The following paragraph may suggest that the writer has a one-track mind:

> In the fall Bethany will be going to college. She is psyched to get out of high school. She is psyched to break away from her small town and live in a big city. She is psyched for meeting new people from all over the country and the world, and she is psyched to get started on a program of studies that she expects will prepare her for law school. But first, she is psyched to take the AP exam.

Every sentence but the first uses the same subject/verb combination. Yet, the overall effect is anything but monotonous. What's memorable is not repetition, but relentlessness. Repeating the verb *psyched* five times emphasizes Bethany's frame of mind. The point could not have been made as emphatically using a different verb in each sentence.

Or take this passage written by an incorrigible bagel freak.

> My taste for bagels knows no bounds. I stop at the bagel shop on my way to school each morning and grab an onion bagel and coffee. Lunch consists of an olive bagel and a couple of veggie bagels smeared with cream cheese. At snack time I'm not picky. Any style bagel will do, but I hate to have dinner without a buttered poppy-seed bagel. Before bed I wash down a plain toasted bagel with a glass of milk, and in case I have insomnia, I stash two or three garlic bagels on my nightstand for a tasty middle-of the-night pick-me-up.

The writer virtually beats you over the head with bagels. But the repetition won't allow you to forget the point—that the writer has eyes not for pizza, not for burritos, not for onion rings—but only for bagels.

A word of caution: Restatements of a word or phrase can also be distracting. Inadvertent repetition obstructs progress by putting useless words in the reader's path. Therefore, stay alert, for accidental repetition, as in:

> In a corner of the room stood a clock. The clock said four o'clock.
> Columbus made three ocean voyages. The voyages took him across the Atlantic Ocean.

Combining such sentences will keep you from ending one sentence and starting the next one with the same words:

> The clock in the corner of the room said four.
> Columbus made three voyages across the Atlantic.

Sentences can also be plagued with a word or a rhyme that draws attention to itself:

> Maybe some people don't have as much freedom as others; but the freedom they do have is given to them for free. Therefore, freedom is proof enough that the best things in life are free.

> The members of the assembly remembered that November was just around the corner.

These writers failed to listen to the sound of their words. Had they read their sentences aloud, they may have noticed that the voices were stuck in a groove. In fact, reading your words aloud allows you to step back and examine word sounds (Hold it! Those two words—*aloud* and *allows*—sound jarring and should not be allowed to stand side by side.) Hearing your written words spoken, you're more apt to notice unwanted repetition. Whenever possible, let each of your practice essays cool for a while. Then enlist a friend to read it aloud. Hearing it in another's voice lends objectivity to the process of self-evaluation.

SHORT AND LONG SENTENCES

Long sentences (like this one) demand greater effort from readers because they must keep track of more words, modifiers, phrases (not to speak of parenthetical asides), and clauses, without losing the writer's main thought, which may be buried amid any number of secondary, or less important, thoughts, while short sentences are usually easier to grasp. A brief sentence can make a point sharply because all its words concentrate on a single point. Take, for example, the last sentence in this passage:

> **TIP**
>
> To fend off monotony, vary the length of your sentences.

> For three days, my parents and I sat in our SUV and drove from college to college to college in search of the perfect place for me to spend the next four years. For 72 hours we lived as one person, sharing thoughts and dreams, stating opinions about each campus we visited, taking guided tours, interviewing students and admissions officials, asking directions a hundred times, eating together in town after town, and even sleeping in the same motel rooms. But mostly, we fought.

A terse closing sentence following a windy, 46-word sentence produces a mild jolt. Indeed, its point is to startle the reader. The technique is easily mastered but should be used sparingly. Overuse dilutes its impact.

A series of short sentences can be as tiresome as a succession of long ones. A balance works best. If you have strung together four or five equally long (or short) sentences, try to separate, or combine, them. Here, to illustrate, is an overweight sentence that needs demolition:

> In the 1870's, the archaeologist, Heinrich Schliemann, dug in the correct spot and discovered not only one ancient city of Troy, but nine of them, one lying on top of the other, since every few centuries a new city had been built upon the ruins of the old, causing Schliemann to dig right past the layer containing the ruins of the famous city of the Trojan Horse without realizing he had done so, a mistake not corrected until almost fifty years later by Carl Blegen of the University of Cincinnati, by which time, unfortunately, it was too late for Schliemann because he had been dead for 40 years.

The sentence is perfectly grammatical, but it carries a big 108-word load. Cut it down to size. Break it into pieces, rearrange it, add verbs, drop an idea or two, change the emphasis and delete words. When you're done, the restyled sentence might sound something like this:

> In the 1870's, the archaeologist, Heinrich Schliemann, dug in the correct spot and discovered not only one ancient city of Troy, but nine of them, one lying on top of the other. He figured out that every few centuries a new city had been built upon the ruins of the old. Without realizing it, he had dug right past the layer he was seeking, the layer containing the ruins of the famous city of the Trojan Horse. His mistake was corrected fifty years later by Carl Blegen of the University of Cincinnati. By then, however, it was too late for Schliemann. He had been dead for 40 years.

Likewise, a string of four or five sentences of almost equal length can be combined to create a more balanced and varied paragraph. Here, for instance, is a paragraph, also about an ancient city, made up of short, choppy sentences:

> Pompeii was an ancient city. It belonged to the Roman Empire. It was near the base of Mount Vesuvius. In 79 A.D. the volcano on Vesuvius erupted. Tons of hot, wet ash fell on Pompeii. In less than a day the city was buried. It just vanished. More than seventeen centuries later an Italian peasant found Pompeii. His discovery was accidental. He was digging in a field. His shovel struck the top of a wall. That was two hundred years ago. Pompeii is still being excavated two hundred years later. About two-thirds of the city has been unearthed. It must have been a beautiful city.

With repetition eliminated and some ideas subordinated to others, here is what you get:

> The ancient Roman city of Pompeii lay near the base of Mt. Vesuvius. In 79 A.D., Vesuvius erupted, burying the city with tons of hot, wet ash. In less than a day the city vanished. More than seventeen centuries later an Italian peasant digging in a field with a shovel accidentally struck the top of a wall. He had found Pompeii. Today, two hundred years later, the city is still being unearthed. The excavation reveals that Pompeii must have been a beautiful city.

> ### Varying Sentences—A Summary
>
> - Use a variety of sentence types: *simple, compound,* and *complex.*
> - Create variety by starting sentences with:
>   1. A prepositional phrase: *From the start, In the first place, At the outset*
>   2. Adverbs and adverbial phrases: *Originally, At first, Initially*
>   3. Dependent clauses: *When you start with this, Because the opening is*
>   4. Conjunctions: *And, But, Not only, Either, So, Yet*
>   5. Adjectives and adjective phrases: *Fresh from, Introduced with, Headed by*
>   6. Verbal infinitives: *To launch, To take the first step, To get going*
>   7. Participles: *Leading off, Starting up, Commencing with*
>   8. Inversions: *Unique is the writer who embarks . . .*
> - Balance long and short sentences.
> - Combine a series of very short sentences.
> - Dismember very long sentences.

Paragraphing

Whoever invented paragraphs deserves a pat on the back because he or she devised a simple way to guide readers through a piece of writing. Each new paragraph alerts readers to get ready for a shift of some kind, just as a car's directional blinker tells other drivers that you're about to turn.

Yet, not every new paragraph signals a drastic change. The writer may simply want to nudge the discussion ahead to the next step. Some paragraphs spring directly from those that preceded them. The paragraph you are now reading, for instance, is linked to the one before by the connecting word *Yet.* The connection was meant to alert you to a change in thought, but it was also intended to remind you that the two paragraphs are related. Abrupt starts may be useful from time to time to keep readers on their toes. But good writers avoid a string of sudden turns that can transform surprise into confusion.

In an essay, paragraphs usually play a primary role and one or more secondary roles. An *introductory paragraph,* for instance, launches the essay and makes the intent of the essay clear to the reader. The *concluding paragraph* leaves the reader with a thought to remember and provides a sense of closure. The majority of paragraphs, however, are *developmental.* They carry forward the main point of the essay by performing any number of functions, among them:

- Adding new ideas to the preceding discussion
- Continuing or explaining in more detail an idea presented earlier
- Reiterating a previously stated idea
- Citing an example of a previously stated idea
- Evaluating an opinion stated earlier
- Refuting previously stated ideas

- Providing a new or contrasting point of view
- Describing the relationship between ideas presented earlier
- Providing background material
- Raising a hypothetical or rhetorical question about the topic

Whatever its functions, a paragraph should contribute to the essay's overall growth. A paragraph that fails to amplify the main idea of the essay should be revised or deleted. Similarly, any idea within a paragraph that doesn't contribute to the development of the paragraph's topic needs to be changed or eliminated.

TOPIC AND SUPPORTING SENTENCES

> **TIP**
>
> Every sentence in a paragraph should help to develop the paragraph's topic.

As you write your AP essays, be sure to include sentences that contain landmarks to help readers know where they are. Such guiding sentences differ from others because they define the paragraph's main topic, hence their name: *topic sentence*. Topic sentences come in many forms, but what they all have in common is their helpfulness. They are like landmarks that tell readers the direction they'll be going for a while.

Most, but not all, paragraphs contain topic sentences. The topic of some paragraphs is so obvious that to state it would be redundant. For instance, a description of a fast-food restaurant might detail the crowd, the noise, the overflowing garbage cans, the smell of cooking oil, the lines of people, the crumb-strewn formica tables, and so on. A reader would certainly get the picture. To state explicitly "It was a busy day at Burger King" would serve no purpose.

No rule governs every possible use of a topic sentence. A sense of what readers need in order to understand the essay must be your guide. Let topic sentences lead the way. Consider your readers as absentminded wanderers who need frequent reminders of where they are and where they are going. If in doubt, grasp their hands too firmly rather than too loosely. Follow the principle that if there is a way to misunderstand or misinterpret your words, readers are sure to find it.

> **GETTING ON TOP OF TOPIC SENTENCES**
>
> Print out or photocopy an essay you've written recently. On one copy underline all the topic sentences. Let a friend do the same on the second copy. Then compare your answers. If you agree, you can be pretty sure that your topic sentences are doing what they are supposed to do.

DEVELOPING PARAGRAPHS

Like essays, paragraphs should have a discernible organization. Ideas can be arranged from general to specific, or vice versa. Sequential arrangements make sense for analytical paragraphs. In a cause-and-effect paragraph, logic dictates that the cause precedes the effect, but the opposite may sometimes be preferable. As always, clarity and intent should govern the sequence of ideas.

Writers shun formulas in creating paragraphs, but they generally concur that paragraphs of only one or two sentences are too scanty. Thorough development of an idea calls for several sentences—most of the time, at least. Journalists, however, often write paragraphs consisting of one or two sentences. But most contemporary nonfiction consists of paragraphs of four to eight sentences. Recognizing that readers need frequent breaks, writers these days almost never write paragraphs of a dozen or more sentences.

Poor essays often suffer from lack of development. The writer states ideas and then drops them. You're not apt to do that, though, if your think of your readers as skeptics who doubt that you're on the level unless you prove that you know what you're talking about. An underdeveloped statement, no matter how strongly worded, usually won't do. That's why you must back up your general ideas with specifics, using illustrative material that can be in any number of forms. In an analytical essay, that means referring frequently to the passage. Paraphrase the passage or use direct quotes, but don't let the quotes constitute the bulk of your essay. Rather, state ideas in your own words, then support them with direct or indirect quotations.

Whatever you do, your analysis must be based on something more solid than your intuition or personal preference. The left side of your brain, the logical side, is being examined along with the right, the creative, side. The best essays reveal that both sides of your brain are in good working order.

> **TIP**
>
> The kind of analytical writing expected on the AP exam is rational discourse, not emotional blabber.

USING TRANSITIONS

Picture your readers as tourists in a foreign country and your essay as a journey they are making from one place to another. Because you can't expect strangers to find their own way, you must lead them. Tell them where they are going (the introduction) and remind them of the progress they're making (the body of the essay).

In long essays readers need more reminders than in short ones. To keep readers well informed, you don't need to repeat what you've already written but rather plant key ideas, slightly rephrased, as milestones along the way. (The sentence you just read contains just such a marker. The phrase *"To keep readers well-informed"* cues you to keep in mind the topic of this paragraph—helping readers find their way.) By regularly alluding to the main idea of the paragraphs, you'll keep readers focused and hold their attention from start to finish.

You can help readers along, too, by choosing words that set up relationships between one thought and the next. This can be done with such words as *this*, which actually ties the sentence you are now reading to the previous one. The word *too* in the first sentence of this paragraph serves the same function; it acts as a link between this paragraph and the one before. Fortunately, the English language is brimming with transitional words and phrases for tying sentences and ideas together.

What follows is a collection of common transitional words and phrases grouped according to their customary use. With a bit of thought, you could probably add to the list.

When you **ADD** ideas: *moreover, in addition (to), further, besides, also, and then, then too, again, next, secondly, equally important . . .*

When you make a **CONTRAST**: *however, conversely, in contrast, on the other hand, on the contrary, but, nevertheless, and yet, still, even so . . .*

When you **COMPARE** or draw a **PARALLEL**: *similarly, likewise, in comparison, in like manner, at the same time, in the same vein . . .*

When you cite an **EXAMPLE**: *for example, for instance, as when, as illustrated by . . .*

When you show **RESULTS**: *as a result, in consequence, consequently, accordingly, therefore, thus, hence . . .*

When you **REINFORCE** an idea: *indeed, in fact, as a matter of fact, to be sure, of course, in any event, by all means . . .*

When you express **SEQUENCE** or the passing of **TIME**: *soon after, then, previously, not long after, meanwhile, in the meantime, later, simultaneously, at the same time, immediately, next, at length, thereafter . . .*

When you show **PLACES**: *here, nearby, at this spot, near at hand, in proximity, on the opposite side, across from, adjacent to, underneath . . .*

When you **CONCLUDE**: *finally, in short, in other words, in a word, to sum up, in conclusion, in the end, when all is said and done . . .*

You don't need a specific transitional word or phrase to bind every sentence to another. Ideas themselves can create strong links. Notice in the paired sentences below that the underlined words in each second sentence echo an idea expressed in the first.

(1) As a kind of universal language, music unites people from age eight to eighty. (2) No matter how old they are, people can lose themselves in melodies, rhythms, tempos, and endless varieties of sound.

(1) At the heart of *Romeo and Juliet* is a long-standing feud between the Capulets and the Montagues. (2) As enemies, the two families always fight in the streets of Verona.

(1) To drive nails into very hard wood without bending them, first dip the points into grease or soap. (2) You can accomplish the same end by moistening the points of the nails in your mouth or in a can of water.

One of your goals on the AP is to assure readers a smooth trip through your essay. Without your help—that is, unless you deliberately tie sentences together with transitions—readers may find themselves lurching from one idea to another. Before long, they'll give up or get lost like travelers on an unmarked road. While not every sentence needs a specific transition, three or four successive sentences without a link of some kind can leave readers wondering whether the trip through your essay is worth taking.

MINI-WORKOUT: TRANSITIONS

Use as many transitions as you can while writing paragraphs on the suggested topics below.

1. Write a paragraph on how to do something—drive a car from home to school, pull a practical joke, avoid doing homework, burn a CD, get on the good side of a teacher, give your cat or dog a bath. Use as many SEQUENCE/TIME transitions as possible, but don't overdo it.

2. Write a paragraph detailing a cause and its effect: the cause and effect of good teaching, of a new fad, of stress in high school students, of taking risks, of lying, of a close friendship. Use as many RESULT transitions as you can, but don't go overboard.

3. Write a paragraph that makes a comparison and contrast—the way people respond to pressure, groups in your school, two athletes, then and now, boredom and laziness, two books, a friend who turned into an enemy, an enemy who became a friend. Use as many COMPARISON/CONTRAST transitions as you can, but don't get carried away.

4. Write a paragraph in which you argue for or against an issue—electronic eavesdropping, school dress codes, educational vouchers, privileges for senior citizens, censoring the Internet, dieting, restrictions on smoking. Use as many ADDITION transitions as you can, but only where they make sense.

Concluding Your Analytical Essay

At the end of your essay, you can lift your pen off the paper and be done with it. Or, if you have the time, you can present your readers with a little gift to remember you by—perhaps a surprising insight, a bit of wisdom, a catchy phrase—something likely to tease the readers' brains, tickle their funny bones, or make them feel smart.

Choose the gift carefully. It should fit the content, style, and mood of your essay and spring naturally from its contents. Because it comes last, the final paragraph leaves an enduring impression. A weak, apologetic, or irrelevant conclusion may dilute or even obliterate the effect you tried so hard to create. Above all, <u>stay away from summary endings</u>. When an essay is short to begin with, it's insulting to review for readers what is evident on the page in front of them. Readers are intelligent people. Trust them to remember what your essay says.

A catchy conclusion isn't always necessary, but even a short ending may be preferable to none at all. Effective endings leave readers fulfilled, satisfied that they have arrived somewhere. A judiciously chosen ending may sway AP readers to judge your essay somewhat more leniently than otherwise. There are no guarantees, of course, but readers are bound to be touched by a memento of your thinking, your sense of humor, or your vision. Even an ordinary thought, uniquely expressed, will leave an agreeable afterglow.

You might try any one of these common techniques:

- Have a little fun with your conclusion; try to put a smile on your reader's face.

- End with an apt quotation drawn from the essay itself, from the prompt, or from another source.

- Finish by clearly re-stating your essay's main point but using new words. Changing the wording, in fact, may shed new light on the main idea—a gesture that your readers will appreciate. If appropriate, add a short tag line, a brief sentence that creates a dramatic effect.

- Bring your readers up to date or project them into the future. Say something about prospects for the months or years ahead.

Although an effective conclusion will add luster to an essay, don't feel obliged to add an ending just for the sake of form. Readers will have developed a fairly accurate sense of your writing ability before reaching your essay's last word. Rest assured that a good but incomplete piece of writing will be graded according to what you have done well instead of what you haven't done at all.

> **TIP**
>
> Stay away from summary endings.

EDITING AND PROOFREADING ESSAYS

Once you've ended your essay, spend whatever time is left editing and proofreading.

Editing for Clarity

Because many words have multiple meanings, do a word-by-word check for clarity. Ask yourself whether a reader could misconstrue a word or find it ambiguous. For example, in an essay about missing teenagers, Paula S. wrote, "The last thing parents should do is talk to their kids." Coming to that sentence, a reader might well wonder whether Paula meant that parents should talk to their kids as a last resort, or, that in a list of what parents ought to do, the final step is talking to their kids.

Later in the essay Paula wrote, "Ellen told her friend Debbie that she had made a serious mistake by running away from home." Paula certainly understood what she intended to say, but readers can't tell whether Ellen took a dim view of Debbie's actions or whether Ellen herself had second thoughts about her own flight. Granted, these sentences have been quoted out of context, but the point remains: What may seem perfectly clear to a writer may send a puzzling message to the reader.

That's why you should work hard to arrange your words in the clearest order. Watch for grammatical perils that interfere with meaning, especially **1) misplaced modifiers, 2) dangling participles,** and **3) lack of parallelism**—all discussed in the pages that follow.

MISPLACED MODIFIERS

Modifiers are words, phrases, and clauses that tell something about or limit the meaning of a particular word or statement. For example:

> The bedroom had a *broken* window.

The adjective *broken* is a modifier because it tells something about the condition of the *window*. In other words, *broken* "modifies" *window*.

Modifiers must be placed so that they modify the correct words:

> Mike only loves Sharon.

Here *only* modifies the verb *loves*. The modifier is appropriate if Mike feels nothing but love for Sharon—no admiration, no awe, no respect, nor any other emotion. If, however, Mike has but one love, and that love is Sharon, then *only* is misplaced. Properly placed, *only* should come either before or after *Sharon*:

> Mike loves *only* Sharon.   or   Mike loves Sharon *only*.

Another example:

> Nora decided *when she had completed her AP English homework* to watch TV.

In this sentence *when she had completed her AP English homework* is the modifier. But it is hard to tell whether it modifies *decided* or *watch*. If it modifies *decided*, Nora finished her essay and then made a decision to watch TV. If it modifies *watch*, Nora worked on her homework and decided at some point that she would watch TV when she had finished.

> When she had finished her AP English homework, Nora decided to watch TV.
>
> While doing her AP English homework, Nora decided to watch TV when she had finished.

Now the meaning of both sentences is unambiguous.

Obviously, misplaced modifiers can cloud a writer's intentions. To avoid the problem, place modifiers as close as possible to the words they modify:

> *Misplaced*: Philip donated his old car to a charity *that no longer ran well*.

The modifier *that no longer ran well* is too far from *car*, the word it modifies.

> *Clear*: Philip donated his old car *that no longer ran well* to a charity.

DANGLING MODIFIERS

In a sentence words must fit together like pieces of jigsaw puzzle. Sometimes, a misplaced word looks as though it fits, but it doesn't say exactly what the writer intended.

> (1) While running to English class, the bell rang.
> (2) Hammering a nail, a crack developed in the board.
> (3) When only eight years old, my father warned me about smoking.

The ludicrous meaning of these sentences may not strike you immediately, but look again. Do you see that these sentences describe a surreal world in which bells run to class, cracks hammer nails, and youthful fathers dispense advice? The problem is that these sentences try to mate two groups of words that can't go together. The parts are mismatched. After the comma in the first sentence, you'd expect to find out who is running, but you aren't told. Likewise, after the commas in sentences 2 and 3, you are not told who was hammering and who is only eight years old. In short, you're left dangling. Hence, the label *dangling modifier* has been given to this type of construction. To correct the error, add the noun or pronoun to be modified, as in:

> While the boys were running to English class, the bell rang.
> Hammering a nail, Rufus cracked the board.
> When I was eight, my father warned me about smoking.

Re-writing the whole sentence is often the best cure for a dangling modifier, as in:

> *Dangling*: While talking on the phone, the stew burned in the pot.
> *Clear*: While I talked on the phone, the stew burned in the pot.

MINI-WORKOUT: MISPLACED AND DANGLING MODIFIERS

Rewrite any of the following sentences that contain an error in modification. Corrections can be made by shifting words around or revising the whole sentence. Some may be correct.

1. The bowling alley lends out shoes to its customers of all sizes.

   _____

2. An old bike was given to a junk man we planned to put in the trash.

   _____

3. At the age of ten, my family and I emigrated from Guatemala to the U.S.

   _____

4. Still sound asleep at noon, my mother thought I was sick.

   _____

5. Totaled beyond repair, Allison knew she'd have to buy another car.

   _____

6. The coach said that canceling the swim meet was the right thing to do under the circumstances.

   _____

7. Used all night to illuminate the steps, I needed new batteries for the flashlight.

   _____

8. A report was submitted about the latest bank heist by the police.

   _____

9. Pausing for a drink of water after the hike, a grizzly bear stood in front of me.

   _____

10. After a quick breakfast, the school bus picked me up at the corner.

   _____

Answers on page 205.

PARALLELISM

Parallel structure keeps equivalent ideas in the same grammatical form. Consider this sentence that lists the contents of a student's locker:

> The locker held a down jacket, aromatic sweatpants, three sneakers, two left-handed gloves, an unused tuna sandwich, a broken ski pole, a hockey puck, six overdue library books, a disposable camera, and a hiking boot.

Every item listed is an object, each expressed in the same grammatical form: a noun preceded by one or two adjectives. When the student wrote a list of his favorite pastimes, though, the sentence lost its parallelism:

> I like skiing, hiking, to take pictures, and running.

The message is clear, but the phrase "to take pictures" is not parallel with the other phrases. To revise it, write "taking pictures":

> I like skiing, hiking, taking pictures, and running.

When you structure the pieces of a sentence in parallel form, you put yourself in the company of world-class stylists. Abraham Lincoln, for one, used parallelism at Gettysburg: "We cannot dedicate, we cannot consecrate, we cannot hallow this ground . . . ." And later, ". . . that government of the people, by the people, and for the people shall not perish from the earth." John F. Kennedy used parallelism in his inaugural speech: "Let every nation know, whether it wishes us good or ill, that we shall pay any price, bear any burden, meet any hardship, support any friend, oppose any foe to assure the survival and the success of liberty."

To apply the essential principles of parallel construction to your prose:

- Express all ideas in a series in the same grammatical form, even when the series consists of only two items:

> Her parents objected to the loud music she played and to the late hours she kept.

Here, parallelism is achieved with prepositional phrases, *to the loud music* and *to the late hours*. Each phrase is followed by the pronoun *she* and the past tense of a verb.

> After graduation she promised to turn the volume down and to come home earlier.

Each parallel idea consists of an infinitive followed by a noun and an adverb.

- Use grammatical equivalents to make comparisons and contrasts. When comparing two ideas, for example, express both ideas in phrases, or pair an idea stated in a clause with a second idea also stated in a clause.

> FAULTY: They are worried more about public opinion than for what the effect of the proposal may be.

The prepositional phrase *about public opinion* may not be paired with the clause *what the effect of the proposal may be.*

> PARALLEL: They are worried more about public opinion than about the effect of the proposal.

Parallelism is achieved by pairing two prepositional phrases.

> FAULTY: Going out to eat no longer thrills me as much as to cook at home.

The gerund *going out* should not be paired with the infinitive *to cook.*

> PARALLEL: Going out to eat no longer thrills me as much as cooking at home.

Parallelism is achieved by pairing two gerunds, *going* and *cooking.*

- Stay alert for pairs of words that signal the need for parallelism, such as *either/or, neither/nor, whether/or, both/and,* and *not only/but also.*

> Alice will attend *neither* NYU *or* Columbia.

Revise by changing *neither* to *either,* or changing *or* to *nor.* Remember to keep the pair of words close to each other in the sentence. If they are too far apart, your sentence may be hard to follow:

> Jake *both* started on the basketball and the volleyball teams.

The signal word *both* is too far removed from the parallel phrase, *basketball and volleyball teams.* Its placement misleads the reader into thinking that the verb *started* is one of the parallel ideas. Correctly worded, the sentence reads:

> Jake started on *both* the basketball and the volleyball teams.

- When an article, preposition, or a conjunction appears before the first in a series of parallel items, repeat the word before the others in the series.

> UNCLEAR: Our mechanic did a better job on my car than his.

Did two mechanics work on the same car or did one mechanic work on two different cars? To clear up the ambiguity, repeat the preposition *on,* as in:

> CLEAR: Our mechanic did a better job on my car than *on* his.

Sometimes repeating both a preposition and an article is necessary:

> UNCLEAR: Before signing the contract, Tiffany spoke with the president and treasurer of the company.

Did Tiffany speak with one person or with two? Repeating *with the* helps to clarify the meaning:

> CLEAR: Before signing the contract, Tiffany spoke with the president and *with the* treasurer of the company.

- Make sure that parallel ideas are logical equivalents.

ABSURD: Terry is six feet tall, kind, and a Texan.

Physical features, traits of character, and place of origin are not logically coordinated.

LESS ABSURD: Terry, a six-foot Texan, is kind.

Still not terribly logical, but at least the revision emphasizes only one of Terry's qualities—his kindness.

ILLOGICAL: San Diego's *harbor* is reported to be more polluted than *any city*.

This sentence is meant to compare pollution in the San Diego harbor with pollution in the harbors of other cities, but it fails to achieve its goal. Instead, it illogically compares San Diego's harbor with a city.

LOGICAL: San Diego's *harbor* is reported to be more polluted than the *harbor of any other city*.

ILLOGICAL: Unlike most *cars* on the street, *Ellie* has her Subaru washed almost every week.

This sentence is intended to compare Ellie's car with other cars on the street, but it manages only to compare Ellie to the other cars, an illogical comparison.

LOGICAL: Ellie's *Subaru*, unlike *most cars* on the street, is washed almost every week.

A lack of parallelism in phrases and clauses is not just bad form but can cause confusion. Sound parallel structure, in contrast, keeps equivalent ideas in the same grammatical form. Take, for example, a sentence that lists the characteristics of a restaurant in which to have a family birthday party:

We are looking for a place that is private, plenty of space, has a friendly staff, and that people like to look at.

The sentence makes some sense, of course, but it's awkward because the four characteristics are not expressed in parallel form. Instead, they are a mix of an adjective, a phrase, and two clauses. One way to fix the problem is to use only adjectives, as in:

We are looking for a place that is private, spacious, friendly, and attractive.

Or use a series of nouns each preceded by an adjective:

We are looking for a place with total privacy, ample space, a friendly staff, and attractive surroundings.

MINI-WORKOUT: PARALLEL STRUCTURE

Look for faulty parallel structure in the following sentences. Write the correct version of the offending word or phrase in the space provided. Some sentences may be correct.

1. This book not only shows what happens to mentally depressed people but it's all right to seek help.

   _____

2. A more easier and direct route exist between Oakland and San Raphael than the one we took.

   _____

3. Jim is tall, kind, and forward on the basketball team.

   _____

4. Whitney prefers to cook at home rather than going out to eat.

   _____

5. Both angry and disappointment at the team's dismal performance, the coach resigned.

   _____

6. The men haven't decided whether canoeing across the lake would better than a sailboat.

   _____

7. The wind had not only knocked down the tree but the electric lines came down, too.

   _____

8. After finding a job, she'll get an apartment, continue playing the guitar, and friends will party with her.

   _____

9. Either the mouse will find a quick way into the attic or will gnaw at the siding for days.

   _____

10. City living is exciting, convenient, and provides amazing entertainment.

   _____

Answers on page 205.

Editing for Interest

Your essay will be read by people—real people who know that essays can be lively and interesting. Like readers everywhere, they'll be bored by writing that is dull.

Therefore, try to enliven your prose by:

- Using *active* instead of *passive* verbs
- Writing *active* instead of *passive* sentences
- Omitting needless words
- Using specific language

ACTIVE VERBS

Because *active* verbs describe or show movement, they excel all other words in pumping vitality into your prose. *Being* verbs, in contrast, have almost no life in them. Their lifelessness is apparent in the common forms of the verb *to be*:

is	are	was
were	am	has been
had been	have been	will be

Being verbs ordinarily join the subject of a sentence to a predicate. They function much like an equal sign in an equation: "Five minus two *is* three" ($5 - 2 = 3$), or "Samantha *was* happy" (Samantha = happy), or "Your AP score *will be* 5" (That = good news!). Because being verbs (and equal signs) lack energy, use active verbs whenever you can.

> **TIP**
>
> Use active verbs whenever you can.

Yes, it's hard to get along in speech and writing without *being* verbs. But be stingy with them. Check a few of your most recent essays. If more than, say, one out of four sentences uses a form of *to be* as its main verb, try the following revision techniques.

1. Substitute an new active verb for the *being* verb:

   Being verb: It *is* not easy for most students to write immortal essays.

   Active verb: Most students *struggle* to write immortal essays.

2. Extract an active verb from a noun in the sentence:

   Being verb: Monica *was* the winner of the essay contest.

   Active verb: Monica *won* the essay contest.

3. Extract an active verb from an adjective:

   Being verb: My weekend at the beach *was* enjoyable.

   Active verb: I *enjoyed* my weekend at the beach.

As you delete *being* verbs, you'll probably notice that some sentences resist change. When that happens, turn subjects into verbs and verbs into nouns. Try also to eliminate unnecessary phrases. Full-scale sentence revisions can result in sentences bearing little resemblance to the originals, but verb-swapping often roots out excess verbiage and improves an essay's readability.

Being verbs are not the only verbs that sap the life out of sentences. They share that distinction with several other verbs, including forms of *to have, to come, to go, to make, to move,* and *to get*—verbs with so many different uses that they creep into our speech and writing virtually unnoticed. *Webster's International Dictionary* lists 16 different meanings for the verb *get* and a dozen more for *make* and *move*. It's true that we can hardly get by without these verbs, but use them only if you can swear that no other words will do. Otherwise, trade them in for more vivid verbs, as in:

> *Dull*: The line to the box office *moved* very slowly.
>
> *Livelier*: The line *crept* (*crawled, inched, poked*) to the box office.

Note that by using a more animated verb, you eliminate the need for "very slowly," which has suddenly become redundant.

> *Dull*: The police officer *gave* drivers permission to turn left on red.
>
> *Livelier*: The police officer *permitted* drivers to turn left on red.

Note that this revision has led not just to a more active sentence but one that contains fewer words—always a stylistic plus.

MINI-WORKOUT: ACTIVE VERBS

Revise each of the following sentences by substituting active verbs for "being" verbs, but try not to change the meaning of the original.

1. Monica and Phil were the highest scorers on the practice AP exam.

   _____

2. Color is the determining factor in choosing a rug for my bedroom.

   _____

3. It is logical that admission to college is the result of a student's effort and achievement.

   _____

4. The monarchy was over after the Revolutionary War.

   _____

5. Since 9/11 there have been many more threats to democracy.

   _____

6. Chaos is a word that is relevant to my math class.

   _____

7. Everyone is scared of Mr. Gill.

   _____

8. The way to the principal's office is down the next corridor.

_____

9. There are students who are excellent in chemistry but not in physics.

_____

10. This novel was the one recommended by the librarian.

_____

Answers on page 206.

ACTIVE AND PASSIVE SENTENCES

To write lively prose, keep in mind the difference between *active* and *passive* sentences. In an active sentence the person or thing performing an action is usually mentioned early in a sentence, so readers know right away who or what you are talking about. In passive sentences the performer of an action is not named or gets less notice than either the receiver of the action or the action itself. For example:

> Two months were spent rehearsing for the concert.

This sentence fails to tell who performed the action—that is, who rehearsed for the concert. The following revision clears up the uncertainty:

> Two months were spent rehearsing for the concert by the marching band.

This version transforms the original, but it still emphasizes the action instead of the performer of the action. To complete the transformation, say something like:

> For two months the marching band rehearsed for the concert.

In the active voice, the performers of the action receive top billing.

Why is the active voice preferable? Mainly because most events in life don't just occur by themselves. Burgers don't just get eaten; people cook and devour them. Marriages don't just happen; couples deliberately go out and marry each other. Goals don't get scored, salmon don't get caught, wallets don't get lost all by themselves. People do these things.

Good essay writers, taking advantage of readers' natural curiosity about others, often strive to make the performer of the action the grammatical subject of their sentences:

> *Passive:* The award was presented to Hildie by the Art Club.
> *Active*: The Art Club presented the award to Hildie.
> *Passive*: Ohio State was attended by my brother, my cousin, and three of my uncles.
> *Active*: My brother, my cousin, and three uncles went to Ohio State.

> **TIP**
> Active sentences, strengthen prose; passive sentences weaken it.

In some contexts, of course, the actor is unknown or irrelevant. That's when a passive sentence works best. For example:

> *Passive:* The curtain was raised at 8:30 sharp.
>
> *Active:* At 8:30 sharp, a stagehand (or Maryanne, the production assistant) raised the curtain.

In the passive version, curtain time is the important fact. Who pulled the rope or pushed the button doesn't matter.

Transforming a passive sentence to an active one takes a bit of editing. As you prepare for the AP, examine your essays for passive sentences. Change them to active sentences unless you have a very good reason not to.

MINI-WORKOUT: REVISING PASSIVE SENTENCES

Put each of the following sentences into active voice:

1. The backyard was covered by dead leaves.

   _____

2. The situation in Lebanon was discussed by us.

   _____

3. Friday's quiz was failed because I had been at a play rehearsal every night that week.

   _____

4. Portland was flown to at the start of our weeklong vacation in Oregon.

   _____

5. The Golden Fleece was pursued by Jason and the Argonauts.

   _____

6. The newspaper was fetched by Rex every morning.

   _____

7. The decision to build a fence on the border was made by immigration officials.

   _____

8. Pizza was ordered by more than twenty diners on Saturday night.

   _____

9. Five of Shakespeare's plays were seen by our group in three days.

_____

10. The voters were urged by the candidate to throw the rascal out of office.

_____

Answers on page 206.

CUTTING NEEDLESS WORDS

Never use two words when one will do. Tell your readers quickly and directly what you have to say. Brevity works best. Cut out verbiage. Readers value economy.

Stop! Have you noticed that the previous paragraph disregards the very advice it dispenses? Do you see repetition and redundancy? Couldn't the point have been made more succinctly?

Here's a word to the wise:

> You should work through all of the sentences you write by examining each one and crossing out all the words you don't definitely need.

To be precise, that's 24 words to the wise—many more than are needed.

> Go through every sentence you write and cross out unnecessary words.

That's better—11 words of free advice, but still too many. The sentence could be trimmed still further:

> Trim unnecessary words out of every sentence.

This seven-word model is less than a third of the original 24 word clunker. But it can be pared even more:

> Omit needless words.

And still more:

> Cut verbosity.

To make every word count, wring your sentences through this four-step word trimmer:

STEP 1. Look for repetition.

> *Wordy*: Elena took Jesse to the movies. Jesse is Elena's brother. (10 words)
> *Trimmed*: Elena took her brother Jesse to the movies. (8 words)

Granted, cutting 10 words to 8 is not much. But consider that it's a 20 percent reduction, and in a 500-word essay, a 20 percent reduction amounts to 100 words—the equivalent of a whole paragraph.

Wordy: When Hannah was 16 years of age she accepted a position at the Moraga Nursery. In this position she learned about plants and about how to handle customers. (28)

Trimmed: At 16 years old, Hannah accepted a position at the Moraga Nursery, where she learned about plants and handling customers. (20)

Re-trimmed: Working at the Moraga Nursery at age 16, Hannah learned to handle both plants and customers. (16)

STEP 2. Hunt for phrases that add words but no meaning, such as *the fact that, due to the fact that, at this point in time, at the present time, that being said*, and comparable usages.

Wordy: Hamlet returned home as a result of his father's death. (10)

Trimmed: Hamlet returned home because his father died. (7).

Wordy: The troops were in danger due to the fact that mines had been planted in the field. (16)

Trimmed: The mine field endangered the troops. (6)

Wordy phrases	Trimmed
what I mean is	I mean
on account of, as a result of	because
in the final analysis	finally
few and far between	few
each and every one	each
this is a subject that	this subject
ten in number	ten
at the age of six years old	at age six
most unique	unique
true fact	fact
biography of her life	biography
in regard to, with regard to, in relation to, with respect to	about

Step 3. Search for redundancies. Innumerable words are wasted on reiteration of what has already been stated, on repeating the obvious, on restating ideas, on saying the same thing again and again and over, driving readers to the brink of madness.

Wordy: A cloud of black soot rose up to the sky. (10)

Soot, by definition, is black, and rising clouds can only go up.

Trimmed: A cloud of soot rose to the sky. (8)

Wordy: He had a smile on his face. (7)

Where else but on a face would a smile appear?

> *Trimmed*: He wore a smile. (4)
>
> *Wordy*: After carefully scrutinizing the X-ray, the doctor seemed fully engrossed in her own train of thought. (16)

S crutinize means "to study carefully," and engrossed means "to think fully." Also, *her own train of thought* is nonsensical because no one can think others' thoughts.

> *Trimmed*: After scrutinizing the X-ray, the doctor seemed engrossed in thought. (10)

After you have pared your sentences to the bone, re-read what remains and discard still more by tracking down little words like *the, a, an, up, down, its,* and *and.* Even though it may hurt to take out what you worked hard to put in, don't whine. Just grit your teeth and be tough!

Step 4. Look for telltale words like *which, who, that, thing,* and *all.* They often signify excess verbiage.

> *Wordy*: Edison was a man who was obsessed by the wonders of electricity. (12)
>
> *Trimmed*: The wonders of electricity obsessed Edison. (6)

Changing the grammatical subject and replacing *was* with an active verb halved the word count.

> *Wordy*: What he most wanted was that the terrorists would release the hostages. (12)
>
> *Trimmed*: He most wanted the terrorists to release the hostages. (9)

MINI-WORKOUT: CUTTING NEEDLESS WORDS

Part A.

Tighten these sentences, but preserve their meaning.

1. The biker, a woman named Mary Roe, wrote a book with the title *A Ride Across America,* about biking across America, which she accomplished after riding 90 miles a day in order to prepare for her ride across America.

_____

_____

2. There is no reason for the chairperson of the committee, who is Carolyn Welles, to take offense at my suggestion, which is aimed at trying to make the meetings more productive and useful to the entire student body at large.

_____

_____

3. Mr. Evans was appointed to be the treasurer of the group in spite of fact that he had once been arrested and tried and sent to jail for a period of six months for embezzling some money from the business he worked for.

_____

_____

4. Harmful criticism is criticism that tears a person down instead of helping the person overcome or deal with a problem.

_____

_____

5. All Americans should try to save gasoline, and the best way they can save gasoline all across the country is to cut down on the number of miles they drive when it's really not necessary to drive.

_____

_____

Part B.

The following paragraph comes from an essay that advocated gaining weight. Please trim its fat.

Such weight-gaining ideas can be used to good advantage by each and every man, woman, and child who is interested in adding pounds of weight to his or her body. They are the latest, most up-to-date set of procedures available anywhere. Owing to the fact that health experts and authorities believe that it is better to be underweight than it is to be overweight, ideas for putting on weight are generally thought to be jokes not taken seriously, which is the reason why such ideas are kept under wraps and not publicized very widely or broadly. Yet, there are many people of all kinds who need to gain weight for a variety of diverse reasons. Here is a quotation that Slim Snyder, who is a graduate of Stanford University, stated during a speech he gave at a meeting of people gathered together at a health conference recently: "Lean people are victims of discrimination, just as obese people are."

_____

_____

_____

_____

_____

_____

_____

_____

Answers on page 206.

BEING SPECIFIC

Specific words are memorable, while hazy words fade quickly away. Tell your garage mechanic vaguely, "This car is broken," and he'll ask for more information. If a patient in the E.R. says, "I feel pain," a doctor wants to know exactly where it hurts.

   In the first draft of an essay for his AP English class, Jeff S. wrote the following about a day he'd like to forget:

> It was an awful day outside. Everything was going wrong. I felt terrible. Things weren't going well in school. I got a below-par grade on a paper, and I was sure that I had failed my Chem quiz. I also had lots of things to do at home and no time to do them. My mother was in a bad mood, too. She yelled at me for all kinds of things. Then Penny called, and we got into a disagreement. I had trouble with my DVD player, and I couldn't pay for repairs. I went to bed early, hoping that tomorrow would be better.

Reviewing this paragraph a few days later, Jeff realized the writing begged for more specificity. Yes, the day had been dreadful, but his account needed specific language to prove it. The next draft took care of that:

> On a cold and rainy November day, my life was as miserable as the weather. I felt chills all day, and my throat was sore. In school I got a D on a history paper about the Bubonic Plague, and I was sure that I had failed the chemistry quiz on molecular modeling. The homework was piling up: two lab reports, more than 150 pages to read in <u>Wuthering Heights</u>, a chapter in the history text, and about a hundred new vocabulary words in Spanish. I didn't have time or energy to do it all, especially when my mother started to pick at

TIP

Specific language is more informative, more interesting, and more desirable.

me about my messy room and the thank you letters I'm supposed to write to my grandparents. Just as she was reminding me that my SAT registration was overdue, Penny called to say that she couldn't come for Thanksgiving after all, so we argued about loyalty and trust and keeping promises. When I tried to watch *Lord of the Rings* one more time, the DVD player kept skipping scenes. The repairman said he would charge $100 just to look at the damn thing, but I don't have that kind of money. By 9:00 P.M. I was in bed, hoping that tomorrow would be better.

This version includes many specific details that vividly illustrate the wretchedness of Jeff's miserable day. Not every paragraph of every essay calls for such detail, but an essay consisting solely of generalities will leave readers at sea.

It's true that vague, shadowy words are easier to think of. But they're often used as a smoke screen to cover up the absence of thought. For example, it's easy to pass judgment on a book by calling it "good" or "interesting." But what readers should be told is precisely why you think so. It's simple to call someone "old" without bothering to show the reader a "round-shouldered, white-haired man hunched in a wheelchair." A student who calls her teacher "ugly" sends a different image of ugliness to each reader. But if the teacher is a "shifty-eyed tyrant who spits when she talks," the specific details create a vivid image. Or if the teacher's personality is ugly, show her arrogant cruelty as she curses her hapless students.

Of course, it's not essential to back up every generalization with specific details. An essay bogged down in detail can be tedious both to read and to write. Every time you mention *dinner*, you don't have to recite the menu. Excessive analysis is boring, but so is too little. A balance is best. No one can tell you precisely how to achieve that balance. To develop the feel of what seems right takes time and practice, like riding a bike or doing a back flip. In the end, the content and purpose of an essay will have to determine how specific it needs to be.

Context determines how abstract your essay should be. Ask yourself what is most important—giving readers a more detailed account of a general idea or pushing on to other more vital matters. Just keep in mind that nobody likes reading essays that fail to deal concretely with anything.

TIP

To develop the knack of writing specifically, study a written passage that you admire. Pick out both details and broad statements. For practice, use the passage as a model for writing a paragraph of your own.

MINI-WORKOUT: WRITING SPECIFICALLY

The following sentences desperately need more specific wording. Please provide the verbal antidote to their vagueness.

1. Missy's score on the AP English exam was high.

_____

2. Mr. Gray possesses a variety of values.

_____

3. Ms. Cronin could care less about my problem doing homework.

_____

4. Sort of violently, Carrie expressed her anger at the other team's player.

_____

5. Mitchell studied hard, but to no avail.

_____

6. Winning the overwhelming approval of the people gave the candidate great satisfaction.

_____

7. People don't care about pollution in the ocean.

_____

8. My science class is pretty useless.

_____

9. The twins were very poor when they were growing up.

_____

10. My parents were happy when I got accepted in college.

_____

Answers on page 207.

Editing for Standard Usage and Mechanics

Save some editing time to proofread your essays for proper spelling, punctuation, and grammar. You won't be penalized for one or two isolated errors, but AP readers are required to deduct credit from papers crowded with mechanical mistakes.

Handwriting Matters

While you're at it, check your essays for legibility. Sloppy, hard-to-read handwriting is not supposed to count against you, but think of your readers: Bogged down in a barely legible paper, they can grow impatient and irritable.

Because a neat hand works in your favor, get into the habit of scrutinizing your penmanship for every letter that doesn't look the way it should. Easier said than done, for sure. But ask a friend to read one of your handwritten essays aloud. Wherever he or she stumbles may be a place where your handwriting needs work.

To minimize writing errors:

1. Write Correct Sentences
2. Use the Correct Verbs
3. Use Adjectives and Adverbs Correctly
4. Choose Correct Pronouns
5. Review Punctuation and Capitalization

WRITING CORRECT SENTENCES

Time won't permit you to meticulously analyze every sentence in your essays. But if you get into the habit of examining sentences in your practice essays and in other schoolwork, you'll soon purge from your writing the three most common sentence errors:

- *Fragments*—incomplete sentences
- *Run-ons*—two or more improperly joined sentences
- *Comma splices*—two complete sentences separated by a comma

FRAGMENTS

Sentence fragments often look remarkably like complete sentences. But looks can be deceptive.

> The bike that Martha often borrowed.

This fragment appears to have all the characteristics of a sentence: It starts with a capital letter and ends with a period, it conveys a complete thought (*Martha often borrowed the bike* is a complete thought), and it seems to contain a subject (*Martha*) and a verb (*borrowed*). What makes it a fragment, though, is that *Martha* isn't the subject. Rather, *bike* is the subject, and the trouble is that *bike* and the verb *borrowed* don't fit together. A bike, after all, is an inanimate object and can't do any borrowing—at least not in the real world. Clearly, Martha did the borrowing, but the noun *Martha* cannot be the subject of the sentence because it is part of the subordinate clause, *that Martha borrowed*. Therefore, *bike* needs a verb of its own.

> The bike that Martha often borrowed was stolen.

With the addition of *was stolen*, the sentence is now complete.

To determine whether a sentence is complete, uncover its "bare bones." That is, eliminate all its dependent clauses, phrases, and verbals. If what remains is a subject and its verb, it's a complete sentence. If not, it's probably a fragment.

To nail down the subject of long sentences may take some doing, but the bare-bones strategy usually works if you remember that the grammatical subject can never be in a prepositional phrase, in a dependent clause, or in a phrase that interrupts the flow of the sentence.

To find the "bare bones" of a sentence:

Step 1: Cross out all prepositional phrases, such as *up the wall, around the corner, to the beach, over the counter*. If you eliminate all the prepositional phrases in these sentences, for instance, only the subject and the verb—the "bare bones"—will remain.

Complete sentence: In the middle of the night, Priscilla slept.

   Bare bones: Priscilla slept.

Complete sentence: One of Frieda's friends is in need of help.

   Bare bones: One is.

Step 2: Delete all the dependent clauses—those parts of sentences which contain a noun and a verb, but which don't qualify as complete sentences because they begin with words and phrases like *although, as, as though, because, before, even though, if, in spite of, regardless of, since, so that, unless, whenever, whether*, and *while*. Other dependent clauses are statements (not questions) that start with *when, where, which, who,* and *what*.

Once the dependent clauses in the following sentences are gone, only the main clauses will remain. That's where to find the bare bones of each sentence.

Complete sentence: Because she missed the bus, Marnie wept.

   Bare bones: Marnie wept.

Complete sentence: While Willie waited for the bus, he studied vocabulary.

   Bare bones: He studied.

Step 3: Delete interrupters—those parts of sentences that impede the smooth flow of the main idea. Interrupters may be just one word (*however, nevertheless*) or dozens. They're often set off by commas.

Complete sentence: Ellen, regardless of the look on her face, rejoiced.

   Bare bones: Ellen rejoiced.

Complete sentence: The boat, a sleek white catamaran, sank.

   Bare bones: Boat sank.

Complete sentence: Marty, who got ticketed for doing 60 in a 30 mph zone, paid the fine.

   Bare bones: Marty paid.

The process of identifying the bare bones of a sentence can be more complex than that suggested by these examples. But by carefully peeling away selected sentence parts, you'll eventually lay bare the subject and verb.

Beware, too, of sentence fragments that can occur when you use the *-ing* form of a verb. The problem is that it won't work as a sentence's main verb, at least not without a helping verb.

> FRAGMENT: Julie, at the box office, *selling* movie tickets to the 7:00 show.
>
> CORRECT: Julie, at the box office, *has been selling* movie tickets to the 7:00 show.

The addition of the helping verb *has been* corrects the error. Other helping verbs include *is, was, will be,* and other forms of the verb *to be.*

RUN-ON SENTENCES

A **run-on sentence** consists of two independent clauses with nothing but a blank space between them:

> Birthstones are supposed to bring good luck mine has never brought me any.

Fill the gap between *luck* and *mine* by inserting the coordinating conjunction *but.*

> Birthstones are supposed to bring good luck, *but* mine has never brought me any.

A comma has also been added because a compound sentence needs a comma between its clauses unless the clauses are very short, as in:

> Carla drove but I walked.

Another way to eliminate run-ons is to write two separate sentences:

> Birthstones are supposed to bring good luck. Mine has never brought me any.

Or you can use a semicolon, which functions like a period.

> Birthstones are supposed to bring good luck; mine has never brought me any.

Note that the initial letter of a sentence that follows a semicolon is never capitalized.

COMMA SPLICES

In a **comma splice**, a comma instead of a period or semi-colon is used to join, or splice, two independent sentences.

> Othello was fooled by a disloyal friend, he should have known better.

Replace the comma with a period and start a new sentence with *He,* or, use a semicolon:

> Othello was fooled by a disloyal friend; he should have known better.

MINI-WORKOUT: WRITING CORRECT SENTENCES

Look for sentence fragments, run-ons, and comma splices. Use the spaces to identify the error and write the sentence correctly. Some items may contain no error.

1. Because Amy is stressed out about the garbage in the back yard.

   _____

2. St. Petersburg was renamed Leningrad after the Russian Revolution, its original name was restored in the 1990s.

   _____

3. My grandmother is 86 years old therefore she walks very slowly.

   _____

4. During the night, the stars that came out like diamonds on black velvet.

   _____

5. There is a belief among superstitious people that birthmarks are caused by influences on the mother before the child is born.

   _____

6. This year's senior class being more involved than last year's.

   _____

7. The American colonists hated the King's tax on British tea they drank Dutch tea instead.

   _____

8. June found a squirrel lying dead in a ditch she didn't tell Henry.

   _____

9. A biologist working in the field of genetic engineering; involved in the controversy surrounding human cloning.

   _____

10. Use the space below to tell one story about yourself to provide the admissions committee, either directly or indirectly, with an insight into the kind of person you are.

   _____

Answers on page 207.

USING CORRECT VERBS

Of all the parts of speech, verbs are the most apt to be used incorrectly. As you edit your AP essays, therefore, ask yourself the following three questions:

Do all nouns and pronouns agree in number with their verbs?
Is every verb in the correct tense?
Is every verb in the correct form?

NOUN-VERB AGREEMENT

Nouns and verbs must agree in *number* and in *person*. A mismatch in number occurs when a singular noun is used with a plural verb, or vice-versa. That's why *the tiger were* and *the tigers was* are nonstandard usages.

A mismatch in *person* occurs when the subject is a pronoun and the writer uses a verb of a different person, as in *he are, you is,* and *they am.*

To avoid errors in noun-verb agreement (often called *subject-verb agreement*), it's useful to know the language constructions that most often cause problems:

- **Intervening words between the subject and verb.**

Few people make agreement errors when the verb comes right after the subject. But clauses and phrases that comes between the noun, or subject, and the verb can cause a problem:

Delivery (singular subject) of today's newspapers and magazines *have been* (plural verb) delayed.

The prepositional phrase *of today's newspapers and magazines* blurs the relationship between subject and verb, and the plural noun *magazines* misleads the writer into using a plural verb. With a correctly matched subject and verb, the sentence reads:

Delivery (singular subject) of today's newspapers and magazines *has been* (singular verb) delayed.

In short, verbs must agree with the subject, not with words mistakenly thought to be the subject.

Take note, too, that such intervening phrases such as *in addition to, along with, as well as, including,* and other similar phrases don't influence the number of the verb.

One (singular subject) of Mike's stories, in addition to several of his poems, was (singular verb) chosen to be published in the school literary magazine.

- **Subjects composed of more than one noun or pronoun.**

Both singular and plural nouns, when joined by *and,* are called compound subjects and need plural verbs:

The *picture and the text* (compound subject) *go* (plural verb) inside this box.
Several *locust trees and a green mailbox* (compound subject) *stand* (plural verb) outside the house.

Compound subjects thought of as a unit need singular verbs:

> Green *eggs and ham* (compound subject as a unit) is (singular verb) Sam's favorite breakfast.

Singular nouns joined by *or* or *nor* take singular verbs.

> A Coke *or* a Pepsi (two nouns joined by *or*) *is* (singular verb) what I thirst for.

When a subject consists of a singular noun and a plural noun joined by *or* or *nor*, the number of the verb is determined by the noun closer to the verb.

> *Either a pineapple or some oranges are* on the table.
> *Neither the linemen nor the quarterback was* aware of the tricky play.

When a subject contains a pronoun that differs in person from a noun or another pronoun, the verb must agree with the closer subject word.

> Neither Meredith nor *you are* expected to finish the work today.
> Either he or *I am* planning to work late on Saturday.

When the subject is singular and the predicate noun is plural, or vice versa, the number of the verb is determined by the subject.

> The *bulk* of Wilkinson's work *is* two novels and a collection of stories.
> Two *novels and a story are* the bulk of Wilkinson's work.

- **Singular subjects containing words that sound plural.**

The names of certain books (*All the King's Men*), teams (New England Patriots), diseases (mumps), course titles (Mathematics), and other singular nouns may sound like plurals because they end in *–s*, but most of the time—although not always—they need a singular verb.

> The *news is* good.
> *Measles is* going around the school.

- **Subjects that are sometimes singular and sometimes plural.**

Collective nouns sound singular but may be plural. A family, for example, is singular. But if you are referring to separate individuals, *family* takes a plural verb.

> The *family* (members) *are* arriving for the wedding at different times.

Other collective nouns include *group, crowd, team, jury, soybeans, audience, herd, public, dozen, class, band, flock, majority, committee, heap,* and *lot.* Other words and expressions governed by the same rule are units of time, money, weight, measurement, and all fractions.

> The *jury is* going to decide today.
> The *jury are* returning to their homes tomorrow.

- **Indefinite pronouns used as subjects.**

Indefinite pronouns such as *everyone, both,* and *any* pose a special problem. Some indefinite pronouns must be matched with singular verbs, some with plural verbs, and some with one or the other, depending on the sense of the sentence. There's no getting around the fact that you need to know which number applies to which pronoun.

1. These words, although they sound plural, get singular verbs: *each, either, neither,* the "ones" (*anyone, no one, everyone, someone*), and the "bodies" (*anybody, everybody, nobody, somebody*).

    Each man and woman in the room *gets* only one vote.

    Everyone who works hard *is* going to earn an "A."

2. These words get plural verbs: *both, many, few, several.*

    In spite of rumors to the contrary, *both are* on the verge of a nervous breakdown.

    Several in the band *are* not going on the trip to Boston.

3. The following words get singular verbs when they refer to singular nouns and plural verbs when they refer to plural nouns: *any, none, some, all, most.*

    Some of the collection is valuable.

    In this sentence *some* is singular because it refers to *collection,* a singular noun.

    Some of the bracelets are fake.

    Here *some* is plural because it refers to *bracelets,* a plural noun.

- **A subject following the verb.**

When the subject of a sentence follows the verb, the verb takes its number from the subject, as usual.

    Behind the building *was* an *alley* (singular subject).

    Behind the building *were* an *alley and a vacant lot* (compound subject).

MINI-WORKOUT: NOUN-VERB AGREEMENT

In some of the sentences below, verbs fail to agree with nouns. Locate the error and write the correct verb in the space provided. Some sentences may be correct.

1. A long line of cars, trucks, SUVs, and motorcycles were stuck in a traffic jam near the construction zone.

    _____

2. Either my sister or one of her boyfriends have always given me a ride to school.

    _____

3. The Board of Trustees are meeting in Springfield this year instead of in Chicago.

   _____

4. The price of gasoline, in addition to the price of home heating oil, are expected to rise this winter.

   _____

5. Lilah and Lucy started an after-school tutoring service which have more customers than they can handle.

   _____

6. There is many levels on which a reader will be able to enjoy this book.

   _____

7. Proceeds from the sale of concert tickets is going to help the victims of the hurricane.

   _____

8. The newspaper reports that a rescue team experienced in climbing rugged mountains are expected to arrive at the site of the crash tomorrow morning.

   _____

9. According to school policy, there is to be two security guards stationed in the playground during recess to protect the children.

   _____

10. Many community members say that the promises made by the principal has not brought about the changes that he predicted.

    _____

Answers on page 208.

USING CORRECT VERB TENSES

Verb tenses convey information about the relative time when an action occurred. To express past action, add *–ed* to the present form: *walk/walked, cry/cried*. To express future action, add *will* before the present tense: *will walk, will cry*. For present perfect, past perfect, and future perfect forms, add *has, have, had* or *will have*, as in *have walked, has cried, had typed, will have arrived*, and so forth.

Verb tenses permit you to indicate time sequence very precisely. But someone not attuned to distinctions between tenses may say something like this:

> There was a condo where the park was.

The meaning may be clear enough, but to state the idea more accurately, it should read:

> There was a condo where the park *had been.*

Using the past perfect verb *had been* indicates that the condo replaced the park, whereas the original sentence states that the condo and park were in the same place at the same time.

This is a subtle difference, but sensitivity to such differences helps you to convey meaning more accurately. Familarity with the following conventions governing verb tenses will help you avoid errors in your AP essays:

- Truisms are expressed in the present tense regardless of other verbs in the sentence.

> Christmas *is* (present) on December 25th.
> Sammy *had been taught* (past perfect) that triangles *contain* (present) 180 degrees.

- In complex sentences, the tense of verbs in the main clause and dependent clause must be in sequence.

> They had driven (past perfect) 20 miles before Chuckie realized (past) that the gas tank was almost empty.

> (Because the driving occurred before Chuckie's realization, the past perfect—not the past tense—in needed to show the sequence of events.)

> Your teacher believes (present) that you will do (future) well on the AP.

- In an *if* clause, don't use *would have* to express the earlier of two actions. Instead use the past perfect.

> *No*: If Linda *would have studied* more, she would have made the Honor Society.
> *Yes*: If Linda *had studied* (past perfect) more, she would have made the Honor Society.
> *No:* The party would have been better if Kit *would have played* the piano.
> Yes: The party would have been better if Kit *had played* (past perfect) the piano.

- The tense of infinitives (*to eat, to snow, to have eaten, to have snowed,* etc.) is governed by the main verb and by the meaning of the sentence.

> Eileen was (main verb in past tense) delighted to receive (present infinitive) the award.

(The present infinitive is used because Eileen received the award before she felt happy about getting it.)

When the infinitive refers to a time before the action described by the main verb, the perfect infinitive should be used.

Eileen is (main verb) happy to have received (perfect infinitive) the award.

- Adjust participles (often ending in *–ing*) according to the tense of the main verb. When the participle describes an action occurring before the action of the main verb, add *having* and then adjust the participle.

No: Working (participle) hard on the essay, Hank opposed cutting the number of words. (Because Hank worked on the essay before he resisted cutting it, the participle needs to be revised.)

Yes: *Having worked* hard on the essay, Hank opposed cutting the number of words.

MINI-WORKOUT: VERB TENSES

In these sentences, the underlined verbs may be in the wrong tense. Write the correct verbs in the spaces provided. Some sentences may contain no error.

1. When he talks with his wife, Macbeth <u>felt</u> overcome with guilt.

   _____

2. When they crossed the country by car, they <u>had visited</u> Mount Rushmore.

   _____

3. In the school parking lot, a policeman stops her and <u>asked</u> to see her driver's license.

   _____

4. <u>Writing</u> a poem every week for a year, Danny finally got one accepted by a literary magazine.

   _____

5. In the afternoon we spotted many friends we <u>saw</u> that morning at the pancake breakfast.

   _____

6. Once the levee had broken, the streets <u>have been</u> flooded.

   _____

7. For anyone with enough brains to have thought about the problem, now <u>is</u> the time to work out a solution.

_____

8. If Susan <u>would have stayed</u> home, she would not have missed Dave's phonecall.

_____

9. Marcy kept the promise she <u>has given</u> to Kenny last summer.

_____

10. The airline pilot <u>expects </u>to have seen the lights of the Jackson airport by now.

_____

Answers on page 208.

CHOOSING ADJECTIVES AND ADVERBS

Errors sometimes occur when an adjective is used where an adverb is required. The reverse—using an adverb in place of an adjective—occurs less often. Check your essay for the proper use of adjectives and adverbs.

Adjectives

Adjectives describe, or modify, nouns and pronouns.

Good is an adjective. Like any adjective, it can be used to descibe a noun, as in *good book, good pie, good night.* That's easy.

Good, along with some other adjectives, causes trouble when used after a verb. Because it won't work after most verbs, avoid using *talks good, sleeps good, writes good,* and so on.

Good, as well as other adjectives, however, can be used after some verbs—those called *linking verbs,* among them, *look, smell, taste, feel, appear, seem, remain,* and all forms of *to be.* So, it's perfectly correct to say *sounds good, feels good,* and *is good.*

What complicates matters is that linking verbs sometimes function as active verbs. *Look,* for instance, is a linking verb when referring to appearance, as in:

The day looks good for flying.

But it is an active verb when it refers to the act of looking, as in:

Margie looked sadly at her sick cat.

If you're not sure whether a verb is being used as a linking verb or an active verb, substitute a form of the verb *to be* in its place. If the sentence retains its basic meaning, the verb may well be a linking verb, as in:

The juice *tastes* good. (The juice *is* good.)

She will *stay* asleep for a century. (She *will be* asleep for a century.)

Because the second version of each sentence pretty well maintains the meaning of the original, *tastes* and *stay* are linking verbs and may be followed by any adjective you choose: *sour, sweet, tart, spoiled,* and a zillion more.

Adverbs

Adverbs, often recognizable by their —*ly* endings, usually describe, or modify, verbs, adjectives, or other adverbs. Much of the time they supply the answer to such questions as How? When? How much? Where? In what sequence? To what exent? In what manner?

> How does Brodie run? Brodie runs well. (The adverb *well* modifies the verb *run.*)
>
> How did the grass look? The grass looked mostly brown. (The adverb *mostly* modifies the adjective *brown.*)
>
> Where did Abigail sit? Abigail sat down. (The adverb *down* modifies the verb *sat.*)
>
> In what manner did she sit down? She sat down quickly. (The adverb *quickly* modifies the verb *sat.*)

If you ever need to choose between an adjective and an adverb while writing your AP essays, follow this simple two-step procedure:

First: Find the verb and determine whether it is a linking verb.

Second: If it is, use the adjective; if not, use the adverb.

Also, if the word modifies an adjective or another adverb, remember to use the adverb. If it modifies a noun or pronoun, use the adjective.

MINI-WORKOUT: ADJECTIVES AND ADVERBS

Check each of these sentences for faulty use of adjectives and adverbs. Write the correct word in the spaces provided. Some sentences may be correct.

1. Annabelle spoke sincere to Tim when she promised to marry him some day.

   _____

2. Rod always feels shyly about speaking in front of the class.

   _____

3. When the batter got hit in the head, the fans thought he had been hurt bad.

   _____

4. "No problem, Mr. Reynolds, I can do both jobs easy."

   _____

5. The audience remained calmly, even when the hall began to fill with smoke.

   _____

6. Later that day, Kirk and Elizabeth spoke frankly about their disagreement.

   _____

7. He walked down the corridor completely oblivious to the trail of papers he left behind.

   _____

8. Be sure to shut the door secure because it tends to swing open by itself.

   _____

9. The tyrant looked down cynical on the crowd assembled in the piazza.

   _____

10. The nurse felt bitterly that she had contracted the flu from a patient.

   _____

Answers on page 208.

USING PRONOUNS CORRECTLY

Skim your essay for pronoun errors. Faulty pronoun usage results most often:

- When pronouns in the wrong "case" are chosen
- When the pronoun reference is unclear or ambiguous
- When pronouns fail to agree in number or gender with their antecedents

Pronoun Case

Most of the time you can probably depend on your ear to tell you what's right and wrong. For example, you'd never say to the bus driver, "Let *I* off at the corner." But you can't always depend on your sense of what sounds right and wrong, especially when pronouns are paired, as in *he and I* and *me and them*. Then, it helps to know that pronouns fall into two groups:

Group 1: *I, he, she, they, we, you*

Group 2: *me, him, her, them, us, you*

The pronouns in the first group are *nominative case* pronouns and are used in grammatical subjects and predicate nominatives. The second group—*objective case* pronouns—are used everywhere else. Because pronouns, when used in pairs, must come from the same case, "*Him* and *I* went to the movies" is a nonstandard usage.

Any time you need a pair of pronouns, and you know that one of them is correct, pick the other from the same group. If you don't know either pronoun, here's a handy rule of thumb to follow: Substitute *I* or *me* for one of them. If *I* seems to fit, choose pronouns from Group 1; if *me* fits better, use Group 2.

Elvis asked that (he, him) and (she, her) practice handstands.

If you insert *me* in place of one of the pronouns, you'll get:

Elvis asked that *me* practice handstands.

Because no one would say that seriously, *I* must be the word that fits. So the pronouns you need come from Group 1, and the sentence should read:

Elvis asked that *he* and *she* practice handstands.

Use objective case pronouns in phrases that begin with prepositions, as in:

<u>between</u> *you* and *me*,
<u>to</u> Sherry and *her*
<u>among</u> *us* women

A Few More Principles of Pronoun Case

- Use objective case pronouns when the pronoun refers to a person to whom something is being done:

   Terry invited *him* to the prom.

   The waiter gave *her* and *me* a piece of cake.

- To find the correct pronoun in a comparison, complete the comparison using the verb that would follow naturally:

   Jackie runs faster than *she* (runs).

   A woman such as *I* (am) could solve the problem.

- When a pronoun appears side by side with a noun (*we* boys, *us* women), deleting the noun will help you pick the correct pronoun:

   (*We, Us*) seniors decided to take a day off from school in late May.
   (Deleting *seniors* leaves <u>We</u> *decided to* . . .).

   This award was presented to (*we, us*) students by the faculty.
   (Deleting *students* leaves *award was presented to* <u>us</u> *by the* . . .).

- Use possessive pronouns (*my, our, your, his, her, their*) before a *gerund*, a noun that looks like a verb because of its *–ing* ending.

   Her asking the question shows that she is alert. (*Asking* is a gerund.)

   Mother was upset about *your* opening the presents too soon.
   (*Opening* is a gerund.)

Gerunds

What is a gerund? It's a verb form that ends in *–ing* and is used as a noun.

Fishing is my grandpa's favorite pastime.
He started *fishing* as a boy in North Carolina.
As a result of all that *fishing* he hates to eat fish.

In all three sentences the gerund is derived from the verb *to fish*. Don't confuse gerunds with the participle form of verbs, as in:

Participle: *Fishing* from the bank of the river, my Grandpa caught a catfish.

Gerund: *Fishing* from the bank of a river is my Grandpa's greatest pleasure.

Not every noun with an *–ing* ending is a gerund. Sometimes it's just a noun, as in *thing, ring, spring.* At other times, *-ing* words are verbs, in particular, they're participles that modify pronouns in the objective case.

I hope you don't mind *my* intruding on your conversation (Here *intruding* is a gerund.)

I hope you don't mind *me* intruding on your conversation. (Here *intruding* is a participle.)

MINI-WORKOUT: PRONOUN CHOICE

Find the pronoun errors in the following sentences. Write the correct pronoun in the space provided. Some sentences may be correct.

1. Josh took my brother and I to the magic show last night.

   _____

2. He said that in my pocket I would find $10 in change to split between me Lucy.

   _____

3. The waiter promised to hold the table for we girls.

   _____

4. Him and me took turns on the treadmill.

   _____

5. They refused to let we boys into the arena without reservations.

   _____

6. When the coins fell out of his sleeve, the audience laughed even harder than us.

   _____

7. Did you hear about him falling and breaking his foot?

   _____

8. Did you stay as long as they at the dance?

   _____

9. I never spoke with them—neither he nor his brother.

   _____

10. If I were he, I'd practice for a long time before the next performance.

    _____

Answers on page 209.

PRONOUN REFERENCES

Check the reference of every pronoun in your essay. Be certain that each refers clearly to its antecedent—usually a noun or another pronoun. Avoid the confusion that results when no clear tie exists or when a pronoun seems to refer to more than one antecedent:

The librarian told Sarah that it was *her* responsibility to shelve the books.

Who is responsible? The librarian or Sarah? It's impossible to tell because the pronoun *her* may refer to either of them. Revised, the sentence reads:

The librarian told Sarah that one of her responsibilities as a library clerk was to shelve books.

A sentence containing two or more pronouns with ambiguous references can be especially troublesome and unclear:

Mike became a good friend of Mark's after *he* helped *him* repair *his* car.

Whose car needed fixing? Who helped whom? To answer these questions, the sentence needs to be rewritten:

Mike and Mark became good friends after Mark helped Mike repair *his* car.

This version is better, but it's still uncertain who owned the car. One way to set the meaning straight is to use more than one sentence:

When Mark needed to repair his car, Mike helped him do the job. Afterwards, Mike and Mark became good friends.

To be correct, a pronoun should refer directly and clearly to a specific noun or another pronoun, or it should refer by implication to an idea. Such implied references frequently involve the pronouns *it*, *they*, and *you*, and the relative pronouns *which*, *that*, and *this*, and cause trouble mostly when the pronoun is used to refer to rather general or ambiguous ideas, as in:

Homeless people allege that the mayor is indifferent to their plight, *which* has been disproved.

What has been disproved? That an allegation was made? That the mayor is indifferent? The intended meaning is unclear because *which* has no distinct antecedent. To clear up the uncertainty, the sentence might read:

Homeless people allege that the mayor is indifferent to their plight, but the allegation has been disproved.

Finally, don't use pronouns to refer to possessives, as in:

In Eminem's latest hit, he stumbles over several words.

The pronoun *he* obviously refers to Eminem, but the word *Eminem* doesn't appear in the sentence. Because the possessive noun *Eminem's* is not a grammatical equivalent to *Eminem*, the revised sentence should be:

In his latest hit, Eminem stumbles over several words.

MINI-WORKOUT: PRONOUN REFERENCE

Revise the following sentences to eliminate pronoun reference problems. Some sentences may be correct.

1. Martha loves to knit and spends most of her spare time doing it.

   _____

2. Mike answered the test questions, collected his pens and pencils, and handed them in.

   _____

3. In Fitzgerald's *The Great Gatsby*, he writes about the American Dream.

   _____

4. Its economy is a mess, but Russia will weather the crisis.

   _____

5. When teens loiter outside the theater on Friday night, they give you a hard time.

   _____

6. His father let him know he had only an hour to get to the airport.

   _____

7. Frankie has been interested in playing major league baseball, and he aspires to be one someday.

   _____

8. Rob has a part-time job at the boatyard and spends every summer on the water, which lies at the root of his interest in going to Annapolis.

   _____

9. If someone buys an old used car, he better be ready to pay for repairs.

_____

10. After the interview, Mike told Tom that he thought Colgate University was a good place for him to spend the next four years.

_____

Answers on page 209.

PRONOUN-ANTECEDENT AGREEMENT

Finally, take a look at the agreement between all the pronouns and their antecedents. Do they agree in gender, number, and person? Problems frequently occur with words like *everyone, anyone*, and *nobody*—singular words that should usually be followed by singular pronouns. Sometimes such words are meant as plurals, however, and should be followed by plural pronouns. (See the earlier discussion on noun-verb agreement, page 148.)

Singular pronouns must have singular antecedents; plural pronouns, plural antecedents. Note the problem of pronoun-antecedent agreement in these sentences:

> Everybody is sticking to *their* side of the story
>
> Anybody can pass this course if *they* study hard.
>
> Neither teacher plans to change *their* policy regarding late papers.

Properly stated, the sentences should read:

> Everybody is sticking to *his* side of the story.
>
> Anybody can pass this course if *she* studies hard.
>
> Neither teacher plans to change *his* policy regarding late papers.

Some people, objecting to the use of specific gender pronouns, prefer the cumbersome and tacky phrase "he or she," but most good writers avoid using it.

Still other words may sound singular but are plural in certain contexts:

> The jury will render *its* verdict tomorrow. /The jury will return to *their* homes tomorrow.
>
> The senior class posed for *its* picture./The senior class had *their* portraits taken for the yearbook.

MINI-WORKOUT: PRONOUN AGREEMENT

Look for errors of agreement between pronouns and antecedents in the sentences below. Use the spaces provided to write the correct pronoun or, if necessary, to revise the sentence. Alter only those sentences that contain errors.

1. The English teacher announced that everyone in the class must turn in their term papers no later than Friday.

   _____

2. The Army, which paid soldiers large bonuses to re-enlist when their tours of duty were over, changed their policy when the budget was cut.

   _____

3. The library put their collection of rare books on display.

   _____

4. Each of my sisters have their own room.

   _____

5. In that class, our teacher held conferences with us once a week.

   _____

6. Everyone on the girls' field hockey team worked as hard as they could to win the championship.

   _____

7. The teacher dictates sentences in French, and each of the students write it down in English and hand it in.

   _____

8. Each horse in the procession followed their riders down to the creek.

   _____

9. The school's chess team has just won their first match.

   _____

10. The person elected to the class presidency will find that the faculty and administration will cooperate with them and help them succeed.

    _____

Answers on page 210.

PUNCTUATION AND CAPITALIZATION

There are many reasons why you should know how to punctuate and when to use capital letters. At present, one of them is that error-free AP essays tend to earn higher scores than those crowded with mistakes. The next few pages cover the basics of everyday punctuation and capitalization.

APOSTROPHES

Apostrophes are used in only three places:

1. **Contractions** such as *won't, it's, could've,* and *where's.* Apostrophes mark places where letters have been omitted.

2. In **plurals** of letters, signs, or numbers, as in *A's* and *B's,* the *1960's,* and *10's* and *20's,* although many experts simplify matters by writing *1960s, Ps* and *Qs,* and so forth.

3. In **possessive nouns** such as the *student's class, women's room,* and in indefinite pronouns such as *anybody's guess.* When the noun is plural and ends in *s,* put the apostrophe after the *s,* as in *leaves' color* and *horses' stable.* Some possessive forms use both an apostrophe and *of,* as in *a friend of the family's;* some others that specify time, space, value, or quantity also require apostrophes, as in *a week's time, a dollar's worth, at my wit's end.*

COMMAS

Commas divide sentences into parts, clarify meaning, and prevent confusion.

1. Use a comma to signal a **pause,** as in:

   No pause: After brushing his teeth gleamed.

   Pause: After brushing, his teeth gleamed.

   Commas are needed after some introductory words and in forms of address:

   Well, you can open it whenever it's convenient.

   The letter will be waiting for you at home, *Jimmy*.

2. Commas set off words that **interrupt the flow** of a sentence, as in

   Carolyn, *regrettably*, was omitted from the roster.

   Jennie, *on the other hand*, was included.

   Commas separate information not essential to the meaning of the sentence:

   The lost hikers, *who had come from New Jersey*, found shelter in a cave.

   The three bikers, *using an out-of-date road map*, arrived two hours late.

   Commas set off **appositives:**

   Samantha, *the prosecutor*, entered the courtroom.

   The judge, *Mr. Peterson*, presided at the trial.

3. Commas separate the clauses of a **compound sentence**:

> The competition is stiff, but it won't keep Miriam from winning.
>
> Pete had better call home, or he'll be in big trouble.

4. Commas separate items in a **series**:

> Rosie's car needs *new tires, a battery, a muffler, and an oil change.*
>
> It was a wonder that Marv could sit through the *long, boring, infantile, and ridiculous* lecture.

Some writers to prefer to skip the comma before the last item in a series, but just in case clarity may suffer, it can't hurt to put it in.

5. Commas separate parts of **addresses, dates, and place names**:

> Who lives at 627 West 115th Street, New York, NY?
>
> Richard was born on May 27, 1990, the same day as Irene.
>
> Dave has lived in Madison, Wisconsin; Seattle, Washington; and Eugene, Oregon.

Note that each location in the last example already contains a comma. So, semicolons were added between the items to avoid confusion.

6. Commas separate quotation from attributions in **dialogue**.

> John said, "Close the window."
>
> "I want it open," protested Ben.

SEMICOLONS

Semicolons may be used between closely related sentences, in effect, shortening the pause that would naturally occur between two separate sentences:

> Mother was worried; her daughters never stay out this late.
>
> The momentum was building; she couldn't be stopped now.

A caution: Because semicolons function like periods, use them only between independent clauses or in a series in which one or more items contains a comma, as in:

> On his trek, Norwood met Allen, a carpenter from Maine; Dr. Jones, a pediatrician from St. Louis; Jonathan, an airline pilot; and me, of course.

QUOTATION MARKS

Quotation marks usually surround direct quotations, as in:

> As the author of the passage pointed out, "George Washington, when naked, weighed at least two hundred pounds."

Quotation marks also enclose the titles of poems, stories, chapter headings, essays, magazine articles, and other short works. Don't use them for longer works. Novels, plays, films, and magazine titles should be underlined in handwritten essays and italicized when they appear in print.

Avoid calling attention to clichés, trite expressions or slang terms by using quotation marks. Rewrite instead, using fresh, original language.

Finally, quotation marks may enclose words that express the silent thoughts of a character, as in:

Carlos glanced at his watch. "I'm going to be late," he thought.

Periods and commas are placed inside close-quotation marks. Question marks and exclamation points go outside the quotation mark unless they are part of the quote itself.

"When will the seminar start?" asked Regis.

Do you understand the meaning of the concept "The end justifies the means"?

MINI-WORKOUT: PUNCTUATION

Part A. Possessives. Check your mastery of possessives by writing the correct possessive form of the italicized word in the space provided. Some items may be correct.

1. *Pauls* reason was personal. _____

2. The future of *Americas* foreign policy is being debated. _____

3. *Teams* from all over the county have gathered at the stadium. _____

4. Luis isn't at all interested in *womens* issues. _____

5. The *girls* locker room is downstairs, but the *boys* is upstairs. _____

6. We are invited to the *Andersons* house for New *Years* Eve. _____

7. All of the *Rosses* are going out to eat. _____

8. Have you seen *Morris* iPod, which he left here yesterday? _____

9. Both of the *computers* keyboards need repair. _____

10. He'll be back in one *months* time. _____

Part B. Commas and semicolons. In the sentences below insert or remove commas and semicolons as necessary. Some sentences may be correct.

1. While Buddy was riding his bike got a flat tire.

2. The mail carrier did not leave the package for Valerie was not at home.

3. After doing homework Mikey as you might expect talked on his cell phone for an hour.

4. His work criticized many commonly held beliefs however and it was strictly censored.

5. The car, that ran into mine at the intersection, was an SUV.

6. I need street maps of Boston; and Portland, Maine.

7. The people who live by the water must be prepared for occasional flooding.

8. The boat, was 75 feet long and 18 feet wide, its mast was about 80 feet tall.

9. To anyone interested in flying planes hold endless fascination.

10. Jeff and Steve left alone for the weekend invited all their friends to a party.

Answers on page 210.

CAPITALIZATION

Capitalization isn't totally standardized, but it's not a free-for-all, either. You won't go wrong following these guidelines:

1. Capitalize the first words of sentences, direct quotations, and lines of poetry (most of the time). This includes sentences that follow colons, as in:

   > He had all the symptoms of love: All day long he could think of nothing but Sherrie.

2. Capitalize proper nouns and adjectives derived from proper nouns: *Victoria, Victorian; Shakespeare, Shakespearean; France, French dressing* (but not *french fries*, which has become a generic term).

3. Capitalize place names: *North America, Lake Moosilauke, Yosemite National Park, Gobi Desert, Mount Rushmore, Panama Canal, the Arctic Ocean, Times Square, Route 66.* Don't capitalize north, east, south, and west unless you are referring to a particular region of the country, as in:

   > They went camping in the *West*.

   Nor should you capitalize the common noun that is not part of the actual place name, as in *the canal across Panama, the city of Moline, the plains of the Midwest.*

4. Capitalize languages, races, nationalities, and religions: *the Hungarian language, Inuit, Argentinian, Hispanic, Muslim.*

5. Capitalize organizations, institutions, and brand names: *United Nations, Pittsburgh Pirates, Library of Congress, Automobile Club of America, Amtrak, Southwest Airlines, the Internet, Toyota.* Don't, however, capitalize the common noun associated with the brand name, as in *Crest toothpaste or Starbuck's coffee.*

6. Capitalize titles of persons that indicate rank, office, or profession when they are used with the person's name: *Congressman Kelly, Doctor Dolittle, Coach McConnell, Judge Judy, Lieutenant Lawlor.* Also, the titles of high officials when they are used in place of the official's name, as in *the Secretary General, the Prime Minister, the Secretary of the Treasury.* Don't capitalize titles when

referring generically to the position: *the superintendent of schools, the assistant librarian, the clerk of the highway department.*

7. Capitalize family relationships, but only when they are used with a person's name, as in *Uncle Wesley, Grandma Jones, Cousin Dave.*

8. Capitalize titles of books, plays, stories, articles, poems, songs, and other creative works, as in *The Grapes of Wrath, Hamlet, "An Occurrence at Owl Creek Bridge," "Ode to a Grecian Urn," "Box of Rain."* Note that articles, conjunctions and prepositions of less than five letters are not capitalized unless they appear as the last or the first words in the title.

9. Capitalize references to the Deity and religious tracts, as in *God, the Gospel, the Torah, the Koran, the Lord, the Prophet.* Also pronouns referring to *Him* or *Her.*

10. Capitalize historical names, events, documents, and periods, as in *Battle of Gettysburg, Alien and Sedition Acts, War of 1812, Bill of Rights, Middle Ages.*

11. Capitalize days of the week, months, and holidays as in *Monday, May, Mothers' Day.* The seasons are not capitalized unless given an identity such as *Old Man Winter.*

12. Capitalize the names of specific courses and schools, as in *History 101, Forensic Science, Brookvale High School, Columbia College.* While course names are capitalized, subjects are not. Therefore, you study *history* in *American History 101* and learn *forensics* in *Forensic Science.* Similarly, you attend *high school* at *Brookvale High School* and go to *college* at *Columbia.*

MINI-WORKOUT: CAPITALIZATION

Add capital letters where they are needed in the following sentences.

1. on labor day bennington county's fire department plans to hold a turkey shoot on the field at miller's pond.

2. the judge gave district attorney lipman a book entitled *the rules of evidence* and instructed her to read it before she ever dared set foot in the court of appeals of the ninth circuit again.

3. the secretary of state greeted the president of austria at the ronald reagan airport in washington, d.c.

4. the shackleton expedition nearly met its doom on georgia island in antarctica.

5. for christmas he got a black & decker table saw from the sears store next to the old bedford courthouse.

6. according to georgetown's high school principal, eugene griffiths, georgetown high school attracts students from the whole west coast. at georgetown students may major in drawing and painting, design, graphics, or sculpture. mr griffiths said, "i attended a similar high school in new england just after the vietnam war."

7. we expect to celebrate new year's eve again this year by renting a movie of an old broadway musical and by settling down in front of the dvd player with some pepsi and a box of oreos.

8. after traveling all the way to the pacific, the corps of discovery rode down the missouri river going east on their way back to st. louis.

9. This irish linen tablecloth was bought at k-mart in the emeryville mall off powell street.

10. yellowstone national park is located in the northwestern corner of wyoming.

Answers on page 210.

Analytical Essay Question with Sample Student Responses

What follows is a typical analytical essay question along with four student responses written by hand under testing conditions: a time limit, no access to a dictionary or other book, and a certain amount of tension. By reading the essays and a reader's comments, you will see what it takes to earn an 8 or a 9, the highest scores. Read the weaker essays, too. They'll alert you to some pitfalls to avoid when you write essays of your own.

QUESTION
(Suggested time—40 minutes)

The passage below is the complete text of a theater review by Henry James entitled "Mr. Henry Irving's Macbeth." It was published in a London newspaper in 1875. After reading it carefully, write a well-organized essay that defines James' rhetorical purpose and analyzes some of the strategies he employs to achieve it.

> Mr. Henry Irving's Macbeth, which, on the actor's first appearance in the part in London some six weeks ago, produced not a little disappointment in the general public, seems to have been accepted as an interesting if not a
> *Line* triumphant attempt, and is exhibited to audiences numerous if not over-
> *(5)* flowing, and deferential if not enthusiastic. Considering the actor's reputation, indeed, the very undemonstrative attitude of the spectators at the Lyceum is most noticeable. Mr. Irving's acting is, to my mind, not of a kind to provoke enthusiasm, and I can best describe it by saying that it strikes me as the acting of a very superior amateur. If Mr. Irving were somewhat
> *(10)* younger, and if there existed in England any such school of dramatic training as the Conservatoire of Paris, any such exemplary stage as the Théâter Français, a discriminating critic might say of him: "Here is an aspirant with the instincts of an artist, and who, with proper instruction, may become an actor." But, thanks to the absence of a school and of any formidable com-
> *(15)* petition, success has come easily to Mr. Irving, and he has remained, as the first tragic actor in England, decidedly incomplete and amateurish. His personal gifts—face, figure, voice, enunciation—are rather meagre; his strong

points are intellectual. He is ingenious, intelligent, and fanciful; imaginative he can hardly be called, for he signally fails to give their great imagina-
(20) tive value to many of the superb speeches he has to utter. In declamation
he is decidedly flat; his voice is without charm, and his utterance without
subtlety. But he has thought out his part, after a fashion of his own, very
carefully, and in the interest of his rendering of it lies in seeing a spare,
refined man, of an unhistrionic—or a rather sedentary—aspect, and with a
(25) thick, unmodulated voice, but with a decided sense of the picturesque,
grappling in a deliberate and conscientious manner with a series of great
tragic points. This hardly gives an impression of strength, of authority, and
it is not for force and natural magic that Mr. Irving's acting is remarkable.
He has been much criticized for his conception of his part—for making
(30) Macbeth so spiritless a plotter before his crime, and so arrant a coward
afterward. But in the text, as he seeks to emphasize it, there is a fair warrant
for the line he follows. Mr. Irving has great skill in the representation of terror, and it is quite open to him to have thrown into relief this side of his
part. His best moment is his rendering of the scene with the bloody dag-
(35) gers—though it must be confessed that this stupendous scene always does
much toward acting itself. Mr. Irving, however, is here altogether
admirable, and his representation of nature trembling and quaking to its
innermost spiritual recesses really excites the imagination. Only a trifle less
powerful is his scene with Banquo's ghost at the feast, and the movement
(40) with which, exhausted with vain bravado, he muffles his head in his mantle and collapses beside the throne. Mr. Irving has several points in common with Edwin Booth, and belongs to the same general type of actor; but
I may say that if, to my thinking, Edwin Booth comes nearer to being a
man of genius, I find Mr. Irving more comfortable to see. Of Miss
(45) Bateman, who does Lady Macbeth, the less said the better. She has good-
will and a certain superficial discretion; but a piece of acting and declaiming of equal pretensions, more charmless in an artistic way, it has not been
my fortune to behold.

Lilah's Response
(Typed as it was written)

Either Henry James was depressed or trying to have fun when he
wrote this review of Macbeth with Mr. Henry Irving playing the lead. He
could have been in a cynical mood because he doesn't have a single praise-
worthy thing to say about the performance or about the audience or about
Mr. Irving as an actor. However, the review is witty in a mean sort of way
and probably caused laughter among the readers of the newspaper that
printed it in 1875. But James might have put humor into his review in
order to prevent himself from sounding like a total curmudgeon.

So how did James amuse his readers and destroyed Mr Irving at the
same time? First, he wrote the entire review in one paragraph which contains an evaluation of five different topics with respect to the performance of Macbeth. He covers the audience, Mr. Irving's training and acting
ability, his physical features and voice, his portrayal of Macbeth, and then
at the end he writes about the performance by Miss Bateman in the role
of Lady Macbeth. The last two sentences about Miss Bateman are the

nastiest ones of all. After the criticism about Mr. Irving, he brings his sarcastic wit to a climax by saying "the less said the better," but then he immediately contradicts his own statement by delivering a knock-out punch with these words: "She has good will . . . but a piece of acting and declaiming of equal pretentions, more charmless in an artistic way, it has not been my fortune to behold." The other things he talks about in the review also come under his brutal criticism in a variety of ways. For example, the audience is called "deferential," implying that they are there more out of duty and respect for the lead actor than because they have any intellectual interest in seeing Macbeth. The general public says the production is "interesting," which is an "interesting" way to put it because when someone doesn't want to say something negative but can't find a positive statement to make "interesting" is the euphemism they use.

When James begins to write about Mr. Irving's acting, he says it is as good as "a very superior amateur," a devastating putdown for a professional actor. The word "amateur" has a negative connotation not only for professionals but also for amateurs because the word suggests incompetence. The insult is compounded in line 16 when James says he is "decidedly incomplete and amateurish." The reason that James gives for Irving's poor acting is related to the education received by English actors. In England there is no school or theater that trains actors the way they do in France. In a way, that excuses Mr. Irving's acting ability due to his country being unable to train him properly.

Now that James has criticized Irving's acting ability and England's deficiency in training actors, he focuses on Irving's physical features and voice and finds both unacceptable, using negative words like "meagre," "flat" and "without charm," and "without subtlety." Then he plays with the word "remarkable," saying that "Mr. Irving's acting is remarkable" (line 28). That could mean the the acting is good or even excellent, but James surprises the reader by using it ironically. What he means but doesnt' say is the acting is remarkably bad.

As he turns his attention to Irving performing Macbeth's part, James finds something good to say about the way Irving played the scene with the bloody daggars. But he undercuts his praise by adding that the scene is so stupendous that it "does much toward acting itself," meaning that the scene is so strong that it helps the actor, including one as bad as Mr. Irving, to perform well. Finally, now that he has almost destroyed Irving's acting, James can't resist one more insulting criticism by describing Irving seeing Banquo's ghost. In that scene Irving is "altogether admirable," but he is really not since he "trembles and quakes . . . muffles his head in his mantle and collapses beside the throne." (lines 40–41) What James is implying that Irving is over-acting and over-emoting; he is playing the part as if he was cast in a melodrama or TV soap.

The readers of this essay in London most likely got a laugh out of Jame's sarcastic humor, but it's a kind of negative humor because it is given at the expense of an actor whose reputation will be smeared by James's superior tone.

Your impressions: _____

_____

_____

_____

Comment to Lilah from an AP Reader

Aside from a few distracting errors in style and mechanics (more attentive proof-reading would no doubt have helped), and an out-of-place allusion to a TV soap opera, your essay is a model of insight and focus. It captures the essence of James' review and analyzes in impressive detail how the author manages to be simultaneously funny and, as you say, devastating. Using apt and specific textual examples, you show how James first attacks Irving and then softens the onslaught by blaming England for the poor man's ineptitude. You also point out correctly that James saves his most brutal assault for Miss Bateman, whose performance exceeds Irving's in its deficiences. The language in your essay not only conveys a sensitive reading of the passage but shows an awareness that diction—the use of "curmudgeon," "euphemism," and "melodrama," to cite a few well-chosen words—is essential to a mature and readable style. References to James' readers in both the opening and concluding paragraphs endow your essay with a sense of unity not always evident in AP essays. Score: 9

Kevin's Response
(Typed as it was written)

Based on the theater review entitled "Mr Henry Irving's Macbeth," Henry James was a sophisticated writer and a strict judge of performers on the stage. His sophistication comes through in his diction, the syntaxes of his sentences, the structure of the passage and a use of irony. His strictness is illustrated by saying only the most critical things about two performers, one being Henry Irving and the second being Miss Bateman, who plays Lady Macbeth. He dismisses Miss Bateman with a wave of his hand by saying "the less said the better" Obviously, to write about her performance is giving it more attention than it deserves. As a matter of fact, James said that he'd never seen a more charmless piece of acting in his life.

James saves most of his abuse for Mr. Irving's Macbeth, using a whole thesaurus of negative words and phrases to describe it, including "very superior amateur," "may become an actor," "decidedly incomplete and amateurish," "fails to give great imaginative value to many of the superb speeches," "without charm," "without subtlety," and many others. He begins the review with some general commentary about the apathetic audience and about Mr. Irving's poor training as an actor. These generalizations are followed up with specific details about his looks, in particular his face and figure, and about his very poor voice, which is "thick" and "unmodulated."

By going from general to specific, he uses a very convincing structure. He introduces general ideas to the reader, getting them ready to find out more, and then wham! he provides the concrete evidence to back up his opinions. He describes Mr. Irving's weaknesses as an actor followed by an evaluation of his performance in playing the role of Macbeth. James agrees with other critics that Irving has made Macbeth a "spiritless plotter before his crime, and so arrant a coward afterward." (lines 30–31).

In terms of syntax, James likes to say things by stating the negative of the reverse of what he wants to say (litotes). For example, he uses "interesting if not triumphant" and "audiences numerous if not overflowing." This kind of sentence structure would appeal to a more sophisticated reader than if he came right out a said the performance was a flop and the audience was small.

The author's irony, however, gives the passage a tone that illustrates his opionion. He quotes an imaginary critic, who is probably James himself in disguise in line 12, who might say "Here is an aspirant with the instincts of an artist, and who, with proper instruction, may become an actor." This is James's way of giving criticism. He makes a negative comment but uses words that seem positive or encouraging, but they are not. Later in the same way he gives the impression that he is praising Irving's "representation of terror," but it is really damning with faint praise because he then slaps him down by saying that any actor can make the stupendous scene with the bloody daggers exciting. Finally, there is a comparison made between Irving and an actor named Edwin Booth, who is "nearer to being a man of genius" than Irving (lines 43–44). Again, he is implying something insulting, namely that Irving is definately not a man of genius.

Your impressions: _____

_____

_____

_____

Comment to Kevin from an AP Reader

The introductory paragraph provides an accurate but conventional blueprint for the essay to follow. True to your word, you deal with each rhetorical feature in turn, and ably support your assessment of James as "a sophisticated writer and strict judge."

Your discussion of structure, complete with the dramatic "wham!" carefully explains the effects of using details to support generalizations. In addition, your analysis of James' diction, introduced with a delightful conceit ("whole thesaurus of negative words and phrases") is thorough and well documented.

Not so, however, the paragraph on syntax. Aside from misidentifying the rhetorical device—James uses antitheses, not litotes—you fail to support the dubious assertion that sophisticated readers prefer one kind of sentence structure to another. You put the essay back on track in the last paragraph, however, by serving up several astute examples of James' irony.

Although you demonstrate an ability to express ideas clearly and forcefully, the essay doesn't exhibit the level of effective writing expected of the very best papers. Score: 7

Danielle's Response

(Typed as it was written)

My mother is British and so my parents go to England every year and go to plays in London. My great grandfather whose name was David Chambers was the owner of a noodle factory near London and could have read the review "Mr Henry Irving's Macbeth" in the London newspaper in 1875. (I don't know if he went to the theater, but he might of gone because he was pretty rich and dressed in elegant clothes in a photo of him and his wife (my great grandmother Jennie) that we have at home on our dining room wall.) If he saw the review by Henry James, he would not have wasted his time and money on going to see <u>Macbeth</u> in the theater.

So Henry James succeeded in accomplishing his purpose. He told readers not to bother with the play because it was "not a little disappointment" as he wrote in line 2.

In all ways, Macbeth was a flop. Henry James uses language that would turn anyone off to the play. For example, he writes about the "undemonstrative attitude of the spectators," meaning the audience. That means they just sat there probably bored out of their minds and maybe didn't even applaud the performance of Mr. Irving and especially Lady Macbeth played by an actress named Miss Bateman.

Mr. Irving strikes the author as "the acting of a very superior amateur," a humorous way to say it because the word <u>amateur</u> is as a surprise at the end of the phrase. <u>Superior</u> sounds like a compliment, but <u>amateur</u> contridicts the compliment. I suppose that readers of the newspaper would find that funny also and would probably enjoy reading the review more than going to the play because the review is filled with comments that could get readers to chuckle or maybe even laugh, while the play would put them to sleep, which I can sympathize with when we read it last year in English class.

"Here is an aspirant with the instincts of an artist, and who, with proper instruction, may become an actor." If that's not a put down, I don't know what it is. It is an awful but also funny remark to say about an actor who is trying to play the lead. Then he adds "His personal gifts—face, figure, voice, enunciation—are rather meagre." Another insult that readers would enjoy.

They'd also get a charge out of the image of a "spare, refined man, of an unhistrionic (?) or rather sedentary—aspect, and with a thick, unmodulated voice, but with a decided sense of the picturesque, grappling in a deliberate and conscientious manner with a series of great tragic points." (lines 26–27)

Henry James then delivers the final blow by saying "Mr. Irving's acting is remarkable" in line 28, but he means remarkably bad, not remarkable good.

At the end of the review James does the same thing he did before when he says that Miss Batemen acting the part of Lady Macbeth is "charmless in an artistic way." A funny phrase because <u>charmless</u> is negative while artistic is positive, and the contradiction is suppose to make a reader laugh. In the last lines (47–48) Henry James concludes his irony by saying "it has not been my fortune to behold" when he really means <u>misfortune</u> because he is referring to Miss Batemen's terrible performance.

Obviously, I don't know if my grandfather read this review but he would probably enjoyed it more than this performance of <u>Macbeth</u>.

Your impressions: _____

_____

_____

_____

Comment to Danielle from an AP Reader

The essay has a distinctive edge over most other essays written in response to this question because of the interesting link you've made with your family history. Imagining that the review may have been read by your relatives helps to make the passage a living document and serves to identify the author's purpose—to entertain readers while also encouraging them to stay away from that production of *Macbeth*.

To your credit, you point out several features of the passage that were meant to amuse readers, not an easy task when the author is Henry James, known for his elegant but convoluted style of writing. Your analysis is perceptive, although you rely on quotations rather heavily—too heavily, in fact. Quoted material is crucial in an analytical essay, but in some places, where it would have been better to use your own words, quotes dominate the text.

Your more-than-adequate analysis of the passage is limited to its humor, but the writing is marked by a rather undisciplined syntax, especially by sentences that go on and on. There are few sentence errors, to be sure, but it's a chore to wade through excessively drawn-out sentences. Marginal control of sentence structure and sentence length detracts from what could have been a more effective essay. Score: 5

Franklin's Response
(Typed as it was written)

In 1875 Henry James wrote a theater review that was published in a London newspaper. It was about Macbeth, Shakespearen play with Mr. Henry Irving receiving top billing as the character Macbeth. The play opened six weeks before the review appeared in the newspaper.

The "general public" which is the name James gives to the audience thought the play was "interesting." They were probably interested in seeing the murder of the king by Macbeth and Lady Macbeth and other things like the three witches and having a whole forest move when the actors put branches in their helmets pretending to be trees.

The public also liked the scene with the bloody daggars when Macbeth came out of the king's room with them and Lady Macbeth called him a coward and takes the daggars back inside and smears blood on the two servants who are supposed to look like they killed the king. Another great scene is when Banquo's ghost comes to the bancquet. The review in line 39 says it was "powerful".

James says the interest of the play was more than what they thought about Mr. Henry Irving. They think he is a "very superior amateur" actor in lines 8–9. James says that he is too old for the part of Macbeth, who should be younger than about 35 or 40 since he and Lady Macbeth have no children, but he should be old enough to be a general in the king's army. In the performance "his voice is without charm" meaning it is dull and flat as if he was reciting the lines from memory and doesn't have an idea of how to build them up with expression and emotion. He (line 25) also has a "think, unmodulated voice".

The performance also has some good things to it. "Mr. Irving has great skill in the presentation of terror." This is important in the play because Macbeth is fighting for his life after Lady Macbeth sleepwalks and comitts suicide. He is scared of Macduff because he has killed his wife and children and when he hears that Macduff did not have natural childbirth and was ripped out of his mother's womb instead he knows that he is soon about to meet his own doom. Macbeth also shows terror at the banquet where Banquo comes in as a ghost and only Macbeth can see him. During that scene Mr. Henry Irving "muffles his head in his mantle and collapses beside the throne (40–41)".

In conclusion, James is full of criticism about the acting of Mr. Henry Irving. He contradicts himself in line 44 when he says that "I find Mr. Irving more comfortable to see". So, it is like James did not really make a decision to like the play or not. The good things and the bad things cancel each other out like an acid and a base in chemistry and the end result is neutral.

Your impressions: _____

_____

_____

_____

Comment to Franklin from an AP Reader

To conclude that Henry James is "neutral" about this production of *Macbeth* suggests that you have misread the passage. Although the author manages to squeeze one or two half-hearted compliments into the review, the tone of James' remarks is mainly sarcastic and disparaging.

Your essay also suggests that you have a weak grasp of literary analysis. Although you are obviously aware of the need to paraphrase key ideas and include quotations, the essay summarizes the content of the passage more than it analyzes the author's diction, tone, imagery, and so forth.

That you are familiar with *Macbeth* is evident. Indeed, the detail with which you discuss certain events in the play demonstrates that, had you been asked to discuss the events of the play, you might have written a winning essay. But here you have overstepped the boundaries of the task and filled the essay with irrelevancies.

Your essay is competently organized, although using the opening paragraph to rephrase the prompt deprives you of an opportunity to say something fresh and appealing. The writing, while grammatically sound, is generally wordy, ungraceful, and mechanically flawed. Score: 3

POINTERS FOR WRITING THE SYNTHESIS ESSAY

- Writing a synthesis essay
- Using sources to your advantage
- Developing a persuasive argument
- Pitfalls to avoid
- Integrating sources into your essay
- Sample question and student responses

The third essay question on the exam calls for a synthesis essay—an essay that argues your point of view on a given issue. Along with a prompt that describes the issue, you are given six sources related to the issue. One of the sources is an image, such as a photo, chart, graph, or cartoon. From three of the sources you are to draw facts, ideas, information—any relevant evidence you can use to bolster your argument.

To write the essay, you are allotted 55 minutes. The first 15 minutes are devoted to reading the sources. During this time, you may mark up the passages with your pen, take notes, write an outline, think about the issue, jot down a tentative thesis—in short, get ready to compose your essay. After the 15-minute prep period, you'll be permitted to open your test booklet and begin writing

Because the prompt contains the topic for your essay, read it carefully with pen in hand to underline the words that tell you what you must do.

TIP
The prompt contains the topic for the synthesis essay. Read it carefully.

SAMPLE PROMPT FOR A SYNTHESIS ESSAY

Since the advent of cell phones, the Internet, e-mail and other wireless connections, we can stay in touch with the world 24/7 wherever we are, whatever we're doing. Does this ability to communicate make life more satisfying or does it lead to greater anxiety and stress?

After carefully reading the sources that follow, write an essay that synthesizes at least three of the sources for support and takes a position that defends, challenges, or modifies the assertion that portable electronic communication has improved our lives.

The first paragraph does little more than introduce the assignment. It may stir up your thinking, but it doesn't tell you how to proceed. It's the second paragraph that actually spells out the instructions: *read the sources and write an essay*—not just any essay but one that *takes a position* that either agrees or disagrees with the proposition that portable electronic communication has improved our lives. It also offers you the option of *modifying* or *qualifying* the statement. That is, you needn't strongly defend nor strongly oppose the statement. You can take a position that falls somewhere in between.

What It's About

A synthesis essay is basically an **argumentative** essay. At the heart of the essay lies a claim, or statement of opinion. Call it a *main idea* or a *thesis statement*. The main idea spells out the overall purpose of the essay. Once you've made clear where you stand on the issue, the rest of the essay should back up your claim. To do that, you need to present a variety of supporting evidence.

The evidence you present is likely to make or break your argument. Solid evidence consists of facts, observations, statistics, the opinions of experts, relevant anecdotes, and more. But you'll get the most mileage from a series of logically presented ideas. No doubt you've had experience trying to convince someone to agree with you—to see an issue your way. Maybe you've tried to talk a teacher into raising a grade. Or how about the time you wanted to drive with your friends to a rap concert 200 miles away, and you had to persuade your parents to let you go? You probably cited reasons why you thought it was a good idea, gave examples of your maturity, reminded them of past instances when you acted responsibly, cited the fact that Scott's and Chris' parents have already given their consent, and so on. In short, you chose and shaped the most convincing evidence you could think of to fit the audience—your parents.

When you write the synthesis essay, you are faced with a similar task. Your audience, of course, will be AP essay readers, and your task is to convince them first, that you understand the essay assignment and second, that you can apply both your own ideas and other ideas you've found in the sources to build a persuasive argument.

Before you begin to write, however, you must read the sources.

Reading the Sources

Some students are blessed with lightning-quick minds that can instantly analyze an issue and articulate a thoughtful position on it. If you happen to be one of them, you're lightyears ahead of the pack. Enjoy your head start and plunge right into the sources to look for the evidence with which to build your case.

The rest of us, unless we happen to have thought about the issue in the past, will start from scratch. We'll begin reading sources with relatively open minds and will weigh all the evidence we can find before making up our minds.

The sources will offer a variety of interpretations and points of view for you to consider. Don't be satisfied that you know what any individual source is all about until you've analyzed it thoroughly and can say clearly what it contributes to the discussion of the issue. If you think it's okay to read only some of the sources in order to find enough ideas for your essay, please think again. In other words, read every source from start to finish before you start to write. After all, the most irresistible idea could pop up in the final paragraph of the last source.

As you read the sources, keep in mind the following purposes:

- **Read to understand what the source has to say.** Quickly underline or circle striking ideas, topic sentences, and other key words and phrases. Use your pencil sparingly, though, or you may end up with most of each passage marked up. A note or two scribbled in the margin can serve later as shorthand reminders of what the passage says.

- **Read to analyze the author's position on the issue.** Read each source to determine where the author stands on the issue. Where the author presents evidence in favor of the claim, put a check in the margin. Where the evidence opposes it, write an X. Later, when you've decided on your own position, these notations will lead you quickly to ideas you may wish to include in your essay.

- **Read for evidence and data that help define your position on the issue.** The position to choose should be the one about which you have the most compelling things to say. The sources will offer a variety of perspectives. Read them in search of evidence that makes the most sense to you. The sooner you know where you stand, the better. If you've read the sources and still can't decide what position to take, make two lists, one for arguments in favor of the issue, one for those opposed. With any luck, the arguments on one side will speak to you more forcefully than those on the other.

  You won't be penalized for taking an unpopular or politically incorrect stance, but you'll get little credit for promoting an unrealistic or illogical position. If you wish, you can straddle the fence on the issue with the "it-all-depends" argument. That approach is safe but not too exciting. But if your judgment tells you that the question warrants a middle-of-the-road response, don't hesitate to write one. In the end, readers will be less impressed by your position than by the potency of your presentation.

- **Interpret the visual source.** The visual source won't require much reading, but it still must be analyzed for what it communicates. Your job is to interpret the graph, the chart, the image, the cartoon, or whatever, and determine its relationship to the other sources. Ask yourself what relevant information it contributes to the discussion of the issue. Once you understand its point, you can use it as evidence in your essay.

  Because visual sources often convey a large amount of information, they can be interpreted in various ways. It all depends on your perspective. Take, for example, the following pie graph that comes from the 2000 census:

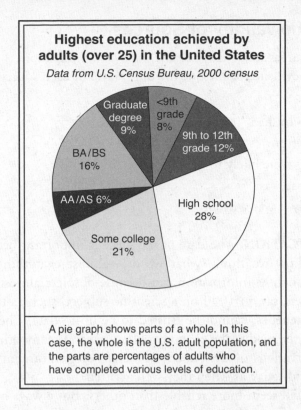

Highest education achieved by adults (over 25) in the United States

Data from U.S. Census Bureau, 2000 census

- Graduate degree 9%
- <9th grade 8%
- 9th to 12th grade 12%
- BA/BS 16%
- High school 28%
- AA/AS 6%
- Some college 21%

A pie graph shows parts of a whole. In this case, the whole is the U.S. adult population, and the parts are percentages of adults who have completed various levels of education.

Analyze what the graph tells you about the level of education of adults in the United States. In the spaces below, write three different conclusions that can be drawn from studying the graph:

1. _____

2. _____

3. _____

One of the more obvious things the graph shows is that the majority of American adults have finished high school. The graph also tells you that more than half the population has gone beyond high school but that more than one out of five students leave college before earning a degree. And so on.

If you were writing an essay on an issue related, say, to school dropouts, you might well focus on the two pieces of the graph that represent the 20 percent who failed to receive high school diplomas. One writer might conclude:

> It's shocking that one-fifth of American adults never finished high school.

Another writer, taking another point of view, might say:

> It's a tribute to America that eight out of ten adults have at least a high school education.

In other words, what you make of a visual source while writing your synthesis essay depends on the topic and your point of view on the issue.

Assessing the Validity of Sources

Because not all sources are equally reliable, it pays to think about their validity before tapping them for evidence to include in your essay. For each source, determine insofar as possible:

When it was published

Where it came from

Who its readers were likely to be

What its purpose was

How objectively it was written

DATE OF PUBLICATION. The date of the piece is important because facts, ideas, what we know, how we think, what we do—almost everything—is perpetually changing. Consequently, information can become obsolete almost before we know it. A source written, say, in 1990 on a scientific subject, such as the exploration of space or human genetics, cannot be trusted to be up-to-date. The same holds true for discussions of the media, the economy, lifestyles, and many other topics. On the other hand, observations of the American system of government written in 1837 may be just as valid today as when they were written.

Some sources will seem more reliable than others. But always be cautious. Don't believe everything you read, and don't depend too heavily on any single source in your essay.

PLACE OF PUBLICATION. A passage that comes from, say, a blogger's Web site, a supermarket tabloid, or the pen of a politician with an axe to grind can't be completely trusted. On the other hand, a passage taken from a scholarly journal, a report published by a foundation, a government document, a popular mass magazine, or a book written by a reputable author is likely to be more reliable. But frankly, there are no guarantees.

> **TIP**
>
> A passage from a blogger's web site can't be completely trusted.

THE INTENDED AUDIENCE. Authors almost always slant their writing to appeal to certain audiences. An article on children's health meant for a mass audience, for example, will be different from an article directed at subscribers to a pediatrics journal. Likewise, an author writing for an audience of nursing home residents will include certain material that would be inappropriate in a publication read mostly by college students. Knowing the intended audience, then, can help you weigh the validity of any source.

AUTHOR'S PURPOSE. An essay you write for school will be different from an email letter you write to a friend, mainly because the reason for writing is different. Every piece of writing has one or more purposes. Think of all the possibilities: to inform, to entertain, to anger, to provoke, to inspire, to move, to convince, to calm down, to compliment, to declare love, and on and on. Knowing why an author has written a particular passage helps you figure out how trustworthy it is.

TONE AND LANGUAGE. Check the source for objectivity. If the author expresses a view in rational terms and supports the idea with sound evidence—even if you don't agree with it—you can pretty well count on the reliability of the material. A source full of passion and inflammatory language, on the other hand, should not be accepted at face value.

For example, which of the following reports of a fire is a more reliable source of information?

> #1: At 3:30 p.m. on September 21, the Bedford Fire Department received a call that a residence at 330 Holly Road was on fire. Ten minutes later, the first fire truck arrived at the site and found a conflagration on an unfinished porch. Firemen promptly extinguished the fire. Damage was limited to the wood frame of the unfinished structure. The cause of the fire is yet to be determined.

> #2: Charlotte Robbins, a 36-year-old widow and mother of four young children wept profusely as she surveyed the charred ruins of the unfinished porch outside her Bedford home last weekend.
>
> "Poor Fred, he would have been devastated," she sobbed, referring to her husband, a disabled mechanic, dead only three weeks, whose dream had long been to build a porch for his loving family. "Why, oh, why did this happen to me?" Charlotte asked, but no one could answer. The cause of the fire remains a mystery, but the misery and heartbreak it caused for Fred's survivors is readily apparent.

The contrast between these two passages is easy to detect. The first account states just the facts; the second gushes with emotion. Sources used for the synthesis essay won't often be as extreme as these sample passages. But you can be sure that analyzing the tone and language of the sources will help you determine their validity.

How to Write a Synthesis Essay

Don't be misled by the heading of this section. It promises more than it can deliver. The reason is that no one learns to master essay writing by reading about how to do it. You learn to write masterful essays by writing essays, by messing around with ideas and words, by experimenting, practicing, and doing. Many of the essays you've written in English, social studies, and other classes have probably been good practice for writing a synthesis essay. And if you've ever written a research paper containing a thesis you had to prove, you've already done it.

In a sense, this AP essay is a mini-research paper. You are given a topic and sources to study. You must devise a thesis and bring in evidence to support it. The AP guidelines require that in one way or other you refer to **at least three** of the sources. In addition, you may use your own knowledge, observations, and experience to support your point of view. In fact, you shouldn't rely solely on the sources. An essay derived partly from your own thinking about the issue stands a greater chance for a top score because your own ideas add a layer of depth that would be absent from an essay drawn completely from the sources.

> **TIP**
>
> Use your own experience **and** the sources in your essay.

WRITING AN ARGUMENT

To write an argumentative essay, follow the same steps recommended for writing analytical essays: pre-writing, composing, editing, and proofreading—all discussed earlier in this book (*see Chapter 4, page 105*). But take note: The process may be similar, but argumentative essays also impose a unique set of demands, including:

- Introducing your position
- Supporting your position with appropriate evidence
- Refuting opposing viewpoints
- Avoiding faulty reasoning
- Incorporating sources
- Citing sources

INTRODUCING YOUR POSITION

Nothing weakens an argument more than an fuzzy, overly-complicated position statement. Therefore, make your position crystal clear with precise, unambiguous language. No rule says that a position statement is limited to a single sentence, although that's not a bad idea. A concise declarative sentence that focuses the reader on the issue may do the trick.

For example, let's assume that a synthesis essay topic deals with the effects of gambling. The issue is whether positive aspects of gambling outweigh its harmful effects, or whether the reverse is true—that gambling causes more harm than good. After weighing the evidence, a student claims:

Gambling is an activity that affects the lives of millions of Americans.

Well . . . the problems with that position statement nearly jump off the page. Just count its flaws:

1) It's too broad.

2) It fails to state a position or express the writer's opinion.

3) It's not arguable (no reasonable person would disagree with it).

4) It ignores the issue raised by the question.

In short, its weaknesses disqualify it as a viable position statement.

Now, look at another position statement on the same topic:

The economic effects of gambling are generally positive.

This position statement works. Why?

1) It's specific enough to be the topic of a short paper.

2) It expresses the writer's opinion.

3) Its controversial—worthy of an argument.

4) It addresses the issue raised by the question.

> ### Use of Qualifying Words
>
> Notice the word *generally* in the position statement, "The economic effects of gambling are generally positive."
>
> *Generally* is a qualifying term that makes the statement less dogmatic. Without the word, the statement implies that gambling *always* has a positive effect on the economy, a claim that is hard to defend and nearly impossible to prove. Just a single exception would destroy its credibility. When you write a position statement, therefore, consider making the claim more difficult to challenge by including an appropriate qualifier, such as *almost, frequently, generally, in most cases, likely, often, might, maybe, probably, sometimes, customarily*, and so forth.

WHERE TO PUT YOUR POSITION STATEMENT

Ordinarily, an essay's thesis or main idea is stated early in the essay. How early? It can be the first sentence, or part of the first sentence, although creating a context for the thesis is often a desirable thing to do. That is, before stating your thesis, search through the sources for interesting ideas that you can adapt for an opening that will draw readers into your essay. Then, consider any of the following introductory techniques, or use one that you've invented.

1. Begin with a brief incident or anecdote related to the point you plan to make in your essay:

    > Until Harrah's introduced casino gambling, Joliet, an Illinois steel town 40 miles from Chicago, was a depressed place, with high unemployment, low wages, and slum conditions. With the coming of the casino, the city enjoyed a remarkable economic rebirth. Jobs were created, opportunities for businesses multiplied, and the place became a magnet for investment in new housing, businesses, restaurants, and motels. While gambling is known to harm millions of Americans, the revitalization of Joliet demonstrates that *its overall effect on a community can nevertheless be positive.* (Thesis statement in italics.)

2. State a provocative idea in an ordinary way or an ordinary idea worded in a provocative way:

    > Gambling casinos pay higher wages to their employees than almost any other businesses except salmon fisheries in Alaska. *In spite of its potential for positive economic effects, however, the gambling industry harms American society more than it helps.* (Thesis statement in italics.)

3. Use a quotation from the prompt, from one of the sources, or from your reading, your experience, your grandmother:

> "All you need is a dollar and a dream." These catchy words have enticed millions of gullible New Yorkers into throwing their money away with the hope that they'll win the state lottery. *Because low-income people play the Lottery more often than well-off people, the lure of gambling harms them more than it does others.* (Thesis statement in italics.)

4. Knock down a commonly held assumption, or define a word in a startling new way:

> Last February, when Sophie Whittaker, a waitress in St. Louis, Missouri, eagerly boarded a Mississippi River boat for an evening of playing slot machines, she had no idea that *winning* really meant *losing.* She won five hundred dollars that night and came back the next weekend to win some more. But the gambling gods had other ideas. Sophie lost, and lost big. To make up for losing nearly a thousand dollars, she returned a few nights later. Two days later she went back once more, and then again and again, sometimes calling in sick to her boss in order to spend the evening hoping for a jackpot. She won a few dollars now and then but slid ever deeper into debt, pulled down by her new-found addiction. Sophie's experience is not unique. Hers is but one of countless similar stories about Americans who have *surrendered to the gambling habit, an unquestionable plague on American society.* (Thesis in italics.)

5. Ask an interesting question or two that you'll answer in the essay:

> Why have Native Americans fought so hard in Washington for the right to run casinos on their tribal lands? The answer is simple. Casinos make their owners rich. In addition, gambling profits can pay the bills for schools, hospitals, roads, and other needs. In effect, *in the right circumstances gambling does more good than harm.* (Thesis in italics.)

An introduction invites your readers into the essay. It enriches the essay and adds a layer of depth, suggesting that your essay hasn't been written merely to fulfill the assignment, but that it has been prepared with care and thought.

But if none of these techniques for writing introductions works for you, or you don't have the time to devise another, just state your position up front. Don't phrase your position like an announcement, however, as in, "In this essay, I am going to prove that gambling does greater harm than good." State your point, as in "Gambling does greater harm than good," and go from there.

SUPPORTING YOUR POSITION WITH APPROPRIATE EVIDENCE

Each paragraph in your essay should contribute to the development of the main idea. It should contain facts, data, examples—reasons of all kinds to corroborate the thesis and to convince readers to agree with you. If you reread what you've written and find that the evidence fails to support the thesis, cross it out or revise it. Be ruthless! Even though you may admire your own words, give them the boot if they don't help to strengthen your case.

HOW MUCH EVIDENCE TO INCLUDE

A rule of thumb is that three distinct and relevant reasons will usually suffice to prove a point. Certainly three is better than one or two, but whether three is enough depends on the issue and the reasons that are cited.

It shouldn't be hard to support your main idea with three secondary ideas. Each of the three ideas may not demand an equal amount of emphasis, however. You might dispose of the weakest idea in just a few sentences, while the others require at least a paragraph or more. But whatever you emphasize, be sure that each idea is separate and distinct. Don't disappoint your readers with an idea that rehashes the first or second in different words. But regardless of the number of reasons, the argument will be weak if the reasons themselves are weak.

> **TIP**
>
> Find at least three distinct ideas to support your thesis.

Here's an outline written by a student in support a thesis that said *the effects of gambling on the economy are generally positive:*

Reason 1: Gambling occurs in many places, including the Internet.

Reason 2: If you can't afford to lose money, you shouldn't gamble.

Reason 3: The money you lose goes into someone else's pocket.

The outline contains three reasons, but they are trite and largely irrelevant to the writer's position statement. Only Reason 3 vaguely refers to the economic consequences of gambling. On the whole, evidence of this caliber would fail to make a sufficient case.

In contrast, analyze these three reasons:

Reason 1: Gambling casinos create jobs, especially in rural areas.

Reason 2: Casinos increase property values in surrounding areas.

Reason 3: Casinos attract tourists who spend money for food, lodging, and services.

Using these three distinct and relevant reasons, a writer could construct a sturdy argument, especially if the reasons are sensibly arranged.

The outline recommended for analytical essays (*see page 111*) will help you sort through your reasons, pick the best ones, and put them in 1-2-3 order of importance. Then decide which reason provides the strongest evidence. That reason may be listed first in your outline, but save it for last in your essay. Giving it away too soon diminishes the impact of the second and third reasons. In other words, it will help you work toward your best point, not away from it. By no means is this the only way to structure an argument, but it's one that works.

> **TIP**
>
> Save your best idea for last.

REFUTING OPPOSING VIEWPOINTS

Another decision you must make in writing a synthesis essay is whether to include a counterargument, or refutation—a paragraph or more that points out weaknesses in the evidence that may be used by someone who disagrees with your position. In order to write a counterargument, you must, of course, anticipate the arguments that a prospective opponent might use to support a point of view contrary to yours. Although it's not essential to present a counterargument, it's recommended, not only because it strengthens your position, but because a thoughtful counterargument adds punch to an essay that can't be achieved in any other way.

Let's return briefly to the issue of gambling and to the claim that the negative economic effects of gambling outweigh its positive effects. Here are three reasons that could be used to support that point of view:

> Reason 1: Gamblers squander money that has better uses, such as education, housing, family life, donations to charity, etc.
>
> Reason 2: Compulsive gambling is a disease that requires costly treatment to cure.
>
> Reason 3: Gambling drains community resources, such as the extra amount spent for law enforcement.

All the reasons sound valid enough, so how can they be refuted? Well, if you focus on Reason 3, you might begin by saying that it makes a good point, but it's not foolproof. You could argue that casinos generate considerable tax revenue that pays for additional law enforcement, or point out that gambling facilities tend to increase the price of nearby housing, thereby raising the standard of living in a community. Since wealthier people usually pay higher taxes, the community should have no trouble paying for a larger police force. While refuting claims made by your opposition, it's important to resist the temptation of tearing them to shreds. Your essay will seem far more rational and circumspect if you concede the possibility that one or two of the reasons offered by the opposition are at least somewhat valid.

WHERE TO PUT A COUNTERARGUMENT

There's no rule governing the location of counterarguments in an essay. Sometimes they belong near the end of an essay, just before the conclusion. At other times they fit better early in the essay. Counterarguments can also be discussed briefly in each paragraph. As you develop your case, anticipate opposing arguments and refute them then and there. In the end, the location of counterarguments is less important than the message they deliver: that your evidence is superior to that of the opposition.

AVOIDING FAULTY REASONING

Evidence must logically support your essay's main idea. To illustrate the point, let's consider a synthesis essay question on another issue—the issue of tracking, or ability grouping, a longtime controversy in high school education. Some educators argue that students make greater educational gains when they are grouped according to ability. Others claim that ability grouping does more harm than good.

To judge the quality of evidence, let's examine an argument that comes from an essay written in favor of ability grouping. The topic sentence of one of its paragraphs reads:

Intelligent and capable students are often bored in mixed classes.

What would you expect the writer of this statement to say next? From the following list, choose the sentence that provides the most logical and appropriate evidence in support of the topic sentence:

1. The quality of education improves when students are homogeneously grouped.

2. Bright students in mixed classes are often left waiting for slow students to catch up.

3. Pity the poor teachers tearing their hair out while trying to teach those godawful mixed classes.

4. No one with his head on straight supports mixed classes.

5. Homogeneous classes usually offer more intellectual stimulation.

All five sentences more or less relate to the subject of the essay. But not all of them offer a logical follow-up to the claim that mixed classes bore smart students.

1. In Sentence 1, the broad generalization for instance, raises issues far beyond the topic sentence.

2. Sentence 2 works well; it provides a relevant detail that supports the writer's view.

3. Sentence 3 is an emotional outburst that has no place in a rational discussion of the topic.

4. Sentence 4 contains inappropriate language that diverts the discussion away from the topic.

5. Sentence 5 provides a point that follows logically from the topic sentence.

Sentences 1, 3, and 4 illustrate three types of faulty reasoning that sometimes creep into essays: over-generalization, emotionalism, and distracting language. In your thinking and writing, try to avoid such pitfalls as well as these other types of faulty reasoning:

1. Irrelevant testimony:

    New York Yankee shortstop Derek Jeter says, "I hated mixed classes in high school."

    Is it logical to cite the classroom experience of a professional baseball player (or any other celebrity) in a serious educational argument?

> **TIP**
>
> Beware of over-generalizations, emotionalism, and inappropriate language.

2. Snob appeal:

> The best AP English students everywhere agree that ability grouping is the way to go.

There's nothing logical about this statement. It is a crude appeal to readers who think they are or wish to be members of an elite group. It adds nothing to a discussion of the pros or cons of ability grouping.

3. Circular reasoning:

> I favor ability grouping because it separates students with different skills and interests.

The fallacy here is that the writer has tried to justified a bias toward ability grouping simply by defining the term. Precisely why the writer prefers ability grouping remains unclear.

4. Absence of proof:

> Grouping has been studied time and again, but I have never seen proof that mixed grouping is educationally superior to ability grouping.

A writer's admitted lack of knowledge can never be logically used as evidence to support a claim.

5. Oversimplification:

> When you get right down to it, ability grouping is like life; people prefer to be with others like themselves.

It's neither logical nor helpful to reduce a controversial and complex issue to a simple platitude.

6. Telling only half the story:

> Ability grouping is better because it serves the educational needs of both the smartest and the slowest students.

The writer has ignored the mass of students in the middle.

7. Going to extremes:

> If ability grouping were abolished, the system of American education as we know it would no longer exist.

This sort of thinking suggests desperation. By offering only the most extreme position, the writer ignores all other possibilities.

INCORPORATING SOURCES

Instructions for the synthesis essay tell you to incorporate at least three sources into your essay. You may refer to more than three but you won't get any extra credit for doing so.

The simplest and most obvious way to use a source in your essay is to state your position and back it up with an idea pulled out of the source. Suppose, for example, that you are writing about the positive (or negative) effects of advertising on our lives, and you wish to make the point that it's virtually impossible to escape from the influence of ads.

One of the sources—call it *Source A*—discusses the growth of advertising in mid-20th century America. It contains this paragraph:

> The most important, and most multidimensional, of the forces shaping youth culture was mass communications . . . . Signs, billboards, store displays, supermarkets, the traditional media, and finally, the new, all-consuming, substitute environment, television, enveloped us in a cocoon of sensory information. I think it is doubtful that anyone who did *not* grow up in this postwar period can appreciate how much the senses of the young were bombarded, as they are today, by messages. Indeed, the media—in the broadest sense of the word—provided a new environment. To those who grew up in the new urban complexes, it virtually *was* the environment.

Ideas from this paragraph can be woven into an essay using any of the following techniques:

- Direct Quotes
- Indirect Quotes
- Paraphrasing
- Commentary

DIRECT QUOTES

Direct quotes are word-for-word reproductions of material found in a source. Everything—grammar, spelling, capitalization—must duplicate the original exactly, and the words must be enclosed in quotation marks:

> Even though most people are unaware of how completely surrounded they have become by advertising, it has an unbelievably profound influence on the environment. In fact, *"To those who grew up in the new urban complexes, it virtually* was *the environment."* (Source A).

If you wish to omit words from the original for grammatical or other reasons, use an ellipsis (. . .) consisting of three periods to mark the place where material has been deleted.

> I think it is doubtful that anyone who did *not* grow up in this postwar period can appreciate how much the senses of the young were bombarded . . . by messages.

If you find it necessary to add words for clarity or any other reason, enclose the words in brackets [like this]. Brackets inform readers that the bracketed words are not part of the original quotation.

> To those who grew up in the new urban complexes, it [advertising] virtually *was* the environment.

INDIRECT QUOTES

An indirect quote reports an idea without quoting it word-for-word. No quotation marks are needed.

> Even though most people are unaware of how completely surrounded they have become by advertising, it has an unbelievably profound influence on the environment. In fact, Source A claims that *it virtually <u>was</u> the environment to those who grew up in urban areas during the postwar period.*

A Word of Caution

In your essay, use direct and indirect quotations sparingly and only as illustrative material. Use them to support ideas that you have first stated in your own words. Although you may be tempted to use lots of quoted material to make your case, don't do it. Don't let quotes dominate your essay. After all, the AP exam is a test of *your* writing ability, not of your ability to quote others.

Notice how the author of the following paragraph relied too heavily on quotations:

Even though most people are unaware of how completely surrounded they have become by advertising, it has a unbelievably profound influence on the environment. *"Signs, billboards, store displays, supermarkets, the traditional media, and finally, the new, all-consuming, substitute environment, television, [have] enveloped us in a cocoon of sensory information. . . ."* It is clear that *"anyone who did not grow up in this postwar period can appreciate how much the senses of the young were bombarded, as they are today, by messages. Indeed, the media—in the broadest sense of the word—provided a new environment."*

PARAPHRASING

Paraphrasing is restating someone else's idea in your own words. A paraphrase contains the same information and should be roughly the same length as the original.

> Even though most people are unaware of how completely surrounded they have become by advertising, it has an unbelievably profound influence on the environment. *In fact, the author of Source A says that advertisements actually became the environment in which young people in cities grew up after the war.*

COMMENTARY

The sources provided on the exam are meant to give you information and to stimulate your thinking about the issue. They also give you ideas to discuss in your essay. With a little practice, you can learn to pick material from a source, transfer it verbatim to your essay, adapt it, or shape it any way you want to build your main idea. But to write a more distinctive essay, one that reveals your ability to interpret and analyze source material, try not only to draw from the sources but also to comment on them. Think of the sources as a one-sided conversation with the authors. Once the authors have their say, it's your turn to respond by commenting on their ideas, their reasoning, their points of view.

Thus, it would be perfectly appropriate to incorporate sources with such comments as:

"The author of Source B offers a short-sighted view of . . ."

"To a point I agree with the author of Source B, although he doesn't carry the argument far enough. To strengthen his case, he should have included . . . ."

"In Source B, the author says that . . . , an assertion that supports my own views. I would add, however, that . . ."

"Clearly, the author of Source B has a bias against . . ., a failing that weakens her argument."

Notice that you need not comment only on sources with which you agree. Feel free to quarrel with authors who ideas differ from yours. Show that they are all wet, out to lunch, or have loose screws—but please use more refined language than that. Avoid name-calling (*moron, airhead, ignoramus,* etc.) and exclamations such as, "That's the dumbest idea I've ever heard!" Refuting the opinions of others can bolster an argument, but treat even wrongheaded opinions with respect.

CITING SOURCES

In your essay, you must cite the source of all direct and indirect quotations. Custom also requires you to give credit to any source from which you borrow, paraphrase, or adapt ideas.

Don't bother to cite the source of everyday factual material that's known by most literate, reasonably alert people. No citation is needed, for example, if you draw from the sources the information that the United States is a republic, that Thanksgiving falls on the fourth Thursday in November, or that most kids like to stay up late at night.

Many different formats exist for citing sources, but on the AP exam you need no more than a brief parenthetical reference within the text of your essay, as in:

According to a school psychologist, "Some children may be better off if they escape their parents' grip, healthier if they grow up wild and free and sort things out on their own" (Source A).

Instead of writing *Source A* inside the parenthesis, you may insert the last name of the author, as in

One panel member summed up the conflict by saying, "Young people want a larger share in the decision-making about their lives" (Collins).

(Note that the end punctuation comes after the close of the parentheses and outside the quotation marks.)

Another technique for naming sources is to integrate the information more fully into the text, as in

> Dean Marcy Denby argues that "the basic purpose of a university education has always been . . . etc."

Which method you use to cite sources on the AP exam is up to you. It's probably better to choose one method and stick to it. Using a variety can make you appear indecisive, maybe even confused.

The Problem of Plagiarism

The one basic rule about plagiarism is this: **Don't do it!**

Why? For one thing, it's dishonest, immoral, and it can get you into a whole mess of trouble. Intentional or not, plagiarism is theft. Stealing someone else's words or ideas and passing them off as your own is, to put it bluntly, a stupid thing to do.

To avoid even the slightest hint of plagiarism on the AP exam, give credit to your sources. It's simple: Whenever you take words or ideas from a source, identify their origin inside a pair of parentheses: *(Source B), (Jones), or ("Title")*. If you forget, your essay score will suffer. Even a brilliant essay that might otherwise earn an 8 or 9 may receive a score of 2 or 3 if you fail to document sources. When in doubt about the need to document a particular idea in your essay, play it safe and smart. Err on the side of inclusion, not exclusion.

Sample Synthesis Essay Question

What follows is a sample synthesis essay question. It is followed by the essays of three students. The essays were handwritten under testing conditions: a time limit of 55 minutes and no access to a computer, a dictionary, or any other book. By reading the essays you'll see what it takes to earn a high score. Read the comments, too. They'll alert you to some pitfalls to avoid when you write a synthesis essay of your own.

(SUGGESTED TIME—
15 MINUTES FOR READING
THE QUESTION AND SOURCES,
40 MINUTES FOR WRITING AN ESSAY)

Instructions: The following essay topic is accompanied by six sources.

Respond to the question below in a well-written, coherent essay that draws on ideas and information found in **at least three** of the sources. Don't simply summarize or paraphrase the sources. Instead, **focus the essay on your point of view,** and use the sources to support or bolster your argument.

Topic: The right to privacy is a fundamental right in a free society. Yet, public figures—from politicians to athletes to entertainers—often have their private lives revealed by the media. Is this fair? Shouldn't celebrities enjoy as much privacy as ordinary citizens? Or should they expect to pay a price for fame by having details of their private lives made public? Is the public's right to know stronger than the right of celebrities to maintain their privacy?

Your task: Read the following sources carefully. **Then, in an essay that synthesizes at least three of the sources, take a position that supports, denies, or modifies the claim that celebrities have the same right to privacy enjoyed by ordinary citizens.**

In your essay, you may refer to the sources simply as Source A, Source B, etc., or by the authors listed below.

Source A (Hilden)
Source B (McElroy)
Source C (DeGrandpré)
Source D (Chart)
Source E (GNL)
Source F (Committee on Freedom of the Press)

SOURCE A

Julie Hilden, *Does Celebrity Destroy Privacy?* published by FindLaw, an online legal news and commentary site for lawyers, businesses, students, and consumers.

The passage below is an excerpt from an article entitled "Is Disclosure of Private Facts About Celebrities Justified?" written in 2002 by Julie Hilden, an attorney and columnist.

Often, it is the intensely private aspects of a celebrity's life—involving drugs, sex, or sexual orientation, marital discord, issues with children or other family members, or similar topics—that the public and the media deem newsworthy. (Illegality only ratchets up the stakes, and increases interest in the story.) But is the public entitled to know such private details about a celebrity, just because that person is a public figure?

Two basic theories are used to justify the exposure of celebrity privacy. One is the "waiver theory," which holds that celebrities have given up their privacy by choosing to appear in the public eye. Those who believe in this theory see celebrities as having made a sort of Faustian bargain: lifelong fame in exchange for the lifelong loss of privacy.

Another widely cited argument for celebrities having forfeited their privacy is what I will call the "hypocrisy theory." It holds that celebrities who, in their statements to the public, have lied about or deceptively omitted a private fact about themselves cannot then complain when the truth becomes known.

Neither of these theories is entirely valid, but the "waiver" theory is by far the weaker of the two. It seems somewhat unfair to say that because a person's gift lies in acting, basketball, or singing, rather than, for example, engineering, architecture, or computer science, that he or she has somehow "chosen" to give up all of his or her privacy.

Indeed, it seems likely that personality type, rather than profession or experience, may often be the best determinant of how painful and damaging a privacy breach will be to a particular person.

SOURCE B

Wendy McElroy, "Clinton and Privacy," published by the Ludwig von Mises Institute, located online at *www.mises.org*.

The following passage is excerpted from an article written in September 1998 during the scandal involving President Bill Clinton and a young White House intern, Monica Lewinsky.

In his four-minute address to the nation that followed his grand jury testimony of August 17th, President Clinton repeatedly made a specious claim: namely, that he has a right to privacy concerning his sexually inappropriate relationship with former White House intern Monica S. Lewinsky. "[I]t is private," he declared. "Now this matter is between me, the two people I love most, my wife and our daughter, and our God…It is nobody's business but ours."

. . . Yet the truth is: President Clinton has no right to privacy—politically, morally, or legally—on the Lewinsky matter. There are at least two political reasons why Clinton has no claim to privacy regarding Lewinsky. First, he has vigorously pursued a policy of using the images of his personal life when they are to his political advantage. From throwing frisbees to his puppy Buddy to dancing on the beach with Hillary in what was widely regarded as a staged display, Clinton has used the media to "leak" his personal life to the American public. Or, rather, he has leaked those images that present him as a man of the people, as a loving husband and father, as just folks.

Having shrewdly used his personal life to further his political career, Clinton cannot object when others question whether the carefully scripted images are accurate. Just as Clinton betrayed associates who accumulated heavy legal bills and endangered their credibility in order to defend him against valid accusations, if Clinton hides behind privacy he will be betraying Democratic candidates in the upcoming election.

SOURCE C

Vincent M. DeGrandpré, "Understanding the Market for Celebrity: An Economic Analysis of the Right of Publicity," published online by Simpson, Thacher & Bartlett, LLP, September 15, 2001.

The following passage is an excerpt from a monograph prepared by a New York law firm.

. . . But what explains the public's interest in celebrities? Several theories have been formulated to explain this phenomenon, of which we can retain a few promising ones. In his provocative work *Life: The Movie*, Neal Gabler argues that entertainment, and the movies in particular, have become so important to our individual existence that American public life itself has evolved to resemble the movies. Gabler argues that this trend has reshaped every sphere of human activity from politics to religion to the arts, all because of the need for these activities to rival readily available entertainment in keeping public attention. Not only have moving pictures become the central metaphor for understanding American public life, they have changed our epistemology, the very understanding of the world in which we live. According to Gabler, we now live in the "lifies." This "lifies" metaphor not only captures the reality that Americans use a significant portion of their income to be entertained; it conveys the idea that we have populated our lives with celebrities, those lead actors whose stories we eagerly watch and weave into our lives.

Our urge to know and associate with celebrities is not only motivated by our desire to be entertained, however. As one author notes, "celebrities have become, in recent decades, the chief agents of moral change in the United States." They have come to embody abstract issues of points of view, and are shorthand forms for ideals or expertise. Theorists have also argued that celebrities attract us because we see them as individuals who stand out in our anonymous, mass society. We seek them because they make us feel in-the-know or on the inside; in our mass society, they humanize our lives. "Stars" attract us because they seem to be free, on-the-go and liberated from the constraints of daily life.

Not surprisingly, Gabler, like others, has argued that the identity of modern Americans is shaped not only by their intimate relationships, but also by their only-superficially intimate ones with well-known personalities. As Kenneth Gergen writes, "[W]e may know more about Merv, Oprah, Johnny, and Phil than we do our neighbors." Consider, for example, the outpouring of sympathy and the personal grief suffered by so many on the death of Princess Diana . . . . As far as movies stars are concerned [says Gergen]:

> It is undoubtedly true that for many people film relationships provide the most emotionally wrenching experience of the average week. The ultimate question is not whether media relationships approximate the normal in their significance, but whether normal relationships can match the power of artifice.

As a result, celebrities have become a sort of "social glue," allowing people from different points of society to converse, to share feelings and essentially to carry on informal relations. In this view, then, the demand for celebrity images and information is driven in large part by society's communication needs and by our respective need to forge personal identity.

SOURCE D

Adapted from "Average Circulation for Top 100 ABC Magazines," Magazine Publishers of America © 2006 Magazine Publishers of America

The table below shows the average circulation of several magazines, listed according to their ranking among the 100 most popular publications.

Rank	Title	Average Circulation Per Issue
1	AARP Magazine	22,675,655
3	Reader's Digest	10,111,773
12	People*	3,734,027
17	Playboy	3,060,376
32	US News & World Report	2,028,167
53	Teen People*	1,525,409
59	STAR*	1,428,767
74	National Enquirer*	1,239,967
87	New Yorker	1,053,019
91	Business Week	986,549
100	Forbes	926,581

*Publications focusing on celebrities

"STAR serves the dish that feeds our insatiable appetite for celebrity news, delivering the makeups, the breakups, the extraordinary and ordinary moments in the lives of the people we most want to watch."

—STAR MediaKit 2006

SOURCE E

GNL, "For Today's Public Figures, Private Lives Really Matter," *Buzzle.com.*, *Intelligent Life on the Web*, November 30, 2004.

The passage below is adapted from an article published in an online British periodical, of general interest to contemporary readers.

Ask yourself this question: do you really—and I mean really—believe that modern politicians are entitled to a private life?

The claim to privacy sounds so reasonable and so right, and at first sight indeed it is. Most of us are not politicians or public figures of any kind, but we all have a clear notion of the difference between our own public lives—where we are answerable to all—and our private ones—where we are answerable only to ourselves and to those closest to us. How much more necessary, we reason, must it be for public figures, exposed to so much more scrutiny, to maintain that distinction?

Why should partners and children have to be in the public eye, we wonder, our decent instincts once again to the fore. Why should the public be entitled to know where the famous go on holiday, or go to dinner, or what they spend their money on? And why, some even assert, do we have any right to know about their private mistakes and their sexual secrets? Nobody denies that such things are often interesting, but surely that is not the point. Would we not all be happier people living in a better society if we drew the line?

. . . [T]he awkward truth is that the way people live their private lives does tell us things that can help to make judgments about them as public people. Their sex lives may be less indicative here than less conveniently dramatic things like how they get on with their children or what they do with their spare time. I'm not sure which is more illuminating: the fact that Tony Blair likes going on holiday in Tuscany or the fact that Gordon Brown doesn't. But each tells me something that I'm glad to know.

That is not the same as saying that the world will only be put to rights if it is run by certified saints. This country was seen through two world wars by leaders who would certainly not qualify on that score; but whatever the human failings of a Lloyd George or a Churchill, they did not include an inability to get the job done.

Crucially, though, the British people were protected from any knowledge of LG's sex life or Churchill's drinking when it mattered. But if today's leaders are to receive the same protection, both they and we will have to renounce habits and instincts that have become second nature. Perhaps that ought to happen, but it seems unlikely that it will.

SOURCE F

"Invasion of Privacy," *First Amendment Handbook*, The Reporter's Committee for Freedom of the Press, Arlington, Virginia, 1992.

The passage below appears in a handbook about freedom of the press written for professional journalists.

The concept of a right to privacy was first articulated in an 1890 Harvard Law Review article by Louis Brandeis and Samuel Warren. It took American courts 15 more years to recognize it. The Georgia Supreme Court was the first to do so in *Pasevich v. New England Life Insurance Co.*, a case involving the use of an individual's photograph without his permission in a newspaper advertisement.

Today, almost every state recognizes some right of privacy, either in statutory or common law. Most state laws attempt to strike a balance between the individual's right to privacy and the public interest in freedom of the press.

. . . Public figures also have a limited claim to a right of privacy. Past and present government officials, political candidates, entertainers, and sports figures are generally considered to be public figures. They are said to have voluntarily exposed themselves to scrutiny and to have waived their right of privacy, at least in matters that might have an impact on their ability to perform their public duties.

Although private individuals can usually claim the right to be left alone, that right is not absolute. For example, if a person who is normally not considered a public figure is thrust into the spotlight because of her participation in a newsworthy event, her claims of a right to privacy may be limited.

A right of privacy can be violated by any means of communication, including spoken words. This tort is usually divided into four categories: intrusion, publication of private facts, false light, and misappropriation.

Sample Student Responses

Whitney's Response
(Typed as it was written)

In dentists waiting rooms and magazine racks all across the United States is <u>People Magazine</u>, one of the most popular magazines in America. The public likes to read about famous people. They are curious about who is going out with who and who is getting divorced or having children. They enjoy photos of movie stars going shopping at the Safeway or visiting Disney World or just walking down the street or washing dishes. That helps them identify with the stars who do the everyday activities of life. It makes them think that being famous is not that big of a deal because even celebrities have to take out the garbage once in a while. In addition when we think of celebrities as just plain folks like us, we "feel in-the-know or on the inside." (Source C) In a way, imagining that we really "know" famous people, the writer of Source C says, in our mass society, celebrities "humanize our lives" by making us feel important.

A problem takes place when the famous person wants to maintain privacy. He or she has the right to do that but the public also has the right to try to find out as much as they want about celebrities. If a famous person wants privacy, they have to take steps to get it. As an example, J.D. Salinger the author of <u>Cather in the Rye</u>. For many years he has escaped in the mountains of Vermont since he wants no part of a public life. He gives no interviews and refuses to show his face in public.

However, Salinger is an exception. Lots of famous people say they want privacy but their actions are not in that direction. As an example, Bill Clinton, former President of the US told the country in August, 1998, that his relation with Monica, his intern, was none of our business. However, as president, everything he does and says is our business. He was elected to his office by the people, and the people have a right to know everything about him. McElroy (Source B) describes some of the images that Clinton chose to make public, such as playing with his puppy on the beach. What McElroy says is true, that Clinton didn't have the right to choose which parts of his personal life would be "leaked" to the public and which aspects were out of bounds. GNL, the author of Source E seemed to agree when he wrote "The way people live their privat lives does tell us things that can help to make judgments about them as public people."

It's not as important to know facts about famous athletes and movie stars, but many of them willingly let themselves be photographed and probably encourage reporters to write stories about them. They even hire publicists to attract attention to themselves. Many people would die for a chance to have their names and faces in the paper. Some people even do heinous things in search of their fifteen minutes of fame. They go on a shooting rampage like the boys at Columbine HS, or could assassinate a famous figure, like the killer of John Lenon. On a less extreme scale they could put themselves through degrading and humiliating experiences on reality television, all for the chance to be noticed or considered out of the ordinary. Some people say that the desire to be different or nonconforming is part of human nature. However, once they make a name for themselves, they often find that fame is not all that great after all.

Once a person has made an effort to become famous, they have given up their rights of privacy. This so-called "waiver theory (Source A) makes sense. It says that the choice that celebrities make to become public figures, they trade privacy for fame. Since nobody forces them to make this "Faustian bargain" (Source A), they have to accept that the eye of the people will be on them all the time and they have no right to complain.

Your impressions: _____

_____

_____

_____

Comment to Whitney
from an AP Reader

You engage your reader immediately by showing that the issue of your essay is current and widespread. By explaining both the desire and the rewards of knowing about famous people, you provide a context for your thesis statement at the beginning of the second paragraph. To support your point of view, you cite examples not only from the sources but from your own fund of knowledge, and set up a particularly apt contrast between the behavior of J.D. Salinger and Bill Clinton. In various ways throughout your essay, you emphasize the public's psychological need to know about the lives of famous figures. That emphasis leaves unaddressed the issue of the public's right to know, although you imply that a *need* to know is tantamount to the *right* to know.

Let me commend you for making the most of your references. You cite the source of the ideas, of course, but also enter into a kind of dialogue with some of the authors. You remark, for example that what "McElroy says is true," and that the "waiver theory" found in Source A "makes sense." This technique astutely integrates the sources into the text of your essay and helps the authors of the sources effectively participate in the development of your main point.

Another strength of your essay is that it discusses issues surrounding the pursuit of fame, including some people's extraordinary efforts to achieve it. The examples you choose are quite startling and lead seamlessly and convincingly to your conclusion that those who have sought fame have no right to complain when their privacy is violated.

Overall, the essay demonstrates your maturity as a thinker. The writing, however, is another story. It contains some sentence errors and a few awkward uses of language. Also, the point of the paragraph about people's craving for fame seems to wander from the essay's main idea. These flaws are relatively minor but they keep the essay from earning the highest possible score. Score: 8

Sonya's Response
(Typed as it was written)

The right to privacy is important. If you know that everthing you do is being watched, you can't be free to do what you like. It is like you are a prisoner which is not right in a free country like ours. This affects especially famous people because they are the ones most watched and put under a microscope by photographers, fans, and reporters.

Source A says, "It seems unfair to say that because a person's gift lies in acting, basketball, or singing, rather than, for example, engineering, architecture, or computer science, that he or she has somehow "chosen" to give up all of his or her privacy." I believe that a person should be free. A person who is a celebrity is entitled to the same freedom as everyone else. Just because a person is a fashion model or a baseball player doesn't mean they should not have the freedom to do what they choose to do.

Source C says that "Stars attract us because they seem to be free, on-the-go and liberated from the constraints of daily life." That statement is not true for many stars. They can't go out without being surrounded by crowds of people. Just to go out of the house requires a plan to trick the photographers and the people who write gossip columns. Just to go to the store for a loaf of bread means avoiding cameras and microphones waiting outside. This is not being free. Its more like an animal trapped inside in a cage in my opinion.

If you read the chart in Source D, it reveals that celebrity magazines sell several millions of copies. To fill up the pages of People and STAR magazine, which are just two examples, many reporters and photographers are hired to watch celebrities. They are basically professional stalkers. An ordinary person can keep their lives private if they want to. Movie stars and other celebrities don't have that right, and that's wrong. In our country everybody is supposed to be equal. I wouldn't go so far as to say that famous people are not equal, but with little right to privacy, equality is much harder to achieve for them.

In conclusion, it is easy for someone to look up to a famous person with envy of their money, looks, house, car, and their lifestyle. But the next time you are tempted to do that, imagine that you are walking in their shoes and you will see that privacy is too valuable to give up.

Your impressions: _____

_____

_____

_____

Comment to Sonya
from an AP Reader

By stating your thesis early and often, you leave no doubt about where you stand on the issue of privacy for celebrities. Your essay's unity, therefore, is one of its obvious strengths, and perhaps a weakness, too. Each paragraph restates the notion that lack of privacy leads to lack of freedom, unquestionably a thoughtful idea. But by limiting yourself to that single notion, you oversimplify the whole right-to-privacy issue and miss a chance to discuss it in depth.

The sources you cite are closely linked to your thesis, but they shape your argument. By leaning on them too heavily, you have abandoned control of the discussion. It would have been preferable to state your positions and then integrate source material as supporting evidence instead of relying on sources for the topic and the starting point of each paragraph.

Your essay follows the popular five-paragraph structure. For that you cannot be faulted, although it turns what could be a fresh and scintillating essay into something more conventional. As it should, the final paragraph brings closure to the essay, but at the same time it raises a new issue—that privacy is too precious to give up for the trappings of celebrity. This is an observation worth pondering, but is only tangentially related to your essay's main concern, the right to privacy. Score: 5.

Ricky's Response
(Typed as it was written)

People like Michael Jackson, Tom Cruise and Jennifer Anniston are celebrities always on TV and in the newspaper. But who cares about their drug habit, sex life, marriage problems, issues with children or other family members, or similar topics? I know I don't. If I asked my friends they would not care either.

When Clinton was president he had a affair with Monica Levinsky. He said I did not have sex with that woman. Some people believed it and some people called Clinton a liar. I did not matter whether he was or not. He declared "Now this matter is between me, the two people I love most, my wife and our daughter and our God. It is nobody's business but ours."

Since the president's sex life is nobody's business, Brad Pitt's romance with —— (forget her name) Jolie is also noone else's business and Brad Pitt is less important than the president. If the people cared about Clinton's sex life they did not have to vote for him, even though he was elected two times.

The question I ask is what explains the public's interest celebrities? The author Neal Galber says that movies are so important that our lives resemble movies, so naturally we are interested in celebrities. We see them as outstanding individuals and so we want to know how they got that way. One author said, they humanize our lives, which means they make us more human. Even so their privacy is not our business so we should stay away from them. When they want to become more popular, some do outrageous things and want their photographs in the paper. Sometimes they put their home addresses on the web. Most of the time they are just regluar people trying to get along, so we should leave them alone.

Your impressions: _____

_____

_____

_____

Comments to Ricky from an AP Reader

Your essay deserves a low score mainly because it lacks unity and fails to synthesize any of the sources. To be sure, you clearly make the point the private lives of celebrities don't matter to you. Yet, you explain that we are curious about celebrities because they are outstanding in some way. At the end you contradict yourself again by declaring that celebrities are "just regular people." Despite the overall incoherence of these and other ideas, the essay, contains occasional insights—your discussion of Neal Gabler's theory, for example. But they remain under-developed and get lost in the confusion.

Your failure to synthesize sources is a particular shortcoming. Synthesis requires documentation of the sources cited. Although some of your ideas are drawn from the sources, you give them no credit. Using others' ideas without acknowledgment is unacceptable in an AP essay. Score: 2

Answer Key to Mini-Workouts

MISPLACED AND DANGLING MODIFIERS, PAGE 128

Answers may vary.

1. The bowling alley lends out shoes of all sizes to its customers.

2. An old bike we planned to put in the trash was given to a junk man.

3. When I was ten, my family and I emigrated from Guatemala to the U.S.

4. Having found me sound asleep at noon, my mother thought I was sick.

5. After totaling the car beyond repair, Allison knew she'd have to buy another one.

6. Correct

7. Used all night to illuminate the steps, the flashlight needed new batteries.

8. A report was submitted by the police about the latest bank heist. (The original sentence is correct if the police have been busy robbing banks.)

9. Pausing for a drink of water after the hike, I found a grizzly bear standing in front of me.

10. The schoolbus picked me up at the corner after I had a quick breakfast.

MINI-WORKOUT: PARALLEL STRUCTURE, PAGE 132

Answers will vary.

1. but explains that it's all right to seek help

2. An easier and more direct route

3. plays forward on the basketball team

4. go out to eat

5. both angry and disappointed

6. better than taking a sailboat

7. knocked down not only the tree

8. and party with friends

9. The mouse will either find a quick way into the attic or gnaw

10. and amazingly entertaining

ACTIVE VERBS, PAGE 134

Answers will vary.

1. Monica and Phil scored highest on the practice AP exam.

2. Color determines my choice of bedroom rug.

3. Logic dictates that a student's effort and achievement govern college admission.

4. The Revolutionary War ended the monarchy.

5. Threats to democracy multiplied after 9/11.

6. The word "chaos" applies to my math class.

7. Mr. Gill scares everyone.

8. The next corridor leads to the principal's office.

9. Some students excel in chemistry but not in physics.

10. The librarian recommended this novel.

REVISING PASSIVE SENTENCES, PAGE 136

Answers will vary.

1. Dead leaves covered the back yard.

2. We discussed the situation in Lebanon.

3. Because I had been at a play rehearsal every night that week, I failed the quiz.

4. We flew to Portland at the start of our weeklong vacation in Oregon.

5. Jason and the Argonauts pursued the Golden Fleece.

6. Rex fetched the newspaper every morning.

7. Immigration officials decided to build a fence on the border.

8. More than 20 diners on Saturday night ordered pizza.

9. Our group saw five of Shakespeare's plays in three days.

10. The candidate urged the voters to throw the rascal out of office.

CUTTING NEEDLESS WORDS, PAGE 139

Part A

Answers may vary.

1. Mary Roe wrote *A Ride Across America*, a book about her cross-country bike ride. To train for her feat, she biked 90 miles a day.

2. My suggestion for making meetings more productive and relevant to all students needn't offend the chairperson, Carolyn Welles.

3. Even though he spent six months in prison for embezzlement, Mr. Evans was appointed treasurer of the group.

4. Harmful criticism hurts more than it helps.

5. By reducing unnecessary driving, Americans everywhere can save gasoline.

Part B

Avoiding discrimination is but one of many reasons for people to gain weight, according to Stanford University graduate Slim Snyder, who, at a recent conference on health, said, "Lean people are victims of discrimination, just as obese people are." Fortunately, many up-to-date weight-gaining procedures are widely available. But they are ridiculed and kept well hidden because health experts agree that being lean is preferable to being obese.

WRITING SPECIFICALLY, PAGE 142

Answers will vary.

1. Missy earned a 5 on the AP English exam.

2. Mr. Gray insists that students study an hour every night, that they be punctual to class, and that they regard math as the epitome of logical thinking.

3. When I told Ms. Cronin that I'm kept from doing homework by driving my brother to piano lessons or Little League, by yearbook meetings on Tuesdays, by work for Peer Leaders and SADD, and by my part-time job at the florist, she muttered, "That's *your* problem."

4. "Get out of my face," Carrie snarled as she punched the Tigers' goalie in the nose.

5. Mitchell's reward for six hours at his desk studying chemistry was a big fat F on the quiz.

6. After winning by a 3 to 1 margin, the senator-elect grinned from ear to ear and told her supporters that she was ready to work in their behalf.

7. Countries bordering the Indian Ocean dump garbage, sewage, and other hazardous waste products into the sea.

8. In science we talk about experiments, but we can't do them because we don't have any equipment.

9. Joey and Teddy, the family twins, couldn't go out at the same time until they were 16 because they shared the same pair of shoes.

10. She met with little success during her high school career.

11. The acceptance letter thrilled my parents. Their worried looks suddenly disappeared, they stopped nagging me about homework, and because the question had been answered, they never again asked what would become of me.

WRITING CORRECT SENTENCES, PAGE 147

Answers may vary.

1. Amy is stressed out about the garbage in the back yard.

2. St. Petersburg was renamed Leningrad after the Russian Revolution. Its original name was restored in the 1990s.

3. My grandmother is 86 years old; therefore, she walks very slowly.

4. During the night, the stars came out like diamonds on black velvet.

5. Correct

6. This year's senior class is more involved than last year's.

7. The American colonists hated the King's tax on British tea; they drank Dutch tea instead.

8. June found the squirrel lying dead in a ditch, but she didn't tell Henry.

9. A biologist working in the field of genetic engineering can get involved in the controversy surrounding human cloning.

10. Correct

NOUN-VERB AGREEMENT, PAGE 150

1. was stuck	The subject is *line*, a singular noun.	
2. has given	The construction *either…or* needs a singular verb.	
3. is meeting	The subject *Board* is a singular noun.	
4. is expected	The subject is *price*, a singular noun.	
5. which has	The pronoun *which* refers to *service*, a singular noun.	
6. There are	The subject is *levels*, a plural noun.	
7. are going	The subject *Proceeds* is a plural noun.	
8. is expected	The noun *team* to which the verb refers is singular.	
9. are to be	The subject *guards* is plural.	
10. have not been	The noun *promises* is plural.	

VERB TENSES, PAGE 153

1. feels	6. were
2. visited	7. No error
3. asks	8. had stayed
4. No error	9. had given
5. had seen	10. expected

ADJECTIVES AND ADVERBS, PAGE 155

1. sincerely	6. Correct
2. shy	7. Correct
3. badly	8. securely
4. easily	9. cynically
5. calm	10. bitter

PRONOUN CHOICE, PAGE 158

1. me
2. correct
3. me
4. He and I
5. us

6. we
7. his falling
8. correct
9. him
10. he

PRONOUN REFERENCE, PAGE 160

Answers will vary.

1. Martha loves knitting and spends most of her spare time doing it.
2. Mike answered the test questions and handed them in. Then he collected his pens and pencils.
3. In *The Great Gatsby* Fitzgerald writes about the American Dream.
4. Correct
5. When teens loiter outside the theater on Friday night, the police give you a hard time.
6. Bob was told by his father, "I have only an hour to get to the airport?"
7. Frankie aspires to play major league baseball someday.
8. Rob wants to go to Annapolis because he has a part-time job at the boatyard and spends every summer on the water.
9. Correct
10. After the interview, Mike told Tom, "I think Colgate University is a good place for you to spend the next four years."

PRONOUN AGREEMENT, PAGE 162

Answers will vary.

1. all the students in the class
2. its policy
3. its collection
4. has her own room
5. Correct
6. as she could
7. write them down . . . and hand them in
8. All the horses
9. its first match.
10. The person elected to the class presidency will find the faculty and administration cooperative and supportive.

PUNCTUATION, PAGE 165

A. POSSESSIVES

1. Paul's	6. Andersons'
2. America's	7. Correct
3. Correct	8. Morris'
4. women's	9. computers'
5. girls'	10. month's

B. COMMAS AND SEMICOLONS

1. While Buddy was riding, his bike got a flat tire.

2. The mail carrier did not leave the package, for Valerie was not at home.

3. After doing homework, Mikey, as you might expect, talked on his cell phone for an hour.

4. His work criticized many commonly-held beliefs, however, and it was strictly censored.

5. The car that ran into mine at the intersection was an SUV.

6. I need street maps of Boston and Portland, Maine.

7. The people who live by the water must be prepared for occasional flooding.

8. The boat was 75 feet long and 18 feet wide; its mast was about 80 feet tall.

9. To anyone interested in flying, planes hold endless fascination.

10. Jeff and Steve, left alone for the weekend, invited all their friends to a party.

CAPITALIZATION, PAGE 167

1. On Labor Day Bennington County's fire department plans to hold a turkey shoot on the field at Miller's Pond.

2. The judge gave District Attorney Lipman a book entitled *The Rules of Evidence* and instructed her to read it before she ever dared set foot in the Court of Appeals of the Ninth Circuit again.

3. The secretary of state greeted the president of Austria at the Ronald Reagan Airport in Washington, D.C.

4. The Shackleton expedition nearly met its doom on Georgia Island in Antarctica.

5. For Christmas he got a Black & Decker table saw from the Sears store next to the Old Bedford Courthouse.

6. According to Georgetown's high school principal, Eugene Griffiths, Georgetown High School attracts students from the whole West Coast. At Georgetown students may major in drawing and painting, design, graphics, or sculpture. Mr. Griffiths said, "I attended a similar high school in New England just after the Vietnam War."

7. We expect to celebrate New Year's Eve again this year by renting a movie of an old Broadway musical and by settling down in front of the DVD player with some Pepsi and a box of Oreos.

8. After traveling all the way to the Pacific, the Corps of Discovery rode down the Missouri River going east on their way back to St.Louis.

9. This irish linen tablecloth was bought at K-Mart in the Emeryville Mall off Powell Street.

10. Yellowstone National Park is located in the northwestern corner of Wyoming.

Practice Tests

CHAPTER 5

- Four full-length tests for practice
- Simulating test conditions
- Why the right answers are right
- How to score your essays
- Calculating your total AP test score

INSTRUCTIONS: Each test in this section lasts three hours and 15 minutes.

As you take each test, allow yourself one hour to answer the multiple-choice questions. Use the answer sheet provided.

Then take a five-minute break and answer the essay questions. Write your essays on standard 8½" × 11" composition paper. Allow yourself 40 minutes each for Essays 1 and 2. For Essay 3, allot 15 minutes to read the sources and 40 minutes to write the essay.

When you are finished, check your answers with the Answer Key that follows each exam. Read the answer explanations for both the questions you missed and those you answered correctly.

To rate your essays, use the Self-Scoring Guide provided with each test.

Worksheets are also provided at the end of each test to help you determine your total score.

Practice Test A
ANSWER SHEET

Multiple-Choice Questions Time—1 hour

1. Ⓐ Ⓑ Ⓒ Ⓓ Ⓔ	21. Ⓐ Ⓑ Ⓒ Ⓓ Ⓔ	41. Ⓐ Ⓑ Ⓒ Ⓓ Ⓔ
2. Ⓐ Ⓑ Ⓒ Ⓓ Ⓔ	22. Ⓐ Ⓑ Ⓒ Ⓓ Ⓔ	42. Ⓐ Ⓑ Ⓒ Ⓓ Ⓔ
3. Ⓐ Ⓑ Ⓒ Ⓓ Ⓔ	23. Ⓐ Ⓑ Ⓒ Ⓓ Ⓔ	43. Ⓐ Ⓑ Ⓒ Ⓓ Ⓔ
4. Ⓐ Ⓑ Ⓒ Ⓓ Ⓔ	24. Ⓐ Ⓑ Ⓒ Ⓓ Ⓔ	44. Ⓐ Ⓑ Ⓒ Ⓓ Ⓔ
5. Ⓐ Ⓑ Ⓒ Ⓓ Ⓔ	25. Ⓐ Ⓑ Ⓒ Ⓓ Ⓔ	45. Ⓐ Ⓑ Ⓒ Ⓓ Ⓔ
6. Ⓐ Ⓑ Ⓒ Ⓓ Ⓔ	26. Ⓐ Ⓑ Ⓒ Ⓓ Ⓔ	46. Ⓐ Ⓑ Ⓒ Ⓓ Ⓔ
7. Ⓐ Ⓑ Ⓒ Ⓓ Ⓔ	27. Ⓐ Ⓑ Ⓒ Ⓓ Ⓔ	47. Ⓐ Ⓑ Ⓒ Ⓓ Ⓔ
8. Ⓐ Ⓑ Ⓒ Ⓓ Ⓔ	28. Ⓐ Ⓑ Ⓒ Ⓓ Ⓔ	48. Ⓐ Ⓑ Ⓒ Ⓓ Ⓔ
9. Ⓐ Ⓑ Ⓒ Ⓓ Ⓔ	29. Ⓐ Ⓑ Ⓒ Ⓓ Ⓔ	49. Ⓐ Ⓑ Ⓒ Ⓓ Ⓔ
10. Ⓐ Ⓑ Ⓒ Ⓓ Ⓔ	30. Ⓐ Ⓑ Ⓒ Ⓓ Ⓔ	50. Ⓐ Ⓑ Ⓒ Ⓓ Ⓔ
11. Ⓐ Ⓑ Ⓒ Ⓓ Ⓔ	31. Ⓐ Ⓑ Ⓒ Ⓓ Ⓔ	51. Ⓐ Ⓑ Ⓒ Ⓓ Ⓔ
12. Ⓐ Ⓑ Ⓒ Ⓓ Ⓔ	32. Ⓐ Ⓑ Ⓒ Ⓓ Ⓔ	52. Ⓐ Ⓑ Ⓒ Ⓓ Ⓔ
13. Ⓐ Ⓑ Ⓒ Ⓓ Ⓔ	33. Ⓐ Ⓑ Ⓒ Ⓓ Ⓔ	53. Ⓐ Ⓑ Ⓒ Ⓓ Ⓔ
14. Ⓐ Ⓑ Ⓒ Ⓓ Ⓔ	34. Ⓐ Ⓑ Ⓒ Ⓓ Ⓔ	54. Ⓐ Ⓑ Ⓒ Ⓓ Ⓔ
15. Ⓐ Ⓑ Ⓒ Ⓓ Ⓔ	35. Ⓐ Ⓑ Ⓒ Ⓓ Ⓔ	55. Ⓐ Ⓑ Ⓒ Ⓓ Ⓔ
16. Ⓐ Ⓑ Ⓒ Ⓓ Ⓔ	36. Ⓐ Ⓑ Ⓒ Ⓓ Ⓔ	
17. Ⓐ Ⓑ Ⓒ Ⓓ Ⓔ	37. Ⓐ Ⓑ Ⓒ Ⓓ Ⓔ	
18. Ⓐ Ⓑ Ⓒ Ⓓ Ⓔ	38. Ⓐ Ⓑ Ⓒ Ⓓ Ⓔ	
19. Ⓐ Ⓑ Ⓒ Ⓓ Ⓔ	39. Ⓐ Ⓑ Ⓒ Ⓓ Ⓔ	
20. Ⓐ Ⓑ Ⓒ Ⓓ Ⓔ	40. Ⓐ Ⓑ Ⓒ Ⓓ Ⓔ	

Practice Test A

SECTION 1

Total time—1 hour

PASSAGE 1

Questions 1–13. Carefully read the following passage and answer the accompanying questions.

The passage below is from a memoir published in the mid-20th century.

You can live a lifetime and, at the end of it, know more about other people than you know about yourself. You learn to watch other people, but you never watch yourself because you strive against loneliness. If you read a
Line book, or shuffle a deck of cards, or care for a dog, you are avoiding your-
(5) self. The abhorrence of loneliness is as natural as wanting to live at all. If it were otherwise, men would never have bothered to make an alphabet, nor to have fashioned words out of what were only animal sounds, nor to have crossed continents—each man to see what the other looked like.

Being alone in an aeroplane even for so short a time as a night and a day,
(10) irrevocably alone, with nothing to observe but your instruments and your own hands in semi-darkness, nothing to contemplate but the size of your small courage, nothing to wonder about but the beliefs, the faces, and the hopes rooted in your mind—such an experience can be as startling as the first awareness of a stranger walking by your side at night. You are a
(15) stranger. It is dark already and I am over the south of Ireland. There are the lights of Cork and the lights are wet; they are drenched with Irish rain, and I am above them and dry. I am above them and the plane roars in a sobbing world, but it imparts no sadness to me. I feel the security of solitude, the exhilaration of escape. So long as I can see the lights and imagine the
(20) people walking underneath them, I feel selfishly triumphant, as if I have eluded care and left even the small sorrow of rain in other hands.

It is a little over an hour now since I left Abingdon, England. Wales and the Irish Sea are behind me like so much time used up. On a long flight distance and time are the same. But there had been a moment when Time
(25) stopped—and Distance too. It was the moment I lifted the blue-and-silver Gull from the aerodrome, the moment the photographers aimed their cameras, the moment I felt the craft refuse its burden and strain toward the earth in sullen rebellion, only to listen at last to the persuasion of stick and elevators, the dogmatic argument of blueprints that said she *had* to fly

(30) because the figures proved it. So she had flown, and once airborne, once she had yielded to the sophistry of a draughtsman's board, she had said, "There, I have lifted the weight. Now, where are we bound?"—and the question had frightened me.

(35) We are bound for a place thirty-six hundred miles from here—two thousand miles of it unbroken ocean. Most of the way it will be night. We are flying west with the night.

So there behind me is Cork; and ahead of me is Berehaven Lighthouse. It is the last light, standing on the last land. I watch it, counting the frequency of its flashes—so many to the minute. Then I pass it and fly out to sea.

(40) The fear is gone now—not overcome nor reasoned away. It is gone because something else has taken its place; the confidence and the trust, the inherent belief in the security of land underfoot—now this faith is transferred to my plane, because land has vanished and there is no other tangible thing to fix faith upon. Flight is but momentary escape from the eternal

(45) custody of earth. . . .

(1942)

1. The rhetorical function of the first sentence (lines 1–2) is best described as

   (A) an assertion against which the entire passage argues
   (B) a piece of common wisdom that the passage will illustrate
   (C) a paradox that the passage will analyze and explain
   (D) the moral of the story that the author is about to tell
   (E) an example that supports the main idea of the passage

2. The author uses all of the following phrases to illustrate the notion of the "abhorrence of loneliness" (line 5) EXCEPT

   (A) "live a lifetime" (line 1)
   (B) "watch other people" (line 2)
   (C) "read a book" (lines 3–4)
   (D) "care for a dog" (line 4)
   (E) "make an alphabet" (line 6)

3. In line 9, the phrase "Being alone" is structurally parallel to the phrase

   (A) "your instruments" (line 10).
   (B) "your own hands" (lines 10–11).
   (C) "nothing to wonder about" (line 12).
   (D) "such an experience" (line 13).
   (E) "the first awareness of a stranger" (line 14)

4. In lines 9–14 of the passage, the author uses an analogy between

    (A) being alone and thinking about the future
    (B) darkness and ignorance
    (C) being brave and contemplating one's beliefs
    (D) flying solo and discovering yourself
    (E) a person's hands and an airplane's instruments

5. The rhetorical purpose of switching from second person to first person in line 15 is primarily to

    (A) explain the meaning of "You are a stranger" (lines 14–15)
    (B) indicate that the author has not been talking about herself in paragraphs 1 and 2
    (C) give an example of the "abhorrence of loneliness" (line 5)
    (D) show that the narrator speaks from first-hand experience about issues raised in paragraphs 1 and 2
    (E) inform the reader that the narrator is an accomplished pilot

6. In paragraph 3 (lines 22–33), which of the following rhetorical devices is most prominent?

    (A) Emphasizing sensual imagery
    (B) Using abstract generalizations
    (C) Mixing facts and impressions
    (D) Appealing to authority
    (E) Employing periodic sentences

7. The tone of the passage as a whole can best be described as

    (A) reflective and philosophical
    (B) objective and informational
    (C) academic and pedantic
    (D) effusive and tumultuous
    (E) terse and impersonal

8. The function of the phrase "sobbing world" (lines 17–18) is primarily to

    (A) describe the rain outside the airplane
    (B) suggest the pulsating sounds of the airplane engine
    (C) explain the sadness of lonely people everywhere
    (D) explain the author's sympathy for the Irish people far below
    (E) indicate that flying serves as a release from everyday cares

9. The sentence in lines 23–24 ("On a long . . . same") has all of the following functions EXCEPT

    (A) to present information about the way pilots think
    (B) to introduce the anecdote that follows in lines 25–30
    (C) to illustrate how pilots on long flights sometimes become disoriented
    (D) to help to contrast the tedium of flying with the thrill of the take-off
    (E) to explain the phrase "like so much time used up" (line 23)

10. The author's observation in lines 24–25 that "Time stopped—and Distance too" is best described as an example of

   I. hyperbole
   II. ironic contrast
   III. mixed metaphor

   (A) I only
   (B) III only
   (C) I and III only
   (D) II and III only
   (E) I, II, and III

11. In the description of the take-off (lines 25–30) the author employs all of the following EXCEPT

   (A) paradox
   (B) parallel structure
   (C) personification
   (D) repetition for emphasis
   (E) shift of pronouns

12. In context, the expression "to fix faith upon" (line 44) is best interpreted as having which of the following meanings?

   (A) To be victorious
   (B) To feel secure
   (C) To gain a sense of direction
   (D) To speed up
   (E) To have the courage of one's convictions

13. The passage as a whole can best be described as

   (A) an extended metaphor
   (B) a metaphysical allegory
   (C) a sentimental evocation of an episode
   (D) an objective narrative
   (E) a personal interpretation

(Questions 14–23) Read the following passage carefully and then answer the questions.

The passage is the text of a newspaper column published in the latter part of the 20th century.

PASSAGE 2

PARRIS ISLAND, S.C.—He is seething, he is rabid, he is wound up tight as a golf ball, with more adrenalin surging through his hypothalamus than a cornered slum rat, he is everything these Marine recruits with their
Line heads shaved to dirty nubs have ever feared or even hoped a drill instructor
(5) might be.

He is Staff Sgt. Douglas Berry and he is rushing down the squad bay of Receiving Barracks to leap onto a table and brace at parade rest in which none of the recruits, daring glances from the position of attention, can see any more of him under the rake of his campaign hat than his lipless mouth

(10) chopping at them like a disaster teletype: WHEN I GIVE YOU THE WORD YOU WILL WALK YOU WILL NOT RUN DOWN THESE STEPS WHERE YOU WILL RUN YOU WILL NOT WALK TO THE YELLOW FOOTMARKS. . . .

Outside, Berry's two junior drill instructors, in raincoats over dress

(15) greens, sweat in a muggy February drizzle which shrinks the view down to this wooden World War II barracks, to the galvanized Butler hut across the company street, the overground steam pipes, a couple of palmetto trees, the raindrops beading on spitshined black shoes. Sgt. Hudson mans the steps, Sgt. Burley the footmarks. They pace with a mannered strut, like men wear-

(20) ing white tie and tails, their hands folded behind their backs, their jaw muscles flexing. One senses there's none of the wisecracking "See Here, Private Hargrove," or "Sgt. Bilko" Army routine here, no hotshot recruits outsmarting dumb sarge for passes to town.

In fact, during his 63 days of training at Parris Island, unless a member

(25) of the immediate family dies, a recruit will get no liberty at all. He will also get no talking, no phone calls, no books or magazines, no television, radio or record players, no candy or gum, one movie, one newspaper a week, and three cigarettes a day. Unless he fouls up, gets sent to the brig or to motivation platoon, and loses the cigarettes.

(30)   WHEN I GIVE YOU THE WORD TO MOVE OUT YOU WILL MOVE OUT DO YOU UNDERSTAND ME? Hudson meets the first one at the steps like a rotary mower ripping into a toad, so psyched he's actually dancing on tiptoe, with his face a choleric three-quarters of an inch from the private FASTER PRIVATE FASTER JUST TAKE YOUR

(35) DUMB TIME SWEETHEART MOVE! MOVE! as this hog, as recruits are colloquially known, piles out of the barracks in a stumble of new boots, poncho, laundry bag and the worst trouble his young ass has ever been in, no doubt about it when Burley meets him just like Hudson, in an astonishment of rage that roars him all the way down to the right front set of yel-

(40) low footprints YOU LOCK YOUR BODY AT ATTENTION YOU LOCK YOUR BODY. . . .

Or maybe Burley writhes up around this private to hiss in his ear—and Burley is very good at this—*you hate me, don't you, you hate me, private, you'd better hate me because I hate you,* or any of the other litanies drill

(45) instructors have been barking and hissing at their charges ever since the first of more than one million Parris Island graduates arrived on the flea-ridden sand barren in 1911.

Until there are 60 of them out there in the drizzle with the drill instructors shouting themselves hoarse, 60 volunteers who had heard from count-

(50) less older brothers and street corner buddies and roommates that it would be exactly like this but they volunteered anyhow, to be Marines.

Right now, with lips trembling, eyes shuttling YOU BETTER STOP THAT EYE-BALLING, PRIVATE! fat and forlorn, they look like 60 sex perverts trapped by a lynch mob. They are scared. They are scared as frater-
(55) nity pledges during a cleverly staged hell week, shaking like boys about to abandon their virginity.

It's a primal dread that drill instructors invoke and exploit in eight weeks (soon to revert to the pre-Vietnam 11 weeks) of folk theater, a spectacle staged on the scale of the Passion Play at Oberammergau, an initiation that
(60) may be the only true rite of passage to manhood that America hasn't yet scoured away as an anthropological anachronism.

(1972)

14. Several sections of the passage appear in capital letters and with almost no punctuation. This can be explained by all of the following reasons EXCEPT

(A) to suggest the volume at which the words are uttered
(B) to indicate a staccato-like manner of speech
(C) to convey the intensity with which the words are spoken
(D) to separate spoken words from narration and description
(E) to heighten dramatic effect

15. In line 8, "daring" modifies

(A) "Berry" (line 6)
(B) "squad bay" (line 6)
(C) "table" (line 7)
(D) "none" (line 8)
(E) "recruits" (line 8)

16. In paragraph 3 (lines 14–18), which of the following rhetorical devices is most in evidence?

(A) Expressionism
(B) Metonymy
(C) Figures of speech
(D) Impressionistic descriptive prose
(E) Visual imagery

17. The principal contrast employed by the author in the passage is between

(A) Sgt. Berry and Sgt. Burley
(B) the drill instructors and the recruits
(C) the reality of boot camp and sitcom versions of military life
(D) modern military training and World War II training
(E) basic training and fraternity hazing

18. The main rhetorical function of the description of Hudson and Burley (lines 19–21) is to

    (A) set the stage for material in the next paragraph
    (B) reinforce a description given earlier in the passage
    (C) prepare for the contrast made in the following sentence
    (D) provide support for a thesis proposed in the first paragraph
    (E) introduce humor into the passage

19. The point of view expressed in "In fact . . . day" (lines 24–28) is that of

    (A) the author
    (B) the recruits
    (C) the Marine Corps
    (D) Sgt. Hudson
    (E) Sgt Berry

20. To create the greatest effect, all of the following rhetorical techniques are used in lines 42–47 EXCEPT

    (A) repetition
    (B) use of highly connotative verbs
    (C) evocation of historical tradition
    (D) vivid adjectives
    (E) subordinate clause set off by dashes

21. In the last paragraph, (lines 57–61), which of the following words is parallel in function to "dread" (line 57)?

    (A) "theater" (line 58)
    (B) "weeks" (line 57)
    (C) "initiation" (line 59)
    (D) "manhood" (line 60)
    (E) "anachronism" (line 61)

22. The passage as a whole might best be described as

    (A) a parable of modern life
    (B) a melodramatic evocation
    (C) a parody
    (D) a dramatic monologue
    (E) an exposé

23. Which of the following best captures the author's attitude toward the events and people described in the passage?

    (A) "Outside . . . barracks" (lines 14–16)
    (B) "One senses . . . town" (lines 21–23)
    (C) "Hudson meets . . . tiptoe" (lines 31–32)
    (D) "They are scared" (line 54)
    (E) "an initiation . . . anachronism" (lines 59–61)

Questions 24–35. Carefully read the following passage and answer the accompanying questions.

This is an excerpt from an essay published in a scholarly journal in the 20th century.

PASSAGE 3

Exile is strangely compelling to think about but terrible to experience. It is the unhealable rift forced between a human being and a native place, between the self and its true home: its essential sadness can never be sur-
Line mounted. And while it is true that literature and history contain heroic,
(5) romantic, glorious, even triumphant episodes in an exile's life, these are no more than efforts meant to overcome the crippling sorrow of estrangement. The achievements of exile are permanently undermined by the loss of something left behind forever.

Exiles look at non-exiles with resentment. *They* belong in their surround-
(10) ings, you feel, whereas an exile is always out of place. What is it like to be born in a place, to stay and live there, to know that you are of it, more or less for ever?

* * *

Although it is true that anyone prevented from returning home is an exile, some distinctions can be made between exiles, refugees, expatriates,
(15) and émigrés. Exile originated in the age-old practice of banishment. Once banished, the exile lives an anomalous and miserable life, with the stigma of being an outsider. Refugees, on the other hand, are a creation of the twentieth-century state. The word "refugee" has become a political one, suggesting large herds of innocent and bewildered people requiring urgent
(20) international assistance, whereas "exile" carries with it, I think, a touch of solitude and spirituality.

Expatriates voluntarily live in an alien country, usually for personal or social reasons. Hemingway and Fitzgerald were not forced to live in France. Expatriates may share in the solitude and estrangement of exile, but they do
(25) not suffer under its rigid proscriptions. Émigrés enjoy an ambiguous status. Technically, an émigré is anyone who emigrates to a new country. Choice in the matter is certainly a possibility. Colonial officials, missionaries, tech- nical experts, mercenaries, and military advisers on loan may in a sense live in exile, but they have not been banished. White settlers in Africa, parts of
(30) Asia, and Australia may once have been exiles, but as pioneers and nation- builders the label "exile" dropped away from them.

Much of the exile's life is taken up with compensating for disorienting loss by creating a new world to rule. It is not surprising that so many exiles seem to be novelists, chess players, political activists, and intellectuals. Each
(35) of these occupations requires a minimal investment in objects and places a great premium on mobility and skill. The exile's new world, logically enough, is unnatural and its unreality resembles fiction. George Lukács, in *Theory of the Novel,* argued with compelling force that the novel, a literary form created out of the unreality of ambition and fantasy, is *the* form of

(40) "transcendental homelessness." Classical epics, Lukács wrote, emanate from settled cultures in which values are clear, identities stable, life unchanging. The European novel is grounded in precisely the opposite experience, that of a changing society in which an itinerant and disinherited middle-class hero or heroine seeks to construct a new world that somewhat resembles an

(45) old one left behind forever. In the epic there is no *other* world, only the finality of *this* one. Odysseus returns to Ithaca after years of wandering; Achilles will die because he cannot escape his fate. The novel, however, exists because other worlds *may* exist, alternatives for bourgeois speculators, wanderers, exiles.

24. The second sentence of the passage, "It is the unhealable . . ." (lines 1–4) functions in all of the following ways EXCEPT

    (A) defining the word "exile"
    (B) introducing the author's attitude toward exile
    (C) highlighting the horrors of exile
    (D) limiting the subject matter of the passage
    (E) developing the emotional tone of the passage

25. Which of the following characteristics of exile are most emphasized in paragraph 1?

    (A) Permanence and bleakness
    (B) Variety and peculiarity
    (C) Risks and rewards
    (D) Burdens and complexities
    (E) Escape and loss

26. The attitude of the author toward exiles is primarily one of

    (A) sympathy.
    (B) superiority.
    (C) pity.
    (D) scorn.
    (E) indifference.

27. The primary rhetorical function of the last sentence in paragraph 2 ("What is it like . . .more or less forever?") is to

    (A) indicate that the author is an authority on the subject of the passage.
    (B) raise the question that the author intends to answer in the next paragraph.
    (C) provide an illustration of exiles' feelings and thoughts.
    (D) define and clarify ideas presented in paragraphs 1 and 2.
    (E) ask a rhetorical question that cannot be answered.

28. In lines 14–29, which of the following best describes the rhetorical strategy used by the author to clarify the meaning of the term, "exile"?

    (A) providing several connotations attached to the word
    (B) comparing it with other terms for people separated from their homes
    (C) recounting the experience of several specific exiles
    (D) analyzing the basic causes and effects of exile
    (E) contrasting the "exile" in reality with "exiles" portrayed in fiction and epic poetry

29. The author mentions settlers in Africa, Asia, and Australia (lines 29–30) chiefly as examples of

    (A) voluntary exiles
    (B) colonists
    (C) mercenaries
    (D) refugees
    (E) military adventurers

30. The sentence structure of the last sentence of paragraph 4 (lines 32–34) is most similar to the sentence structure of

    (A) the first sentence of paragraph 1 (line 1)
    (B) the first sentence of paragraph 3 (lines 13–15)
    (C) the last sentence of paragraph 3 (lines 18–21)
    (D) the seventh sentence of paragraph 4 (lines 27–29)
    (E) the second sentence of paragraph 5 (lines 33–34)

31. Which of the following best describes the first sentence in paragraph 5 (lines 32–33)?

    (A) The author's interpretation of why some people leave their homelands permanently
    (B) A reference to the similarity between "exile" and "banishment"
    (C) A statement of the main idea of the paragraph that follows
    (D) A review of the content of the discussion so far
    (E) A more specific restatement of a generalization made in the previous paragraph

32. In the sentence "Classical epics . . . life unchanging" (lines 40–41) which of the following words is parallel in function to "unchanging" (line 41)?

    (A) "Classical" (line 40)
    (B) "settled" (line 41)
    (C) "values" (line 41)
    (D) "clear" (line 41)
    (E) "life" (line 41)

33. The author's allusion to classical epics (lines 40–49) serves primarily to

    (A) show that the phenomenon of exile has existed for a long time
    (B) review the history of exile
    (C) contrast epic tales with European novels
    (D) describe a major theme of classical literature
    (E) emphasize the courage of classical heroes

34. The description of a hero or heroine seeking to "construct a new world" (line 44) contributes to the unity of the passage in which of the following ways?

    (A) As a restatement of the idea expressed by "efforts meant to overcome the crippling sorrow of estrangement" (line 6)
    (B) As a contrast to the exiles' feeling "out of place" (line 10)
    (C) As an allusion to Hemingway and Fitzgerald (line 23)
    (D) As a parallel to sharing in "the solitude and estrangement of exile" (line 24)
    (E) As an echo of "investment in objects and places" (line 35)

35. The passage as a whole can best be characterized as

    (A) a tribute to exiles
    (B) an analysis of the problems faced by exiles
    (C) an objective report on exiles
    (D) a literary appreciation of exiles
    (E) a sociological study of exiles

Questions 36–44. Carefully read the following passage and answer the accompanying questions.

The passage is an excerpt from a 20th-century book.

PASSAGE 4

Both the city and the Italian Colony were progressing steadily when the 1906 earthquake and fire struck. San Francisco had been razed by fires six times from 1849 to 1851, and each time the ruins had been swept away and
Line the city rebuilt in a much finer fashion. This time, however, the damage was
(5) far too extensive. The tragedy was compounded by the great number of people and buildings which were concentrated along the path of the fault.[31]

The destruction caused by the earthquake and the ensuing fire in the Italian Quarter resulted in the complete loss of the district. The Italian Quarter, as other parts of the city hit by the disaster, had been reduced to
(10) a knotted, tangled mass of bent steel frames, charred bricks, and ashes. In North Beach, only a small part of the community remained. The Italians on Telegraph Hill had been luckier than most, although they suffered losses since insurance companies were not interested in insuring remote areas of the Hill. The scattered fire hydrants and water cisterns were not to be found
(15) east of Dupont Street and the insurance companies were not willing to

gamble. It was reported in the Italian press that some 20,000 Italians lost their homes in the conflagration.[32]

One of the priests from the church of Sts. Peter and Paul had managed to save the consecrated host, vestments, and holy vessels[33] and said Mass
(20) under the inflamed sky. After the fires had died, the Italians quietly returned to North Beach and tried to find the confidence to rebuild Little Italy.[34]

Approximately five to six hundred Italians had definitely left San Francisco due to this tragic event, while over six thousand new immigrants
(25) arrived and helped the survivors clear the ruins. Seven hundred building permits were granted to North Beach Italian residents and businessmen[35] to expedite the construction of the Colony. Several real estate firms, such as the J. Cuneo Company in North Beach, demonstrated their confidence in the determination of the Italians by investing $400,000 in the reconstruc-
(30) tion of apartments, stores, flats, and business offices.[36]

Temporary buildings were cheaply erected for immediate occupancy, while the leaders of the Colony were busily engaged in drawing up plans for a modern Little Italy. The buildings would be simple, small, neat, and airy, which combined both functional and classical lines.[37] One writer
(35) described this new architecture as a reflection of the Italian immigrants' acceptance of American ways.[38] The most picturesque features of the flats and apartments were the roof-top sun decks with flower gardens.[39] Part of the planning for the new Colony included the renaming of two of the main thoroughfares of the Italian Quarter. In 1907, one-half of Dupont Street
(40) was renamed Grant Avenue, and by the end of 1908 all of Dupont became Grant Avenue. By 1910, Montgomery Avenue was renamed Columbus Avenue and still retained its fame as "The Avenue." The changes in these street names denoted a change in the geographic character of the Italian Quarter.

---

[32] *"La Infernale Catastrofe de San Francisco,"* L'Italia, *p. 1. April 1906.*

[33] *"The Frightful Calamity on the Pacific Coast,"* Leslie's Weekly, *102:418. May 3, 1906.*

[34] *"La Riconstruzione de San Francisco,"* La Voce del Popolo, *p, 1. May 12, 1906.*

[35] *"Facts and Figures Worthy of Consideration,"* L'Italia, *p. 1. April 28, 1906.*

[36] *"J. Cuneo Co."* L'Italia, *July 2, 1906. In deposit, Bank of America NT&SA Archives, San Francisco.*

[37] *"Curious Tour of City Leaves Telegraph Hill for Fisherman's Wharf,"* San Francisco Chronicle, *p. 12. Feb. 16, 1932.*

[38] *Peixotto,* Scribner's, *48:82. July, 1910.*

[39] *J.M. Scanland, "On the Roofs of the Latin Quarter,"* Overland Monthly, *57:330. March, 1911.*

36. The speaker's main focus in the passage is

    (A) the effects of the 1906 San Francisco earthquake on the Italian community
    (B) the economic consequences of the 1906 San Francisco earthquake and fire
    (C) why Italians came to San Francisco after the 1906 earthquake
    (D) how the San Francisco earthquake transformed the Italian Colony
    (E) the courage and fortitude of Italians in San Francisco during the 1906 earthquake and fire

37. Which of the following describes the rhetorical purpose of the first paragraph (lines 1–6)?

    (A) It suggests that San Franciscans were unaware of the dangers of earthquakes.
    (B) It raises questions that will be discussed in the remainder of the passage.
    (C) It provides a thesis that will be challenged later in the passage.
    (D) It explains the uniqueness of the 1906 earthquake.
    (E) It introduces the reader to the intense emotion generated by the tragic events discussed in the passage.

38. The sequence of detailed images in line 10 are meant to illustrate all of the following EXCEPT

    (A) "The tragedy" (line 5)
    (B) "the fault" (line 6)
    (C) "The destruction" (line 7)
    (D) "complete loss" (line 8)
    (E) "the disaster" (line 9)

39. Which of the following best describes the primary rhetorical purpose of the sentence, "The scattered . . .to gamble" (lines 14–16)?

    (A) to develop an idea presented in the previous sentence
    (B) to provide background for understanding information contained in the next sentence
    (C) to specify the location where the earthquake did the greatest damage
    (D) to clarify the author's attitude toward insurance companies
    (E) to suggest that the earthquake destroyed the hydrants and water cisterns

40. Taken as a whole, the footnotes show that

    (A) it is crucial to consult published books while doing historical research
    (B) almost all news about the earthquake was reported in Italian by the Italian press
    (C) only a small amount of material about the earthquake was published after 1911
    (D) in doing historical research about an event, it is best to use work published close to the time the event occurred
    (E) the author of the passage relied heavily on sources contemporary to the earthquake

41. Which of the following is a proper interpretation of footnote 38 (line 36)?

    (A) The author found the material to be footnoted between pages 48 and 82.
    (B) *Scribner's* is the name of a book published in 1910.
    (C) The work by Peixotto has been cited in a previous footnote.
    (D) In 1910, Scribner's published Peixotto's book.
    (E) References to *Scribner's* can be found on pages 48 and 82 of an article by Peixotto.

42. The development of the passage can best be described as

    (A) an analysis of how people in 1906 reacted to misfortune and tragedy
    (B) a detailed examination of a group that shared a common heritage
    (C) a compilation of information about the effects of the earthquake
    (D) a narrative of the earthquake and its aftermath
    (E) an explanation of why the earthquake had been so damaging

43. Which of the following sources cited by footnotes 37–39 express a favorable view of the housing being planned for "a modern Little Italy" (lines 31–34) ?

     I. The source cited in footnote 37
    II. The source cited in footnote 38
    III. The source cited in footnote 39

    (A) I only
    (B) II only
    (C) I and III only
    (D) II and III only
    (E) I, II and III

44. Lines 39–41 contain which of the following?

    (A) An illustrative anecdote
    (B) Subordinate clauses
    (C) A single compound sentence
    (D) Antithesis
    (E) An extended metaphor

45. The tone of the passage is best described as

    (A) reverent but remorseful
    (B) disapproving but respectful
    (C) excited and energetic
    (D) unemotional and informative
    (E) admiring and awe-struck

Questions 46–55. Carefully read the following passage and answer the accompanying questions.

The passage is a segment of a book written early in the 20th century.

PASSAGE 5

In a recent bulletin of the Superintendent of the Census for 1890 appear these significant words: "Up to and including 1880 the country had a frontier of settlement, but at present the unsettled area has been so broken into
Line by isolated bodies of settlement that there can hardly be said to be a fron-
(5) tier line. In the discussion of its extent, its westward movement, etc., it cannot, therefore, any longer have a place in the census reports." This brief official statement marks the closing of a great historic movement. Up to our own day American history has been in a large degree the history of the colonization of the Great West. The existence of an area of free land, its con-
(10) tinuous recession, and the advance of American settlement westward, explain American development.

Behind institutions, behind constitutional forms and modifications, lie the vital forces that call these organs into life and shape them to meet changing conditions. The peculiarity of American institutions is the fact
(15) that they have been compelled to adapt themselves to the changes of an expanding people—to the changes involved in crossing a continent, in winning a wilderness, and in developing at each area of this progress out of the primitive economic and political conditions of the frontier into the complexity of city life. Said Calhoun in 1817, "We are great, and rapidly—I was
(20) about to say fearfully—growing!" So saying, he touched the distinguishing feature of American life. All peoples show development; the germ theory of politics has been sufficiently emphasized. In the case of most nations, however, the development has occurred in a limited area; and if the nation has expanded, it has met other growing peoples whom it has conquered. But in
(25) the case of the United States we have a different phenomenon. Limiting our attention to the Atlantic coast, we have the familiar phenomenon of the evolution of institutions in a limited area, such as the rise of representative government in complex organs; the progress from primitive industrial society, without division of labor, up to manufacturing civilization. But we
(30) have in addition to this a recurrence of the process of evolution in each western area reached in the process of expansion. Thus American development has exhibited not merely advance along a single line, but a return to primitive conditions on a continually advancing frontier line, and a new development for that area. American social development has been continu-
(35) ally beginning over again on the frontier. This perennial rebirth, this fluidity of American life, this expansion westward with its new opportunities, its continuous touch with the simplicity of primitive society, furnish the forces dominating the American character. The true point of view in the history of this nation is not the Atlantic coast, it is the Great West. Even the slav-
(40) ery struggle, which is made so exclusive an object of attention by writers like Professor von Holst, occupies its important place in American history because of its relation to westward expansion.

In this advance, the frontier is the outer edge of the wave—the meeting point between savagery and civilization. Much has been written about the *(45)* frontier from the point of view of border warfare and the chase, but as a field for the serious study of the economist and the historian it has been neglected.

The American frontier is sharply distinguished from the European frontier—a fortified boundary line running through dense populations. The *(50)* most significant thing about the American frontier is, that it lies at the hither edge of free land. In the census reports it is treated as the margin of that settlement which has a density of two or more to the square mile. The term is an elastic one, and for our purposes does not need sharp definition.

46. In the context of the passage as a whole, the quotation from the Superintendent of the Census (lines 1–6) presents

    (A) an analogy that illustrates the theme of the passage.
    (B) an anecdote that introduces the main subject of the passage.
    (C) a problem for which the author of the passage will offer a solution.
    (D) a statement on which the passage will build.
    (E) an opinion that emphasizes the gravity of the issue discussed in the rest of the passage.

47. In its context, the phrase "vital forces" (line 13) refers to

    (A) the Census Bureau.
    (B) the U.S. Constitution.
    (C) new laws and regulations passed to deal with changing social and economic conditions.
    (D) the natural obstacles faced by settlers in the West.
    (E) the people's urge to go west and to settle there.

48. Which of the following phrases illustrates "the germ theory of politics" (lines 21–22)?

    (A) "and rapidly—I was about to say fearfully—growing" (lines 19–20)
    (B) "development . . . in a limited area" (line 23)
    (C) "rise of representative government" (lines 27–28)
    (D) "process of evolution" (line 30)
    (E) "return to primitive conditions" (lines 32–33)

49. The "different phenomenon" mentioned in line 25 refers to all of the following EXCEPT

    (A) a return to a primitive style of life.
    (B) new development in unsettled areas.
    (C) a recurrence of historical events.
    (D) growth within a limited geographical area.
    (E) the potential for further expansion.

50. The dominant rhetorical feature of the sentence, "This perennial . . . character" (lines 35–38) is:

    (A) the use of repetition and rhythm
    (B) alliteration
    (C) a pronounced change in tone from the preceding sentence
    (D) a sudden shift in the author's point of view
    (E) a balance of overstatement and understatement

51. In context, the word "chase" (line 45) is best interpreted to mean

    (A) the hunt for food
    (B) survival in primitive conditions
    (C) the question of slavery in the new territories
    (D) the expulsion of the indigenous population
    (E) settlers' competition for free land

52. In the passage the author employs which of the following rhetorical strategies?

    (A) Extended analogy
    (B) Appeal to patriotism
    (C) Testimony from authority
    (D) Inspiring language
    (E) Statistical support

53. The function of the sentence in lines 48–49 ("The American frontier . . . . populations") is to

    (A) draw a contrast between American and European frontiers.
    (B) show the superiority of the American frontier.
    (C) reveal the uniqueness of the American frontier.
    (D) help summarize the passage.
    (E) present arguments in opposition to those in the previous paragraph.

54. The attitude of the author toward the closing of the frontier is primarily one of

    (A) regret.
    (B) historical interest.
    (C) disapproval.
    (D) hopefulness about the future.
    (E) satisfaction.

55. Which of the following best captures the main theme of the passage?

    (A) An industrial society has superseded a primitive society on the frontier.
    (B) America's frontier differs sharply from frontiers elsewhere.
    (C) Expansion to the West has helped to define America's character.
    (D) Criteria for taking the U.S. census must remain flexible.
    (E) America's frontier has been characterized by violence.

SECTION II
Three Essay Questions
Total time—Two hours and 15 minutes

Write your essays on standard 8½" × 11" composition paper. At the exam you will be given a bound booklet containing 12 lined pages.

ESSAY QUESTION 1

(Suggested time—40 minutes. This question counts as one third of the total score for Section II.)

Here are two passages from the essays of the renowned physicist Albert Einstein. After reading them carefully, write an essay that analyzes and compares Einstein's use of language and rhetoric in each.

PASSAGE A

Physics deals with "events" in space and time. To each event belongs, besides its place coordinates x, y, z, a time value t. The latter was considered measurable by a clock (ideal periodic process) of negligible spatial extent. This

Line
(5)
clock C is to be considered at rest at one point of the coordinate system, e.g., at the coordinate origin ($x = y = z = 0$). The time of an event taking place at a point P (x,y,z) is then defined as the time shown on the clock C simultaneously with the event. Here the concept "simultaneous" was assumed as physically meaningful without special definition. This is a lack of exactness which seems harmless only since with the help of light (whose velocity is practically

(10) infinite from the point of view of daily experience) the simultaneity of spatially distant events can apparently be decided immediately.

PASSAGE B

I am convinced there is only one way to eliminate these grave ills, namely through the establishment of a socialist economy, accompanied by an educational system which would be oriented toward social goals. In such an

(15) economy, the means of production are owned by society itself and are utilized in a planned fashion. A planned economy, which adjusts production to the needs of the community, would distribute work to be done among all those able to work and would guarantee a livelihood to every man, woman and child. The education of the individual, in addition to promot-

(20) ing his own innate abilities, would attempt to develop in him a sense of responsibility for his fellow men in place of the glorification of power and success in our present society.

Nevertheless, it is necessary to remember that a planned economy is not yet socialism. A planned economy as such may be accompanied by the com-

(25) plete enslavement of the individual. The achievement of socialism requires the solution of some extremely difficult socio-political problems: is it possible, in view of the far-reaching centralization of political and economic power, to prevent bureaucracy from becoming all-powerful and overweening? How can the rights of the individual be protected and therewith a dem-

(30) ocratic counterweight to the power of the bureaucracy be assured?

ESSAY QUESTION 2

(Suggested time—40 minutes. This question counts as one third of the total score for Section II.)

The German poet Goethe once wrote, "Treat people as if they were what they ought to be and you help them to become what they are capable of being."

Goethe's statement might be applied to schools, government, social services, business, even to families—anyplace, really, where people interact with each other. Is Goethe just expressing pretty-sounding, idealistic nonsense, or does his ideal have real-life applicability? In a well-organized essay, comment on the validity of Goethe's statement as a realistic guide to human relationships. To support your point of view, you may draw evidence from your reading, studies, observation, and personal experience.

ESSAY QUESTION 3

Time—15 minutes to read the sources, 40 minutes to write the essay.

Instructions: The following essay topic is accompanied by six sources.

Respond to the question below in a well-written, coherent essay that draws on ideas and information found in **at least three** of the sources. Don't simply summarize or paraphrase the sources. Instead, **focus the essay on your point of view**, and use the sources to support or bolster your argument.

Topic: Many people worldwide devote huge amounts of time, money, and energy opposing the use of animals in laboratory research. Many others take the view that animals should be used in research for the overall benefit of humankind.

Your task: Read the following sources carefully. Then, in an essay that synthesizes at least three of the sources, take a position that supports, challenges, or modifies the claim that animals should not be used in research.

In your essay, you may refer to the sources simply as Source A, Source B, etc., or by the key words in parentheses below.

Source A (AALAS)
Source B (Andre and Velasquez)
Source C (Pie graph)
Source D (Derbyshire)
Source E (Nuffield)
Source F (Haggarty)

SOURCE A

"What Benefits Have Come From Medical Research Using Animals?" American Association for Laboratory Animal Science (AALAS).<*www.foundation.aalas.org*>

The following comes from the web site of a foundation that provides funding to promote awareness of research in animal care and animal contributions to biomedical research, safety testing, and education.

. . . Today's children routinely receive a vaccine that provides a lifetime of protection against polio. Children are also immunized against typhus, diphtheria, whooping cough, smallpox, and tetanus. Untold millions of people around the world are healthy adults because of these vaccines made possible through animal research.

Diabetes is another example of the importance of biomedical research. Approximately 6.2% of the population (17 million people) has diabetes. Nearly 1 million new cases of diabetes are diagnosed every year, and based on death certificate data, diabetes contributed to 209,664 deaths in 1999 alone. Without insulin treatments to regulate blood sugar levels, many more diabetics would die. Dogs were crucial to the research that identified the cause of diabetes, which led to the development of insulin. Recently, researchers have developed insulin pumps to replace injections, and current transplant research offers the hope that diabetes can be cured.

The importance of animal research to those suffering from heart and circulatory diseases cannot be overlooked. About 50 million Americans age six and older have high blood pressure, which can cause strokes, heart attacks, and heart disease. Research involving animals has helped identify the causes of high blood pressure and develop more effective drugs to control the problem. Other research has resulted in treatments for strokes and heart attacks that save thousands of lives and reduce recovery time. Dogs have been especially important to researchers who developed open-heart surgery, pacemakers, and heart transplants. These techniques have revolutionized therapy for people who have severe heart disease.

. . . Animals benefit from biomedical research as well. Feline immunodeficiency virus (FIV) and feline leukemia virus (FeLV) infections are major causes of death in cats. Surveys show that up to 15 percent of sick cats are infected with one or both of these viruses, and that even healthy cats may harbor infections and spread them to other cats. A vaccine is available to prevent these diseases, but much additional work is necessary to explain these diseases and their treatment.

Sometimes research can have unexpected benefits. In 1978, there was a sudden, worldwide outbreak of a virus among dogs, which caused vomiting, diarrhea, dehydration, and, frequently, death. Researchers soon discovered that this disease, called canine parvovirus, was similar to the feline panleukopenia virus. Since a vaccine was already available for the feline panleukopenia virus, a vaccine for parvovirus was developed, tested, and made available for distribution within a year. Now recognized as one of the most significant success stories of modern veterinary science, the parvovirus vaccine checked the spread of the disease among adult dogs in the United States almost immediately.

SOURCE B

Claire Andre and Manuel Velasquez, "Of Cures and Creatures Great and Small," Issues in Ethics, v.1, No. 3, Spring, 1988, published by Markkula Center for Applied Ethics, Santa Clara University.

The passage below comes from a position statement published by an organization active in the field of ethical issues.

About 20 million animals are experimented on and killed annually, three-fourths for medical purposes and the rest to test various products. An estimated eight million are used in painful experiments. Reports show that at least 10 percent of these animals do not receive painkillers. Animal rights advocates are pressing government agencies to impose heavy restrictions on animal research. But this growing criticism of painful experimentation on animals is matched by a growing concern over the threat restrictions on the use of animals would pose to scientific progress. Whether such experiments should be allowed to continue has become a matter for public debate.

Those who argue that painful experimentation on animals should be halted, or at least curtailed, maintain that pain is an intrinsic evil, and any action that causes pain to another creature is simply not morally permissible. Pointing to the words of the nineteenth-century utilitarian, Jeremy Bentham, animal welfare advocates claim that the morally relevant question about animals is not, "Can they reason? nor Can they talk? but, Can they suffer?" And, animals do in fact suffer, and do in fact feel pain. The researcher who forces rats to choose between electric shocks and starvation to see if they develop ulcers does so because he or she knows that rats have nervous systems much like humans and feel the pain of shocks in a similar way. Pain is an intrinsic evil whether it is experienced by a child, an adult, or an animal. If it is wrong to inflict pain on a human being, it is just as wrong to inflict pain on an animal.

Moreover, it is argued, the lives of all creatures, great and small, have value and are worthy of respect. This right to be treated with respect does not depend on an ability to reason. An insane person has a right to be treated with respect, yet he or she may not be able to act rationally. Nor does the right to be treated with respect rest on being a member of a certain species. Restricting respect for life to a certain species is to perform an injustice similar to racism or sexism. Like the racist who holds that respect for other races does not count as much as respect for his or her own race, those who support painful experimentation on animals assume that respect for other species does not count as much as respect for members of his or her own species. "Speciesism" is as arbitrarily unjust as racism or sexism. The right to be treated with respect rests, rather, on a creature's being a "subject of a life," with certain experiences, preferences, and interests. Animals, like humans, are subjects of a life. Justice demands that the interests of animals be respected, which includes respect for their interest to be spared undeserved pain.

SOURCE C

"Numbers of animals used in research in the United Kingdom" Home Office (2004) *Statistics of Scientific Procedures on Living Animals, Great Britain 2003.*

The pie graph below comes from a British government agency.

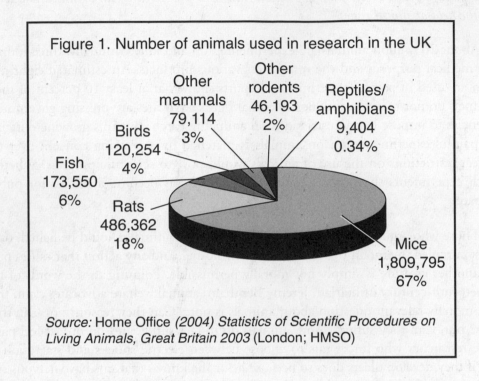

Figure 1. Number of animals used in research in the UK

Other mammals 79,114 3%

Other rodents 46,193 2%

Reptiles/ amphibians 9,404 0.34%

Birds 120,254 4%

Fish 173,550 6%

Rats 486,362 18%

Mice 1,809,795 67%

Source: Home Office *(2004) Statistics of Scientific Procedures on Living Animals, Great Britain 2003* (London; HMSO)

SOURCE D

Stuart Derbyshire, PhD., "Animal Experimentation," Speech at Edinburgh Book Festival, 19 August 2002.

Below are excerpts from a talk given at a book festival by a faculty member in the School of Psychology, University of Birmingham.

. . .Ongoing research with a wide variety of animals includes investigations of AIDS, cancer, heart disease, cystic fibrosis, and muscular dystrophy. The development of artificial arteries, the possibility of reversing spinal cord injury, and the aging process are all being investigated using animal models. The best hopes to cure malaria, Parkinson's and Alzheimer's diseases, epilepsy, clinical obesity, infertility, and a variety of birth defects all rely on current animal experiments.

Without doubt there are many experiments that will fail or lead to no useful therapy—such is the nature of all science. But to suggest that scientists are pointlessly pursuing experiments and models that do not work is just wrong-headed. The process of peer review and grant allocation certainly has its problems, but it is not that bad! If there were good alternatives to animals that worked better or as well, for less money and hassle, scientists would use them. We can be stubborn but we are not totally bananas.

. . . Tom Regan and Richard Ryder argue that animals are like us, that they share with us the capacity for seeing, hearing, believing, remembering, and anticipating and for experiencing pleasure and pain. They suggest that animals are "subjects of a being."

There is a trivial sense in which Regan and Ryder are undoubtedly correct; animals certainly do possess the biological properties necessary for processing information. But, in every important sense, they are flat out wrong. Animals and humans do not think alike, feel alike, or experience alike. Humans and animals are not on the same scale.

. . . The bottom line is that humans are special, but this is not a popular outlook— and for good reason. The twentieth century saw a series of calamities and disasters that battered our self-belief. . . and left humanity feeling sorry for itself. We look in the mirror and see something a lot more brutish than it truly is, and we look at the animals and see more that is human than is truly there. The campaign for animal rights has gained greater purchase as pessimism surrounding the human condition has increased.

Scientists share this pessimism as much as any other group and their defensiveness on the question of animal experimentation has sadly contributed to the increasing anti-human sentiment. . . .

I wonder how it ever got so difficult. For me, humans trump animals every time and it is right and proper that animals be sacrificed for the cause of humanity. If all animal experimentation were stopped, the slowdown would be real and the cost would be high. Right now, for example, there are at least four compounds undergoing animal testing as a potential vaccine against malaria. Malaria kills 2.7 million people every year, over five people every minute, most of them children under the age of five. A delay in developing a vaccine by just one month would kill 225,000 people. Are we really so fed up with humanity that we would sacrifice ourselves and our children to save the monkeys?

SOURCE E

"The Ethics of Research Involving Animals: A Guide to the Report," Nuffield Council on Bioethics, 25 May 2005.

The following is an excerpt from a report issued by a foundation that studies and reports on ethical issues involving biological and medical research.

The question of defining the moral status of humans and animals often arises in the debate on research involving animals. Are humans morally more important than all animals? Is there a sliding scale with humans at the top and the simplest animals at the bottom? Or are humans and animals morally equal?

We suggest that the proper moral treatment of a being depends on the characteristics it possesses, rather than simply on the species to which it belongs. We identify five morally relevant features:

- Sentience (the capacity to feel pleasure and pain)
- Higher cognitive capacities (for example, the ability to use language and learn complicated tasks, such as making and using tools)
- The capacity to flourish (the ability to satisfy species—specific needs)
- Sociability (being a member of a community)
- Possession of a life (attributing value to life itself)

What weight should be given to each of the morally relevant features in considering whether or not research is acceptable? Are there factors to be weighed against human benefit? Should they be understood as absolute constraints? For example, should any use of animals that are capable of suffering be prohibited, or only the use of those that have higher cognitive capacities?

Many people seem to support a "hybrid" approach. This involves a combination of laying down definite limits for what should and should not happen (for example: "animals with higher cognitive capacities such as chimpanzees should never be used in research") and weighing up the costs and benefits of a particular action (for example, "research that causes minimum pain to a mouse is acceptable if it helps to ascertain the safety of an important and frequently used chemical"). This approach can also be found in the Animals (Scientific Procedures) Act 1986: the costs and benefits have to be weighed for each project and there are specific policies that prevent the use of Great Apes and the use of animals in the testing of new cosmetics.

The ethical debate comes down to disagreement on two questions:

- What are the definite limits?
- How do we weigh the different morally relevant factors within the permitted limits?

SOURCE F

Clare Haggarty, "Animals in Scientific Research: The Ethical Argument," National Anti-Vivisection Society, <*www.navs.org*>

The following comes from the web site of an organization devoted to protecting animals and their rights.

. . .Being sentient beings, which means the ability to experience sensation or feelings, animals caught in the web of scientific research suffer enormously both physically and psychologically. Even those few "laboratory" animals that escape outright physical pain and discomfort are almost always subjected to isolation, depression, and anxiety. In fact the worst atrocity we inflict upon animals condemned to scientific research may be the act of removing them from the natural habitat, or breeding them in captivity, and then placing them in the artificial environment of a laboratory cage, where they have no hope of having the kind of life nature intended for them.

In the end, we as a society have a choice. Do we treat our fellow creatures with cruelty and callousness? Or with compassion, respect and justice? As humans, we have the freedom to make that choice. With this freedom comes the moral obligation to make responsible decisions.

Animals have no such choice. Because they cannot say no, they are completely vulnerable to whatever the researcher has in store for them, no matter how much pain and suffering is involved. Animals are unable to understand or claim their right to be alive, to be free from pain and suffering, and fulfill their biological potential. Therefore, it is up to humans to recognize and protect those rights for them, just as we are morally obligated to protect infants, the developmentally disabled, and the mentally ill.

It has been said that the moral progress of our society can be measured by the way it treats animals. Animal experimentation—an institutionalized form of exploitation—stands in the way of moral progress. Now is the time to extend our sphere of ethical concern to all creatures.

END OF PRACTICE TEST A

Answer Key
PRACTICE TEST A

Answers to Multiple-Choice Questions

1. B	21. C	41. C
2. A	22. B	42. C
3. D	23. E	43. C
4. D	24. D	44. C
5. D	25. A	45. D
6. C	26. A	46. D
7. A	27. C	47. C
8. E	28. B	48. A
9. C	29. A	49. D
10. A	30. D	50. A
11. A	31. C	51. D
12. B	32. D	52. C
13. E	33. C	53. D
14. D	34. A	54. B
15. E	35. B	55. C
16. E	36. A	
17. B	37. D	
18. C	38. B	
19. C	39. A	
20. E	40. E	

Summary of Answers in Section I (Multiple-Choice)

Number of correct answers _____

Number of incorrect answers _____

Number of questions not answered _____

Use this information when you calculate your score on this exam. See page 252.

Answer Explanations

PASSAGE 1—AN EXCERPT FROM BERYL MARKHAM, *WEST WITH THE NIGHT*

1. **(B)** The author alludes directly and indirectly to the sentiment expressed in the aphoristic opening sentence. She is surprised to meet the "stranger" (herself) in the cockpit of her plane (lines 14–15).

2. **(A)** All the phrases except that in (A) identify activities that people have contrived to keep loneliness at bay.

3. **(D)** "Being alone" is a verbal phrase that starts out as the grammatical subject of the sentence. But the verb of the sentence—"can be"—does not appear until line 13, after several intervening prepositional phrases and infinitives. By that time, the writer has chosen to recast the sentence with a new grammatical subject—"such an experience." Consequently, the two phrases together serve as the subject of the sentence.

4. **(D)** The author compares the experience of piloting an airplane all alone to discovering a stranger—that is, solo flying is like finding a side of yourself that you hadn't known about.

5. **(D)** The first paragraph consists of generalizations about man's abhorrence of loneliness. The second paragraph cites an example of extreme loneliness. In the third paragraph, the narrator feels obliged to explain that her thoughts about loneliness are based on her own experience. Thus, she relates a personal anecdote about a solo flight she once made.

6. **(C)** After telling where she is and what she sees, the author describes the feelings and thoughts that the situation evokes.

7. **(A)** During much of the passage, the author reflects on loneliness. She also discloses her thoughts and fears about flying.

8. **(E)** Piloting a plane provides the "security of solitude, the exhilaration of escape" (lines 18–19). These feelings contrast with those of the cares of the world below and "the small sorrow of rain" (line 21).

9. **(C)** The sentence explains why distance is compared to "so much time used up." But it also serves all the other functions except to show that equating time and distance is an indication of pilot disorientation.

10. **(A)** The observation dramatizes a moment during the take-off—a moment so riveting that it seemed unreal. To capture that sense of unreality, the author uses exaggeration, or hyperbole. The notion that time and distance can stop has metaphorical implications, too, but the metaphor used here is consistent, not mixed. Choice II does not apply.

11. **(A)** A paradox is a valid statement that seems to fly in the face of logic. The lines contain no such feature. (B) and (D) are evident in the piling up of phrases beginning with "the moment." (C) can be found in lines that suggest the airplane has a will of its own, as in "refuses its burden." (E) is seen when the narrator shifts from the impersonal "it" to "she."

12. **(B)** The speaker is describing how fear vanishes once she is airborne. Because she can no longer depend on the "security of land underfoot," security comes from the plane itself.

13. **(E)** Throughout the passage the author assigns meanings to particular moments in her flight and interprets the general experience of flying. None of the other choices accurately describe the passage.

PASSAGE 2—AN EXCERPT FROM HENRY ALLEN, "THE CORPS"

14. **(D)** The capitalized words convey the effect of the drill instructor's speech pattern and loudness.

15. **(E)** The phrase "daring glances" is a participial modifying the noun "recruits."

16. **(E)** The paragraph is filled with visual images, climaxed by the vivid reference to "raindrops beading on spitshined black shoes."

17. **(B)** Most of the passage is devoted to describing the behavior of the omnipotent drill instructors. Their power contrasts starkly with the haplessness of the recruits.

18. **(C)** Hudson and Burley, proud, tough Marines, stand in stark contrast to the goofy, wisecracking Hargrove and Bilko of television fame.

19. **(C)** While not an exact quote from Marine Corps regulations, the material in these lines is a paraphrase of the rules governing recruits during their basic training.

20. **(E)** The paragraph contains all of the techniques except a subordinate clause set off by dashes. The material between the dashes (lines 42–43) is an independent clause embedded in another independent clause.

21. **(C)** Because the word "dread" names the subject of the sentence ("It"), it is a predicate nominative. Other words in the sentence that serve the same function are "spectacle" and "initiation."

22. **(B)** Each of the choices has possibilities, but the purpose of the passage is best described as the author's attempt to recreate life at Parris Island. The extreme emotions and often inflammatory choice of words contain ample evidence of melodrama.

23. **(E)** All the choices are descriptive except the last one, in which the author implies his approval of the methods used by the Marine Corps to train its recruits.

PASSAGE 3—AN EXCERPT FROM EDWARD SAID, "REFLECTIONS ON EXILE"

24. **(D)** The sentence in question, while defining the word "exile," also conveys the author's attitude toward his subject. It does not limit the subject matter of the passage, however.

25. **(A)** Such words as "unhealable," "permanently," and "forever" indicate the endlessness of exile; words such as "terrible," "sadness," "sorrow," and "loss" speak for its woefulness. (C), (D), and (E) each contain a word that characterizes exile, but the correct answer requires that both words apply.

26. **(A)** In describing exiles, the author seems to understand their plight. He recognizes that exile is an altogether painful experience.

27. **(C)** The sentence, phrased as a question, briefly puts the reader inside the mind of an exile, wondering what it would be like not to be exiled.

28. **(B)** To make clear what he means by "exile," the author compares exiles with "refugees," "expatriates," and "émigrés."

29. **(A)** The settlers participated in the adventure of nation-building and pioneering in far-off lands. In the passage, the author uses them as examples of people who chose to exile themselves.

30. **(D)** The sentence in question is a complex sentence that includes a dependent clause beginning with the subordinating conjunction *but*. The other sentence with similar characteristics is that which immediately precedes it.

31. **(C)** The sentence serves as the topic sentence of the paragraph, which offers several examples of how exiles make up for the loss of their homelands.

32. **(D)** The word "unchanging" is an adjective that modifies the noun "life." Similarly, "clear" is an adjective that modifies a noun—"values." Both appear in a series of parallel adjective clauses.

33. **(C)** The passage says that European novels are "grounded in precisely the opposite experiences" (line 42) from that of classical epics. The point is to show that exiled heroes in European novels differ from the heroes of ancient epics.

34. **(A)** One of the unifying elements in the passage is the notion that exiles are forced to recreate, or construct, a new life in order to compensate for the loss they have suffered. This idea is stated or alluded to throughout the passage.

35. **(B)** The author stresses the emotional tolls of exile. While objective in parts, the passage consists primarily of one man's thoughts about the phenomenon.

PASSAGE 4—AN EXCERPT FROM DEANNA PAOLI GUMINA, *THE ITALIANS OF SAN FRANCISCO*

36. **(A)** Although each of the choices is mentioned somewhere in the passage, the speaker's overall purpose in the passage is to tell the story of how the earthquake affected the Italian residents of the city.

37. **(D)** The details in the first paragraph emphasize the unusual nature of the 1906 earthquake. (E) may sound like a promising choice because the author calls the earthquake a "tragedy" (line 5). But overall, the author's rhetorical stance in the paragraph is largely straightforward and objective.

38. **(B)** The "knotted, tangled mass" of rubble depicts all the choices except the fault line—the underground crack where the earthquake was centered.

39. **(A)** The sentence is meant to explain why the people on Telegraph Hill suffered losses in spite of being "luckier than most" (line 12).

40. **(E)** Because five of the eight footnotes cite sources written soon after the earthquake, (E) is the only logical choice. All the other choices are assumptions based on too little evidence. All the other choices are incorrect because the numbers refer to the volume and page number of a periodical—in this case *Scribner's*, which is neither a book nor a publisher.

41. **(C)** The absence of a book title in the footnote signifies that the work by Peixotto has appeared in a previous footnote.

42. **(C)** To inform readers about the effects of the earthquake on the Italian community in San Francisco is the main purpose of the passage. (A) is too broad because the passage focuses on the Italians of San Francisco. (B) is inaccurate because the passage covers how the Italian community fared in the earthquake but does not scrutinize or examine the community in detail. (D) suggests an account of the entire event, but the passage begins only after the quake has occurred. (E) is slightly valid because the first paragraph of the passage mentions why the quake had been so deadly, but fails to take into account the rest of the passage.

43. **(C)** Sources I and II say complimentary things about the design of the buildings. The author of the remaining source (Footnote 38) neither approves or disapproves, commenting instead on what the architecture implies about Italians' experience in America.

44. **(C)** The first sentence is a compound sentence that is made up of two independent clauses joined by the conjunction *and*. None of the other features are found in these lines of the passage.

45. **(D)** The author's intent in the passage is to write a serious, informative account of the events described. Because her approach is that of an objective historian, evidence of her personal feelings is hardly noticeable.

PASSAGE 5—AN EXCERPT FROM FREDERICK JACKSON TURNER, *THE FRONTIER IN AMERICAN HISTORY*

46. **(D)** The quotation announces a change in the manner in which census reports are made. In the remainder of the passage, the author details this change and explains its historic implications.

47. **(C)** According to the author, "vital forces" generate institutional changes.

48. **(A)** The author alludes to the "germ theory" in the context of a discussion about growth and development, described vividly by Calhoun's words. The quotation suggests that in 1817 the nation was expanding uncontrollably—not an altogether sanguine situation in Calhoun's words, but rather, the author believes, like a plague of "germs."

49. **(D)** Growth in a limited geographical area is characteristic of Europe and of the original American settlement along the Atlantic coast. All the other features pertain to the frontier in the American West.

50. **(A)** The most notable feature is the rhythmic piling up of similar phrases that constitute the subject of the sentence.

51. **(D)** According to the paragraph in question, the frontier has been the "meeting point between savagery and civilization," and has been marked by "border warfare." Both phrases imply the existence of a clash between the settlers and those who interfered with their progress—namely the native inhabitants of the land. Indeed, much has been written about the conflict between settlers and the Indians.

52. **(C)** Twice in the passage, the author quotes authority figures—the Superintendent of the Census (lines 2–6) and Calhoun (lines 19–20)—and then refers to Professor von Holst (line 41). In all instances, the words serve as a springboard to further discussion.

53. **(D)** While the sentence points out that the European and American frontiers differ from each other, the purpose of the entire last paragraph of the passage is to summarize what came before. Thus, the sentence introduces and contributes to a summary of the passage.

54. **(B)** The author analyzes the historical meaning of the end of the frontier in America. He expresses no strong feelings about it. Rather, he presents his interpretation of a great historical event.

55. **(C)** Throughout the passage, the author refers to the frontier's influence on American life. In the first paragraph he states that American development can be explained by the westward expansion. In the next paragraph, he states that America's institutions have adapted to the needs of expansion. In lines 35–38, the author states outright that the frontier has furnished "the forces dominating the American character."

Answers to Essay Questions

For an overview of how essays are graded, turn to "How Essays Are Scored," on page 27.

Although answers to the essay questions will vary greatly, the following descriptions suggest a possible approach to each question and contain ideas that could be used in a response to the question. Perhaps your essay contains many of the same ideas. If not, don't be alarmed. Your ideas may be no less, or could be even more, insightful than those presented below.

ESSAY QUESTION 1, BASED ON PASSAGES BY ALBERT EINSTEIN

Although the two passages were written by the same person, they are dramatically different from each other. In the first, Einstein explains a phenomenon in physics, a world in which he is very much at home. Much of the passage is factual, precise, and impersonal. He writes, for example, "The latter was considered measurable . . .," using a passive construction in order to avoid using the first person. The technical nature of the passage is evident in several symbols and formulas and in the specialized language of physics, e.g., "negligible spatial extent" and "the simultaneity of spatially distant events."

Unlike the first passage, the second is written speculatively. Gone is the voice of authority and the technical language and formulas—replaced herein by vague generalizations couched in the language of economics and sociology. Consider such phrases as "an educational system . . . oriented toward social goals," and "the education of the individual . . . would attempt to develop . . . a sense of responsibility." This sort of language may sound good, but it lacks substance. It's jargon, plain and simple. We are hearing the views of someone who may be a thoughtful human being, but the words resemble empty platitudes. Instead of stating his case forcefully, Einstein resorts to the repeated use of *would,* a word that suggests tentativeness. Had he been more confident and well-informed on the topic, his language would have reflected greater certainty. He would have used *will,* a far more decisive word.

ESSAY QUESTION 2, BASED ON A STATEMENT BY GOETHE

The task in this question is to support, challenge, or qualify Goethe's statement. If you agree with Goethe, your essay should contain examples—possibly in anecdotal form—of people living up to expectations because they were treated with respect and dignity. You may remember a time, for example, when you were treated like an adult, and so you behaved like one, or in contrast, because you were treated as a child, you acted silly or immature.

If you cannot subscribe to Goethe's point of view, you should cite examples of people being treated well but acting badly. A striking example occurred not long ago when a high school student in New York murdered his English teacher after the teacher had gone out of his way to help the student deal with both academic and personal problems. One could argue, of course, that because this case was an aberration, it cannot reasonably support a generalization about human behavior. In fact, beware of drawing any broad conclusions based on a single event or example—both in your essay writing and in life.

ESSAY QUESTION 3

On this issue, it's unusual to take an extreme position, although those who do probably come down on the side of animal protection. But not always.

If you believe that there should be no prohibition against using animals in laboratory research, you might have incorporated some of these ideas found in the sources:

- Millions of people owe their good health to vaccines developed with the help of animals. (Source A)

- Many diseases, from diabetes to heart disease, can be treated with drugs developed in laboratories using animals. (Source A)

- Scientific progress depends on animal research. (Source B)

- The vast majority of animals used in research—mice and rats—are of a lower order than humans and most other mammals. (Source C)

- Animals and humans should not be equated because they are not on the same scale; humans are special. (Source D)

On the other hand, if you claim that research using animals should be banned, these are some of the arguments you might have used.

- Imposing pain on helpless animals is intrinsically evil. (Source B)

- Using animals for experimentation is unjust and shows a wanton disregard of the value of life. (Source B)

- Literally millions of animals are used in research in just one year in just one country—England. (Source C)

- Employing animals for research should not be undertaken without considering several morally relevant features, among them the cognitive level of the animal. (Source E)

- The treatment of animals in the lab is cruel and callous. (Source F)

- The moral position of a society can be measured by the way its animals are treated. (Source F)

Self-Scoring Guide—Practice Test A

SCORING SECTION 2 ESSAYS

After referring to "How Essays Are Scored," on pages 27–30 of this book, use this guide to help you evaluate each essay. Do your best to evaluate your performance in each category by using the criteria spelled out below. Because it is hard to achieve objectivity when assessing your own writing, you may improve the validity of your score by having a trusted and well-informed friend or experienced teacher read and rate your essay.

On the following Rating Chart, enter a number (from 1 to 6) that you think represents your level of performance in each category (A–F).

Category A: OVERALL PURPOSE/MAIN IDEA

6 extremely well-defined and insightful

5 clearly defined and generally insightful

4 mostly clear

3 somewhat clear but occasionally confusing

2 generally unclear and confusing

1 virtually incomprehensible

Category B: HANDLING OF THE PROMPT

6 self-evident or extremely clear throughout

5 mostly clear

4 somewhat clear

3 somewhat unclear

2 generally unclear or ambiguous

1 confusing or nonexistent

Category C: ORGANIZATION AND DEVELOPMENT

6 insightfully organized; fully developed with excellent supporting evidence

5 reasonably well organized; developed with appropriate supporting material

4 appropriately organized; developed with some relevant material

3 inadequately organized; weak development

2 poorly organized; little or no development

1 no discernible organization; no relevant development

Category D: SENTENCE STRUCTURE

6 varied and engaging

5 sufficiently varied to create interest

4 some variety

3 little variety; minor sentence errors

2 frequent sentence errors that interfere with meaning

1 serious sentence errors that obscure meaning

Category E: USE OF LANGUAGE

6 precise and effective word choice

5 competent word choice

4 conventional word choice; mostly correct

3 some errors in diction or idiom

2 frequent errors in diction or idiom

1 meaning obscured by word choice

Category F: GRAMMAR AND USAGE

6 error-free or virtually error-free

5 occasional minor errors

4 basically correct but with several minor errors

3 meaning somewhat obscured by errors

2 meaning frequently obscured by errors

1 meaning blocked by several major errors

RATING CHART

Rate your essay:	Essay 1	Essay 2	Essay 3
Overall Purpose/Main Idea			
Handling of the Prompt			
Organization and Development			
Sentence Structure			
Use of Language			
Grammar and Usage			
Composite Scores (Sum of each column)			

By using the following scale, in which composite scores are converted to the nine-point AP rating scale, you may determine the final score for each essay:

Composite Score	AP Essay Score
33–36	9
29–32	8
25–28	7
21–24	6
18–20	5
15–17	4
10–14	3
7–9	2
6 or below	1

AP Essay Scores Essay 1 _____ Essay 2 _____ Essay 3 _____

TEST SCORE WORKSHEET FOR PRACTICE TEST A

The scores you have earned on the multiple-choice and essay sections of the exam may now be converted to the AP five-point scale by performing the following calculations:

I. Determine your score for Section I (Multiple Choice)

Step A: Number of correct answers _____

Step B: Number of wrong answers _____ (Note: Do not count unanswered questions.)

Step C: Multiply the number of wrong answers by .250 and enter the figure here _____ .

Step D: Subtract the figure in Step C from the figure in Step A _____ .

Step E: Multiply the figure in Step D by 1.2500 to find your Multiple-Choice Score _____ (If less than zero, enter zero.)

II. Determine your score for Section II (Essays)

Step A: Enter your score for Essay 1 (out of 9) _____

Step B: Enter your score for Essay 2 (out of 9) _____

Step C: Enter your score for Essay 3 (out of 9) _____

Step D: Add the figures in Steps A, B, and C _____

Step E: Multiply the figure in Step D by 3.0556 _____. (Do not round.) This is your Essay Score.

III. Determine Your Total Score

Add the scores for I and II to find your composite score _____ .

To convert your composite score to the AP five-point scale, use the chart below. The range of scores only approximates what you would earn on the actual test because the exact figures may vary from test to test. Be aware, therefore, that your score on this test, as well as on other tests in this book, may differ slightly from your score on an actual AP exam.

Composite Score	AP Grade
108–150	5
93–107	4
72–92	3
43–71	2
0–42	1

AP essays are ordinarily judged in relation to other essays written on the same topic at the same time. Therefore, the scores you assign yourself for these essays may not be the same as the scores you would earn on an actual exam.

Practice Test B
ANSWER SHEET

Multiple-Choice Questions Time—1 hour

1. Ⓐ Ⓑ Ⓒ Ⓓ Ⓔ
2. Ⓐ Ⓑ Ⓒ Ⓓ Ⓔ
3. Ⓐ Ⓑ Ⓒ Ⓓ Ⓔ
4. Ⓐ Ⓑ Ⓒ Ⓓ Ⓔ
5. Ⓐ Ⓑ Ⓒ Ⓓ Ⓔ
6. Ⓐ Ⓑ Ⓒ Ⓓ Ⓔ
7. Ⓐ Ⓑ Ⓒ Ⓓ Ⓔ
8. Ⓐ Ⓑ Ⓒ Ⓓ Ⓔ
9. Ⓐ Ⓑ Ⓒ Ⓓ Ⓔ
10. Ⓐ Ⓑ Ⓒ Ⓓ Ⓔ
11. Ⓐ Ⓑ Ⓒ Ⓓ Ⓔ
12. Ⓐ Ⓑ Ⓒ Ⓓ Ⓔ
13. Ⓐ Ⓑ Ⓒ Ⓓ Ⓔ
14. Ⓐ Ⓑ Ⓒ Ⓓ Ⓔ
15. Ⓐ Ⓑ Ⓒ Ⓓ Ⓔ
16. Ⓐ Ⓑ Ⓒ Ⓓ Ⓔ
17. Ⓐ Ⓑ Ⓒ Ⓓ Ⓔ
18. Ⓐ Ⓑ Ⓒ Ⓓ Ⓔ
19. Ⓐ Ⓑ Ⓒ Ⓓ Ⓔ
20. Ⓐ Ⓑ Ⓒ Ⓓ Ⓔ

21. Ⓐ Ⓑ Ⓒ Ⓓ Ⓔ
22. Ⓐ Ⓑ Ⓒ Ⓓ Ⓔ
23. Ⓐ Ⓑ Ⓒ Ⓓ Ⓔ
24. Ⓐ Ⓑ Ⓒ Ⓓ Ⓔ
25. Ⓐ Ⓑ Ⓒ Ⓓ Ⓔ
26. Ⓐ Ⓑ Ⓒ Ⓓ Ⓔ
27. Ⓐ Ⓑ Ⓒ Ⓓ Ⓔ
28. Ⓐ Ⓑ Ⓒ Ⓓ Ⓔ
29. Ⓐ Ⓑ Ⓒ Ⓓ Ⓔ
30. Ⓐ Ⓑ Ⓒ Ⓓ Ⓔ
31. Ⓐ Ⓑ Ⓒ Ⓓ Ⓔ
32. Ⓐ Ⓑ Ⓒ Ⓓ Ⓔ
33. Ⓐ Ⓑ Ⓒ Ⓓ Ⓔ
34. Ⓐ Ⓑ Ⓒ Ⓓ Ⓔ
35. Ⓐ Ⓑ Ⓒ Ⓓ Ⓔ
36. Ⓐ Ⓑ Ⓒ Ⓓ Ⓔ
37. Ⓐ Ⓑ Ⓒ Ⓓ Ⓔ
38. Ⓐ Ⓑ Ⓒ Ⓓ Ⓔ
39. Ⓐ Ⓑ Ⓒ Ⓓ Ⓔ
40. Ⓐ Ⓑ Ⓒ Ⓓ Ⓔ

41. Ⓐ Ⓑ Ⓒ Ⓓ Ⓔ
42. Ⓐ Ⓑ Ⓒ Ⓓ Ⓔ
43. Ⓐ Ⓑ Ⓒ Ⓓ Ⓔ
44. Ⓐ Ⓑ Ⓒ Ⓓ Ⓔ
45. Ⓐ Ⓑ Ⓒ Ⓓ Ⓔ
46. Ⓐ Ⓑ Ⓒ Ⓓ Ⓔ
47. Ⓐ Ⓑ Ⓒ Ⓓ Ⓔ
48. Ⓐ Ⓑ Ⓒ Ⓓ Ⓔ
49. Ⓐ Ⓑ Ⓒ Ⓓ Ⓔ
50. Ⓐ Ⓑ Ⓒ Ⓓ Ⓔ
51. Ⓐ Ⓑ Ⓒ Ⓓ Ⓔ
52. Ⓐ Ⓑ Ⓒ Ⓓ Ⓔ
53. Ⓐ Ⓑ Ⓒ Ⓓ Ⓔ
54. Ⓐ Ⓑ Ⓒ Ⓓ Ⓔ

Practice Test B

Total time—1 hour

Questions 1–10. Carefully read the following passage and answer the accompanying questions.

The passage comes from the quill of a renowned essayist of the 16th century.

Passage 1

I am not excessively fond of salads or fruit, with the exception of melons. My father hated every kind of sauce; I like them all. Eating too much makes me uncomfortable; but in respect of its properties I am not yet very certain
Line that any kind of food disagrees with me. Nor have I noticed that I am
(5) affected by full or new moons, by autumn or spring.

We are subject to fickle and inexplicable changes. For example, radishes, which I first found to agree with me, afterwards disagreed, and now they agree again. In several things I have found my stomach and palate to vary in the same way: I have changed more than once from white wine to claret,
(10) and back again from claret to white wine.

I have a dainty tooth for fish, and the meatless days are my meat-days; my fasts are my feasts. Besides, I believe that it is, as some people say, more easily digested than meat. As it goes against my conscience to eat meat on fish-days, so my taste rebels against mixing meat and fish; the difference
(15) seems to me too wide.

From my youth up I have occasionally skipped a meal; either to sharpen my appetite for the next day (for, as Epicurus used to fast and make lean meals in order to accustom his greed to dispense with plenty, I do so, on the contrary, in order to train my greed to take better advantage of plenty
(20) and to enjoy it more cheerfully); or I used to fast to keep my strength for the performance of some mental or bodily action; for both my body and mind are made cruelly sluggish by repletion. . . . To cure my ailing digestion, I say that we should not so much look to what we eat as to whom we eat with.

(25) To me no dressing is so acceptable, and no sauce so appetizing, as that derived from good company. I think it is more wholesome to eat more at leisure with a good friend, and less, and to eat oftener. But I would give hunger and appetite their due; I should take no pleasure in dragging

through three or four wretched repasts a day, restricted by doctors' orders.
(30) Who will assure me that I can recover at supper-time the good appetite I
had this morning? Let us old men especially take the first opportunity that
comes our way. Let us leave the making of dietaries to doctors and almanac
makers . . . .

I do not cover my legs and thighs more in winter than in summer: sim-
(35) ple silk hose. For the relief of my colds I gave way to the habit of keeping
my head warmer, and my belly on account of the colic. But in a few days
my ailments became accustomed to them and scorned my ordinary precautions: from a cap I advanced to a kerchief, and from a bonnet to a lined hat.
The wadding of my doublet is now only ornamental. All that would be of
(40) no avail unless I added a hare's skin or a vulture's plumage, with a skull-cap
for the head. Continue this gradual progress and you will go a long way. I
shall take care not to do so, and would gladly go back to where I began, if
I dared. "Have you developed a new ailment? Is the remedy no longer of
any avail? You have grown accustomed to it? Then try another." In this way
(45) they ruin their health who allow themseves to be fettered by enforced rules,
and superstitiously adhere to them; they need more and more, and after
that more again. There is no end.

1. Which of the following best describes the rhetorical function of the last
   sentence of paragraph 1 (lines 4–5)?

   (A) It helps to establish the speaker's credentials as an expert on the topic of
       the passage.
   (B) It challenges a commonly held superstition to be discussed later in the
       passage.
   (C) It introduces a major theme of the passage.
   (D) It refers to an old saying about the consequences of overeating.
   (E) It creates a rhetorical link between paragraph 1 and the first sentence of
       paragraph 2.

2. The author's references to radishes and to claret (second paragraph) function
   in all of the following ways EXCEPT to

   (A) prove the validity of the second paragraph's topic sentence
   (B) identify changes that the author has experienced
   (C) define the word "fickle" (line 6)
   (D) add to the litany of the author's personal quirks
   (E) hint that the author has switched from a serious to an ironic tone

3. The description of the speaker's "dainty tooth for fish" (line 11) contributes
   to the unity of the passage by

   (A) contrasting the taste of two different foods
   (B) adding further details to the speaker's portrait of himself
   (C) condemning those who do not observe meatless days
   (D) drawing a parallel between different kinds of cooking
   (E) commenting of the absurdity of the speaker's taste in food

4. Lines 11–15 contain all of the following EXCEPT

   (A) alliteration
   (B) parallel syntax
   (C) synecdoche
   (D) a paradox
   (E) onomatopoeia

5. In lines 16–24, the speaker uses which of the following reasons to justify his occasional fasting?

   I. To increase his appetite
   II. To overeat without feeling guilty
   III. To derive greater enjoyment from his meals

   (A) I only
   (B) II only
   (C) I and III only
   (D) II and III only
   (E) I, II, and III

6. The passage as a whole can best be described as

   (A) a prescription for a better diet
   (B) an anecdote about old-fashioned eating customs
   (C) an account of one man's tastes
   (D) a comparison of the author and his father
   (E) a reflection on unhealthful eating habits

7. Which of the following best describes the rhetorical function of lines 25–27 in the passage?

   (A) They serve as a transition between the paragraphs that come before and after.
   (B) They support the author's assertion that he likes all sauces (line 2).
   (C) They provide evidence contrary to material in a previous paragraph.
   (D) They reiterate an idea presented in the previous paragraph.
   (E) They state a logical conclusion based on statements in the previous paragraph.

8. The speaker's allusion to going back to "where I began" (line 42) refers to

   (A) looking for relief from a head cold.
   (B) an earlier unspecified time of life.
   (C) wearing a skull cap.
   (D) putting on a cap to keep his head warm.
   (E) covering his legs with silk hose.

9. Which of the following phrases is probably exaggerated for effect?

   (A) "from white wine to claret, and back again" (lines 9–10)
   (B) "body and mind are made cruelly sluggish" (lines 21–22)
   (C) "three or four wretched repasts a day" (line 29)
   (D) "from a bonnet to a lined hat" (line 38)
   (E) "a hare's skin or a vulture's plumage" (line 40)

10. The principal contrast drawn by the author of the passage is between

    (A) theory and fact.
    (B) conventions and individual preferences.
    (C) old wives' tales and modern practices.
    (D) idealism and realism.
    (E) restraint and freedom.

Questions 11–22. Carefully read the following passage and answer the accompanying questions.

The passage is an excerpt from a book by a 20th century author.

Passage 2

Does history repeat itself? In our Western world in the eighteenth and nineteenth centuries, this question used to be debated as an academic exercise. The spell of well-being which our civilization was enjoying at the time
Line had dazzled our grandfathers into the quaint pharisaical notion that they
(5) were "not as other men are"; they had come to believe that our Western society was exempt from the possibility of falling into those mistakes and mishaps that have been the ruin of certain other civilizations whose history, from the beginning to end, is an open book. To us, in our generation, the old question has rather suddenly taken on a new and very practical signifi-
(10) cance. We have awakened to the truth (how, one wonders, could we ever have been blind to it?) that Western man and his works are no more invulnerable than the now extinct civilizations of the Aztecs and the Incas, the Sumerians and the Hittites. So today, with some anxiety, we are searching the scriptures of the past to find out whether they contain a lesson that we
(15) can decipher. Does history give us any information about our own prospects? And, if it does, what is the burden of it? Does it spell out for us an inexorable doom, which we can merely await with folded hands— resigning ourselves, as best we may, to a fate that we cannot avert or even modify by our own efforts? Or does it inform us, not of certainties, but of
(20) probabilities, or bare possibilities, in our own future? The practical difference is vast, for, on this second alternative, so far from being stunned into passivity, we should be aroused to action. On this second alternative, the lesson of history would not be like an astrologer's horoscope; it would be like a navigator's chart, which affords the seafarer who has the intelligence
(25) to use it a much greater hope of avoiding shipwreck than when he was sailing blind, because it gives him the means, if he has the skill and courage to use them, of steering a course between charted rocks and reefs.

It will be seen that our question needs defining before we plunge into an attempt to answer it. When we ask ourselves, "Does history repeat itself?"

(30)   do we mean no more than, "Does history turn out to have repeated itself, on occasions, in the past?" Or are we asking whether history is governed by inviolable laws which have not only taken effect in every past case to which they have applied, but are also bound to take effect in every similar situation that may arise in the future? On this second interpretation, the word

(35)   "does" would mean "must"; on the other interpretation it would mean "may." On this issue, the writer of the present article may as well put his cards on the table at once. He is not a determinist in his reading of the riddle of human life. He believes that where there is life there is hope, and that, with God's help, man is master of his own destiny, at least to some

(40)   extent, in some respects.

11. The author of the passage can best be characterized as someone who

    (A) is interested in theorizing about history.
    (B) is critical of historical researchers.
    (C) studies first-hand accounts of historical events.
    (D) believes in the influence of fate in shaping human events.
    (E) is not hopeful about the future of the human race.

12. In the context of the first paragraph, "grandfathers" (line 4) probably refers to all of the following EXCEPT

    (A) bygone observers of society.
    (B) ancestors of the author.
    (C) 18th and 19th century historians.
    (D) European and American thinkers and writers of the past.
    (E) scholars of previous generations.

13. In line 8, the phrase "an open book" refers to

    (A) the Western world of the 18th and 19th centuries.
    (B) our grandfathers' notion of history.
    (C) the lessons taught by ancient civilizations.
    (D) the debates of academicians.
    (E) the mistakes of civilizations now fallen into ruin.

14. Which of the following best describes the rhetorical function of the sentence "To us, in our generation . . . ." (lines 8–10)?

    (A) It reiterates the main idea of the passage.
    (B) It answers the question asked in the first line of the passage.
    (C) It introduces a contrast between the past and the present.
    (D) It offers a point of view with which the author disagrees.
    (E) It prepares the reader for the discussion of extinct civilizations.

15. The primary function of the author's observation made in the parentheses (lines 10–11) is

    (A) to counterbalance the question asked in line 1 of the passage.
    (B) to introduce an issue addressed later in the passage.
    (C) to briefly inject a change in the tone of the passage.
    (D) to summarize a different perspective on the topic of the passage.
    (E) to imply that the passage deals with a question that cannot be adequately answered.

16. In line 14 the word "scriptures" is best interpreted to mean

    (A) religious beliefs.
    (B) the laws.
    (C) the record.
    (D) the written record.
    (E) artifacts.

17. The end of the first paragraph (lines 22–27) contains all of the following rhetorical features EXCEPT

    (A) an antithesis.
    (B) an extended simile.
    (C) a metaphor.
    (D) alliteration.
    (E) hyperbole.

18. The phrase "this second alternative" (line 21) refers to which of the following?

    (A) History's ability to suggest the future.
    (B) The fate we cannot avert or modify.
    (C) Predictable events.
    (D) Our unknown future.
    (E) A navigation chart.

19. By comparing an "astrologer's horoscope" (line 23) and a "navigator's chart" (line 24), the author intends to convey the idea that

    (A) unlike our ancestors, we have the wherewithal to avoid mistakes of the past.
    (B) our ancestors were more superstitious than we are.
    (C) knowledge of navigation would have saved past civilizations.
    (D) science is superior to superstition.
    (E) astrology is a dying art.

20. In its context, the word "intelligence" (line 24) can best be defined as

    (A) an understanding of history.
    (B) probabilities.
    (C) formal education.
    (D) foresight and information.
    (E) techniques used to solve problems.

21. For which of the following reasons does the writer use the expression, "put his cards on the table" (lines 36–37)?

      I. To win the reader's confidence
    II. To indicate that he hasn't yet made up his mind on the question
  III. To acknowledge a personal bias

    (A) II only
    (B) I and II
    (C) II and III
    (D) I and III
    (E) I, II, and III

22. Which of the following most accurately describes the author's intent throughout the passage?

    (A) To solve a logical problem faced by historians
    (B) To refute theories espoused by other historians
    (C) To speculate on the validity of a historical principle
    (D) To prove an important historical theory
    (E) To define several terms used by historians

Questions 23–34. Carefully read the following passage and answer the accompanying questions.

The passage is taken from a work written in the twentieth century.

Passage 3

What are the practical results of the modern cult of beauty? The exercises and the massages, the health motors and the skin foods—to what have they led? Are women more beautiful than they were? Do they get something for
Line the enormous expenditure of energy, time, and money demanded of them
(5) by the beauty cult? These are questions which it is difficult to answer. For the facts seem to contradict themselves. The campaign for more physical beauty seems to be both a tremendous success and a lamentable failure. It depends how you look at the results.

It is a success insofar as more women retain their youthful appearance to
(10) a greater age than in the past. "Old ladies" are already becoming rare. In a few years, we may well believe, they will be extinct. White hair and wrinkles, a bent back and hollow cheeks will come to be regarded as medievally old-fashioned. The crone of the future will be golden, curly, and cherry-lipped, neat-ankled and slender. The Portrait of the Artist's Mother will
(15) come to be almost indistinguishable, at future picture shows, from the Portrait of the Artist's Daughter. This desirable consummation will be due in part to skin foods and injections of paraffin wax, facial surgery, mud baths, and paint, in part to improved health, due in its turn to a more rational mode of life. Ugliness is one of the symptoms of disease; beauty, of
(20) health. Insofar as the campaign for more beauty is also a campaign for more health, it is admirable and, up to a point, genuinely successful. Beauty that is merely the artificial shadow of these symptoms of health is

intrinsically of poorer quality than the genuine article. Still, it is a sufficiently good imitation to be sometimes mistakable for the real thing. The

(25) apparatus for mimicking the symptoms of health is now within the reach
of every moderately prosperous person; the knowledge of the way in which
real health can be achieved is growing, and will in time, no doubt, be universally acted upon. When that happy moment comes, will every woman
be beautiful—as beautiful, at any rate, as the natural shape of her features,

(30) with or without surgical and chemical aid, permits?

   The answer is emphatically: No. For real beauty is as much an affair of
the inner as of the outer self. The beauty of a porcelain jar is a matter of
shape, of color, of surface texture. The jar may be empty or tenanted by spi-
ders, full of honey or stinking slime—it makes no difference to its beauty

(35) or ugliness. But a woman is alive, and her beauty is therefore not skin deep.
The surface of the human vessel is affected by the nature of its spiritual contents. I have seen women who, by the standards of a connoisseur of porcelain, were ravishingly lovely. Their shape, their color, their surface texture
were perfect. And yet they were not beautiful. For the lovely vase was either

(40) empty or filled with some corruption. Spiritual emptiness or ugliness shows
through. And conversely, there is an interior light that can transfigure forms
that the pure aesthetician would regard as imperfect or downright ugly.

23. The word "cult" (line 1) as used in the passage means primarily

   (A) a group with a particular obsession
   (B) a subculture dedicated to a pagan rite
   (C) a movement sponsored by patrons of beauty salons
   (D) the devotees of a unique ideology
   (E) the followers of a charismatic leader

24. The first paragraph raises expectations that the remainder of the passage
   will be

   (A) a biting indictment.
   (B) an objective description.
   (C) a "pro" and "con" kind of discussion.
   (D) praise for the perpetuation of youthfulness.
   (E) advice on maintaining good health.

25. Which of the following is most likely a deliberate exaggeration?

   (A) "tremendous success and lamentable failure" (line 7)
   (B) "It is a success" (line 9)
   (C) "they will be extinct" (line 11)
   (D) "a bent back and hollow cheeks" (line 12)
   (E) "old-fashioned" (line 13)

26. The primary rhetorical strategy used to develop the idea that old ladies are becoming rare is best described as

    (A) a series of metaphors.
    (B) rhetorical questions and answers.
    (C) examples with repetitive sentence structure.
    (D) parallel and periodic sentences.
    (E) allusions and analogies.

27. The author of the passage can be described in all of the following ways EXCEPT

    (A) probing.
    (B) intellectually curious.
    (C) somewhat condescending.
    (D) scientifically objective.
    (E) perceptive.

28. Which of the following best characterizes the tone of the phrase "crone of the future" (line 13)?

    (A) Anger
    (B) Bitterness
    (C) Sympathy
    (D) Ridicule
    (E) Irony

29. In the development of the last paragraph (lines 31–42), the rhetorical device most in evidence is

    (A) extended analogy.
    (B) compound subject.
    (C) appeal to authority.
    (D) emotional exclamation.
    (E) antithesis.

30. "The surface of the human vessel is affected by the nature of its spiritual contents" (lines 36–37) is a statement best decribed as

    (A) an epigram.
    (B) a simile.
    (C) a platitude.
    (D) a witticism.
    (E) a symbol.

31. The point at which the author turns to the principal theme of the passage is

    (A) at the beginning of paragraph 2.
    (B) when he refers to the Portrait of the Artist's Mother (line 14).
    (C) the last sentence of paragraph 1.
    (D) the beginning of paragraph 3.
    (E) the last two sentences of paragraph 3.

32. The passage contains all of the following EXCEPT

   (A) a description of the success of the cult of beauty.
   (B) a discussion of the link between beauty and health.
   (C) a comparison of inner and outer beauty.
   (D) a sympathetic presentation of the yearning for eternal youth.
   (E) the personal feelings of the author toward the phenomena described.

33. Which of the following represents the author's main purpose?

   (A) To highlight the successful aspects of the beauty cult.
   (B) To comment on a phase of female psychology.
   (C) To describe a change of values in contemporary society.
   (D) To expose the shortcomings and omissions of the beauty cult.
   (E) To extol the virtues of aging.

34. The principal contrast employed by the author of the passage is between

   (A) crones and fair ladies.
   (B) inner beauty versus outer beauty.
   (C) health and good looks.
   (D) staying young and living longer.
   (E) youth and age.

Questions 35–44. Carefully read the following passage and answer the accompanying questions.

The passage was written early in the 20th century.

Passage 4

A hundred years ago a crusty old bachelor of fifty-seven, so deaf that he could not hear his own music played by a full orchestra, yet still able to hear thunder, shook his fist at the roaring heavens for the last time, and died as
Line he had lived, challenging God and defying the universe. He was Defiance
(5) Incarnate: he could not even meet a Grand Duke and his court in the street without jamming his hat tight down on his head and striding through the very middle of them. He had the manners of a disobliging steamroller (most steamrollers are abjectly obliging and conciliatory); and he was rather less particular about his dress than a scarecrow: in fact he was once arrested
(10) as a tramp because the police refused to believe that such a tatterdemalion could be a famous composer, much less a temple of the most turbulent spirit that ever found expression in pure sound. It was indeed a mighty spirit; but if I had written the mightiest, which would mean mightier than the spirit of Handel, Beethoven himself would have rebuked me; and what
(15) mortal man could pretend to a spirit mightier than Bach's? But that Beethoven's spirit was the most turbulent is beyond all question. The impetuous fury of his strength, which he could quite easily contain and control, but often would not, and the unroariousness of his fun, go beyond anything of the kind to be found in the works of other composers.
(20) Greenhorns write of syncopation now as if it were a new way of giving the

utmost impetus to a musical measure; but the rowdiest jazz sounds like *The Maiden's Prayer* after Beethoven's third *Leonora* overture; and certainly no jazz ensemble that I ever heard could propel even the most eager dancer into action as the last movement of the *Seventh Symphony*. And no other

(25) composer has ever melted his hearers into complete sentimentality by the tender beauty of his music, and then suddenly turned on them and mocked them with derisive trumpet blasts for being such fools. Nobody but Beethoven could govern Beethoven; and when, as happened when the fit was on him, he deliberately refused to govern himself, he was ungovernable.

(30) It was this turbulence, this deliberate disorder, this mockery, this reckless and triumphant disregard of conventional manners, that set Beethoven apart from the musical geniuses of the ceremonious seventeenth and eighteenth centuries. He was a giant wave in that storm of the human spirit which produced the French Revolution. He called no man master. Mozart,

(35) his greatest predecessor in his own department, had from his childhood been washed, combed, splendidly dressed, and beautifully behaved in the presence of royal personages and peers. His childish outburst at the Pompadour, "Who is this woman who does not kiss me? The Queen kisses me," would be incredible of Beethoven, who was still an unlicked cub even

(40) when he had grown into a very grizzly bear.

35. Which of the following best describes the rhetorical function of the second sentence of the passage (lines 4–7)?

(A) It contrasts a man and the environment in which he lived.
(B) It conveys the tragic tone of the passage.
(C) It restates the main idea of the passage.
(D) It provides a specific example to illustrate the preceding generalization.
(E) It adds a new dimension to the portrait of the person being described.

36. The author uses all of the following phrases to illustrate his subject's rebellious spirit EXCEPT

(A) "old bachelor" (line 1).
(B) " shook his fist" (line 3).
(C) "challenging God" (line 4).
(D) "Defiance Incarnate" (lines 4–5).
(E) "striding through . . .the middle of them" (lines 6–7).

37. In describing Beethoven's social behavior and appearance (lines 7–12), the author makes use of which rhetorical devices?

(A) symbolic references
(B) metaphors and similes
(C) everyday clichés
(D) caustic sarcasm
(E) slang expressions and euphemisms

38. Which of the following words is parallel in function and theme to "fury" (line 17)?

    (A) "turbulent" (line (16)
    (B) "impetuous" (line 17)
    (C) "strength" (line 17)
    (D) "unroariousness" (line 18)
    (E) "fun" (line 18)

39. In describing Beethoven's works (lines 17–28), the principal contrast employed by the author is between

    (A) music played by an orchestra and music played by a jazz band
    (B) loud, vigorous music and soft, tender music
    (C) revolutionary music and conventional music
    (D) Beethoven's style and the style of other composers
    (E) formal, structured music and free-form, impressionistic music

40. The author mentions the *Leonora* overture and the *Seventh Symphony* (lines 22–24) as examples of which of the following?

    (A) Outstanding achievements that have never been fully appreciated
    (B) Unique pieces that other composers have tried to imitate, but unsuccessfully
    (C) Well-known selections that helped Beethoven establish his reputation
    (D) Classical music that contains elements of jazz
    (E) Forceful musical compositions marked by high energy and powerful rhythm

41. In context, the expression "the fit was on him" (lines 28–29) is best interpreted to have which of the following meanings?

    (A) That he couldn't control himself
    (B) That he had a one-track mind
    (C) That he lacked faith in his ability to compose
    (D) That he was under severe pressure to write music
    (E) That he had fallen prey to his hot temper

42. The tone conveyed by the author's description of Mozart (lines 34–37) can best be described as

    (A) slightly disparaging
    (B) mildly ironic
    (C) astonished
    (D) vaguely annoyed
    (E) apprehensive

43. The final sentence of the passage (lines 38–40) contains which of the following rhetorical devices?

    I. paradox
   II. metaphor
  III. personification

(A) I only
(B) III only
(C) I and II only
(D) II and III only
(E) I, II, and III

44. Which of the following best states the subject of the passage?

(A) Beethoven's place in the history of music
(B) Beethoven as a symbol of the time in which he lived
(C) The influence of Beethoven on modern classical music
(D) Beethoven's incomparable genius
(E) How Beethoven the man is reflected in his music

Questions 45–54. Carefully read the following passage and answer the accompanying questions.

The passage is an excerpt from a book on world history written late in the 20th century.

Passage 5

    In the United States on the opening of Congress in January, 1890, a newly elected Speaker of the House of Representatives was in the Chair. A physical giant, six feet three inches tall, weighing almost three hundred
Line pounds and dressed completely in black, "out of whose collar rose an enor-
(5) mous clean-shaven baby face like a Casaba melon flowering from a fat black stalk, he was a subject for a Franz Hals, with long white fingers that would have enraptured Memling."*[1] Speaking in a slow drawl, he delighted to drop cool pearls of sarcasm into the most heated rhetoric and to watch the resulting fizzle with the bland gravity of a New England Buddha. When a
(10) wordy perennial, Representative Springer of Illinois, was declaiming to the House his passionate preference to be right rather than President, the Speaker interjected, "The gentleman need not be disturbed; he will never be either." When another member, notorious for ill-digested opinions and a halting manner, began some remarks with, "I was thinking, Mr. Speaker,
(15) I was thinking . . ." the Chair expressed the hope that "no one will interrupt the gentleman's commendable innovation." Of two particularly inept speakers, he remarked, "They never open their mouths without subtracting from the sum of human knowledge." It was said that he would rather make an epigram than a friend. Yet among the select who were his chosen friends
(20) he was known as "one of the most genial souls that ever enlivened a company," whose conversation, "sparkling with good nature, was better than

the best champagne." He was Thomas B. Reed, Republican of Maine, aged fifty. Already acknowledged after fourteen years in Congress as "the ablest running debater the American people ever saw," he would, before the end

(25) of the session, be called "the greatest parliamentary leader of his time, . . . far and away the most brilliant figure in American politics."

Although his roots went back to the beginning of New England, Reed was not nurtured for a political career by inherited wealth, social position or landed estate. Politics in America made no use of these qualities, and

(30) men who possessed them were not in politics. Well-to-do, long-established families did not shoulder—but shunned—the responsibilities of government. Henry Adams' eldest brother, John, "regarded as the most brilliant of the family and the most certain of high distinction," who made a fortune in the Union Pacific Railroad, "drew himself back" from government,

(35) according to his brother. "He had all he wanted; wealth, children, society, consideration; and he laughed at the idea of sacrificing himself in order to adorn a Cleveland Cabinet or get cheers from an Irish mob."[2] This attitude was not confined to the rather worn-out Adamses. When the young Theodore Roosevelt announced his intention of entering politics in New

(40) York in 1880, he was laughed at by the "men of cultivated and easy life" who told him politics were "low" and run by "saloon-keepers, horse-car conductors and the like," whom he would find "rough, brutal and unpleasant to deal with."

Hals: Dutch painter 1582–1666; Memling: Flemish painter of 15th century. Both specialized in portraits.

[1]*DE CASSERES, BENJAMIN, "Tom Reed," American Mercury, February, 1930. The following quotations in this paragraph, in order, are from CLARK, CHAMP, My Quarter Century of American Politics, 2 vols., New York, Harper, 1920, I, 287; LEUPP, FRANCIS E., "Personal Recollections of Thomas Brackett Reed," Outlook, September 3, 1910; McCALL, SAMUEL, The Life of Thomas Brackett Reed, Boston, Houghton Mifflin, 1914, 248; DUNN, ARTHUR WALLACE, From Harrison to Harding, 2 vols. New York, Putnam's 1922, I, 165; FOULKE, WILLIAM DUDLEY, A Hoosier Autobiography, Oxford Univ. Press, 1922, 110; PORTER, ROBERT P., "Thomas Brackett Reed of Maine," McClure's, October, 1893. "The ablest running debater" was said by Rep. John Sharp Williams, Democratic Leader of the House; "the greatest parliamentary leader" by Lodge; "far and away the most brilliant" by CLARK, II, 10.*

[2]*HENRY ADAMS on his brother John: Sept. 1, 1894, Letters, ed. Worthington Chauncey Ford, 2 vols. Boston, Houghton Mifflin, 1930–38, II, 55.*

45. The development of the first paragraph of the passage can best be described as

(A) a chronological account of a public servant's career.
(B) a compilation of background information on the life of an influential public figure.
(C) a report on the aspirations of a 19th-century politician.
(D) the description of a character based on the testimony of others.
(E) the presentation of conflicting views regarding a well-known American.

46. Which of the following rhetorical effects does the author achieve by delaying the disclosure of the Speaker's name until line 22?

    (A) It emphasizes that the name is irrelevant to the passage
    (B) It creates a tentative transition from the first paragraph to the second
    (C) It highlights a contradiction between the man's words and his actions
    (D) It keeps the reader in suspense about the identity of an unusual man
    (E) It illustrates the kind of rhetoric used by political figures

47. The structure of lines 7–13 ("Speaking . . . either'") can best be described as

    (A) a generality supported by a specific example.
    (B) a questionable statement of fact followed by an explanation of its source.
    (C) the movement from a cause to an effect.
    (D) a claim followed by a qualifying statement.
    (E) an assumption and an conclusion based on that assumption.

48. Overall, the writers whose words are documented by footnote 1 viewed Speaker Reed as

    (A) an extraordinary political figure.
    (B) a politician who could not be corrupted.
    (C) a representative dedicated to his constituents.
    (D) a fighter for liberal causes.
    (E) the driving force behind many new laws.

49. Taken as a whole, footnote 1 suggests that the author of the passage

    (A) researched the daily newspapers published while Reed served in Congress.
    (B) relied heavily on official documents related to Reed's work.
    (C) used few sources contemporary with Reed's first term as a Congressman.
    (D) interviewed members of Congress who worked with Reed.
    (E) studied speeches delivered by Reed in the House of Representatives.

50. The author's use of the phrase "New England Buddha" (line 9) refers mainly to the man's

    (A) appearance and demeanor.
    (B) intelligence and sense of humor.
    (C) background and family history.
    (D) energy and ambition.
    (E) stubbornness and perseverance.

51. Which of Reed's characteristics does the author illustrate with the quotations in lines 12–18?

     I. Reed's quick wit
    II. Reed's fondness for sarcasm
  III. Reed's dislike of pretentiousness

(A) I only
(B) III only
(C) I and II only
(D) II and III only
(E) I, II, and III

52. In context, the phrase "ill-digested" (line 13) is best interpreted to mean

(A) sincere but stupid.
(B) contradictory.
(C) sickening.
(D) poorly thought-out.
(E) illogical.

53. Which of the following is an accurate reading of information in footnote 2 (line 37)?

(A) It attributes the quotations in lines 32–37 to Henry's brother, John.
(B) *Letters* was published in Boston in 1894.
(C) A letter from John Adams to Worthington Chauncey Ford was dated Sept. 1, 1894.
(D) A book published in two volumes contains the letters of Henry Adams.
(E) From 1930 to 1938, John and Henry Adams wrote letters that were published in Boston.

54. The author's reference to Roosevelt (lines 38–43) is meant to illustrate

(A) a famous government officeholder.
(B) an old New England family.
(C) a politician from a wealthy family.
(D) a man with great ability.
(E) a member of an American political dynasty.

SECTION II
Three Essay Questions
Total time—Two hours and 15 minutes

Write your essays on standard 8½" × 11" composition paper. At the exam you will be given a bound booklet containing 12 lined pages.

Essay Question 1

Time—15 minutes to read the sources
     40 minutes to write the essay

Instructions: The following essay topic is accompanied by six sources.

Respond to the question below in a well-written, coherent essay that draws on ideas and information found in **at least three** of the sources. Don't simply summarize or paraphrase the sources. Instead, **focus the essay on your point of view**, and use the sources to support or bolster your argument.

Topic: In response to the events of September 11, 2001, there has been considerable discussion and debate about creating a national ID card. Some people argue that our country would be more secure if everyone were required to carry ID cards. Others say that ID cards could take away our rights and liberties.

Your task: Read the following sources carefully. Then, in an essay that synthesizes at least three of the sources, take a position that supports, challenges, or modifies the claim the United States should create a system of national ID cards.

In your essay, you may refer to the sources simply as Source A, Source B, etc., or by the key words in parentheses below.

Source A (Barber)
Source B (Dershowitz)
Source C (Etzioni)
Source D (Cartoon)
Source E (Clement)
Source F (Fussell)

SOURCE A

Grayson Barber, "Would National ID Cards Increase Safety and Preserve Civil Liberties"? American Civil Liberties Union of New Jersey, <*www.aclu.org/safeand free*>

The following statement was written by an attorney and member of the Board of Trustees of the ACLU of New Jersey.

The best argument in favor of national ID cards is their exculpatory value. If an airline passenger has dark skin, for example, and an Islamic-sounding last name, he or she could simply flash the card and avoid being hassled at the airport. Advocates in favor of ID cards argue that the inconvenience of having to register with the government would be spread across all social groups, and ethnic profiling would end because disfavored groups would not be singled out for negative treatment. National ID cards would streamline governmental administration and, if adopted by the private sector, provide useful links between commercial and government institutions.

The difficulty with national ID cards is that they inevitably increase police powers. They are used in about 100 countries around the world, for a variety of purposes, from determining eligibility for government benefits to eliminating border controls. They do not cut crime rates, but they do improve governmental efficiency.

An important question, therefore, is what national ID cards would be used for in this country. If the goal is to track people with criminal records, for example, the magnetic strip could carry information about arrests and convictions. Failure to carry one's ID could be grounds for arrest, and the police could perform spot-checks on undesirables everywhere.

Another question is whether national ID cards would achieve their purpose. They would not have identified the September 11 hijackers who had valid driver's licenses (not to mention frequent flyer miles). Moreover, ID cards are only as good as the documentation supporting them. Biometric chips can be embedded in a card, but if the card is issued based on a forged birth certificate, it is still fraudulent. Problems that arise from illegal immigration cannot be cured with a single ID card strategy. For example, it is easy to stay in this country after a student visa expires, because colleges and universities are not required to track, monitor, retrieve, and deport students from other countries.

The American Association of Motor Vehicle Administrators (AAMVA) has proposed to turn state driver's licenses into de facto national IDs. The plan is to use digital photos, holographic images, and magnetic strips to compare licenses against a national criminal information database. Under current law, if you're pulled over while driving, the police can only check to see if your car is stolen or if there are any warrants outstanding for your arrest. The AAMVA proposal would inevitably strengthen the state's police powers.

SOURCE B

Alan Dershowitz, "Small Compromises," *Boston Review*, Dec 2002/Jan 2003
<*www.bostonreview.net*>

The following is an excerpt from a Harvard Law School professor's piece that appeared in a publication that calls itself "a political and literary forum."

If there must be compromises with liberty, it is far better in a democracy that small ones be required of everyone (of the "we's") than that large compromises be imposed only on outsiders ("they's"). That is one reason why, as a civil libertarian, I strongly prefer a limited national ID card to racial profiling. The limited national ID card as proposed would contain only the name, photograph, Social Security number, address, and a finger- or retinal print that would prevent identity theft. The card I would favor would be optional. No one would have to carry it. And no one would be asked to show it on the street. The police would not be able to stop citizens and demand "Your papers, please." But this national telemetric card with a print would be the only identification acceptable in places—such as airports and government buildings—that now appropriately require identification. Anyone who did not show such a card would be subject to far more intrusive inquiries.

Such a limited card would eliminate much of the justification now offered for racial or ethnic profiling. When I first came to Harvard Law School in the 1960s, the few African-American students were often harassed by security officers since they didn't "look" as if they "belonged" on or near the Harvard campus. ID cards helped them to solve that problem. African-American students, by showing their cards, were generally able to avoid being hassled. Of course they were asked to show their cards more frequently than students who looked like they belonged, and that surely is not appropriate. But ID cards clearly reduced the amount of inappropriate hassling of minority students. I suspect the same would be true for Arab and Muslim Americans. By showing the telemetric card they could probably avoid much of the harassment that many have experienced on airplanes and other places.

As I wrote in my book *Why Terrorism Works*, As a general proposition, I think it far better for everybody to be deprived of a little bit of anonymity than for one specific ethnic group to bear a disproportionate part of the burden. I prefer "we-we" compromises over "we-they" compromises.

"We-we" intrusions provide a more effective check on abuses, since those whose rights are being compromised have more political power than the "they's." An optional national ID card is a "we-we" intrusion, since those who deliberately opt out of the national ID system have made a decision to endure more intrusive searches in exchange for not having to carry the card. In some respects, this is a little like the trade-off people make when they agree to have their automobile identified by a radio computer when crossing bridges and tunnels, rather than stopping and paying an anonymous toll.

SOURCE C

Amitai Etzioni, "You'll Love Those National ID Cards," *Christian Science Monitor*, January 14, 2002.

The following is part of an opinion piece by a professor at George Washington University and author of The Limits of Privacy *(Basic Books, 1999).*

Beyond making it much harder for terrorists to abuse our free society, tamper-proof, national ID card should be embraced for all the other good service they will do. Currently, there are some 300,000 criminals on the lam in the US. These are not mere suspects, but convicts who somehow escape the jurisdiction of the courts, say, by fleeing prison. Many of them commit additional crimes, because they know they're heading for a stiff jail sentence anyhow. One of the best ways to get them off the streets is to introduce foolproof ID cards.

Such cards will also help ensure that people who work in child-care centers and schools are not child abusers or sex offenders. This is not an idle threat. When six states did screen such employees, more than 6,200 individuals convicted of serious crimes were found among those seeking child-care jobs. Elder-care facilities face a similar challenge when they try to screen out people with a record of violence. No ID—no valid screening.

Also, validated IDs would greatly curtail the price of identify theft, which cost the public at least $750 million in 1997. They would also shave income tax fraud committed by those who file multiple tax returns at an estimated cost of more than $1 billion per year, and welfare fraud amounting to $10 billion annually in entitlement programs alone.

Indeed, the public is wising up. While in 1993 a minority (39 percent) favored ID cards and a majority (53 percent) objected to them, a post 9/11 poll finds a sea change. Now 70 percent favor a national identity card to show police upon request and only 1 out of 4 (26 percent) oppose it. You may say all this makes sense if one could really have a foolproof ID card. The good news is that new ways of identifying people do not involve old-fashioned pieces of paper with ugly mug shots. Now they're based on biometrics. Luckily, no two people—even identical twins—have identical faces or irises. Computers can now recognize these.

We live in a new world, and now must make some careful adjustments to our way of life. To require everyone within our borders to identify themselves is a reliable manner is a reasonable step in the right direction.

SOURCE D

Cartoon: "The Americans Oppressed Card" The Cobra's Lair, 2005. *<the cobraslair.com/images/ NATIONAL-ID-CARD-STREAM.gif>*

The illustration below appeared on the web site of the Cobra's Lair.

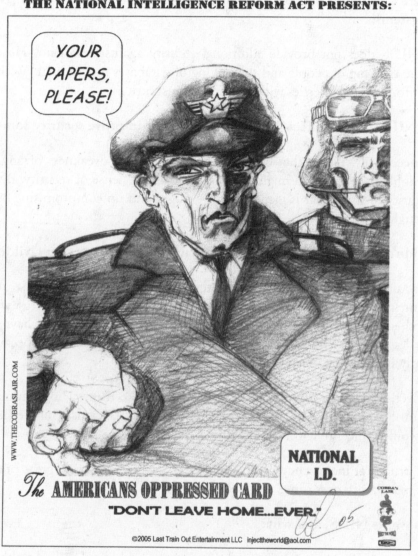

SOURCE E

Andrew Clement, et al., "National Identification Schemes: FAQ," Openflows Network, Ltd., 11/13/01. <*www.openflows.org*>

The following is part of a series of questions and answers posted online by an organization that publishes material of interest on a multitude of topics.

6. Is there a trade-off between civil liberties and security with NIDS [National ID System]?

No, NIDS does not provide additional security against terrorism. However, it makes the tracking of people and the linking of databases much easier. With NIDS we compromise civil liberties without increasing security.

7. OK, NIDS is not perfect, but doesn't it at least improve security somewhat?

Not necessarily. Given the somewhat hidden systemic weakness of any NIDS, such a highly visible system might well produce a false sense of security. By relying on a security measure that is inadequate, we might end up compromising our security through NIDS.

8. Wouldn't a voluntary NIDS improve security while preserving civil liberties?

No, actually, it would be even worse than a mandatory system. First, it would make untrustworthy anyone who does not have a card. A lot of energy would be wasted checking people who are only suspects because they don't have a card. Second, less time would be spent checking people who have a card because they apparently have already been cleared.

In effect, it would make life easier for terrorists like those who committed the attacks on September 11 because they could use their ID cards while security personnel would concentrate on those without one.

This structural inefficiency of a voluntary system would create great pressure to make it mandatory over time.

9. Who wants NIDS, and why?

Two groups: The law enforcement community would like a tool to make it easier to identify people on routine checks and to link their databases by using the national ID card as a unique identifier. This has little to do with the fight against terrorism but a lot to do with the expansion of police powers.

Smart-card identification systems have also been promoted by large information technology vendors. For them, a multi-billion dollar system would be a great business opportunity. The most prominent promoters. . . have been Scott McNealy, CEO of Sun Microsystems, and Larry Ellison, CEO of Oracle.

SOURCE F

Jim Fussell, "Group Classification on National ID Cards as a Factor in Genocide and Ethnic Cleansing," published on the web site of Prevent Genocide International.

The following is part of a talk delivered at a seminar at Yale University's Genocide Studies Program, November 15, 2001.

. . .Once the 1994 genocide in Rwanda began, an ID card with the designation "Tutsi" spelled a death sentence at any roadblock. No other factor was more significant in facilitating the speed and magnitude of the 100 days of mass killing in Rwanda.

National ID cards of all kinds are controversial. In recent years in the United States, Britain, Canada, and Australia, proposals for introducing national ID cards and registry systems have raised debate about governmental control and privacy issues. Classification of ethnic, racial, or religious groups on ID cards, however, is a distinctly different issue. Group classification on ID cards or other official personal documents (passports, residence permits, etc.) forces a person to be affiliated with a governmentally-defined group and exposes the person to profiling and human rights abuses based upon their group identity. In times of crisis, such classifications facilitate the targeting of persons on the basis of group affiliation, making individuals readily identifiable for possible detention, deportation, or death.

ESSAY QUESTION 2

Suggested time—40 minutes. This question counts as one third of the total score for Section II.

Read the following passage, an excerpt from an email written to friends and family by an American soldier fighting in Iraq, 2003–2004. Then write an essay in which you analyze the rhetorical strategies used by the author to explain his experience and convey his attitude toward that experience.

I know a number of you have been curious about what it's like over here, so we are going to take a small mental voyage. First off, we are going to prepare our living area. Go to your vacuum, open the canister, and pour it all
Line over you, your bed, clothing, and your personal effects. Now roll in it until
(5) it's in your eyes, nose, ears, hair, and . . .well, you get the picture. You know it's just perfect when you slap your chest and cough from the dust cloud you kicked up. And so, there is no escape, trust me. You just get used to it.

OK, pitch a tent in your driveway, and mark off an area inside it along one wall about six feet by eight feet (including your bed). Now pack every-
(10) thing you need to live for four months— without Wal-Mart—and move in. Tear down the three walls of your tent seen from the street and you have about as much privacy as I have.

If you really want to make this accurate, bring in a kennel full of pugs; the smell, snoring, and social graces will be just like living with my nine
(15) tentmates. Also, you must never speak above a whisper because at all times at least four of your tentmates will be sleeping. That's where the flashlight comes in handy; you are going to use it to navigate a pitch-dark tent, 24 hours a day.

Time for hygiene. Walk to the nearest bathroom. In my case, it's a thou-
(20) sand-foot trudge over loose gravel. Ever stagger to the john at 0400? Try it in a frozen rock garden. Given the urges that woke you at this hour, taking the time to put on your thermals and jacket might not be foremost in your mind. But halfway there, it's too late. So dress warmly. It gets really freakin' cold here at night.

(25) I don't even feel like talking about the latrine experience. All I have to say is that, after the first time, I went back to the tent and felt like either cry-ing or lighting myself on fire to remove the filth.

ESSAY QUESTION 3

(Suggested time—40 minutes. This question counts as one third of the total score for Section II.)

After you have read the following passages—the first by Maxwell Anderson, a playwright and novelist; the other by Susanne Langer, a philosopher and teacher— write an essay that compares the ways in which the two authors convey their views about art. You might consider such rhetorical and stylistic devices as diction, figurative language, point of view, repetition, and sentence structure.

Passage A

Line
(5)

(10)

(15)

To the young people of this country I wish to say: if you practice an art, be proud of it and make it proud of you; if you now hesitate on the threshold of your maturity, wondering what rewards you should seek, wondering perhaps whether there are any rewards beyond the opportunity to feed and sleep and breed, turn to the art which has moved you most readily, take what part in it you can, as participator, spectator, secret practitioner, or hanger-on and waiter at the door. Make your living any way you can, but neglect no sacrifice at your chosen altar. It may break your heart, it may drive you half mad, it may betray you into unrealizable ambitions or blind you to mercantile opportunities with its wandering fires. But it will fill your heart before it breaks it; it will make you a person in your own right; it will open the temple doors to you and enable you to walk with those who have come nearest among men to what men may sometime be. If the time arrives when our young men and women lose their extravagant faith in the dollar and turn to the arts we may then become a great nation, nurturing great artists of our own, proud of our own culture and unified by that culture into a civilization worthy of our unique place on this rich and lucky continent between its protecting seas.

(1947)

Passage B

(20)

(25)

Art is, indeed, the spearhead of human development, social and individual. The vulgarization of art is the surest symptom of ethnic decline. The growth of a new art or even a great and radically new style always bespeaks a young and vigorous mind, whether collective or single.

What sort of thing is art, that it should play such a leading role in human development? It is not an intellectual pursuit, but is necessary to intellectual life; it is not religion, but grows up with religion, serves it and in large measure determines it (as Herodotus said, "Homer made the gods," and surely the Egyptian deities grew under the chisels of sculptors in strangely solemn forms).

(30)   We cannot enter here on a long discussion of what has been claimed as the essence of art, the true nature of art, or its defining function; in a single lecture dealing with one aspect of art, namely its cultural significance, I can only give you by way of preamble my own definition of art, with categorical brevity. That does not mean that I set up this definition in a cat-

(35) egorical spirit, but only that we have no time to debate it, so you are asked to accept it as an assumption underlying these reflections.

Art, in the sense intended—that is, the generic term subsuming painting, sculpture, architecture, music, dance, literature, and drama—may be defined as the practice of creating perceptible forms expressive of human

(40) feeling. I say "perceptible" rather than "sensuous" forms because some works of art are given to imagination rather than to the outward senses. A novel, for instance, usually is read silently with the eye, but is not made for vision, as a painting is; and though sound plays a vital part in poetry, words even in poetry are not essentially sonorous structures like music. Dance

(45) requires to be seen, but its appeal is to deeper centers of sensation. The difference between dance and mobile sculpture makes this immediately apparent. But all works of art are purely perceptible forms that seem to embody some sort of feeling.

(1957)

END OF PRACTICE TEST B

Answer Key
PRACTICE TEST B

Answers to Multiple-Choice Questions

1. E	21. D	41. A
2. E	22. C	42. A
3. B	23. A	43. C
4. E	24. C	44. E
5. C	25. C	45. D
6. C	26. C	46. D
7. D	27. D	47. A
8. D	28. E	48. A
9. E	29. A	49. C
10. B	30. A	50. A
11. A	31. D	51. E
12. B	32. D	52. D
13. E	33. D	53. D
14. C	34. B	54. C
15. C	35. D	
16. C	36. A	
17. E	37. B	
18. A	38. D	
19. A	39. B	
20. D	40. E	

Summary of Answers in Section I (Multiple-Choice)

Number of correct answers _____

Number of incorrect answers _____

Number of questions not answered _____

Use this information when you calculate your score on this exam. See page 293.

Practice Test B

Answer Explanations

PASSAGE 1—AN EXCERPT FROM MICHEL DE MONTAIGNE, "THE ENJOYMENT OF LIVING"

1. **(E)** The speaker presents himself as a quirky, unpredictable gentleman. The sentence in question, which seems unrelated to the topic of eating, illustrates exactly what the first sentence of the second paragraph is about: "fickle and inexplicable changes."

2. **(E)** The first sentence of the paragraph is the topic sentence. The remainder of the paragraph supports the topic sentence and adds to the self-portrait of the author. There is no evidence of a change in the author's tone.

3. **(B)** The speaker's explanation of his preference for fish contributes to his portrait as a careful and fastidious eater.

4. **(E)** Line 12 contains an alliteration ("my fasts are my feasts"). Two clauses in the last sentence of the paragraph are parallel in structure ("As it goes against . . ." and ". . . my taste rebels against . . ."). The phrase "dainty tooth" is a synecdoche—a figure of speech in which a part stands for the whole. "My fasts are my feasts" is a paradox. Only onomatopoeia is missing.

5. **(C)** The author enjoys eating and never feels guilty about consuming too much.

6. **(C)** The discussion of eating habits appears in the context of a description of how the author manages to lead a pleasurable life—by acceding to his whims and fancies.

7. **(D)** According to the previous paragraph, one's dining companions at a pleasurable meal are at least as important as the quality of the food. Lines 25–26 reiterate that sentiment.

8. **(D)** To stay warm, the speaker keeps donning additional layers of clothing. His body, however, shortly craves more layers. Having grown weary of putting on more and more, the speaker would like to return to the time before he first put on a cap to keep his head warm.

9. **(E)** In the next to last paragraph, the author describes the methods he uses to keep warm. He knows that it would be ridiculous to resort to "a hare's skin or a vulture's plumage." Yet he uses the terms to emphasize the lengths to which he is forced to go in order to remain comfortably warm.

10. **(B)** The passage is devoted to descriptions of the author's preferences, particularly in food and health care. Although his preferences often fly in the face of convention, he makes no apology.

**PASSAGE 2—AN EXCERPT FROM ARNOLD TOYNBEE,
"DOES HISTORY REPEAT ITSELF?"**

11. **(A)** The author is a theorist. Throughout the passage, he ponders the degree to which we can intelligently use and benefit from lessons taught by history.

12. **(B)** In the context, "grandfathers" refers to 18th- and 19th-century people who may have occasionally talked over whether history repeats itself, but who deceived themselves into believing that they were unique—that is, that they were exempt from the lessons that history teaches. The passage does not mention or allude to the author's own actual grandfathers.

13. **(E)** Because the "open book" records mistakes of past civilizations, readers can infer the lessons that history teaches. The "open book" itself, however, refers to the history of past civilizations, in particular the mistakes and mishaps that led to their downfall.

14. **(C)** Early in the passage the author discusses our grandfathers' view of the question of whether history repeats itself. With this sentence, the author begins to present a more up-to-date perspective.

15. **(C)** By asking the question enclosed by parentheses, the author expresses an opinion that, in effect, rebukes himself and his fellow historians for their past shortsightedness. The question is different in tone—far more informal and personal—from the discussion that precedes and follows it.

16. **(C)** As we study past civilizations, we have little to go on except the ruins that have been left behind. From the ruins, we infer lessons that have the force of scripture.

17. **(E)** Lines 19–20 contain an example of an antithesis. The discussion of a navigator's chart (line 24) appears in the context of an extended simile. The phrase "charted rocks and reefs" comprises a metaphor. Combinations of words such as "probabilities/possibilities" and "rocks/reefs" contain alliteration.

18. **(A)** The "second alternative" refers to our ability to study history to infer what lies in store.

19. **(A)** The horoscope tells what fate has in store for us. The navigation chart, in contrast, enables us to steer "a course between charted rocks and reefs." In other words, we can learn from the mistakes of past civilizations. Because we know the perils, we can take steps to avoid them.

20. **(D)** A seafarer with "intelligence" uses the data on the navigator's chart to avoid rocks and reefs. In other words, he realizes how the information he has before him can guide him safely into the future.

21. **(D)** The colloquial expression tends to create the impression that the writer is going to confide his true feelings to the reader; in short, he's going to be frank and forthright. At the same time, the writer implies that he has definite views on the subject.

22. **(C)** Throughout the passage the author ruminates on the notion of history repeating itself. He contrasts current thinking about the issue with the debates of earlier times. While he does not prove the theory that history repeats itself, he is optimistic that it does.

PASSAGE 3—AN EXCERPT FROM ALDOUS HUXLEY, "MUSIC AT NIGHT"

23. **(A)** The second sentence of the passage suggests what the author means. Those who make up a "cult" have an extreme devotion—an obsession, really—to a particular belief or set of activities; in this case it is the desire to create, preserve, or restore physical beauty.

24. **(C)** The unanswered questions and the uncertainties expressed in the first paragraph ("difficult to answer"; "It depends") prepare the reader for a discussion that weighs both sides of the issue.

25. **(C)** The notion that "old ladies" will become extinct overstates the case. In fact, the author retracts the idea in the next sentence by asserting that the characteristics typically attributed to aging women will become "old fashioned," but they won't altogether disappear. The exaggeration helps the author emphasize his point—that the cult of beauty is gradually changing women's overall appearance.

26. **(C)** Several examples of changes in women's appearance are expressed in similarly structured sentences, each beginning with the grammatical subject followed by the verb "will be."

27. **(D)** The style and content of the passage reveal that the author possesses all the traits listed except scientific objectivity.

28. **(E)** The dubious title "crone of the future" is meant ironically—comparable, in a way, to an accolade like "serial killer of the year" or "airhead of the month."

29. **(A)** The paragraph is dominated by an analogy that compares beauty in a woman with the beauty of a porcelain jar.

30. **(A)** In its context, the statement is a concise, thoughtful, and memorable idea. Thus, it can be labeled an *epigram*.

31. **(D)** The author uses the first two paragraphs to provide a context for his main concern, which is the difference between inner and outer beauty. Therefore, paragraph 3 contains the heart of the passage.

32. **(D)** The first paragraph describes the cult of beauty; the second, the beauty/health connection. Inner and outer beauty are compared in the final paragraph. Throughout the passage, the author assumes a somewhat condescending attitude. What is missing from the passage, then, is a sympathetic discussion of the yearning for eternal youth.

33. **(D)** By emphasizing the differences between inner and outer beauty, the author makes clear his disapproval of the commercial cult of beauty, which concerns itself only with the superficial, surface appearance of its clientele.

34. **(B)** The first paragraph questions the efficacy of the "modern cult of beauty." The second paragraph discusses women's techniques for making themselves beautiful. These two paragraphs merely serve as a prelude to the final paragraph, in which the author raises his main concern—the difference between inner and outer beauty.

PASSAGE 4—AN EXCERPT FROM GEORGE BERNARD SHAW, *SHAW ON MUSIC: A SELECTION FROM THE MUSIC CRITICISM OF GEORGE BERNARD SHAW,* 1927.

35. **(D)** The opening sentences generalizes about the man's stormy, defiant personality and state of mind. The sentence shows the man behaving defiantly in a specific situation.

36. **(A)** That Beethoven, the subject of the passage, was unmarried does not reflect his rebelliousness. All the other choices suggest feistiness, including (E), which shows Beethoven refusing to step aside to let the Grand Duke and his company pass on the street.

37. **(B)** The author compares Beethoven manners to a steamroller (line 7), his dress to that of a scarecrow (line 9).

38. **(D)** A word that is parallel to the noun "fury" must also be a noun and must precede a prepositional phrase. To be thematically parallel, it must suggest something unfriendly. The word "unroariousness" fits the bill because it is a noun preceding a prepositional phrase, and although you won't find "unroarious" in the dictionary, it is clearly meant to convey the opposite of "uproariousness"—in other words, something dark and mopey.

39. **(B)** The author contrasts the energy and power in parts of Beethoven's music with the soft sentimentality of other parts.

40. **(E)** The author's references to "syncopation" (line 20), "musical measure" (line 21), and propelling an "eager dancer into action" (line 23) are clues that his concern is a foot-tapping, rowdy element in some of Beethoven's music.

41. **(A)** The author is referring to Beethoven's ungovernable nature; Beethoven, in short, surrendered himself to an uncontrollable passion to compose.

42. **(A)** The author clearly prefers the personality of Beethoven to the personality of Mozart, who is portrayed as an arrogant, impeccably-groomed snob.

43. **(C)** The notion that Beethoven was an "unlicked cub" and a "grizzly bear" at the same time is paradoxical. Calling him either a "cub" or a "bear" is metaphorical. There is no personification in this segment of the passage.

44. **(E)** What the author focuses on throughout the passage is Beethoven's defiance of convention, both in his personality and his music.

PASSAGE 5—AN EXCERPT FROM BARBARA TUCHMAN, *THE PROUD TOWER*, 1962.

45. **(D)** The author's intent is to introduce Reed to the reader. Although describes the man, much of what we learn about him comes from those who knew him personally or studied his work and career.

46. **(D)** By providing several intriguing details about the man, the author heightens curiosity about who this man might be. Readers presumably will keep reading to find out his identity.

47. **(A)** The author describes Reed's manner of speaking in general terms. This is followed by an specific example of a caustic comment directed at a long-winded Congressman.

48. **(A)** Collectively, the quotations portray Reed as an exceptional man in both appearance and style.

49. **(C)** By 1890, Reed had been in Congress for 14 years (line 23), but the footnote cites quotations related largely to Reed's tenure as Speaker of the House.

50. **(A)** Buddha symbolizes many different things to many different people, but in general a Buddha represents wisdom, inscrutability, contemplation, and peace of mind. The author of the passage depicts Reed sitting back rather pleased with himself after cleverly knocking a pompous speaker off his high horse. Also, the physical description in lines 3–6 attributes a Buddha-like look to Reed.

51. **(E)** The quotations show that Reed had little tolerance for long-winded, pompous, or bumbling orators. To shut them up and deflate their egos, he apparently perfected the art of the scathing and sarcastic wisecrack.

52. **(D)** The phrase is used to describe hastily-expressed opinions—that is, opinions that haven't been thoroughly examined.

53. **(D)** The author of the passage drew the quotes about John from Volume II of *Letters*, a collection of the letters of Henry Adams, edited by Worthington Chauncey Ford and published by Houghton Mifflin in Boston. The first volume probably came out in 1930, and the second in 1938.

54. **(C)** The author makes the point that men with great inherited wealth did not usually go into politics. Theodore Roosevelt was an exception.

Practice Test B

Answers to Essay Questions

Although answers to the essay questions will vary greatly, the following descriptions suggest a possible approach to each question and contain ideas that could be used in a response to the question. Perhaps your essay contains many of the same ideas. If not, don't be alarmed. Your ideas may be no less, or even more, insightful than those presented below.

ESSAY QUESTION 1 ON NATIONAL ID CARDS

ARGUMENTS IN FAVOR OF NATIONAL ID CARDS MAY INCLUDE:

- National ID cards would enable the police to increase their authority and function more efficiently. (Source A) (*Note*: To some, this is an argument *against* national ID cards.)
- Those most likely to be stopped or questioned at airports, etc., would avoid being detained/harassed. (Sources A and B)
- Government administration could be streamlined. (Source A)
- Racial profiling would be reduced or eliminated. (Source B)
- Performing acts of terrorism would be much harder. (Source C)
- Criminals and other lawbreakers could be more easily apprehended. (Source C)
- Applicants for sensitive jobs could be screened more easily and efficiently. (Source C)

ARGUMENTS AGAINST NATIONAL ID CARDS MAY INCLUDE:

- National ID cards would increase the power of the police. (Sources A and D) (Note: To some, this is an argument *in favor* of national ID cards.)
- Our liberties and privacy would diminish. (Sources B and E)
- Cards fail to provide greater security against terrorists. (Source E)
- Cards create a false sense of security. (Source E)
- In other countries the use of ID cards has led to abuse and persecution of certain groups. (Source F)

ESSAY QUESTION 2, BASED ON A PASSAGE BY EDWARD P. GYOKERES

The author intends to recreate his experience in Iraq for a homefront audience that he assumes has no idea what it's like being a soldier in a war zone. As he tells his story, the author addresses the reader as "you," a device that establishes intimacy between himself and the recipients of his e-mail. In addition, he speaks frankly and informally, using the common, down-to-earth parlance of a soldier—for example, "personal effects" (line 4), "0400" (line 20), "really freakin' cold" (lines 23–24).

The author could easily have summarized his life in Iraq by stating simply, "It's wretched." Instead, however, he tries to make the account as vivid as possible by employing the rhetorical device of a "small mental voyage" (line 2). Rather than tell what he sees, feels, hears, and smells, he helps his readers recreate the experience by instructing them to do outrageous things with everyday objects: empty the contents of a vacuum cleaner bag onto yourself, tear apart the walls of a small tent you've set up on your driveway, and so forth.

Recognizing that a reader's imaginings will leave a more powerful impression than any words he can write, the author deliberately avoids going into minute detail, interjecting instead "...well, you get the picture" (line 6) and "trust me" (line 8). He uses a similar tactic at the end of the passage by briefly describing his nighttime "latrine experience." Again, he stops short of piling on details, saying, "I don't even feel like talking about" it (line 25). Again, he expects that a reader's imagination will fill in the blanks. But just in case, he describes what happened after returning to his tent: He feels the urge to light himself on fire, a claim that may seem like hyperbole. But everything in his existence is so dreadful that readers might well believe he means it.

ESSAY QUESTION 3, BASED ON PASSAGES BY MAXWELL ANDERSON AND SUSANNE LANGER

Both passages promote art as a desirable, even a necessary, dimension of life. The first author, Maxwell Anderson, speaks directly to young people. Using imperative verbs, he tells the audience what to do: "be proud," "make it proud," "take what part in it you can," and so on. But not to appear too overbearing, he tempers his comments by repeatedly using "may": "It may break your heart . . . may drive you half mad, may betray you." He also uses several conditional sentences that say, in effect, "If you do X, then Y will happen," adopting the tone of a well-meaning advisor.

To suggest his reverence for art, and to encourage his listeners to become active in artistic endeavors, Anderson, like an evangelist, employs the language of religion: "neglect no sacrifice at your chosen altar," "it will open the temple doors," "lose . . . extravagant faith in the dollar."

Langer's more scholarly—although equally fervent—support of art, which she terms "the spearhead of human development," also asserts a relationship between art and religion: "It is not religion," she declares, "but grows up with religion."

All told, Langer's approach is more academic than Anderson's. She is concerned about defining art and explaining its various categories. Whereas Anderson clumps all forms of expression into a broad category he calls "art," Langer names the arts she has in mind: painting, sculpture, etc.

Both authors refer to themselves in the first person and address their audiences as "you." But Langer is more aloof, more business-like: ". . . we have no time to debate [a definition of art]. . ., so you are asked to accept it." Notice that she does not say "I ask you to accept it," a locution that sounds more conciliatory. Rather, she sets herself a task—to explain the importance of art—and won't be forsworn.

Self-Scoring Guide—Practice Test B

SCORING SECTION 2 ESSAYS

After referring to "How Essays Are Scored" on page 27 of this book, use this guide to help you evaluate each essay. Do your best to evaluate your performance in each category by using the criteria spelled out below. Because it is hard to achieve objectivity when assessing your own writing, you may improve the validity of your score by having a trusted and well-informed friend or experienced teacher read and rate your essay.

On the following Rating Chart, enter a number (from 1 to 6) that you think represents your level of performance in each category (A–F).

Category A: OVERALL PURPOSE/MAIN IDEA

6 extremely well-defined and insightful

5 clearly defined and generally insightful

4 mostly clear

3 somewhat clear but occasionally confusing

2 generally unclear and confusing

1 virtually incomprehensible

Category B: HANDLING OF THE PROMPT

6 self-evident or extremely clear throughout

5 mostly clear

4 somewhat clear

3 somewhat unclear

2 generally unclear or ambiguous

1 confusing or nonexistent

Category C: ORGANIZATION AND DEVELOPMENT

6 insightfully organized; fully developed with excellent supporting evidence

5 reasonably well organized; developed with appropriate supporting material

4 appropriately organized; developed with some relevant material

3 inadequately organized; weak development

2 poorly organized; little or no development

1 no discernible organization; no relevant development

Category D: SENTENCE STRUCTURE

6 varied and engaging

5 sufficiently varied to create interest

4 some variety

3 little variety; minor sentence errors

2 frequent sentence errors that interfere with meaning

1 serious sentence errors that obscure meaning

Category E: USE OF LANGUAGE

6 precise and effective word choice

5 competent word choice

4 conventional word choice; mostly correct

3 some errors in diction or idiom

2 frequent errors in diction or idiom

1 meaning obscured by word choice

Category F: GRAMMAR AND USAGE

6 error-free or virtually error-free

5 occasional minor errors

4 basically correct but with several minor errors

3 meaning somewhat obscured by errors

2 meaning frequently obscured by errors

1 meaning blocked by several major errors

RATING CHART

Rate your essay:	Essay 1	Essay 2	Essay 3
Overall Purpose/Main Idea			
Handling of the Prompt			
Organization and Development			
Sentence Structure			
Use of Language			
Grammar and Usage			
Composite Scores (Sum of each column)			

By using the following scale, in which composite scores are converted to the nine-point AP rating scale, you may determine the final score for each essay:

Composite Score	AP Essay Score
33–36	9
29–32	8
25–28	7
21–24	6
18–20	5
15–17	4
10–14	3
7–9	2
6 or below	1

AP Essay Scores Essay 1 _____ Essay 2 _____ Essay 3 _____

TEST SCORE WORKSHEET FOR PRACTICE TEST B

The scores you have earned on the multiple-choice and essay sections of the exam may now be converted to the AP five-point scale by performing the following calculations:

I. Determine your score for Section I (Multiple Choice)

Step A: Number of correct answers _____

Step B: Number of wrong answers _____ (Note: Do not count unanswered questions.)

Step C: Multiply the number of wrong answers by .250 and enter the figure here _____ .

Step D: Subtract the figure in Step C from the figure in Step A _____ .

Step E: Multiply the figure in Step D by 1.2500 to find your Multiple-Choice Score _____ (If less than zero, enter zero.)

II. Determine your score for Section II (Essays)

Step A: Enter your score for Essay 1 (out of 9) _____

Step B: Enter your score for Essay 2 (out of 9) _____

Step C: Enter your score for Essay 3 (out of 9) _____

Step D: Add the figures in Steps A, B, and C _____

Step E: Multiply the figure in Step D by 3.0556 _____ (Do not round.) This is your Essay Score.

III. Determine Your Total Score

Add the scores for I and II to find your composite score _____ .

To convert your composite score to the AP five-point scale, use the chart below. The range of scores only approximates what you would earn on the actual test because the exact figures may vary from test to test. Be aware, therefore, that your score on this test, as well as on other tests in this book, may differ slightly from your score on an actual AP exam.

Composite Score	AP Grade
108–150	5
93–107	4
72–92	3
43–71	2
0–42	1

AP essays are ordinarily judged in relation to other essays written on the same topic at the same time. Therefore, the scores you assign yourself for these essays may not be the same as the scores you would earn on an actual exam.

Practice Test C
ANSWER SHEET

Multiple-Choice Questions
Time—1 hour

1. Ⓐ Ⓑ Ⓒ Ⓓ Ⓔ
2. Ⓐ Ⓑ Ⓒ Ⓓ Ⓔ
3. Ⓐ Ⓑ Ⓒ Ⓓ Ⓔ
4. Ⓐ Ⓑ Ⓒ Ⓓ Ⓔ
5. Ⓐ Ⓑ Ⓒ Ⓓ Ⓔ
6. Ⓐ Ⓑ Ⓒ Ⓓ Ⓔ
7. Ⓐ Ⓑ Ⓒ Ⓓ Ⓔ
8. Ⓐ Ⓑ Ⓒ Ⓓ Ⓔ
9. Ⓐ Ⓑ Ⓒ Ⓓ Ⓔ
10. Ⓐ Ⓑ Ⓒ Ⓓ Ⓔ
11. Ⓐ Ⓑ Ⓒ Ⓓ Ⓔ
12. Ⓐ Ⓑ Ⓒ Ⓓ Ⓔ
13. Ⓐ Ⓑ Ⓒ Ⓓ Ⓔ
14. Ⓐ Ⓑ Ⓒ Ⓓ Ⓔ
15. Ⓐ Ⓑ Ⓒ Ⓓ Ⓔ
16. Ⓐ Ⓑ Ⓒ Ⓓ Ⓔ
17. Ⓐ Ⓑ Ⓒ Ⓓ Ⓔ
18. Ⓐ Ⓑ Ⓒ Ⓓ Ⓔ
19. Ⓐ Ⓑ Ⓒ Ⓓ Ⓔ
20. Ⓐ Ⓑ Ⓒ Ⓓ Ⓔ

21. Ⓐ Ⓑ Ⓒ Ⓓ Ⓔ
22. Ⓐ Ⓑ Ⓒ Ⓓ Ⓔ
23. Ⓐ Ⓑ Ⓒ Ⓓ Ⓔ
24. Ⓐ Ⓑ Ⓒ Ⓓ Ⓔ
25. Ⓐ Ⓑ Ⓒ Ⓓ Ⓔ
26. Ⓐ Ⓑ Ⓒ Ⓓ Ⓔ
27. Ⓐ Ⓑ Ⓒ Ⓓ Ⓔ
28. Ⓐ Ⓑ Ⓒ Ⓓ Ⓔ
29. Ⓐ Ⓑ Ⓒ Ⓓ Ⓔ
30. Ⓐ Ⓑ Ⓒ Ⓓ Ⓔ
31. Ⓐ Ⓑ Ⓒ Ⓓ Ⓔ
32. Ⓐ Ⓑ Ⓒ Ⓓ Ⓔ
33. Ⓐ Ⓑ Ⓒ Ⓓ Ⓔ
34. Ⓐ Ⓑ Ⓒ Ⓓ Ⓔ
35. Ⓐ Ⓑ Ⓒ Ⓓ Ⓔ
36. Ⓐ Ⓑ Ⓒ Ⓓ Ⓔ
37. Ⓐ Ⓑ Ⓒ Ⓓ Ⓔ
38. Ⓐ Ⓑ Ⓒ Ⓓ Ⓔ
39. Ⓐ Ⓑ Ⓒ Ⓓ Ⓔ
40. Ⓐ Ⓑ Ⓒ Ⓓ Ⓔ

41. Ⓐ Ⓑ Ⓒ Ⓓ Ⓔ
42. Ⓐ Ⓑ Ⓒ Ⓓ Ⓔ
43. Ⓐ Ⓑ Ⓒ Ⓓ Ⓔ
44. Ⓐ Ⓑ Ⓒ Ⓓ Ⓔ
45. Ⓐ Ⓑ Ⓒ Ⓓ Ⓔ
46. Ⓐ Ⓑ Ⓒ Ⓓ Ⓔ
47. Ⓐ Ⓑ Ⓒ Ⓓ Ⓔ
48. Ⓐ Ⓑ Ⓒ Ⓓ Ⓔ
49. Ⓐ Ⓑ Ⓒ Ⓓ Ⓔ
50. Ⓐ Ⓑ Ⓒ Ⓓ Ⓔ
51. Ⓐ Ⓑ Ⓒ Ⓓ Ⓔ
52. Ⓐ Ⓑ Ⓒ Ⓓ Ⓔ
53. Ⓐ Ⓑ Ⓒ Ⓓ Ⓔ

Practice Test C

PASSAGE 1

Question 1–12. Carefully read the following passage and answer the questions.

The passage is an excerpt from an essay by a 19th-century American author.

But it is mostly my own dreams I talk of, and that will somewhat excuse
me for talking of dreams at all. Everyone knows how delightful the dreams
are that one dreams one's self, and how insipid the dreams of others are. I
Line had an illustration of the fact, not many evenings ago, when a company of
(5) us got telling dreams. I had by far the best dreams of any; to be quite frank,
mine were the only dreams worth listening to; they were richly imaginative,
delicately fantastic, exquisitely whimsical, and humorous in the last degree;
and I wondered that when the rest could have listened to them they were
always eager to cut in with some silly, senseless, tasteless thing that made
(10) me sorry and ashamed for them. I shall not be going too far if I say that it
was on their part the grossest betrayal of vanity that I ever witnessed.

But the egotism of some people concerning their dreams is almost incredible. They will come down to breakfast and bore everybody with a recital
of the nonsense that has passed through their brains in sleep, as if they were
(15) not bad enough when they were awake; they will not spare the slightest
detail; and if, by the mercy of Heaven, they have forgotten something, they
will be sure to recollect it, and go back and give it all over again with added
circumstance. Such people do not reflect that there is something so purely
and intensely personal in dreams that they can rarely interest anyone but
(20) the dreamer, and that to the dearest friend, the closest relation or connection, they can seldom be otherwise than tedious and impertinent. The habit
husbands and wives have of making each other listen to their dreams is
especially cruel. They have each other quite helpless, and for this reason
they should all the more carefully guard themselves from abusing their
(25) advantage. Parents should not afflict their offspring with the rehearsal of
their mental maunderings in sleep, and children should learn that one of
the first duties a child owes its parents is to spare them the anguish of hearing what it has dreamed about overnight. A like forbearance in regard to the
community at large should be taught in the first trait of good manners in
(30) public schools, if we ever come to teach good manners there.

Certain exceptional dreams, however, are so imperatively significant, so vitally important, that it would be wrong to withhold them from the knowledge of those who happened not to dream them, and I could scarcely forgive myself if I did not, however briefly, impart them. It was only last

(35) week, for instance, that I found myself one night in the company of the Duke of Wellington, the great Duke, the Iron one, in fact; and after a few moments of agreeable conversation on topics of interest among gentlemen, his Grace said that now, if I pleased, he would like a couple of those towels. We had not been speaking of towels, that I remember, but it seemed the

(40) most natural thing in the world that he should mention them in the connection, whatever it was, and I went at once to get them for him. At the place where they gave out towels, and where I found some very civil people, they told me that what I wanted was not towels, and they gave me instead two bath-gowns, of rather scanty measure, butternut in color, and

(45) Turkish in texture. The garments made somehow a very strong impression upon me, so that I could draw them now, if I could draw anything, as they looked when they were held up to me. At the same moment, for no reason that I can allege, I passed from a social to a menial relation to the Duke, and foresaw that when I went back to him with those bath-gowns he would

(50) not thank me as one gentleman to another, but would offer me a tip as if I were a servant. . . .

This seemed to end the whole affair, and I passed on to other visions, which I cannot recall.

1. In the first paragraph, the primary contrast made by the speaker is between

   (A) pleasant dreams and nightmares.
   (B) his own dreams and the dreams of others.
   (C) vanity and modesty.
   (D) realistic dreams and fantastical dreams.
   (E) dreams of the past and dreams of the present.

2. Which of the following best describes the rhetorical function of the second sentence in the second paragraph (lines 13–18)?

   (A) It provides details to support the preceding generalization
   (B) It reiterates the main idea of the passage
   (C) It presents an alternate view of the passage's main subject
   (D) It undercuts an assertion made in the first paragraph
   (E) It introduces an question that will be answered later in the passage

3. In context, the word "reflect" (line 18) is best interpreted to mean

   (A) imitate
   (B) take into account
   (C) show off
   (D) mull over
   (E) mirror

4. The speaker in the passage can be described as a person with all of the following qualities EXCEPT

   (A) self-centered hypocrisy
   (B) the ability to see himself as others see him
   (C) blindness to the fact that he is the very sort of person he scorns
   (D) a belief that he is a well-mannered gentleman
   (E) unawareness that the more he says the more he reveals his shortcomings

5. In line 21, "they" refers to which of the following?

   I. "people" (line 18)
   II. "dreams" (line 22)
   III. "husbands and wives" (line 22)

   (A) I only
   (B) II only
   (C) I and II only
   (D) II and III only
   (E) I, II, and III

6. The last sentence of the second paragraph (lines 28–30) can best be described as

   (A) a generalization followed by a specific example.
   (B) a suggestion followed by the reason for making it.
   (C) a statement about a cause and its effect.
   (D) a reasonable assumption and a logical conclusion.
   (E) a recommendation followed by an editorial comment.

7. That the speaker declares that some dreams "are so imperatively significant, so vitally important" (lines 31–32) is ironic mainly because

   (A) the speaker has been railing against the telling of dreams
   (B) some dreams are "exceptional" (line 31)
   (C) the speaker has characterized dreams as "intensely personal" (line 19)
   (D) irrational events occur in dreams as well as in reality
   (E) people rarely remember their dreams

8. The speaker's report of his nighttime encounter with the Duke of Wellington (lines 34–51) contributes to the unity of the passage in which of the following ways?

   (A) As proof of the fleeting nature of dreams
   (B) As a deliberate example of a "silly, senseless, tasteless thing" (line 9)
   (C) As a description of the speaker's social status
   (D) As evidence that dreams leave permanent impressions on the dreamer
   (E) As an illustration of the speaker's conviction that his own dreams are "worth listening to" (line 6)

9. The speaker's tone in the passage as a whole can best be described as

   (A) crude and unsentimental.
   (B) mournful and bleak.
   (C) arrogant and condescending.
   (D) grouchy and reckless.
   (E) troubled and anxious.

10. The change in the speaker's attitude toward the Duke of Wellington (lines 47–51) is most accurately described as going from

   (A) devoted to rebellious.
   (B) friendly to violently contemptuous.
   (C) helpful to profoundly defiant.
   (D) respectful to slightly disconcerted.
   (E) courteous to angry.

11. In line 45, "Turkish" modifies

   (A) "towels" (line 43)
   (B) "bath-gowns" (line 44)
   (C) "measure" (line 44)
   (D) "color" (line 44)
   (E) "garments" (line 45)

12. The passage as a whole can best be described as

   (A) a dramatic monologue.
   (B) a statement of principles.
   (C) a soliloquy.
   (D) an expression of opinion.
   (E) an offer of advice.

PASSAGE 2

Questions 13–24. Carefully read the following passage and answer the accompanying questions.

The passage is part of a talk delivered by a renowned 20th-century poet.

I hold no diploma, certificate, or other academic document to show that I am qualified to discuss this subject. I have never taught anybody of any age how to enjoy, understand, appreciate poetry, or how to speak it. I have

Line known a great many poets, and innumerable people who wanted to be told
(5) that they were poets. I have done some teaching, but I have never "taught poetry." My excuse for taking up this subject is of wholly different origin. I know that not only young people in colleges and universities, but secondary school children also, have to study, or at least acquaint themselves with, poems by living poets; and I know that my poems are among those studied.
(10) This fact brings some welcome supplement to my income; and it also brings an increase in my correspondence, which is more or less welcome, though not all the letters get answered. These are the letters from children themselves, or more precisely, the teenagers. They live mostly in Britain, the United States, and Germany, with a sprinkling from the nations of Asia. It
(15) is in a spirit of curiosity, therefore, that I approach the subject of teaching poetry: I should like to know more about these young people and about their teachers and the methods of teaching.

For some of my young correspondents seem to be misguided. Sometimes I have been assigned to them as a "project," more often they have made the
(20) choice themselves—it is not always clear why. (There was one case, that of an Egyptian boy, who wanted to write a thesis about my work, and as none of my work was locally available and as he wanted to read it, asked me to send him all my books. That was very exceptional, however.) Very often the writers ask for information about myself, sometimes in the form of a ques-
(25) tionnaire. I remember being asked by one child whether it was true that I only cared to associate with lords and bishops. Sometimes a photograph is asked for. Some young persons seem to want me to provide them with all the material for a potted biography, including mention of my interests, tastes, and ways of amusing myself. Are these children studying poetry, or
(30) merely studying poets? Very often they want explanations, either of a whole poem ("what does it mean") or of a particular line or phrase; and the kind of question they ask often suggests that their approach to that poem has been wrong, for they want the wrong kind of explanation, or ask questions which are simply unanswerable. Sometimes, but more rarely, they are avid
(35) for literary sources, which would seem to indicate that they have started too early on the road to Xanadu.

Now, when I was young, this sort of thing did not happen. I did study English at school, beginning, thank God, with grammar, and going on to "rhetoric"—for which also I am grateful. And we had to read a number of
(40) set books of prose and verse—mostly in school editions which made them look peculiarly unappetizing. But we never were made to read any literature which could be called "contemporary."

No. Not only were we not encouraged to take an interest in the poetry actually being written, but even had we been, I doubt whether we should
(45) have thought of entering into correspondence with the authors. Some of the juvenile correspondence I receive seems to be instigated by the teachers, but the greater part does not. Indeed, some of my letters, I suspect, are inspired by a desire to score off the teacher in the hope of getting some statement from the horse's mouth which will be a direct contradiction of
(50) what has been taught. (I confess that this last type of letter is one which I sometimes take pleasure in answering—when the teacher seems to have been wrong.) But my point is that this pressure upon the poet from young people who have been compelled to read his work is a modern phenomenon. I don't believe that Tennyson and Browning, Longfellow and Whittier
(55) (to say nothing of Poe and Whitman, poets whose works we did not study) were embarrassed by juvenile correspondence choking up their letter boxes. The teaching of the contemporary literature, the introduction of the young to poetry by living poets, is something that came about in my time without my being aware of what was happening.

13. The rhetorical purpose of the speaker's statement that he has no experience teaching poetry is mainly to

(A) win the audience's sympathy
(B) highlight the division between poetic theory and practice
(C) present a problem for which he will propose solutions
(D) contrast his lack of expertise in one area with his profound insights in another
(E) prepare the audience for the subject he intends to talk about

14. The phrase "innumerable people who wanted to be told they were poets" (lines 4–5) probably refers to

(A) aspiring poets who have asked Eliot to comment on their work.
(B) students given a class assignment to write a poem.
(C) college and university students majoring in poetry.
(D) writers who have submitted poems for publication.
(E) frustrated literary critics.

15. In line 23, the word "That" refers to

(A) the overall purpose of the Egyptian boy's letter.
(B) the fact that Eliot received a letter from Egypt.
(C) the boy's claim that he wanted to read all of Eliot's books.
(D) the unavailablity of Eliot's books in Egypt.
(E) the boy's claim that he wanted to write a thesis about Eliot's works.

16. Based on the sentence beginning in line 25 ("I remember . . . lords and bishops"), the speaker in the passage is acknowledging that

    (A) he plays an official role in church affairs.
    (B) his poetry is difficult to understand.
    (C) he has an undeserved reputation as an elitist.
    (D) he believes that schoolchildren are ignorant.
    (E) he comes from a family of nobility.

17. The tone of the second paragraph can best be described as

    (A) didactic
    (B) amused
    (C) resigned
    (D) nostalgic
    (E) confident

18. The statement "they have started too early on the road to Xanadu" (lines 35–36) contains an example of

    (A) an epithet.
    (B) pathetic fallacy.
    (C) a metaphorical allusion.
    (D) metonymy.
    (E) hyperbole.

19. Which of the following best characterizes the rhetorical function of the first sentence of paragraph 3 (line 37)?

    (A) It provides a logical transition between paragraphs 3 and 4.
    (B) It restates the main idea of the previous paragraph.
    (C) It bolsters the main point made by paragraph 3.
    (D) It introduces a change in the speaker's attitude toward the topic of the passage.
    (E) It briefly summarizes the main idea of the passage.

20. In context, all of the following describe the speaker's rhetorical intent in using the expression "thank God" (line 38) EXCEPT

    (A) to indicate that he is a devout, God-fearing individual.
    (B) to suggest that writing letters to poets is less valuable than studying grammar.
    (C) to express skepticism about the usefulness of some current educational practices.
    (D) to imply that knowledge of grammar is essential to a good education.
    (E) to encourage his audience to master English grammar.

21. The last paragraph (lines 43–59) include all of the following rhetorical strategies EXCEPT

    (A) the use of allusion.
    (B) an interjection used for emphasis.
    (C) a metaphorical usage.
    (D) a parenthetical digression.
    (E) a rhetorical question.

22. In context, the expression "to score off" (line 48) is best interpreted to mean which of the following?

    (A) To embarrass
    (B) To take advantage of
    (C) To annoy
    (D) To slander
    (E) To scold

23. The speaker mentions Tennyson, Browning, Longfellow, and other poets (lines 54–55) as examples of which of the following?

    (A) Poets whose work is often studied in English classes
    (B) Famous writers who enjoy corresponding with their readers
    (C) Poets whose experience differs from that of the speaker
    (D) Authors whom the speaker admires
    (E) Poets who declined to answer students' letters

24. The speaker's tone in the passage as a whole can best be described as

    (A) hypercritical and agitated.
    (B) tactful and restrained.
    (C) sentimental but detached.
    (D) rigorous but sympathetic.
    (E) authoritative and demanding.

PASSAGE 3

Questions 25–40. Carefully read the following passage and answer the accompanying questions.

The passage comes from the pen of a well-known 19th-century writer.

The changes wrought by death are in themselves so sharp and final, and so terrible and melancholy in their consequences, that the thing stands alone in man's experience, and has no parallel upon earth. It outdoes all
Line other accidents because it is the last of them. Sometimes it leaps suddenly
(5) upon its victims, like a Thug; sometimes it lays a regular siege and creeps upon their citadel during a score of years. And when the business is done, there is sore havoc made in other people's lives, and a pin knocked out by which many subsidiary friendships hung together. There are empty chairs, solitary walks, and single beds at night. Again, in taking away our friends,
(10) death does not take them away utterly, but leaves behind a mocking, tragical, and soon intolerable residue, which must be hurriedly concealed. Hence a whole chapter of sights and customs striking to the mind, from the pyramids of Egypt to the gallows and hanging trees of medieval Europe. The poorest persons have a bit of pageant going towards the tomb; memo
(15) rial stones are set up over the least memorable; and, in order to preserve some show of respect for what remains of our old loves and friendships, we must accompany it with much grimly ludicrous ceremonial, and the hired undertaker parades before the door.

Although few things are spoken of with more fearful whisperings than
(20) this prospect of death, few have less influence on conduct under healthy circumstances. We have all heard of cities in South America built upon the side of fiery mountains, and how, in this tremendous neighbourhood, the inhabitants are not a jot more impressed by the solemnity of mortal conditions than if they were delving gardens in the greenest corner of England.
(25) There are serenades and suppers and much gallantry among the myrtles overhead; and meanwhile the foundation shudders underfoot, the bowels of the mountain growl, and at any moment living ruin may leap sky-high into the moonlight, and tumble man and his merry-making in the dust. In the eyes of very young people, and very dull old ones, there is something
(30) indescribably reckless and desperate in such a picture. It seems not credible that respectable married people, with umbrellas, should find appetite for a bit of supper within quite a long distance of a fiery mountain; ordinary life begins to smell of high-handed debauch when it is carried on so close to a catastrophe; and even cheese and salad, it seems, could hardly be relished in
(35) such circumstances without something like defiance of the Creator. It should be a place for nobody but hermits dwelling in prayer and maceration, or mere born-devils drowning care in perpetual carouse.

And yet, when one comes to think upon it calmly, the situation of these South American citizens forms only a very pale figure for the state of ordi
(40) nary mankind. This world itself, travelling blindly and swiftly in overcrowded space, among a million other worlds travelling blindly and swiftly

in contrary directions, may very well come by a knock that would set it into explosions like a penny squib[1]. And what, pathologically looked at, is the human body with all its organs, but a mere bagful of petards[2]? The least of
(45)   these is as dangerous to the whole economy as the ship's powder-magazine to the ship; and with every breath we breathe, and every meal we eat, we are putting one or more of them in peril. Think with what a preparation of spirit we should affront the daily peril of the dinner table: a deadlier spot than any battlefield in history, where the far greater proportion of our
(50)   ancestors have left their bones! What woman would ever be lured into marriage, so much more dangerous than the wildest sea? And what would it be to grow old? For, after a certain distance, every step we take in life we find the ice growing thinner below our feet, and all around us and behind us we see our contemporaries going through.

---

[1]*squib: a small firecracker*
[2]*petards: a) intestinal gases; b) a case containing explosives*

25. Which of the following phrases does the speaker use to develop the notion that "death has no parallel" (line 4)?

(A) "changes . . . are . . . sharp" (line 1)
(B) "changes . . . are . . .terrible and melancholy" (lines 1–2)
(C) "outdoes all other accidents" (lines 3–4)
(D) "leaps suddenly" (line 4)
(E) "lays a regular siege" (line 5)

26. The primary rhetorical function of the sentence "There are . . .at night" (lines 8–9) is to

(A) illustrate a generalization made in the previous sentence.
(B) contradict an assertion made in the first sentence of the paragraph.
(C) discuss the connotation of words to be used later in the passage.
(D) provide a brief digression from the main idea of the passage.
(E) prove the validity of the passage's opening sentence.

27. The two sentences in lines 4–8 contain all of the following EXCEPT

(A) simile.
(B) dramatic irony.
(C) personification.
(D) unifying repetition.
(E) metaphor.

28. In the first paragraph, the speaker's primary purpose is to

(A) discuss the gravity and after-effects of death.
(B) ridicule the social customs associated with dying.
(C) propose a hypothesis about humankind's fear of death.
(D) comfort readers who have recently lost friends or loved ones.
(E) convince readers that death is a topic that must be discussed openly.

29. In line 5, "it" refers to

    (A) "the thing" (line 2).
    (B) "man's experience" (line 3).
    (C) "no parallel" (line 3).
    (D) "earth" (line 3).
    (E) "a Thug" (line 5).

30. The speaker uses the phrase "a whole chapter of sights and customs striking to the mind" (line 12) to refer to

    (A) physical reminders of death.
    (B) lost friends.
    (C) inevitable thoughts about one's own death.
    (D) mourners.
    (E) hired undertakers.

31. Lines 19–21 contain all of the following EXCEPT

    (A) a complex sentence.
    (B) an extended analogy.
    (C) a paradoxical idea.
    (D) a subordinate clause.
    (E) parallel syntax.

32. In line 25, "serenades and suppers and much gallantry among the myrtles" most directly alludes to

    (A) "fearful whisperings" (line 19).
    (B) "conduct under healthy circumstances" (lines 20–21).
    (C) "solemnity" (line 23).
    (D) "mortal conditions" (lines 23–24).
    (E) "gardens in . . . England" (line 24).

33. The use of which rhetorical device is most in evidence in lines 25–28 ("There are serenades . . . in the dust")?

    (A) Deductive reasoning
    (B) Overdone sentimentality
    (C) Alliteration
    (D) Fantasy
    (E) Antithesis

34. The function of the sentences in lines 25–28 ("There are serenades . . . in the dust") might best be described as

    (A) presenting a problem and offering an immediate solution.
    (B) balancing an overstatement and an understatement.
    (C) citing two examples of natural perils.
    (D) contrasting man's weaknesses and nature's power.
    (E) developing in more detail the main ideas of the previous sentence.

35. Which of the following best describes how paragraph 2 (lines 19–37) is developed?

    (A) With an elaborate metaphor
    (B) With an abstract statement followed by a concrete explanation
    (C) With a narrative about events in a South American city
    (D) With factual information from which the main idea of the passage can be inferred
    (E) With a series of paradoxical statements about human behavior

36. In context, the speaker uses the phrase "with umbrellas" (line 31) to suggest that

    (A) it is customary for British people to carry umbrellas.
    (B) keeping up an appearance of respectability is important to married couples.
    (C) the people are prepared for a bit of rain but not for real disaster.
    (D) umbrellas often symbolize old age.
    (E) umbrellas provide a false sense of security.

37. For which of the following reasons does the speaker associate "hermits" (line 36) with "born-devils" (line 37)?

    I. Neither puts value on their present existence
    II. They lead unconventional lives
    III. Both are oblivious to mortal dangers

    (A) I only
    (B) III only
    (C) I and II only
    (D) II and III only
    (E) I, II, and III

38. The pronoun "them" (line 47) refers to

    (A) "South American citizens" (line 39).
    (B) "a million other worlds" (line 41).
    (C) "organs" (line 44).
    (D) "petards" (line 44).
    (E) "every breath" and "every meal" (line 46).

39. In the last paragraph of the passage (lines 38–54) the speaker uses all of the following rhetorical devices to characterize the perils awaiting us EXCEPT

    (A) repetition for emphasis.
    (B) an analogy.
    (C) a rhetorical question.
    (D) an anecdote.
    (E) a metaphor.

40. In the passage, the speaker's primary focus is

    (A) fear of violent death.
    (B) the thrill of living dangerously.
    (C) humanity's inability to cope with the constant threat of death.
    (D) the thin dividing line between life and death.
    (E) the impermanence of life.

PASSAGE 4

Questions 41–53. Carefully read the following passage and answer the accompanying questions.

The passage is an excerpt from a contemporary book.

So he bought it.[1] Everyone knows that. Peter Minuit purchased
Manhattan Island from a group of local Indians for sixty guilders worth of
goods, or as the nineteenth-century historian Edmund O'Callaghan calcu-
Line lated it, twenty-four dollars. From the seventeenth through the early twen-
(5) tieth century thousands of real estate transactions occurred in which native
Americans sold parcels—ranging in size from a town lot to a midwestern
state—to English, Dutch, French, Spanish, and other European settlers.
But only one sale is legend; only one is known by everyone. Only one has
had the durability to be riffed on in Broadway song ("Give It Back to the
(10) Indians," from the 1939 Rodgers and Hart musical *Too Many Girls*), and,
at the end of the twentieth century, to do service as a punchline in a column by humorist Dave Barry (". . . which the Dutch settler Peter Minuit
purchased from the Manhattan Indians for $24, plus $167,000 a month in
maintenance fees").[2]

(15) It's pretty clear why this particular sale lodged in the cultural memory,
why it became legend: the extreme incongruity, the exquisitely absurd
price. It is the most dramatic illustration of the whole long process of strip-
ping the natives of their land. The idea that the center of world commerce,
an island packed with trillions of dollars' worth of real estate, was once
(20) bought from supposedly hapless Stone Age innocents for twenty-four dollars' worth of household goods is too delicious to let slip. It speaks to our
sense of early American history as the history of savvy, ruthless Europeans
conniving, tricking, enslaving, and bludgeoning innocent and guileless
natives out of their land and their lives. It's a neatly packed symbol of the
(25) entire conquest of the continent that was to come.

Beyond that, the purchase snippet is notable because it is virtually the
only thing about Manhattan colony that has become part of history. For
this reason, too, it deserves exploring.

So, who were the Indians who agreed to this transaction, and what did
(30) they think it meant? The ancestors of the people whom European settlers
took to calling Indians (after Columbus, who at first thought he had arrived
at the outer reaches of India) traveled the land bridge from Siberia to Alaska
that existed during the last ice age, more than twelve thousand years ago,
then spread slowly through the Americas. They came from Asia; their
(35) genetic makeup is a close match with Siberians and Mongolians.[3] They
spread out thinly across the incomprehensible vastness of the American
continents to create a linguistic richness unparalleled in human history: it
has been estimated that at the moment Columbus arrived in the New
World twenty-five percent of all human languages were North American
(40) Indian.[4]

There are two rival, hardened stereotypes that get in the way of understanding these people: the one that arose from the long cultural dismissing of American Indians as "primitive," and the modern dogma that sees them as Noble and Defenseless. Both are cartoon images. Recent work in genetics, archaeology, anthropology, and linguistics makes plain what should be (45) obvious: that the Mohican, Mohawk, Lenape, Montauk, Housatonic, and other peoples occupying the lands that for a time were called New Netherland, as well as the Massachusett, Wampanoag, Sokoki, Pennacook, Abenaki, Oneida, Onondaga, Susquehannock, Nanticoke, and others who (50) inhabited other parts of what became the states of New York, Massachusetts, Pennsylvania, Connecticut, Vermont, New Hampshire, Maine, Delaware, Maryland, and New Jersey, were biologically, genetically, intellectually, all but identical to the Dutch, English, French, Swedish, and others who came in contact with them in the beginning of the seventeenth (55) century. The Indians were as skilled, as duplicitous, as capable of theological rumination and technological cunning, as smart and as pig-headed, and as curious and cruel as the Europeans who met them. The members of the Manhattan-based colony who knew them—who spent time among them in their villages, hunted and traded with them, learned their languages— (60) knew this perfectly well. It was later, after the two had separated into rival camps, that the stereotypes set. The early seventeenth century was a much more interesting time than the Wild West era, a time when Indians and Europeans were something like equal participants, dealing with one another as allies, competitors, partners.

---

[1] *The order of events is far from clear, and historians debate whether Verhulst or Minuit was the one who purchased Manhattan Island. My account is based on my own reading of all relevant primary source material, as well as arguments made by various historians. I side against those who in recent decades removed Minuit from his legendary position as purchaser of the island, and with those who reassign him to that position . . . .*

[2] *Dave Barry, "A Certified Wacko Rewrites History's Greatest Hits,"* Milwaukee Journal-Sentinel, *26 December 1999.*

[3] *Brian Sykes,* The Seven Daughters of Eve: The Science That Reveals Our Genetic Ancestry, *279–280.*

[4] *J.C.H. King,* First People, First Contacts: Native Peoples of North America, *8.*

41. The passage as a whole can best be described as

    (A) the dramatization of a legendary occurrence.
    (B) an example of an "irony of history".
    (C) an interpretation of a historical event.
    (D) a historical document.
    (E) the depiction of a particular geographical place.

42. The speaker's tone of the first two sentences of the passage (line 1) is best described as

    (A) scornful.
    (B) confidential.
    (C) undoubting.
    (D) ill-tempered.
    (E) argumentative.

43. Footnote 1 (line 1) suggests that

    (A) the passage is theoretical, not factual.
    (B) the story of the purchase of Manhattan is most likely fictitious.
    (C) information about long-ago events cannot be trusted.
    (D) historians sometimes draw different conclusions from the same set of facts.
    (E) the name of the buyer is historically more significant than the fact of the purchase itself.

44. The speaker's reference to a Broadway song (line 9) serves chiefly to

    (A) illustrate the uniqueness of the sale of Manhattan Island.
    (B) distinguish between several momentous land acquisitions.
    (C) comment on the price that was paid for the island.
    (D) explain a cause of hostility between European settlers and Indians.
    (E) commend Peter Minuit for outsmarting the Indians.

45. All of the following phrases are used to support the idea that the "sale lodged in the cultural memory" (line 15) EXCEPT

    (A) "is known by everyone" (line 8).
    (B) "durability to be riffed on" (line 9).
    (C) "do service as a punchline" (line 11).
    (D) "too delicious to let slip" (line 21).
    (E) "ruthless Europeans" (line 22).

46. In line 21, the pronoun "our" refers to

    (A) Native-Americans.
    (B) specialists in early American history.
    (C) everyone familiar with the details of the purchase of Manhattan Island.
    (D) schoolchildren who have studied the history of New York.
    (E) authors who write books about colonial America.

47. Which of the following inferences can be drawn from a reading of footnotes 3 and 4?

    (A) That the information designated by footnote 3 (line 35) and footnote 4 (line 40) appeared in the works of both Sikes and King
    (B) That *First People, First Contacts: Native Peoples of North America* is an eight-page pamphlet
    (C) That the works of Sikes and King have been cited earlier in the book from which this passage has been taken
    (D) That Sykes' work, *The Seven Daughters of Eve . . .* , is an article published in an unnamed periodical
    (E) That the absence of a copyright dates in both footnotes suggests that the works of Sykes and King were published before the advent of copyright laws

48. The primary rhetorical purpose of the sentence "For this reason . . ."(lines 27–28) is to

    (A) express a causal relationship between the sale of Manhattan and the island's future growth.
    (B) link the idea expressed in the preceding sentence with the next paragraphs.
    (C) restate the main idea of the passage.
    (D) introduce important information that was deliberately left out of the second paragraph.
    (E) suggest a symbolic interpretation of the events surrounding the sale of Manhattan.

49. In which of the following does the speaker exaggerate in order to create certain effects?

    I. "Everyone knows that" (line 1)
    II. "the most dramatic illustration . . . of their land" (lines 17–18)
    III. "linguistic richness unparalleled in human history" (line 37)

    (A) I only
    (B) III only
    (C) I and II only
    (D) II and III only
    (E) I, II, and III

50. In describing the Indians who lived in areas that now are eastern states (lines 55–57), the speaker emphasizes their

    (A) human qualities.
    (B) cooperative nature.
    (C) antagonism toward white settlers.
    (D) courage in the face of danger.
    (E) deceitfulness.

51. Which of the following best describes the footnoted material in the passage?

    (A) It all contains ideas that originated in primary historical sources.
    (B) Footnote 1 (line 1) refers to material that the author of the passage has paraphrased from his sources.
    (C) Footnotes 1 (line 1) and 2 (line 14) refer to material containing general historical information.
    (D) Footnotes 3 (line 35) and 4 (line 40) refer to material containing subjective interpretations of historical events.
    (E) Footnote 2 (line 14) refers to material that contains a direct quotation.

52. In the sentence beginning "The Indians were . . ." (lines 55–57), all of the following words are parallel in function to "capable" (line 55) EXCEPT

  (A) "skilled" (line 55).
  (B) "duplicitous" (line 55).
  (C) "technological" (line 56).
  (D) "smart" (line 56).
  (E) "cruel" (line 57).

53. The main rhetorical function of the last sentence of the passage (lines 61–64) is to

  (A) offer a specific answer to the question that begins paragraph 4 (lines 29–30).
  (B) put to rest a misconception that is discussed in the last paragraph of the passage.
  (C) summarize the main idea of the passage.
  (D) provide a series of generalizations that are drawn from evidence in the passage.
  (E) introduce a new twist on the subject that readers would do well to think about.

SECTION II
Three Essay Questions
Total time—Two hours and 15 minutes

Write your essays on standard 8½" × 11" composition paper. At the exam you will be given a bound booklet containing 12 lined pages.

Essay Question 1

Time—15 minutes for reading the question and sources
    40 minutes for writing an essay

Instructions: The following essay topic is accompanied by six sources.

Respond to the question below in a well-written, coherent essay that draws on ideas and information found in **at least three** of the sources. Don't simply summarize or paraphrase the sources. Instead, **focus the essay on your point of view**, and use the sources to support or bolster your argument.

Topic: In 2004, Michael Newdow, an avowed atheist, brought a case to the Supreme Court that challenged the daily recitation of the Pledge of Allegiance in his daughter's third-grade class. Newdow claimed that the presence of "under God" in the Pledge violated the separation of church and state provided by the Constitution. The Court declined to rule on the issue, saying that Newdow lacked the legal authority to speak for his daughter because he was then involved in a child custody dispute.

Therefore, "under God" remains in the Pledge, although it is sure to be challenged again.

Your task: Read the following sources carefully. Then, in an essay that synthesizes at least three of the sources, take a position that supports, challenges, or modifies the claim that "under God" should be eliminated from the Pledge of Allegiance.

In your essay, you may refer to the sources simply as Source A, Source B, etc., or by the key words in parentheses below.

> Source A (DeMar)
> Source B ("About")
> Source C (Pinkerton)
> Source D (Graph)
> Source E (Sekulow)
> Source F (Elder)

SOURCE A

Gary DeMar, "The Pledge of Allegiance Goes to Trial," American Vision web site,<*www.americanvision.com*>

The following is an excerpt from an article by an author and lecturer on religious and Bible-related issues.

Many who are arguing for "under God" to remain in the Pledge of Allegiance are doing so by declaring that the phrase has no particular religious meaning for our nation today. This was the view of Solicitor General Theodore Olson when the Pledge issue first came before the Supreme Court in 2004. "Olson argued that the phrase is viewed as an 'acknowledgment' of religion's role in the lives of America's founders." It's not that our nation is actually under the sovereign rule of God but only that people once believed that it was. Olson is not alone in using this line of argument:

Many pledge proponents offer secular justifications to fit Supreme Court rulings. They claim "under God" isn't any sort of religious exercise or prayer but simply a factual acknowledgment of the nation's past heritage of faith, for patriotic rather than religious reasons.

Given this line of argument, why not rewrite the Pledge to read, "I pledge allegiance to the Flag of the United States of America, and to the Republic for which it stands, which people used to believe was one nation under God, indivisible, with liberty and justice for all."

History tells a different story. "Under God" was added to the Pledge because Congress wanted to distinguish America from atheistic Communism. The goal wasn't an acknowledgment that America at one time had been religious. If that's all it was, then the Soviet Union could have a similar pledge, since at one time Russia was very religious, some would even say Christian. "Under God" was a statement that America at that time, in 1954, was officially theistic.

SOURCE B

Austin Kline, "Defending 'under God' in the Pledge of Allegiance," posted on the "About" web site, March 30, 2004, *<www.atheism.about.com>*

Catholic League president William Donohue comments:

> *"It cannot be seriously maintained that the words 'under God' in the Pledge of Allegiance constitute the establishment of religion. Surely there is a dramatic difference between the collective acknowledgment of our religious heritage and the formal establishment of religion. While it is not surprising that Mr. Newdow cannot understand the difference— he is a devout atheist—the American people have every right to expect that the high court can make such a distinction."*

This argument, that the phrase "under God" merely acknowledges the nation's religious heritage, is a common argument. It's also a profoundly bad one—so bad, in fact, that one has to wonder whether it is not being offered dishonestly by people who know that it isn't true.

If this were simply an acknowledgment of the influence of religion and religious beliefs on American history, why isn't the phrase set in the *past tense?* Something like " . . .one nation, believed in at times by many to have been under God . . ." would serve such a function, though its awfully awkward.

What we have instead, is a *declaration* about the state of the nation in the *present tense*, not an *observation* about the beliefs of some in the *past tense*. What this means, I believe, is that it cannot reasonably be regarded as a mere acknowledgment about the nation's past religious history. . . .

Because it is in the present tense, it is referring to a current, ongoing situation— not the heritage of the past. This declaration informs students of *how things are* and, by virtue of its context, *how things must be.* It is, in many ways, a "Keep Off the Grass" sign for nonbelievers.

SOURCE C

James Pinkerton, "On the God Issue, Let's Take the Pledge," *Los Angeles Times*, June 28, 2002.

The following is part of a newspaper editorial.

[I]f the words "under God" are so vital, why weren't they in the Pledge until 1954? The U.S. managed to get along for nearly two centuries without asking for God's help every morning in homeroom—indeed, the Pledge didn't exist in any form until 1892.

To be sure, oaths are a good idea, for this nation and for every nation. As the French sociologist Emile Durkheim observed: "There can be no society, which does not feel the need of upholding and reaffirming at regular intervals the collective sentiments and the collective ideas which make its unity." But if so, we might think hard about what sort of unity we strive for.

Forget the moment that plenty of folks are left out of the "under God" formulation—atheists, pantheists, polytheists. Think instead of those whose faith, be it Baptist, Catholic or Wahhabi, might come ahead of state. That's why the national motto *e pluribus unum*—"out of many, one"— is far more valuable for a complex country than "In God We Trust."

The events of Sept. 11 should have heightened concern about the national well-being, not about God's will. The firefighters at the World Trade Center didn't die for God; they died for the people of New York, and for the U.S. in general. It might be nice to think that they're all in heaven, but of course fans of Mohamed Atta think that he and the other 18 Al Qaeda hijackers are in heaven, too.

It could be that the whole flap is nothing more than a ritualized exercise in civic hypocrisy, in which politicians seek to expand their own power at the expense of the liberty that comes from the separation of church and state. Is that an unreasonable conclusion in watching lawmakers scramble to be pledgier than thou?. . .

. . . In pledging, it's best to keep the state and God separate, no matter how desperate politicians might be to combine the two devotions into one aggrandizing state-religion.

SOURCE D

"Pledge Protection Act, H.R. 2028," Dr. Dave web site, Institute for Local Self-Reliance, <*http.www.newrules.org/*>

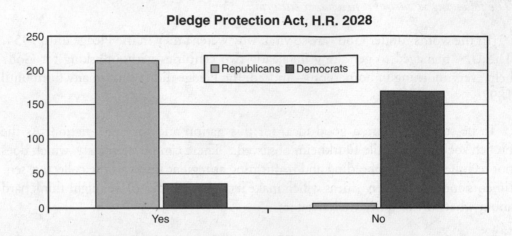

SOURCE E

Jay Sekulow, "Keep the Pledge of Allegiance Intact," American Center for Law and Justice.

The following is an excerpt from an essay written by the Chief Council of the ACLJ, a public interest law firm specializing in constitutional law.

As our nation battles terrorism—at home and abroad—there is a very real threat that millions of students in the U.S. will no longer have an opportunity to express their patriotism by voluntarily reciting the Pledge of Allegiance with the phrase "one nation under God."

. . . While the Supreme Court has never ruled directly on the constitutionality of the Pledge, there are numerous cases over the years where justices concluded that the phrase "one nation under God" is not an establishment of religion, but merely a way for the government to acknowledge our religious heritage.

In 1962 in *Engel v. Vitale*, Justice Potter Stewart referred to the Pledge of Allegiance as an example of governmental recognition when he quoted a 1952 finding by the court (*Zorach v. Clauson*) that "[w]e are a religious people whose institutions presuppose a Supreme Being."

In *Abingdon v. Schempp*, Justice William Brennan wrote in 1963 that such patriotic exercises like the Pledge do not violate the Establishment Clause of the First Amendment because such a reference, as he put it, "may merely recognize the historical fact that our nation was believed to have been founded 'under God.' Thus reciting the Pledge may be no more of a religious exercise than the reading aloud of Lincoln's Gettysburg Address . . ."

In 1984, the Court in *Lynch v. Donnelly* recognized that "there is an unbroken history of official acknowledgment by all three branches of government of the role of religion in American life." Among the many examples of our government's acknowledgment of our religious heritage, according to the court, is the phrase "one nation under God."

And in 1985, Justice Sandra Day O'Connor argued in *Wallace v. Jaffree* that the inclusion of the words "under God" in the Pledge is not unconstitutional because the words "serve as an acknowledgment of religion with 'the legitimate secular purpose of solemnizing public occasions, and expressing confidence in the future.'"

SOURCE F

Lindsey Elder, "Keep the Pledge in School," *The Daily Collegian—Online*, posted 4/29/03

The following is an excerpt from a column that appeared in an online newspaper.

For those who claim the phrase "under God" as being another example of American enforcement of certain beliefs and faiths, keep in mind that the founders opposed the institutionalization of religion. They kept the Constitution free of references to God, as to not forget that the purpose of their coming to this country in the first place was freedom from religious persecution. The document mentions religion only to guarantee that godly belief would never be used as a qualification for holding office—a departure from many existing state constitutions. Erecting a church/state wall was a first priority when the Bill of Rights was added to the Constitution.

The main reason for the Supreme Court intervention in June 2002, the first since the Pledge's last revision in 1954, was the case of Michael A. Newdow, an atheist from Sacramento, Calif. He was against his daughter in second grade being required to recite the Pledge of Allegiance, in turn, because he felt she was forced to acknowledge the existence of God. Did they actually think the recitation of the Pledge, including the words "under God," by thousands of schoolchildren each day would somehow lead to the establishment of a state or federal religion?

This lacks common sense. You are an American, and saying the Pledge does not make you any more of a supporter of a certain religion than it does for his daughter to acknowledge the existence of a church on her way home from school. A generic two-word reference to God tucked inside a rote civic exercise is not a prayer . . .

People rage at being emotionally wounded by having to say "under God," and groups like the ACLU immediately jump to their aid. If they are claiming offense at a national tradition, what will be next? That we are not supposed to sing "God Bless America"? All U.S. currency is inscribed with "In God We Trust", but I'd be willing to bet no one who claims to be offended by the Pledge of Allegiance would pass up a $20 bill on a matter of principal [sic].

Essay Question 2

Suggested time—40 minutes. This question counts as one third of the total score for Section II.

What follows is part of an essay, "Our March to Washington," written by Theodore Winthrop (1828–1861) about going off to fight in the Civil War. Carefully read the excerpt and then write an essay which analyzes the rhetorical strategies Winthrop uses used to convey his feelings about the experience.

Line

(5)

(10)

(15)

(20)

(25)

(30)

At three o'clock in the afternoon of Friday, April 19, we took our peace-maker, a neat twelve-round brass howitzer, down from the Seventh Regiment Armory, and stationed it in the rear of the building. The twin peacemaker is somewhere near us, but entirely hidden by this enormous crowd.

An enormous crowd! of both sexes, of every age and condition. The men offer all kinds of truculent and patriotic hopes; the women shed tears, and say, "God bless you, boys."

This is a part of the town where baddish cigars prevail. But good or bad, I am ordered to keep all away from the gun. So the throng stands back, peers curiously over the heads of its junior members, and seems to be taking the measure of my coffin.

At a great house on the left, as we pass the Astor Library, I see a handkerchief waving for me. Yes! it is she who made the sandwiches in my knapsack. They were a trifle too thick, as I afterwards discovered, but otherwise perfection. Be these my thanks and the thanks of hungry comrades who had bites of them!

At the corner of Great Jones Street we halted for half an hour,—then, everything ready, we marched down Broadway.

It was worth a life, that march. Only one who passed, as we did, through that tempest of cheers, two miles long, can know the terrible enthusiasm of the occasion. I could hardly hear the rattle of our own gun-carriages, and only once or twice the music of our band came to me muffled and quelled by the uproar. We knew now, if we had not before divined it, that our great city was with us as one man, utterly united in the great cause we were marching to sustain.

This grand fact I learned by two senses. If hundreds of thousands roared it into my ears, thousands slapped it into my back. My fellow-citizens smote me on the knapsack, as I went by at the gun-rope, and encouraged me each in his own dialect. "Bully for you!" alternated with benedictions, in the proportion of two "bullies" for one blessing.

I was not so fortunate as to receive more substantial tokens of sympathy. But there were parting gifts showered on the regiment, enough to establish a variety-shop. Handkerchiefs, of course, came floating down upon us from the windows like a snow. Pretty little gloves pelted us with love-taps. The (35) sterner sex forced upon us pocket-knives new and jagged, combs, soap, slippers, boxes of matches, cigars by the dozen and the hundred, pipes to smoke shag and pipes to smoke Latakia,[1] fruit, eggs, and sandwiches. One fellow got a new purse with ten bright quarter-eagles.

---

[1] *a type of tobacco*

Essay Question 3

Suggested time—40 minutes. This question counts as one third of the total score for Section II.

The following passage was written by Sidney Smith (1771–1845), an English clergyman known as the wittiest man of his time. It has been adapted from Smith's review of *The Book of Fallacies* by Jeremy Bentham, published in London in 1824.

Once you have read the passage, write an essay in which you support, refute, or qualify Smith's claim that to invoke our ancestors as a justification to act in a certain way is to rely on an "absurd and mischievous" fallacy. Use evidence from your reading, study, observation, or personal experience to develop your argument.

There are a vast number of absurd and mischievous fallacies, which pass readily in the world for sense and virtue, while in truth they tend only to fortify error and encourage crime. Mr. Bentham has enumerated the most conspicuous of these in the book before us . . .

Line

(5) OUR WISE ANCESTORS—*The Wisdom of Our Ancestors—The Wisdom of the Ages—Venerable Antiquity—Wisdom of Old Times—*This mischievous and absurd fallacy springs from the grossest perversion of the meaning of words. Experience is certainly the mother of wisdom, and the old have, of course, greater experience than the young; but the question is (10) who are the old? and who are the young?

Of *individuals* living at the same period, the oldest has, of course, the greatest experience; but among *generations* of men the reverse is true. Those who come first (our ancestors) are the young people, and have the least experience. We have added to their experience the experience of many cen- (15) turies; and, therefore, as far as experience goes, are wiser and more capable of forming an opinion than they were. The real feeling should be, *not* can we be so presumptuous as to put our opinions in opposition to those of our ancestors? but can such young, ignorant, inexperienced persons as our ancestors necessarily were, be expected to have understood a subject as well (20) as those who have seen so much more, lived so much longer, and enjoyed the experience of so many centuries?

END OF PRACTICE TEST C

Answer Key
PRACTICE TEST C

Answers to
Multiple-Choice
Questions

1. B	21. E	41. C
2. A	22. A	42. C
3. B	23. C	43. D
4. B	24. B	44. A
5. B	25. C	45. E
6. E	26. A	46. C
7. A	27. B	47. C
8. E	28. A	48. B
9. C	29. A	49. E
10. D	30. A	50. A
11. B	31. B	51. E
12. D	32. E	52. C
13. E	33. C	53. B
14. A	34. E	
15. A	35. E	
16. C	36. C	
17. B	37. E	
18. C	38. C	
19. A	39. D	
20. A	40. C	

Summary of Answers in Section I (Multiple-Choice)

Number of correct answers _____

Number of incorrect answers _____

Number of questions not answered _____

Use this information when you calculate your score on this exam. See page 334.

Answer Explanations

PASSAGE 1—AN EXCERPT FROM WILLIAM DEAN HOWELLS' "I TALK OF DREAMS"

1. **(B)** The speaker's focus is on the delightfulness of his own dreams compared to the pointlessness of others' dreams.

2. **(A)** In the first sentence of the paragraph the speaker generalizes about the incredible "egotism of some people." In the next sentence he explains exactly what he means.

3. **(B)** The speaker finds fault with people who fail to realize how dull their dreams can be to others.

4. **(B)** Throughout the passage the speaker inadvertently reveals shortcomings in his own personality and character. Primarily, he criticizes others' flaws while remaining unaware that he is flawed in the very same ways.

5. **(B)** The pronoun "they" refers to the dreams that can interest only the person who dreamt them. The people who tell their dreams may be just as "tedious and impertinent" as the dreams themselves, but grammatically speaking, "they" refers to dreams, not to people.

6. **(E)** The verb, "should be taught," is a clue that the speaker is proposing a course of action. In the second clause, the speaker adds a gratuitous slur.

7. **(A)** After criticizing people for imposing their dreams on others, it is ironic that the speaker is about to do just what he insists should not be done—tell the story of a dream.

8. **(E)** By telling about his dream, the speaker supports his claim, made in the first paragraph, that unlike the dreams of others, his own dreams are worth hearing about. (B), the only other reasonable choice, refers specifically to the dreams of other people.

9. **(C)** The speaker finds fault with everyone but himself. Only the Duke of Wellington is beyond reproach, and that's because the Duke is, after all, a duke, not to mention the one who defeated Napolean, and therefore too high-ranking to be criticized.

10. **(D)** Out of respect for the Duke's status, the speaker does what "his Grace" requests, fetching a couple of towels. When the Duke treats him like a servant, however, the speaker seems slightly put off—although the passage ends before the speaker can go into detail.

11. **(B)** The adjective "Turkish" describes the two bath-gowns given to the speaker.

12. **(D)** The speaker devotes almost the entire passage to passing judgments on several matters, particularly people's propensity to relate their dreams to others. (A) cannot be the answer because the speaker in a dramatic monologue addresses a particular person or audience and responds to their cues. (B) and (E) apply only to minor segments of the passage. (C) is not a good answer because, in a soliloquy, the speaker customarily talks aloud to himself.

PASSAGE 2—AN EXCERPT FROM T. S. ELIOT, "ON TEACHING THE APPRECIATION OF POETRY."

13. **(E)** Because the speaker has never "taught poetry," he cannot advise his audience on how to teach it. Rather, he can talk with authority about what he has observed, from a distance, about the teaching of poetry in schools.

14. **(A)** The speaker is alluding to the plight of many renowned poets and authors—namely unsolicited requests by struggling writers for advice and critiques of their work.

15. **(A)** In contrast to the Egyptian boy, who boldly stated his purpose (he wants books), many youngsters did not make clear why they had written to him.

16. **(C)** The child's innocent question amuses the speaker. That he is able to laugh about it suggests that rumors of his elitism are unfounded, or at least overstated.

17. **(B)** A gentle, ironic humor pervades the speaker's account of his correspondence with students.

18. **(E)** Eliot questions teaching methods (lines 15–17), states that students are "misguided" (line 18), and asks rhetorically whether children are studying poetry at all (lines 29–30).

19. **(A)** The sentence marks a slight change in the direction of the passage, but by using the phrase "this sort of thing" the speaker ties paragraph 3 to what he intends to say in paragraph 4.

20. **(A)** To some degree, all the choices except (A) are implied by the speaker's brief interjection.

21. **(E)** (A) refers to the names of past poets; (B) is found in "No," the first word of the paragraph. (C) is exemplified by "horse's mouth" (line 49), and (D) is used in lines 50–52. Only a rhetorical question is missing from the paragraph.

22. **(A)** The speaker surmises that some letters are motivated not by students' desire to learn, but by a hope to put their teachers down.

23. **(C)** The speaker mentions these poets of the past to stress the point that receiving letters from students is a development that only contemporary poets like himself have experienced.

24. **(B)** Although the speaker expresses misgivings over the way poetry is being taught, his criticism is tempered with gentle humor and understanding.

PASSAGE 3—AN EXCERPT FROM ROBERT LOUIS STEVENSON, "AES TRIPLEX."

25. **(C)** Both phrases suggest the uniqueness of death. That is, among life's experiences, there is nothing else like it.

26. **(A)** The "empty chairs" and "solitary walks," etc., are examples of the "sore havoc" (line 7) that follows the death of a friend or loved one.

27. **(B)** The phrase "like a Thug" is a simile. Personification occurs in "it leaps suddenly upon its victims" and "it lays regular siege." The repetition of "sometimes" serves to unify the first of the two sentences. The "pin," a device for holding things together, is an example of a metaphor. Only dramatic irony, a circumstance in which the reader knows more about a situation than a character in a story, is missing.

28. **(A)** The paragraph deals first with the seriousness of death for both the deceased and the survivors, and then with various consequences associated with dying. At the end of the paragraph, the speaker bemoans the fact that daily life leaves little time to reflect on the meaning of death.

29. **(A)** "It" refers to death, or as it is called in line 2, "the thing."

30. **(A)** The speaker cites the pyramids of Egypt, gallows, and hanging trees as "residue" that reminds us of death. Also "empty chairs, solitary walks, and single beds at night" (lines 8–9)—all sights and customs that help keep us constantly aware of death.

31. **(B)** Because the sentence is constructed of a subordinate clause and a main clause, it is a complex sentence. It describes a paradox of human behavior: We fear death terribly but act as though it did not exist. The sentence also contains parallel phrases: "few things are spoken of" and "few have less influence." The lines don't contain an analogy.

32. **(E)** The adjective "tremendous" refers to a city built on the side of a volcano. In context, therefore, "tremendous" suggests a dreadful, frightful place.

33. **(C)** The repetition of initial consonant sounds—particularly the *s* and *m* sounds—is noteworthy.

34. **(E)** The sentences develop the idea that residents of cities built on the side of fiery mountains appear to be indifferent to the mortal dangers of volcanic eruption.

35. **(E)** The opening sentence of the paragraph states a basic paradox: death frightens people, but it has no influence on their behavior. Much of the paragraph continues to discuss details about the inhabitants of cities built on the "side of fiery mountains." Paradoxically, the people are "not a jot more impressed by the solemnity of mortal conditions than if they were delving gardens . . . ." In other words, they lead ordinary lives, taking part in "serenades and suppers . . . etc.," in spite of the dangers lurking underfoot.

36. **(C)** The speaker alludes to umbrellas to suggest that these married couples take pains to protect themselves from the rain but mindlessly put themselves in harm's way by having "a bit of supper" on the side of a fiery mountain.

37. **(E)** Hermits pray for their own souls, are solitary figures, and suffer through their present lives in exchange for a heavenly life after death. The "born-devils" as described in the passage mindlessly drown their cares and sorrows in drink, unmindful of the consequences or longterm effects.

38. **(C)** The speaker is saying that much of what we do in life jeopardizes the health of our organs, hence our very lives.

39. **(D)** The repetition of "travelling blindly and swiftly" (line 40) conjures the chaotic movement of a million worlds. The comparison of the human body and a ship is an analogy. Among the rhetorical questions are, "What woman would ever be lured into marriage . . . etc.?" (lines 50–51). In the last sentence "ice" is a metaphor for life. Only an anecdote is missing; nowhere does the speaker tell a story.

40. **C** The first and third paragraphs discuss the omnipresence of death. In the rest of the passage the speaker observes that, although death is a constant threat, people conduct their lives as though death were a phenomenon that has nothing to do with them. In effect, they ignore it because they can't control it.

PASSAGE 4—AN EXCERPT FROM RUSSELL SHORTO, *THE ISLAND AT THE CENTER OF THE WORLD.*

41. **(C)** While explaining the circumstances surrounding the purchase of Manhattan Island from the Indians, the speaker interprets the famous event and expresses opinions about it.

42. **(C)** The pair of terse back-to-back sentences convey the impression that the speaker has no doubt about the validity of his claim that Peter Minuit bought Manhattan Island.

43. **(D)** The footnote explains that historians differ on who actually purchased Manhattan Island. The speaker, after reading various accounts of the transaction, sides with those who believe it was Peter Minuit, but evidently no one knows for sure.

44. **(A)** In context, the reference to the song is meant to show that the story of Peter Minuit's purchase of Manhattan Island is unusually famous and well-remembered.

45. **(E)** All the phrases except "ruthless Europeans" to some degree develop the speaker's assertion that the story of Manhattan Island's purchase has become a well-known piece of America's cultural history.

46. **(C)** The speaker, explaining the legendary quality of the story, says that the "sale lodged in the cultural memory" (line 15). The pronoun "our" refers to those who make up the "cultural memory," namely anyone who knows the terms of sale agreed to by the Dutch and the Indians.

47. **(C)** The omission of information such as the publisher and date of publication indicates that a complete citation most likely appears earlier in the book.

48. **(B)** The speaker uses this brief sentence as a transition between the first and second halves of the passage. He has told the story of the purchase of Manhattan in general terms and is preparing to dig deeper into certain aspects of the event.

49. **(E)** Each statement is an exaggerated generalization that cannot be proven or disproven. Each is powerful and dramatic, leaving readers with a sense that this passage consists of weighty, well-researched material.

50. **(A)** The speaker notes characteristics that are typically human: possession of technical and thinking skills, a capacity for cruelty and deception, curiosity about the world.

51. **(E)** Note 2 refers specifically to a quotation by comedian Dave Barry.

52. **(C)** All the words except (C) are predicate adjectives that describe "Indians," the subject of the sentence. "Technological" is also an adjective, but it modifies, or describes, "cunning," an object of the preposition *of*.

53. **(B)** The speaker uses the last sentence to clear up various stereotyped impressions of American Indians. In all respects, says the speaker, the Indians had many of the same characteristics—both favorable and unfavorable—as European settlers.

Answers to Essay Questions

Although answers to the essay questions will vary greatly, the following descriptions suggest a possible approach to each question and contain ideas that could be used in response to the question. Perhaps your essay contains many of the same ideas. If not, don't be alarmed. Your ideas may be no less—or perhaps even more—insightful than those presented below.

ESSAY QUESTION 1, BASED ON THE ISSUE OF KEEPING "UNDER GOD" IN THE PLEDGE OF ALLEGIANCE.

SOME ARGUMENTS __IN FAVOR__ OF ELIMINATING "UNDER GOD" FROM THE PLEDGE:

- The words, in effect, say that in America anyone who doesn't believe in God does not count. (Source C)
- It's a non-issue generated by politicians who tell voters whatever they want to hear, even at the expense of breaking the barrier between church and state. (Source C)
- Religion has nothing to do with the issue. Opinions are based on ideological differences between Democrats and Republicans. (Source D)
- The founders of the U.S. opposed the institutionalization of religion. (Source F)
- We must not forget that many people came to America to escape religious persecution. (Source F)

SOME ARGUMENTS __AGAINST__ ELIMINATING "UNDER GOD" FROM THE PLEDGE:

- The words do not cross the divide that separates church and state; they merely acknowledge the role that religion has played in the history of America. (Source A)
- America is basically a Christian country; the words recognize that fact. (Source A)
- The use of the words does not constitute the "establishment of religion" prohibited by the Constitution. Instead, the words declare the current state of our country. (Source B)
- According to Supreme Court rulings, the words are not unconstitutional for a variety of reasons. (Source E)
- The two words do not constitute a prayer. (Source F)

QUESTION 2, BASED ON AN EXCERPT FROM THEODORE WINTHROP'S "OUR MARCH TO WASHINGTON," 1861

The first-person narrator of this episode is a young man on his way to war. He and his regiment are parading through a city where people have gathered to send them off.

First he is assigned to keep onlookers away from a large cannon, a howitzer, named a "peacemaker." Whether he is aware of the irony of applying that label to a machine of war remains unclear, but in all likelihood he isn't, because he seems too caught up in the spirit of the moment.

Indeed, he is impressed by the size of the cheering crowd. Twice he uses the phrase "enormous crowd" (lines 4 and 5), once with an exclamation point for additional emphasis. He notes the men's expressions of "truculent and patriotic hopes" (line 6). He also notices that the "women shed tears and say, 'God bless you, boys'" (line 7), but he seems unmindful of the feelings that evoke such responses. In other words, this is not a time for subtle observation or reflection. Yet, he reads in the faces of onlookers that they seem "to be taking the measure of my coffin" (lines 10–11). In other words, before continuing his description of the parade, the speaker senses briefly the dark implications behind the noisy celebration.

"It was worth a life, that march" (line 20), he says, an opinion that can be interpreted in two ways. It could mean simply that the march was an experience of a lifetime. On the other hand, it suggests that the speaker knows that he, as well as many of his comrades, will soon be giving up their lives—a thought reinforced by the phrase "terrible enthusiasm" (line 20), in which "terrible" seems to be used in the sense of "terrifying" or "horrible," although at that time the word also carried a connotation of "awe-inspiring."

What is more, the speaker uses the term "tokens of sympathy" (line 31) for the small gifts—handkerchiefs, gloves, combs, soaps, etc.—that the crowd bestows on the troops. In a sense, this could also be the speaker's way of drawing attention to the discrepancy between the sacrifice he and his comrades may be about to make in battle and the trivial price paid by the people left behind. Or the seemingly insignificant gifts may also be interpreted as more personal expressions of support.

On one level, then, the passage is a rather superficial depiction of a typical farewell march of troops going to fight. On a deeper level, though, readers are privy to the apprehension felt by one young soldier. His fears and anxieties are presented not as blatant statements but by hints and indirections. Like most of the crowd—more inclined to shout "'bullies'" than "benedictions" (lines 29–30)—he puts up a brave front at a time of great uncertainty.

QUESTION 3, BASED ON SIDNEY SMITH'S REVIEW OF
THE BOOK OF FALLACIES

If you were to agree with Smith, your essay might begin with a rationale such as this: Young people need to make decisions on their own. Self-reliance is a sign of maturity. Therefore, on the verge of adulthood, the young will disregard the wisdom of the past. Beyond that, you could probably name several situations and endeavors in which young people are likely to be better informed than their elders. When it comes to modern electronic and digital technology, for instance, it's a truism that the young folks are far more savvy than the geezers. The same principle applies to such everyday activities as going to bed and getting up in the morning. Traditional wisdom says, "Early to bed and early to rise . . .," but modern youth knows better. They have the advantage of research into enzymes and body chemistry showing that most teenagers, biologically, tend to function more efficiently later in the day than early in the morning. No doubt you can think of additional ways in which to support Smith's surprising assertion that our ancestors are "the young people, and have the least experience."

If, on the other hand, you choose to poke holes in Smith's argument, you might cite several examples of the reliability of old-time wisdom and experience. You might argue that governmental decisions and policies must be based on historical evidence. From World War II the world has learned, if nothing else, to be far more alert to the threats of genocide. From Vietnam and Iraq, America has presumably learned to be wary of political and military quagmires. In addition, in crisis after crisis, the wisdom of America's founders has proved to be a solid foundation for decision-making. Then there are ancient religious texts thousands of years old that still serve as moral compasses for individuals as well as groups. Back in the 17th century, Rouchefoucauld said, "Nothing is given so profusely as advice," and, "The true way to be deceived is to think oneself more clever than others"—just two pieces of wisdom among countless others that are as apt today as they were generations ago.

Or let your essay take the middle ground between these two extremes. A strong case could be made that the past can serve as a beacon in some areas of life, but is hopelessly irrelevant in others. Certainly our ancestors can teach us little about treating cancer or AIDS. Their knowledge of diseases, health, nutrition, and genetics now seems quaint. Their understanding of the physical world was relatively primitive. But, when it comes to common sense about character and human relations, getting and spending money, morals and values, and so on, the wisdom of "old times" may still be instructive and useful.

Self-Scoring Guide—Practice Test C

SCORING SECTION 2 ESSAYS

After referring to "How Essays Are Scored" on page 27 of this book, use this guide to help you evaluate each essay. Do your best to evaluate your performance in each category by using the criteria spelled out below. Because it is hard to achieve objectivity when assessing your own writing, you may improve the validity of your score by having a trusted and well-informed friend or experienced teacher read and rate your essay.

On the following Rating Chart, enter a number (from 1 to 6) that you think represents your level of performance in each category (A–F).

Category A: OVERALL PURPOSE/MAIN IDEA

6 extremely well-defined and insightful

5 clearly defined and generally insightful

4 mostly clear

3 somewhat clear but occasionally confusing

2 generally unclear and confusing

1 virtually incomprehensible

Category B: HANDLING OF THE PROMPT

6 self-evident or extremely clear throughout

5 mostly clear

4 somewhat clear

3 somewhat unclear

2 generally unclear or ambiguous

1 confusing or nonexistent

Category C: ORGANIZATION AND DEVELOPMENT

6 insightfully organized; fully developed with excellent supporting evidence

5 reasonably well organized; developed with appropriate supporting material

4 appropriately organized; developed with some relevant material

3 inadequately organized; weak development

2 poorly organized; little or no development

1 no discernible organization; no relevant development

Category D: SENTENCE STRUCTURE

6 varied and engaging

5 sufficiently varied to create interest

4 some variety

3 little variety; minor sentence errors

2 frequent sentence errors that interfere with meaning

1 serious sentence errors that obscure meaning

Category E: USE OF LANGUAGE

6 precise and effective word choice

5 competent word choice

4 conventional word choice; mostly correct

3 some errors in diction or idiom

2 frequent errors in diction or idiom

1 meaning obscured by word choice

Category F: GRAMMAR AND USAGE

6 error-free or virtually error-free

5 occasional minor errors

4 basically correct but with several minor errors

3 meaning somewhat obscured by errors

2 meaning frequently obscured by errors

1 meaning blocked by several major errors

RATING CHART

Rate your essay:	Essay 1	Essay 2	Essay 3
Overall Purpose/Main Idea	_____	_____	_____
Handling of the Prompt	_____	_____	_____
Organization and Development	_____	_____	_____
Sentence Structure	_____	_____	_____
Use of Language	_____	_____	_____
Grammar and Usage	_____	_____	_____
Composite Scores (Sum of each column)	_____	_____	_____

By using the following scale, in which composite scores are converted to the nine-point AP rating scale, you may determine the final score for each essay:

Composite Score	AP Essay Score
33–36	9
29–32	8
25–28	7
21–24	6
18–20	5
15–17	4
10–14	3
7–9	2
6 or below	1

AP Essay Scores Essay 1 _____ Essay 2 _____ Essay 3 _____

TEST SCORE WORKSHEET FOR PRACTICE TEST C

The scores you have earned on the multiple-choice and essay sections of the exam may now be converted to the AP five-point scale by performing the following calculations:

I. Determine your score for Section I (Multiple Choice)

Step A: Number of correct answers _____

Step B: Number of wrong answers _____ (Note: Do not count unanswered questions.)

Step C: Multiply the number of wrong answers by .250 and enter the figure here _____ .

Step D: Subtract the figure in Step C from the figure in Step A _____ .

Step E: Multiply the figure in Step D by 1.2500 to find your Multiple-Choice Score _____ (If less than zero, enter zero.)

II. Determine your score for Section II (Essays)

Step A: Enter your score for Essay 1 (out of 9) _____

Step B: Enter your score for Essay 2 (out of 9) _____

Step C: Enter your score for Essay 3 (out of 9) _____

Step D: Add the figures in Steps A, B, and C _____

Step E: Multiply the figure in Step D by 3.0556 _____ (Do not round.) This is your Essay Score.

III. Determine Your Total Score

Add the scores for I and II to find your composite score _____ .

To convert your composite score to the AP five-point scale, use the chart below. The range of scores only approximates what you would earn on the actual test because the exact figures may vary from test to test. Be aware, therefore, that your score on this test, as well as on other tests in this book, may differ slightly from your score on an actual AP exam.

Composite Score	AP Grade
108–150	5
93–107	4
72–92	3
43–71	2
0–42	1

AP essays are ordinarily judged in relation to other essays written on the same topic at the same time. Therefore, the scores you assign yourself for these essays may not be the same as the scores you would earn on an actual exam.

Practice Test C

Practice Test D
ANSWER SHEET

Multiple-Choice Questions
Time—1 hour

1. Ⓐ Ⓑ Ⓒ Ⓓ Ⓔ
2. Ⓐ Ⓑ Ⓒ Ⓓ Ⓔ
3. Ⓐ Ⓑ Ⓒ Ⓓ Ⓔ
4. Ⓐ Ⓑ Ⓒ Ⓓ Ⓔ
5. Ⓐ Ⓑ Ⓒ Ⓓ Ⓔ
6. Ⓐ Ⓑ Ⓒ Ⓓ Ⓔ
7. Ⓐ Ⓑ Ⓒ Ⓓ Ⓔ
8. Ⓐ Ⓑ Ⓒ Ⓓ Ⓔ
9. Ⓐ Ⓑ Ⓒ Ⓓ Ⓔ
10. Ⓐ Ⓑ Ⓒ Ⓓ Ⓔ
11. Ⓐ Ⓑ Ⓒ Ⓓ Ⓔ
12. Ⓐ Ⓑ Ⓒ Ⓓ Ⓔ
13. Ⓐ Ⓑ Ⓒ Ⓓ Ⓔ
14. Ⓐ Ⓑ Ⓒ Ⓓ Ⓔ
15. Ⓐ Ⓑ Ⓒ Ⓓ Ⓔ
16. Ⓐ Ⓑ Ⓒ Ⓓ Ⓔ
17. Ⓐ Ⓑ Ⓒ Ⓓ Ⓔ
18. Ⓐ Ⓑ Ⓒ Ⓓ Ⓔ
19. Ⓐ Ⓑ Ⓒ Ⓓ Ⓔ
20. Ⓐ Ⓑ Ⓒ Ⓓ Ⓔ

21. Ⓐ Ⓑ Ⓒ Ⓓ Ⓔ
22. Ⓐ Ⓑ Ⓒ Ⓓ Ⓔ
23. Ⓐ Ⓑ Ⓒ Ⓓ Ⓔ
24. Ⓐ Ⓑ Ⓒ Ⓓ Ⓔ
25. Ⓐ Ⓑ Ⓒ Ⓓ Ⓔ
26. Ⓐ Ⓑ Ⓒ Ⓓ Ⓔ
27. Ⓐ Ⓑ Ⓒ Ⓓ Ⓔ
28. Ⓐ Ⓑ Ⓒ Ⓓ Ⓔ
29. Ⓐ Ⓑ Ⓒ Ⓓ Ⓔ
30. Ⓐ Ⓑ Ⓒ Ⓓ Ⓔ
31. Ⓐ Ⓑ Ⓒ Ⓓ Ⓔ
32. Ⓐ Ⓑ Ⓒ Ⓓ Ⓔ
33. Ⓐ Ⓑ Ⓒ Ⓓ Ⓔ
34. Ⓐ Ⓑ Ⓒ Ⓓ Ⓔ
35. Ⓐ Ⓑ Ⓒ Ⓓ Ⓔ
36. Ⓐ Ⓑ Ⓒ Ⓓ Ⓔ
37. Ⓐ Ⓑ Ⓒ Ⓓ Ⓔ
38. Ⓐ Ⓑ Ⓒ Ⓓ Ⓔ
39. Ⓐ Ⓑ Ⓒ Ⓓ Ⓔ
40. Ⓐ Ⓑ Ⓒ Ⓓ Ⓔ

41. Ⓐ Ⓑ Ⓒ Ⓓ Ⓔ
42. Ⓐ Ⓑ Ⓒ Ⓓ Ⓔ
43. Ⓐ Ⓑ Ⓒ Ⓓ Ⓔ
44. Ⓐ Ⓑ Ⓒ Ⓓ Ⓔ
45. Ⓐ Ⓑ Ⓒ Ⓓ Ⓔ
46. Ⓐ Ⓑ Ⓒ Ⓓ Ⓔ
47. Ⓐ Ⓑ Ⓒ Ⓓ Ⓔ
48. Ⓐ Ⓑ Ⓒ Ⓓ Ⓔ
49. Ⓐ Ⓑ Ⓒ Ⓓ Ⓔ
50. Ⓐ Ⓑ Ⓒ Ⓓ Ⓔ
51. Ⓐ Ⓑ Ⓒ Ⓓ Ⓔ
52. Ⓐ Ⓑ Ⓒ Ⓓ Ⓔ

Practice Test D

SECTION 1

Total time—1 hour

PASSAGE 1

Questions 1–14. Carefully read the following passage and answer the accompanying questions.

The passage is an excerpt from the autobiography of a 19th-century American literary figure.

One day in June, 1854, young Adams walked for the last time down the steps of Mr. Dixwell's school in Boylston Place, and felt no sensation but one of unqualified joy that this experience was ended. Never before or
Line afterwards in his life did he close a period so long as four years without
(5) some sensation of loss—some sentiment of habit—but school was what in after life he commonly heard his friends denounce as an intolerable bore. He was born too old for it. The same thing could be said of most New England boys. Mentally they were never boys. Their education as men should have begun at ten years old. They were fully five years more mature
(10) than the English or European boy for whom schools were made. For the purposes of future advancement, as afterwards appeared, these first six years of a possible education were wasted in doing imperfectly what might have been done perfectly in one, and in any case would have had small value. The next regular step was Harvard College. He was more than glad
(15) to go. For generation after generation, Adamses and Brookses and Boylstons and Gorhams had gone to Harvard College, and although none of them, as far as known, had ever done any good there, or thought himself the better for it, custom, social ties, convenience, and above all, economy, kept each generation in the track. Any other education would have
(20) required a serious effort, but no one took Harvard College seriously. All went there because their friends went there, and the College was their ideal of social self-respect.

Harvard College, as far as it educated at all, was a mild and liberal school, which sent young men into the world with all they needed to make
(25) respectable citizens, and something of what they wanted to make useful ones. Leaders of men it never tried to make. Its ideas were altogether different. The Unitarian clergy had given to the College a character of moderation, balance, judgment, restraint, what the French called *mesure;*

(30) excellent traits, which the College attained with singular success, so that its graduates could commonly be recognized by the stamp, but such a type of character rarely lent itself to autobiography. In effect, the school created a type but not a will. Four years of Harvard College, if successful, resulted in an autobiographical blank, a mind on which only a water-mark had been stamped.

(35) The stamp, as such things went, was a good one. The chief wonder of education is that it does not ruin everybody concerned with it, teachers and taught. Sometimes in after life, Adams debated whether in fact it had not ruined him and most of his companions, but, disappointment apart, Harvard College was probably less hurtful than any other University then

(40) in existence. It taught little, and that little ill, but it left the mind open, free from bias, ignorant of facts, but docile. The graduate had few strong prejudices. He knew little, but his mind remained supple, ready to receive knowledge.

What caused the boy most disappointment was the little he got from his

(45) mates. Speaking exactly, he got less than nothing, a result common enough in education. Yet the College Catalogue for the years 1854–1861 shows a list of names rather distinguished in their time. Alexander Agassiz and Phillips Brooks led it. H. H. Richardson and O. W. Holmes helped to close it. As a rule the most promising of all die early, and never get their names

(50) into a Dictionary of Contemporaries which seems to be the only popular standard of success. Many died in the war. Adams knew them all, more or less; he felt as much regard, and quite as much respect for them then, as he did after they won great names and were objects of a vastly wider respect; but, as help toward education, he got nothing whatever from them or they

(55) from him until long after they had left College. Possibly the fault was his, but one would like to know how many others shared it. Accident counts for as much in companionship as in marriage. Life offers perhaps only a score of possible companions, and it is mere chance whether they meet as early as school or college, but it is more than a chance that boys brought up

(60) together under like conditions have nothing to give each other.

1. Taken as a whole, the passage is best described as

   (A) a series of anecdotes about college life in the past.
   (B) a summary of academic customs during a particular era.
   (C) an assessment of a young man's educational experiences.
   (D) an indictment of an obsolete educational system.
   (E) a description of a historical period.

2. In line 3, the phrase "this experience" refers to Adams'

   (A) lack of sensation.
   (B) attendance at Mr. Dixwell's school.
   (C) walk down the steps.
   (D) graduation after four years.
   (E) boredom.

3. Which of the following best describes the rhetorical effect of the sentence in line 7 ("He was born too old for it")?

   (A) It succinctly summarizes all the ideas contained in the passage thus far.
   (B) It contrasts starkly to the structure and diction of the preceding sentence.
   (C) It suggests the simpleminded mentality of most New England boys.
   (D) It completely reverses the the tone of the passage.
   (E) It serves as a dramatic climax to the story of Adams' education.

4. The idea expressed in "He was born too old for it" (line 7) is reinforced by all of the following phrases EXCEPT

   (A) "some sentiment of habit" (line 5).
   (B) "an intolerable bore" (line 6).
   (C) "never boys" (line 8).
   (D) "education as men should have begun at ten" (line 8).
   (E) "fully five years more mature" (line 9).

5. The speaker mentions the "Adamses and Brookses and Boylstons and Gorhams" (lines 15–16) as examples of which of the following?

   I. Families that helped Harvard maintain its reputation as an exclusive finishing school for young men
   II. New England families that had traditionally sent their sons to Harvard
   III. Students whose names assured them of preferential treatment in Harvard's admission process

   (A) I only
   (B) I and II only
   (C) II and III only
   (D) III only
   (E) I, II, and III

6. The two sentences beginning with "Harvard College" and ending with "tried to make" (lines 23–26), employ all of the following EXCEPT

   (A) a compound subject.
   (B) predicate adjectives.
   (C) subordinate clause.
   (D) parallel syntax.
   (E) inverted sentence structure.

7. The effects of a Harvard education discussed in lines 23–26 are referred to elsewhere as which of the following?

   (A) "above all, economy" (lines 18–19)
   (B) "serious effort" (line 20)
   (C) "less hurtful" (line 39)
   (D) "ready to receive knowledge" (lines 42–43)
   (E) "less than nothing" (line 45)

8. In context, the word "stamp" (line 30) is best interpreted to mean

   (A) a seal of approval.
   (B) a credential.
   (C) habit.
   (D) harmony.
   (E) a uniform image.

9. "[A] mind on which only a water-mark had been stamped" (lines 33–34) is best understood as a metaphor for

   (A) an inhibited imagination.
   (B) an imperceptible amount of learning.
   (C) a lack of basic common sense.
   (D) a set of attitudes and values.
   (E) misinformation and confusion.

10. Which of the following best describes the tone of the sentence in lines 35–37 ("The chief . . . and taught")?

   (A) Cynical
   (B) Combative
   (C) Ironic
   (D) Resigned and contemplative
   (E) Agitated and moralistic

11. The rhetorical device most in evidence in lines 40–42 is best described as

   (A) oxymoron.
   (B) pun.
   (C) antithesis.
   (D) hyperbole.
   (E) allusion.

12. The function of the sentences "Yet the College Catalogue . . . close it" (lines 46–49) is primarily to

   (A) qualify a statement made in the previous paragraph.
   (B) spell out the paragraph's main idea.
   (C) offer an explanation for the idea expressed in the previous sentence.
   (D) deny the truth of the first two sentences in the paragraph.
   (E) provide evidence that contrasts with an idea stated in the previous sentences.

13. The speaker employs an analogy between companionship and marriage (lines 56–59) mainly to

   (A) foreshadow Adams' marital difficulties.
   (B) analyze Adams' problems with friends.
   (C) argue in favor of co-education.
   (D) reflect on the unpredictability of life.
   (E) discuss life's losses and gains.

14. The speaker in the passage can best be described as a person inclined to believe all of the following EXCEPT that

(A) a Harvard education in the mid-19th century left much to be desired.
(B) the maturity of boys from abroad tended to lag behind the maturity of boys from New England.
(C) to be a Harvard student was socially desirable and advantageous.
(D) Harvard graduates were virtually indistinguishable from one another.
(E) Harvard's administration and faculty ought to have been held accountable for the College's deficiencies.

PASSAGE 2

Questions 15–25. Carefully read the following passage and answer the accompanying questions.

The passage is from an essay written by an early 20th-century feminist British poet.

Play is not for every hour of the day, or for any hour taken at random. There is a tide in the affairs of children. Civilization is cruel in sending them to bed at the most stimulating time of dusk. Summer dusk, especially,
Line is the frolic moment for children, baffle them how you may. They may have
(5) been in a pottering mood all day, intent upon all kinds of close industries, breathing hard over choppings and poundings. But when late twilight comes, there comes also the punctual wildness. The children will run and pursue, and laugh for the mere movement—it does so jolt their spirits.

What remembrances does this imply of the hunt, what of the predatory
(10) dark? The kitten grows alert at the same hour, and hunts for moths and crickets in the grass. It comes like an imp, leaping on all fours. The children lie in ambush and fall upon one another in the mimicry of hunting. The sudden outbreak of action is complained of as a defiance and a rebellion. Their entertainers are tired, and the children are to go home. But, with
(15) more or less of life and fire, the children strike some blow for liberty. It may be the impotent revolt of the ineffectual child, or the stroke of the conqueror; but something, something is done for freedom under the early stars.

This is not the only time when the energy of children is in conflict with the weariness of men. But it is less tolerable that the energy of men should
(20) be at odds with the weariness of children, which happens at some time of their jaunts together, especially, alas! in the jaunts of the poor.

Of games for the summer dusk when it rains, cards are most beloved by children. Three tiny girls were to be taught "Old Maid" to beguile the time. One of them, a nut-brown child of five, was persuading another to play.
(25) "Oh, come," she said, "and play with me at 'New Maid.'"

The time of falling asleep is a child's immemorial and incalculable hour. It is full of traditions, and beset by antique habits. The habit of prehistoric races has been cited as the only explanation of the fixity of some customs in mankind. But if the inquirers who appeal to that beginning remembered

(30) better their own infancy, they would seek no further. See the habits in falling to sleep which have children in their thralldom. Try to overcome them in any child, and his own conviction of their high antiquity weakens your hand.

Childhood is antiquity, and with the sense of time and the sense of mys-
(35) tery is connected for ever to the hearing of a lullaby. The French sleep-song is the most romantic. There is in it such a sound of history as must inspire any imaginative child, falling to sleep, with a sense of the incalculable; and the songs themselves are old. "Le Bon Roi Dagobert" has been sung over French cradles since the legend was fresh. The nurse knows nothing more
(40) sleepy than the tune and the verse that she herself slept to when a child. The gaiety of the thirteenth century, in "Le Pont d'Avignon," is put mysteri-ously to sleep, away in the *tête à tête* of child and nurse, in a thousand lit-tle sequestered rooms at night. "Malbrook" would be comparatively modern, were not all things that are sung to a drowsing child as distant as
(45) the day of Abraham.

If English children are not rocked to many such aged lullabies, some of them are put to sleep to strange cradle-songs. The affectionate races that are brought into subjection sing the primitive lullaby to the white child. Asiatic voices and African persuade him to sleep in the tropical night. His closing
(50) eyes are filled with alien images.

15. The sentence "There is a tide in the affairs of children" (line 2) functions chiefly as

   (A) the topic sentence of the first paragraph.
   (B) an expression of the main idea of the passage.
   (C) a fact discussed in more detail later in the passage.
   (D) an analogy used to make an abstraction concrete.
   (E) an introduction to a paradox to be discussed later.

16. By using the word "tide" (line 2), the speaker emphasizes that

   (A) children are more changeable than adults.
   (B) consistency is difficult for children to learn.
   (C) some children follow parental rules; others don't.
   (D) children can be taught that there is a time and place for everything.
   (E) children's energy regularly comes and goes.

17. As used in line 4 "baffle" most nearly means

   (A) constrain.
   (B) confuse.
   (C) puzzle.
   (D) instruct.
   (E) schedule.

18. In lines 9–12, the speaker associates the wildness she observes in children at summer dusk with

    (A) ancient survival techniques.
    (B) a primitive impulse to kill.
    (C) the instinctual behavior of predators.
    (D) aggressive intimidation.
    (E) extinct mammals.

19. The speaker's observation in the sentences, "But, with more or less . . . early stars" (lines 14–17) can best be described as an example of

    (A) an expert's advice to parents.
    (B) an objective analysis of disobedient children.
    (C) an interpretation of children's behavior.
    (D) an appeal to authority.
    (E) an objection to excessively strict parental discipline.

20. Which of the following descriptions apply to paragraph 5 (lines 26–33)?

    I. Its language is more concrete than that in the other paragraphs of the passage
    II. It contains an illustrative anecdote
    III. It includes relevant dialogue

    (A) I only
    (B) III only
    (C) I and II only
    (D) II and III only
    (E) I, II, and III

21. The primary rhetorical purpose of the sixth paragraph (lines 34–45) is to

    (A) refute a widely held assumption.
    (B) develop an emotionally appealing argument.
    (C) provide a perspective on a common, everyday phenomenon.
    (D) cite specific examples to prove an abstract argument.
    (E) propose a theory to be studied in the future.

22. In line 30, the pronoun "their" refers to

    (A) "prehistoric races" (lines 27–28).
    (B) "customs" (line 28).
    (C) "inquirers" (line 29).
    (D) "habits" (line 30).
    (E) "children" (line 31).

23. The speaker's central rhetorical strategy in the seventh paragraph (lines 46–50) can best be described as

    (A) introducing a series of generalizations that will be supported later.
    (B) citing specific examples to illustrate an abstract concept.
    (C) comparing and contrasting a pair of suppositions.
    (D) challenging a controversial thesis proposed earlier.
    (E) anticipating objections raised by ideas presented in lines 35–37.

24. Which of the following phrases does the speaker use to illustrate the "mystery" (lines 33–34) associated with lullabies?

    (A) "The French sleep song" (line 35)
    (B) "the most romantic" (line 36)
    (C) "a sound of history" (line 36)
    (D) "a sense the incalculable" (line 37)
    (E) "the tune and the verse" (line 40)

25. The author's tone in the passage as a whole is best described as

    (A) contemplative and tender.
    (B) casual and meandering.
    (C) strict and dogmatic.
    (D) scientific and aggressive.
    (E) enthusiastic and extravagant.

PASSAGE 3

Questions 26–38. Carefully read the following passage and answer the accompanying questions.

The passage is from a essay written by a well-known novelist of the late 19th and early 20th centuries.

There is a certain evening that I count as virtually a first impression— the end of a wet, black Sunday, twenty years ago, about the first of March. There had been an earlier vision, but it had turned gray, like faded ink, and
Line the occasion I speak of was a fresh beginning. No doubt I had a mystic pre-
(5) science of how fond of the murky Babylon I was one day to become; cer- tain it is that as I look back I find every small circumstance of those hours of approach and arrival still as vivid as if the solemnity of an opening era had breathed upon it. The sense of approach was already almost intolerably strong at Liverpool, where, I remember, the perception of the English char-
(10) acter of everything was as acute as a surprise, though it could only be a surprise without a shock. It was expectation exquisitely gratified, superabundantly confirmed. There was a kind of wonder indeed that England should be as English as, for my entertainment, she took the trou- ble to be; but the wonder would have been greater, and all the pleasure
(15) absent, if the sensation had not been violent. It seems to sit there again like a visiting presence, as it sat opposite me at breakfast at a small table in a window of the old coffee-room of the Adelphi Hotel—the unextended (as it then was), the unimproved, the unblushingly local Adelphi. Liverpool is not a romantic city, but that smoky Saturday returns to me as a supreme
(20) success, measured by its association with the kind of emotion in the hope of which, for the most part, we betake ourselves to far countries.

It assumed this character at an early hour—or rather indeed twenty-four hours before—with the sight, as one looked across the wintry ocean, of the strange, dark, lonely freshness of the coast of Ireland. Better still, before we
(25) could come up to the city, were the black steamers knocking about in the

yellow Mersey, under a sky so low that they seemed to touch it with their funnels, and in the thickest, windiest light. Spring was already in the air, in the town; there was no rain, but there was still less sun—one wondered what had become, on this side of the world, of the big white splotch in the

(30) heavens; and the gray mildness, shading away into black at every pretext, appeared in itself a promise. This was how it hung about me, between the window and the fire, in the coffee-room of the hotel—late in the morning for breakfast, as we had been long in disembarking. The other passengers had dispersed, knowingly catching trains for London (we had only been a

(35) handful); I had the place to myself, and I felt as if I had an exclusive property in the impression. I prolonged it, I sacrificed to it, and it is perfectly recoverable now, with the very taste of the national muffin, the creak of the waiter's shoes as he came and went (could anything be so English as his intensely professional back? it revealed a country of tradition), and the rus-

(40) tle of the newspaper I was too excited to read.

    I continued to sacrifice for the rest of the day; it didn't seem to me a sentient[1] thing, as yet, to inquire into the means of getting away. My curiosity must indeed have languished, for I found myself on the morrow in the slowest of Sunday trains, pottering up to London with an interruptedness

(45) which might have been tedious without the conversation of an old gentleman who shared the carriage with me and to whom my alien as well as comparatively youthful character had betrayed itself. He instructed me as to the sights of London, and impressed upon me that nothing was more worthy of my attention than the great cathedral of St. Paul. "Have you seen

(50) St. Peter's in Rome? St. Peter's is more highly embellished, you know; but you may depend upon it that St. Paul's is the better building of the two." The impression I began with speaking of was, strictly, that of the drive from Euston, after dark, to Morely's Hotel in Trafalgar Square. It was not lovely—it was in fact rather horrible; but as I move again through dusky

(55) tortuous miles, in the greasy four-wheeler to which my luggage had compelled me to commit myself, I recognize the first step in an initiation of which the subsequent stages were to abound in pleasant things.

---

[1]*sentient: aware; conscious; capable of making fine distinctions*

26. The speaker in the passage focuses primarily on

    (A) changes that have occurred since he arrived in London
    (B) a recollection of his state of mind upon arriving in England
    (C) memorable qualities that characterize England and the English people
    (D) his affection for all things English
    (E) the significance of his return to his ancestral homeland

27. In line 5, the phrase "murky Babylon" can best be described as

    (A) an analogical comparison.
    (B) an example of verbal irony.
    (C) an elliptical construction.
    (D) a metaphorical allusion.
    (E) anecdotal development.

28. In paragraphs 1 and 2 (lines 1–40), the speaker's depiction of the setting emphasizes its

    (A) dark gloominess.
    (B) visual surprises.
    (C) distant views.
    (D) variety of color.
    (E) bustling activity.

29. In the first paragraph, all of the following contribute to the speaker's anticipation of a "fresh beginning" (line 4) EXCEPT

    (A) "the end of a wet, black Sunday" (line 2).
    (B) "a mystic prescience" (lines 4–5).
    (C) "the sense of approach" (line 8).
    (D) that "everything was as acute as a surprise" (line 10).
    (E) "a visiting presence" (line 16).

30. The sentence "It was expectation . . . confirmed" (lines 11–12) functions in all the following ways EXCEPT

    (A) it characterizes one of the speaker's reactions to setting foot on English soil.
    (B) it suggests that the speaker was well informed about England.
    (C) it helps to clarify the precise meaning of "surprise without a shock" in the preceding sentence.
    (D) it helps to reveal another dimension of the speaker's feelings.
    (E) it confirms that the speaker had lost control of his emotions.

31. To the speaker, the "Adelphi Hotel" (line 17) is associated with

    (A) the dreariness of traveling alone.
    (B) a fondly remembered feeling.
    (C) a shattered expectation.
    (D) a welcome relief.
    (E) a temporary bout with depression.

32. The "kind of emotion" mentioned in line 20 refers to

    (A) nostalgia.
    (B) "surprise without a shock" (line 11).
    (C) self-satisfaction.
    (D) gratification over having successfully achieved a long-sought goal.
    (E) a sense of wonder.

33. In line 22, the pronoun "It" refers to

   (A) "a first impression" (line 1).
   (B) "an earlier vision" (line 3).
   (C) "the English character" (lines 9–10).
   (D) "a kind of wonder" (line 12).
   (E) "the coast of Ireland" (line 24).

34. The second paragraph (lines 22–40) derives its unity primarily through

   (A) an abundant use of sensual imagery.
   (B) using details to support a generalization.
   (C) a comparison of the land and the sea.
   (D) its emphasis on the weather.
   (E) contrasting the speaker's impressions of the night and the day.

35. In context, the phrase "sacrificed to it" (line 36) is best understood to mean that the speaker

   (A) abandoned his fellow passengers.
   (B) gave up his customary reading of the daily paper.
   (C) found himself being shunned by other passengers.
   (D) had given up a great deal in order to travel to England.
   (E) decided to linger in Liverpool before continuing his journey.

36. Which of the following best describes the tone of the parenthetical remark "could anything . . . of tradition" (lines 38–39)?

   (A) curious and questioning
   (B) smug and worldly-wise
   (C) uncertain and troubled
   (D) puzzled and wary
   (E) uncomfortable and insulting

37. The rhetorical function of the last sentence of the passage (lines 53–57) is to

   (A) bring the passage to an unexpected climax.
   (B) present a realistic picture of the speakers's emotional state.
   (C) unify the passage by reiterating its main theme.
   (D) reveal an inconsistency in the character of the speaker.
   (E) strengthen the coherence of the passage by alluding to the "earlier vision" (line 3).

38. The speaker in the passage can best be described as a person who

   (A) habitually boasts of his past successes.
   (B) nostalgically recalls earlier days.
   (C) tends to test the validity of his conjectures.
   (D) writes in order to recreate the pathos of a misspent youth.
   (E) promotes the advantages of traveling alone.

PASSAGE 4

Questions 39–52. Carefully read the following passage and answer the questions.

The passage is an excerpt from a book written during the 20th century.

In Massillon, Brown's rules had served as a sort of social welfare, teaching high-school boys to develop self-control and discipline. In Cleveland, his dress codes, his curfews, and his strict study regimen with playbooks, con-
Line   stant lectures, and testing, served a different postwar ethic: it enhanced an
(5)   image, the image of a well-run organization. His model turned out to be less a throwback to wartime army discipline than a look forward to a new style of corporate control.

"We want you to reflect a special image in pro football," Brown told his players in a speech at the opening of each season.[45] They were not to smoke
(10)   or drink *in public*; they were to wear jackets and ties, slacks and polished shoes *in public*; they were to display a proper "decorum" and not curse *in public*; if they so much as lounged on the ground during a game, they were fined; above all, they were never to behave in a manner that would make the team look "low class"—in other words, that would remind anybody of
(15)   the league's origins in the mills and mines.

Brown demonstrated the seriousness of all this at the first opportunity: two days before the new league's first title game, he fired the team's captain, Jim Daniell, after the tackle had a few drinks and got into a minor spat with some local policemen. "I'll take my players high class, cold, deadly," Brown
(20)   repeated in his seasonal speech. "We don't want any butchers on this team. No T-shirts in the dining hall. Don't eat with your elbows on the table and eat quietly." He told *Time* magazine in 1947, "There's no place on my team for Big Butch who talks hard and drinks hard. I like a lean and hungry look." When a young college lineman whom Brown was planning to recruit
(25)   arrived at the team's training camp unshaven and "dressed like a laborer," Brown took one look, told him that he had been summoned mistakenly, and dismissed him at once.[46]

"Class always shows," Brown maintained, and what he wanted his men to show was the face of the new, white-collar bourgeoisie. "I didn't want
(30)   them to look like the stereotype of the old-time pros," Brown said. "College players had a good reputation, but the public perception of the professional football player back then was of a big, dumb guy with a potbelly and a cheap cigar. That kind of person disgusted me, and I never wanted anyone associating our players with that image."[47] What Brown wanted was a man-
(35)   agerial look: polished and uniform, college-educated but not effetely so, aspiring but conformist. What he wanted was a team represented by organization men. It was the sort of look he himself exemplified. With his contained demeanor, trim frame, and bland corporate suits, he looked like the archetypal suburban husband about to board the commuter train to his
(40)   desk job in the city. While Brown was insistent on his men flying first class and staying in fine hotels, it turned out this was not so much for their sakes as for the public profile of the team. He was intent on turning pro football

into a sort of respectable middle class occupation that fit with the new white-collar bureaucracies and the rising corporate management ethic of
(45) postwar America.

---

45 *Brown*, PB, p. 148.
46 *Ibid.*, pp.16, 148; *Clary*, Cleveland Browns, p. 18; "Football: Brown Ohio," Newsweek, Dec. 30, 1946, p. 66; *Byrne, et al.*, The Cleveland Browns, p. 17; *Maule*, "A Man for This Season," p. 32; "Praying Professionals," Time, Oct. 27, 1947, pp. 55–56.
47 *Clary*, The Gamesmakers, p. 32; *Clary*, Cleveland Browns, p. 19; *Brown*, PB, p. 15.

39. Which of the following best states the subject of this passage?

    (A) Professional football at the crossroads
    (B) The role of a football coach
    (C) A football coach's vision of his team
    (D) The transformation of professional football teams
    (E) Turning college players into professionals

40. Which of the following rhetorical strategies does the author use in paragraph 1 of the passage?

      I. parallel syntax
     II. repetition of sentence structure
    III. antithesis

    (A) I only
    (B) II only
    (C) I and II only
    (D) II and III only
    (E) I, II, and III

41. Which of the following best describes the rhetorical function of the second sentence (lines 2–5) of the passage?

    (A) It amends the tone of the first sentence.
    (B) It puts an idea expressed at the start of the passage into different words.
    (C) It presents a specific example in support of the preceding generalization.
    (D) It states the main idea of the passage.
    (E) It analyzes the author's purpose.

42. Which of the following phrases does the author use to reiterate the notion of a "different postwar ethic" (line 4)?

    (A) "social welfare" (line 1)
    (B) "self-control" (line 2)
    (C) "discipline" (line 2)
    (D) "playbooks" (line 3)
    (E) "image of a well-run organization" (line 5)

43. In lines 10–12 of the passage, the author uses repetition in order to emphasize Brown's concern about

    (A) good manners.
    (B) the image of the players.
    (C) neatness.
    (D) the future of pro football.
    (E) physical conditioning.

44. In line 14, "low class" implies all of the following EXCEPT

    (A) a family living in poverty.
    (B) a lack of breeding.
    (C) a blue-collar background.
    (D) coarse manners.
    (E) the absence of self-respect.

45. Footnote 46 (line 27) gives readers all of the following information EXCEPT

    (A) the incident of the young college lineman was widely reported.
    (B) the words "dressed like a laborer" were quoted by Clary and Byrne.
    (C) Brown discusses the dismissal of the young college lineman early in his book and then again later in the book.
    (D) *The Cleveland Browns* was written by more than one author.
    (E) the authors of articles published in *Newsweek* and *Time* received no bylines.

46. In context, the expression "a lean and hungry look" (lines 23–24) is best interpreted as having which of the following meanings?

    (A) unobtrusive and civilized
    (B) determined to succeed
    (C) starved for affection
    (D) versatile and adaptable
    (E) physically and emotionally well-balanced

47. The author's observation that Brown wanted his players to show "the face of the new, white-collar bourgeoisie" (line 29) is best described as an example of

    (A) poetic license
    (B) the author's explanation of Brown's values
    (C) the use of sarcasm
    (D) Brown's inflated way of speaking
    (E) the author's dismissal of a false claim

48. Which of the following is being referred to by the abstract term "bourgeoisie" (line 29)?

    (A) "'dressed like a laborer'" (line 25)
    (B) "stereotypes of the old-time pros" (line 30)
    (C) "'good reputation'" (line 31)
    (D) "'big, dumb guy'" (line 32)
    (E) "organization men" (lines 36–37)

49. Which of the following pieces of information can be inferred from footnote 47?

    (A) That all of the works listed in the footnote have been cited in earlier footnotes
    (B) That Clary writes articles for sports publications
    (C) That *The Gamesmakers* was published prior to both *Cleveland Browns* and *PB*
    (D) That Brown, the author of *PB*, interviewed Brown, the coach, while doing research
    (E) That Clary collaborated with other authors in writing *The Gamesmakers* and *The Cleveland Browns*

50. The sentence structure and diction of lines 34–40 ("What Brown wanted . . . in the city") suggest that the author views herself primarily as

    (A) an impartial observer of human behavior.
    (B) an interpreter of words and actions.
    (C) a suspicious commentator.
    (D) a well-meaning but selfish friend.
    (E) a flattering admirer of celebrities.

51. Taken all together, the footnotes suggest that

    (A) sports historians depend more on books than on news magazines as sources of information.
    (B) Ohio is the center for publishing books about football and other sports.
    (C) most of the material in the passage is anecdotal.
    (D) Brown's work was a fertile source for the author of the passage.
    (E) the passage was written roughly in the middle of the 20th century.

52. The development of the last paragraph (lines 28–45) can best be described as

    (A) a selection of details leading to a generalized summary.
    (B) a series of examples arranged chronologically.
    (C) a statement of opinion followed by supporting evidence.
    (D) an accumulation of generalizations.
    (E) the movement from theory to a factual conclusion.

SECTION II
Three Essay Questions
Total time—Two hours and 15 minutes

Write your essays on standard 8½" × 11" composition paper. At the exam you will be given a bound booklet containing 12 lined pages.

Essay Question 1

Suggested time—40 minutes.
This question counts as one third of the total score for Section II.

The following sketch, "A Fair and Happy Milkmaid," written in 1615 and credited to two possible authors—Thomas Overbury and John Webster—pays tribute to a lovely young lass.

Read the passage carefully. Then write an essay in which you analyze how the speaker uses rhetorical strategies and stylistic devices to convey his affection for the milkmaid.

> A fair and happy milkmaid is a country wench, that is so far from making herself beautiful by art, that one look of hers is able to put all outsides face-physic out of countenance. She knows a fair look is but a dumb orator to
> *Line* commend virtue, therefore minds it not. All her excellencies stand in her so
> *(5)* silently, as if they had stolen upon her without her knowledge. The lining of her apparel . . . is far better than the outsides of tissue: for though she be not arrayed in the spoil of the silk-worm, she is decked in innocency, a far better wearing. She doth not, with lying long abed, spoil both her complexion and conditions; nature hath taught her, too immoderate sleep is rust to the
> *(10)* soul: she rises therefore with chanticleer, her dame's cock, and at night makes the lamb her curfew. In milking a cow, and straining the teats through her fingers, it seems that so sweet a milk-press makes the milk the whiter or sweeter; for never came almond glove or aromatic ointment on her palm to taint it. The golden ears of corn fall and kiss her feet when she reaps them,
> *(15)* as if they wished to be bound and led prisoners by the same hand that felled them. Her breath is her own, which scents all the year long of June, like a new made haycock. She makes her hand hard with labour, and her heart soft with pity: and when winter evenings fall early (sitting at her merry wheel), she sings a defiance to the giddy wheel of fortune. She doth all things with
> *(20)* so sweet a grace, it seems ignorance will not suffer her to do ill, being her mind is to do well. She bestows her year's wages at next fair; and in choosing her garments, counts no bravery in the world, like decency. The garden and the bee-hive are all her physic[1] and chirurgery,[2] and she lives the longer for it. She dares go alone, and unfold sheep in the night, and fears no man-
> *(25)* ner of ill, because she means none: yet to say truth, she is never alone, for she is still accompanied with old songs, honest thoughts, and prayers, but short ones; yet they have their efficacy, in that they are not palled with ensuing idle cogitations. Lastly, her dreams are so chaste, that she dare tell them; only a Friday's dream[3] is all her superstition: that she conceals for fear of
> *(30)* anger. Thus lives she, and all her care is that she may die in the spring time, to have store of flowers stuck upon her winding sheet.

---

[1]*physic: medicine, cures*
[2]*chirurgery: surgery*
[3]*Friday's dream: Christ's passion took place on a Friday; hence, Friday's dreams are ominous*

Essay Question 2

Suggested time—40 minutes.

This question counts as one-third of the total score for Section II.

What follows are the remarks of the two candidates for President made on the same day during the 2004 election campaign. Read the passages carefully. Then write an essay in which you analyze how each speaker uses rhetorical strategies to win the votes of his audience.

President George Bush in Janesville, Wisconsin:

"I met with the prime minister of Iraq yesterday. He's willing to do the hard work, too. He came to our country—he came to our country to thank the American people. He came to our country to thank the moms and dads
Line and husbands and wives of those who have sacrificed for his freedom and
(5) America's security. That's what he came to do. He gave a strong speech. He's a strong man. The fellow—he woke up one night in London, England—he'd been in exile. And there was two people by his bed with axes sent by Saddam Hussein—seriously—to chop him up. And he survived. And now he's the prime minister of that country. He is going to lead this country. No
(10) matter how hard it gets, he will lead this country to a better day. He believes in the people of Iraq.

He spoke to the Congress. He gave a great speech to the Congress. He talked about his strategy of defeating the insurgents, of holding the elections in January. Afghanistan is going to have them in October, and they'll
(15) be held in January.

And my opponent chose to criticize the prime minister of Iraq. This great man came to our country to talk about how he's risking his life for a free Iraq, which helps America, and Senator Kerry held a press conference and questioned Prime Minister Allawi's credibility.

(20) You can't lead this country if your ally in Iraq feels like you question his credibility."

Senator John Kerry at Temple University, Philadelphia

"Let me be as blunt and direct with the American people as I can be. Let me tell you the truth, which is what America deserves.

The invasion of Iraq was a profound diversion from the battle against our
Line greatest enemy, Al Qaeda, which killed more than 3,000 people on 9/11
(5) and which still plots our destruction today. And there's no question about it; the president's misjudgment, miscalculation, and mismanagement of the war in Iraq all make the war on terror harder to win.

Iraq is now what it was not before the war: a haven for terrorists. George Bush made Saddam Hussein a priority. I would have made Osama bin
(10) Laden the priority.

As president, I pledge to you, America will finish the job in Iraq. And I will refocus our energies on the real war on terror. I will wage this war relentlessly, with a single-minded determination to capture or kill the terrorists, crush their movement and free the world from fear.

(15)   But to destroy our enemy, we have to know our enemy. We have to understand—we have to understand that we are facing a radical fundamentalist movement with global reach and a very specific plan.

They are not just out to kill us for the sake of killing us, they want to provoke a conflict that will radicalize the people of the Muslim world, turning *(20)* them against the United States and the West. And they hope to transform that anger into a force that will topple the region's governments and pave the way for a new empire, an oppressive, fundamentalist superstate stretching across a vast area from Europe to Africa, from the Middle East to Central Asia. That's their goal.

(25)   And the American people have the right to hear the answer to a fundamental question: How are we going to win this war?"

Essay Question 3

Time—15 minutes to read the sources
    40 minutes to write the essay

Instructions: The following essay topic is accompanied by six sources.

Respond to the question below in a well-written, coherent essay that draws on ideas and information found in **at least three** of the sources. Don't simply summarize or paraphrase the sources. Instead, **focus the essay on your point of view**, and use the sources to support or bolster your argument.

Topic: In December 2000, Congress passed the Children's Internet Protection Act (CIPA), a law meant to eliminate children's access to offensive material on the Internet in schools and libraries. Supporters of CIPA claim that public schools and libaries have an obligation to keep dangerous and harmful material away from children. Opponents argue that the law amounts to government censorship and treads on our First Amendment rights.

Your task: Read the following sources carefully. Then, in an essay that synthesizes at least three of the sources, take a position that supports, challenges, or modifies the claim that the government should continue to limit children's access to the Internet in schools and libraries.

In your essay, you may refer to the sources simply as Source A, Source B, etc., or by the key words in parentheses below.

Source A (Depken)
Source B (Sagall)
Source C (Hughes)
Source D (Pie Graph)
Source E (Kaminer)
Source F (Magid)

SOURCE A

Craig A. Depken, "Who Supports Internet Censorship?" *First Monday, Peer Review Journal on the Net*, March 6, 2006, *<www.firstmonday.org>*

The following is an excerpt from an article by a member of the University of Texas at Arlington economics department.

The first discussions on the need to limit Internet content followed the Oklahoma City bombing in April of 1995. At the time, concern centered on the availability of information on how to prepare explosives and the increasing number of Web sites dedicated to extreme views and so-called hate speech. In February 1996, the U.S. Congress passed the Communications Decency Act (CDA), as a portion of the 1996 Telecommunications Act. The CDA made it illegal to view pornography and other "indecent" material on computer networks on which no attempt had been made to restrict access by those less than eighteen years of age. Within weeks, a Federal court injunction suspended its execution. On June 26, 1997, the U.S. Supreme Court, in *Reno v. ACLU*, struck down the CDA as an unreasonable infringement on free speech.

Although the CDA was deemed unconstitutional for its particular wording, those who supported Internet censorship soon crafted new legislation to limit access and publication of certain information. In 1998, Senator John McCain proposed the Internet School Filtering Act to require public schools to filter all material deemed "inappropriate" for children. Although a Federal court ruled in 1998 that forcing Virginia schools to use Internet filtering software violated the First Amendment, in October of that year, Congress passed the Child Online Protection Act (COPA), which required those who publish pornography and other material deemed "harmful to minors" on the Internet to limit access by using some form of age verification system. In December 2000 the Congress passed the Children's Internet Protection Act (CIPA) requiring public primary and secondary schools and public libraries to install Internet filtering software or risk losing federal funds. In June 2003, the U.S. Supreme Court upheld CIPA, although it was unclear how many libraries would comply with the law; immediately after the decision, many public librarians registered their dissatisfaction with the decision. In July 2004, the Court determined that COPA likely violated the First Amendment but did not rule on the constitutionality of the law but sent the underlying case back to a lower court for trial.

While pornography, hate speech, or other materials might be deemed offensive to some and acceptable to others, the strong desire to limit access to such material by all or a majority of individuals is at the heart of the Internet censorship debate.

SOURCE B

Richard J. Sagall, "Internet Censorship," *Pediatrics for Parents*, May 1995, posted on the Web at *www.looksmart.com.*

The exerpt below was published online by a periodical containing articles of general public interest.

Those who are concerned about pornography and other material they have decided isn't appropriate for children seek, via the Communications Decency Act, a way to protect users, particularly children, from this material.

The American Civil Liberties Union, the Electronics Frontier Foundation, and other groups believe this bill is an unacceptable form of censorship. They contend the bill contains unconstitutional restrictions on online free speech and privacy rights.

It's important to remember that there's nothing available on the Internet that isn't available other places. Pornography, sexually explicit material, "dirty talk," and everything else those in favor of censoring the Internet fear is available in many local bookstores, through catalogs, and from other sources. Some of the material those in favor of censoring the Internet want to restrict are available in local libraries.

It's practically impossible for large ISPs to monitor everything posted on their computer. With the hundreds of thousands of messages posted on ISPs, there is no way a ISP can police them for "indecent, lewd, lascivious, or filthy material."

It's important to understand the way most Internet users access any material, including what some might call pornography. The user has to make an effort to find it—request it from the provider or find the place the information is stored and go there. The process is a lot like shopping, just perhaps a little easier. But it's rare that something pornographic is sent to someone without requesting it.

I am not a proponent of pornography, nor do I favor children reading it. But I don't want others, particularly those who are sure they know what's best for me to read, making decisions for me.

Can a parent keep their child away from this type of material? I doubt it. Children are resourceful and willing to take a risk. I remember the very respectable father of one of my childhood friends who thought he had hidden well his copies of Playboy. Well, he didn't.

What parents can and should do is talk with their children about this type of material. It's the parents' responsibility to educate their children about the real world, and pornography is a part of the real world. Protecting children from pornography by trying to deny them access to it doesn't work. Talking with your children about pornography, the "sick" people they may encounter, and helping them learn how to deal with these situations is the best way to protect them. Trying to censor what's on the Internet is just passing the buck.

SOURCE C

Donna Rice Hughes, "Sexual Predators Online," *www.ProtectKids.com*, 2001.

The following passage was written by one of the country's leading proponents of shielding children from harmful Internet materials.

One of the attractions of the Internet is the anonymity of the user, and this is why it can be so dangerous. A child doesn't always know with whom he or she is interacting. Children may *think* they know, but unless it's a school friend or a relative, they really can't be sure. Often we think of pedophiles as having access to children out on the playground and other places, but because of the way the Internet works, children can actually be interacting on their home computers with adults who pretend to be children.

Child sexual exploitation occurs in every economic, social, ethnic, and religious group. With the explosion of the Internet into a powerful, worldwide medium, the danger to children, whether they are from New York or New Zealand, has drastically increased. Pedophiles and other sexual predators can use the Internet, with no precautions, to exchange names and addresses of other pedophiles and of potential child victims. Hidden behind screen names that are pseudonyms, they gather online and swap child pornography with amazing speed and in amounts beyond our wildest imagination, which excites them to molest even more.

Offline, pedophiles typically operate in isolation. *Never before have pedophiles had the opportunity to communicate so freely and directly with each other as they do online.* Their communication on the Internet provides validation, or virtual validation, for their behavior. They share their conquests, real and imagined. They discuss ways to contact and lure children online and exchange tips on seduction techniques. They are using the technology of the Internet to train and encourage each other to act out sexually with children. The Internet also serves as a tool for predators to exchange tips on the avoidance of law enforcement detection.

The most common means by which sexual predators contact children over the Internet is through chat rooms, instant messages, and email. In fact, 89% of sexual solicitations were made in either chat rooms or instant messages and one in five youth (ages 10–17 years) has been sexually solicited online. Considering that 25% of kids online participate in real time chat and 13 million use instant messaging, the risks of such children, either knowingly or unknowingly, interacting with a predator is alarming.

SOURCE D

Elena Kozakewich, "Adolescent Computer Use and Preferences for Leisure Time," *Psychology of Adolescence*, *<www.students.haverford.edu>*

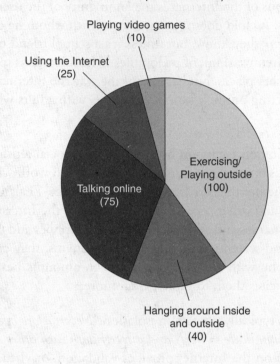

What activity would be the hardest to give up for two weeks?
(Number of respondents: 250)

Playing video games (10)

Using the Internet (25)

Exercising/ Playing outside (100)

Talking online (75)

Hanging around inside and outside (40)

Question asked of 250 adolescents: What activity would be the hardest to give up?

SOURCE E

Wendy Kaminer, *Secret Censors*, The Boston Globe, March 13, 1997, p. 19.

The passage below is an excerpt from an article by a feminist writer and social critic. She is the president of the National Coalition Against Censorship.

Imagine this: The mayor of Boston hires a private corporation to remove all books from the public libraries that the corporation deems unsuitable for children. The mayor and many parents believe that the corporation will protect kids from hard-core pornography, and the corporation (let's call it Book Police) promises to keep all sexually explicit material off shelves.

But executives at Book Police believe that even libraries shorn of pornography are dangerous places for children. Book Police makes a unilateral decision to censor a broad range of information and ideas, removing books about feminism, gun control and the Second Amendment, animal rights, environmentalism, homosexuality, as well as censorship and free speech.

These offensive books are locked up in a secret place. Adults are not even told that such bad books exist, but those who do somehow learn of their existence may be granted access to the books if the city's chief information officer decides that they are needed for "legitimate research."

This may seem like a farfetched scenario, but recently, it came true. The mayor summarily ordered blocking software installed on computers in the public libraries. Created by a private corporation, Cyber Patrol, the software will sweep as broadly through the Internet as my imaginary Book Police would sweep through the library shelves. It will deprive both children and adults of information about sex and gender roles as well as access to political debates—notably debates about free speech.

The mayor's action has so far enjoyed considerable support, partly because it is not very well understood. News stories and editorials have described this as a reasonable effort to protect children from pornography without reporting on the scope of materials that will be censored by Cyber Patrol. Nor has it been made clear that employees at Cyber Patrol will be the people deciding which sites to block.

Instead, we've been told that librarians or city officials may pick and choose among the 12 categories of material that Cyber Patrol blocks. If they want only to block pornography, not information about animal rights or feminism, they can choose to block only the sexually explicit category.

That's true—but terribly misleading. The sexually explicit category will not just encompass "pornography." It may well include feminist sites (which some consider pornographic anyway). The sexually explicit category is also likely to block discussions of free speech that refer to the censorship of pornography, discussions of sexual harassment cases or speech codes, as well as educational sites focusing on sexuality.

SOURCE F

Larry Magid, "Study Outlines Safety Tips for Kids: Online study finds perpetrators are younger than you'd expect," San José *Mercury News*, June 11, 2000.

The following excerpt is from a newspaper article summarizing the findings of a research study on the experience of children while online.

If you're worried about dirty old men sexually soliciting your children on the Internet, you can relax. That's the good news from an "online victimization" study released last week by the National Center for Missing and Exploited Children that provides some interesting, though not terribly surprising, insights about the online experiences of youth between the ages of 10 and 17.

The bad news is that a significant percentage are being sexually solicited, but the age and the gender of the perpetrators might surprise you. The vast majority—96 percent—of those who solicit teens are under 25 and nearly half—48 percent—are themselves children under the age of 18. Some 20 percent are female.

What we have here is not unlike the halls of any high school where, rightly or wrongly, students are frequently hitting on other students. In the physical world that can be something as innocuous or even flattering as a genuine expression of affection. But when it happens online, especially from someone you've never met, it somehow seems more ominous. . . .

According to the survey results, one in four young people has had "unwanted exposure to pictures of naked people or people having sex." These are not cases where the young person admits to looking for such pictures, but situations where they have come upon them while searching for material, or where links to such material were sent via e-mail.

That number hardly surprised me and it certainly didn't surprise my 13-year-old son Will who, since he was 9, has been getting unsolicited advertisements for sex sites in his e-mail. It also won't surprise anyone who has ever used a search engine such as Yahoo or Alta Vista to look for words like "whale" or "Bambi," or those of us who have accidentally mis-typed the name of a Web site. Enter .com instead of .org or .gov on some popular sites and you'll be exposed to what could be an unpleasant surprise by adult Web site operators who deliberately mislead Web surfers into stumbling on their sites.

END OF PRACTICE TEST D

Answer Key
PRACTICE TEST D

Answers to Multiple-Choice Questions

1. C	21. C	41. D
2. B	22. D	42. E
3. B	23. B	43. B
4. A	24. D	44. A
5. B	25. A	45. B
6. A	26. B	46. A
7. D	27. D	47. B
8. E	28. A	48. E
9. D	29. A	49. A
10. A	30. E	50. B
11. C	31. B	51. D
12. E	32. E	52. A
13. D	33. D	
14. E	34. A	
15. B	35. E	
16. E	36. B	
17. A	37. C	
18. C	38. B	
19. C	39. C	
20. E	40. E	

Summary of Answers in Section I (Multiple-Choice)

Number of correct answers _____

Number of incorrect answers _____

Number of questions not answered _____

Use this information when you calculate your score on this exam. See page 373.

Answer Explanations

PASSAGE 1—AN EXCERPT FROM HENRY ADAMS, *THE EDUCATION OF HENRY ADAMS*

1. **(C)** Through most of the passage, the speaker appraises the evolution of Adams' education from his last day at Mr. Dixwell's school through his graduation from Harvard and beyond.

2. **(B)** The experience is young Adams' career at Mr. Dixwell's school. The boy is overjoyed that it has come to an end.

3. **(B)** Coming on the heels of two lengthy introductory sentences, this stark seven-word, seven-syllable sentence stands out startlingly and tersely.

4. **(A)** All the phrases except (A) in one way or other develop the idea that Adams was too mentally and emotionally advanced for the school he attended.

5. **(B)** The names are those of old and influential New England families that enjoyed long affiliations with Harvard and helped to build the stature of the college. It would be reasonable to assume that applicants bearing those names would be given preferential treatment, but the passage does not discuss the admissions process.

6. **(A)** Neither sentence contains a compound subject. The words "mild" and "liberal" are predicate adjectives; "which" (line 24) begins a subordinate clause; that portion of the sentence beginning with "with" (line 24) contains parallel syntax; and in the second sentence the predicate precedes the subject, indicating inverted word order.

7. **(D)** The phrase "something of what they wanted to make useful ones" (lines 25–26) suggests that a Harvard degree was not the end of a young man's education. Rather, it marked just the start. Once the graduate left Harvard, he was "ready to receive knowledge"—that is, he could now begin to acquire the knowledge needed to make something of himself.

8. **(E)** The speaker maintains that Harvard graduates project a certain uniform and easily identifiable image.

9. **(D)** Graduates of Harvard became recognizable types, inevitably endowed with a certain set of qualities, among them supple, but docile, minds and few strong prejudices (lines 41–42).

10. **(A)** The sentence, which is a broad statement about the deleterious effects of education, reveals a cynical state of mind. It reflects both the speaker's and Adams' attitude.

11. **(C)** The speaker uses a succession of antitheses: "taught little . . . but left the mind open," "free from bias . . . but docile," and "knew little . . . but . . . remained supple."

12. **(E)** The conjunction "Yet" at the beginning of the sentence is a clue that the speaker is about to offer a contradiction or contrast to a preceding idea. Indeed, the sentence offers evidence meant to show that Adams' experience at Harvard could not have been caused by the absence of distinguished fellow students.

13. **(D)** The speaker uses the analogy to emphasize the effect of "accident" or "chance" in human life. In other words, no one can predict when one will meet one's lifelong friends or one's future spouse. It is a matter completely out of our hands.

14. **(E)** The speaker holds many opinions, but in the passage he makes no judgments about Harvard's administrators or teachers.

PASSAGE 2—AN EXCERPT FROM ALICE MEYNELL, "UNDER THE EARLY STARS"

15. **(B)** The sentence introduces the main topic of the paragraph—that like the tide, the behavior of children is regular but uncontrollable.

16. **(E)** In its context, the word "tide" is used as a metaphor to suggest the ebb and flow of children's moods, energy, and inclinations to play. In the remainder of the paragraph the speaker discusses a problem caused by such changes.

17. **(A)** According to the speaker, children will frolic at dusk in the summertime regardless of what may be done to constrain or control them.

18. **(C)** The wildness of children conjures thoughts of predatory creatures, including prehistoric man, although a kitten on the prowl also manifests the primitive hunting instinct and is a more appropriate example in a passage about the behavior of children.

19. **(C)** The speaker sees in children's activities at twilight a struggle for freedom. Others, of course, may interpret the children's wild behavior as something else.

20. **(E)** Each description fits the paragraph. Of all the paragraphs in the passage, it contains the least amount of interpretation and analysis of children and their lives. In addition, no other paragraph contains any sort of anecdote.

21. **(C)** There is no way to account for the time that a child falls asleep. The speaker advances the theory, however, that the falling-asleep habits of children have been passed along from both the long-ago past—from "antiquity"—and from the more recent past, when today's adults were themselves little children.

22. **(D)** Grammatically, the pronoun refers to "habits," which, according to the speaker, are virtually unbreakable.

23. **(B)** The paragraph's main idea is that lullabies have their origins in antiquity and are imbued with mystery and a sense of timelessness. To support that assertion, the speaker comments on three popular lullabies.

24. **(D)** The phrase implies something unknowable, something mysterious and puzzling.

25. **(A)** The speaker observes children affectionately, almost sentimentally. Her interpretations of children's behavior appear to have been thoughtfully developed over a long period of being with and watching small children.

PASSAGE 3—AN EXCERPT FROM HENRY JAMES, *FROM LONDON*

26. **(B)** Most of the passage discusses the speaker's emotions as he arrives in England and makes his way to London.

27. **(D)** The phrase alludes to Babylon, an ancient city that has become a metaphor for a large, luxurious metropolis given to gratifying the senses of its inhabitants and visitors.

28. **(A)** Beginning with the phrase "wet, black Sunday" (line 2) until the description of "the gray mildness, shading away into black" (line 30), the speaker stresses the bleakness of the land and sky.

29. **(A)** All the phrases except "the end of a wet, black Sunday" suggest the speaker's high level of emotional anticipation as he approached London. In contrast, a "wet, black Sunday, . . . about the first of March" is primarily a piece of incidental information.

30. **(E)** Although arriving in England evoked strong feelings, there is no evidence that the speaker's emotions leapt beyond his control.

31. **(B)** At breakfast in the hotel soon after his arrival in England, the speaker realized with a sense of wonder how "English" it was in England (lines 12–18).

32. **(E)** As the speaker says, it's the kind of emotion (line 20) that often makes us yearn for strange and faraway places—in other words a sense of wonder.

33. **(D)** Through much of the first paragraph the speaker describes his sense of wonder. The pronoun "It" carries the discussion into the next paragraph.

34. **(A)** Pervasive throughout the paragraph are sensual images evoking sights, sounds, smells, tastes, and physical sensations; for example: "strange, dark, lonely freshness of the coast" (line 24), "the gray mildness, shading away into black" (line 30), and "the creak of the waiter's shoes" (lines 37–38).

35. **(E)** In order to remain on an emotional high a while longer, the speaker stays put for a day, thereby sacrificing, as it were, the pleasure and anticipation of a timely arrival in London, his final destination.

36. **(B)** The remark is somewhat boastful. It sends a message to the reader that says: Look how clever I am to make this witty and perceptive observation about the waiter's back.

37. **(C)** The last sentence contains another reference to the speaker's fondness for London. Even the "rather horrible" ride on the "greasy fourwheeler" could not keep him from recognizing the start of a beautiful friendship with the city.

38. **(B)** Not only is the speaker similar to a memoirist, he actually *is* one, fondly recalling his arrival in England about twenty years before (line 2) when he was still "comparatively youthful" (line 47).

PASSAGE 4—AN EXCERPT FROM SUSAN FALUDI, *STIFFED*

39. **(C)** Although an element of each choice appears in the passage, the main focus is on Coach Brown and his effort to reshape the image of the players on his team.

40. **(E)** Parallel syntax is exemplified by the series phrases in lines 3 and 4. The structure of the first two sentences of the passage is virtually identical: Both begin with prepositional phrases, and both contain the same verb, *served*. The last sentence of the paragraph employs antithesis (not a "throwback" but a "look forward").

41. **(D)** The passage is devoted to a discussion of the ideas stated in this sentence—how Brown went about reshaping the image of the players on his team.

42. **(E)** Choices (A), (B), and (C) refer to Brown's days as a high-school football coach. In Cleveland, Brown's plan for a "well-run organization" more fully refers to the new ethic he had in mind for his players.

43. **(B)** The author's repeated use of the italicized phrase "in public" is meant to show that Brown's paramount interest was the team's public image.

44. **(A)** What mattered most to Brown was that his players reflected conventional middle-class values, or as the author puts it in line 29, "the face of the new, white-collar bourgeoisie." The economic condition of their families didn't matter.

45. **(B)** Where the author of the passage found the quotation "dressed like a laborer" remains unclear.

46. **(A)** In context, the expression describes someone just the opposite of a "Big Butch who talks hard and drinks hard" (line 23)—in other words, someone whose behavior is discreet and restrained.

47. **(B)** Throughout the passage, the author illuminates and expands the meaning of Brown's ideas.

48. **(E)** The author explains the term in lines 34–43. What Brown wanted was a team full of bland, corporate types—in other words, men who looked and acted in a particular way, who gave up some of their individuality for the team, i.e., for the organization.

49. **(A)** Because the works cited contain only the author, title, and page number, it's reasonable to infer that each of the works has been listed before. The previous citations probably contained full information about each work. (It's also possible that the author of the book used another documentation method in which all footnotes refer to works listed in a separate bibliography.)

50. **(B)** The author analyzes Brown's words and spells out what she thinks Brown is really saying. In other words, she examines the implications of Brown's down-to-earth ideas and articulates them in the more sophisticated language of, say, a sociologist or historian.

51. **(D)** All three footnotes cite Brown, suggesting that the author of the passage found Brown's work fruitful.

52. **(A)** The paragraph contains a number of quotations amplified by the author's commentary. The last sentence summarizes Brown's intentions and generalizes the overall point of the passage.

Answers to Essay Questions

Although answers to the essay questions will vary greatly, the following descriptions suggest a possible approach to each question and contain ideas that could be used in response to the question. Perhaps your essay contains many of the same ideas. If not, don't be alarmed. Your ideas may be no less, or perhaps even more, insightful than those presented below.

ESSAY QUESTION 1, BASED ON "A FAIR AND HAPPY MILKMAID" BY EITHER THOMAS OVERBURY OR JOHN WEBSTER

The equivalent of a prose poem, this sketch idealizes the subject's appearance, behavior, and state of mind. Using the language and sentence structure of his day—the 17th century—the speaker compiles a list of the young maid's virtues, endowing her with the qualities of a saint.

The girl embodies excellence. She is innocent, beautiful, natural, and good in every way. And best of all she is unaware of these extraordinary assets: Her "excellencies stand in her so silently, as if they had stolen upon her without her knowledge" (lines 4–5). To create this portrait of near-perfection the speaker relies mainly on images taken from nature and rural life: the girl rises "with chanticleer" (rooster) and retires with the lambs. Her breath smells fresh like a "new made haycock" (lines 15–16); the "garden and the beehive" assure her good health. What's more, she is devout. Spinning at her wheel on winter evenings, she sings a "defiance to the giddy wheel of fortune," (lines 18–19) implying her belief that God is watching over her.

Using hyperbole, the speaker gives the maid her own godlike qualities: Ears of corn, for example, "fall and kiss her feet when she reaps them" (lines 13–14); milk that passes through her fingers becomes whiter and sweeter. Because she "fears no manner of ill" (line 24), she is immune to worry and apprehension. In spite of such qualities, however, she is still subject to human anxieties. She fears being overcome with anger (lines 28–29) toward those who crucified Jesus, and she has concerns about death. The maid even displays a touch of vanity, for she hopes to die in the springtime in order have flowers available to decorate her "winding sheet," (line 31) the garment in which corpses are wrapped.

ESSAY QUESTION 2, BASED ON CAMPAIGN SPEECHES BY PRESIDENT BUSH AND SENATOR KERRY

Although the prompt doesn't say that you must compare the rhetorical strategies of the two candidates, it makes sense to do so. You can write an essay that analyzes each passage point by point, or you can analyze each passage separately, in which case the comparison may be more subtle—implied rather than stated outright. Either way, these are some of the features to notice about each passage:

Bush appears to have shaped his remarks to fit his audience. He speaks simply, using a folksy manner that is likely to resonate with his small-town, rural listeners. At the outset, he creates rapport with specific members of the audience by referring to "moms and dads and husbands and wives" (lines 3–4). In contrast, Kerry, speaking at a university, ignores the crowd in front of him and addresses "the American people" (line 25), an abstraction that keeps the assembled audience at a distance. In fact, this sets the pattern for his entire speech. Kerry says that his remarks will be "blunt and direct," but they consist mostly of hollow generalities, certainly not the "truth" (line 2) that he claims "America deserves" (line 2). Kerry's use of repetition and alliteration in line 6 ("misjudgment, miscalculation, and mismanagement") might add force and coherence to a passage written for another purpose, but in the context of a campaign appearance, the words sound forced and phony—chosen only for effect, not for stating the blunt and direct truth.

In addition, Kerry's reach far exceeds his grasp. In a few dozen lines, he criticizes the President, tries to explain what he would have done, and reassures America that he will defeat the enemy. He fills his text with numerous references to killing, destruction, terror, conflict—words meant to incite fear. At the same time, however, he's taken on an overwhelming challenge—to say something meaningful and reassureing about America's future in less than five minutes. He's not up to the task, and in fact, confounds his audience by asking at the end, "How are we going to win this war?" To win votes, he should comfort his audience, not leave them guessing.

Bush, on the other hand, goes to extremes in the opposite direction. He presents himself not as a man just talking about vague ideas but a man focused on performing the specific duties of his office. Yesterday, for example, he "met with the prime minister of Iraq" (line 1). Instead of sounding as though he's giving a canned stump speech, Bush tries to sound sincere and down-to-earth, as though he's talking with friends in the kitchen. He uses many short, simple sentences, repeats words, backtracks, throws in parenthetical comments. He tells part of an anecdote about a threat to the prime minister's life, deliberately leaving out the details, but using it later to emphasize that the minister is a brave fellow, "risking his life for a free Iraq" (line 20). Unlike Kerry, Bush doesn't make grandiose or provocative statements about America's future. Rather, he focuses his remarks on his current work, trying to give the impression that in his hands the country is in good hands.

ESSAY QUESTION 3, BASED ON THE ISSUE OF RESTRICTING CHILDREN'S ACCESS TO THE INTERNET

Arguments in favor of continuing the restrictions on children's access to the Internet in schools and libaries include the following:

- Kids need to be safe online. (Several sources imply that, even those that oppose restrictions)

- Pornography and hate speech are offensive and harmful. (Source A)
- Sexual predators roam the Internet looking for innocent victim to exploit. (Source C)
- A survey in 2000 showed that 25% of the adolescents interviewed had been exposed to unwanted lewd images while online. (Source F)

Arguments against the restrictions on children's Internet access to the Internet schools and libraries include the following:

- Some courts have declared the limitations on Internet access unconstitutional. (Source A)
- The Internet contains nothing that is not available elsewhere, including the public library. (Source B)
- Children have a way of finding the material they want regardless of restrictions. (Source B)
- Let parents educate their children about proper usage of the Internet. (Source B)
- Censorship blocks innocent material that contains nothing pornographic or harmful. (Source E and Source F)

Self-Scoring Guide—Practice Test D

SCORING SECTION 2 ESSAYS

After referring to "How Essays Are Scored" on page 27 of this book, use this guide to help you evaluate each essay. Do your best to evaluate your performance in each category by using the criteria spelled out below. Because it is hard to achieve objectivity when assessing your own writing, you may improve the validity of your score by having a trusted and well-informed friend or experienced teacher read and rate your essay.

On the following Rating Chart, enter a number (from 1 to 6) that you think represents your level of performance in each category (A–F).

Category A: OVERALL PURPOSE/MAIN IDEA

6 extremely well-defined and insightful

5 clearly defined and generally insightful

4 mostly clear

3 somewhat clear but occasionally confusing

2 generally unclear and confusing

1 virtually incomprehensible

Category B: HANDLING OF THE PROMPT

6 self-evident or extremely clear throughout

5 mostly clear

4 somewhat clear

3 somewhat unclear

2 generally unclear or ambiguous

1 confusing or nonexistent

Category C: ORGANIZATION AND DEVELOPMENT

6 insightfully organized; fully developed with excellent supporting evidence

5 reasonably well organized; developed with appropriate supporting material

4 appropriately organized; developed with some relevant material

3 inadequately organized; weak development

2 poorly organized; little or no development

1 no discernible organization; no relevant development

Category D: SENTENCE STRUCTURE

6 varied and engaging

5 sufficiently varied to create interest

4 some variety

3 little variety; minor sentence errors

2 frequent sentence errors that interfere with meaning

1 serious sentence errors that obscure meaning

Category E: USE OF LANGUAGE

6 precise and effective word choice

5 competent word choice

4 conventional word choice; mostly correct

3 some errors in diction or idiom

2 frequent errors in diction or idiom

1 meaning obscured by word choice

Category F: GRAMMAR AND USAGE

6 error-free or virtually error-free

5 occasional minor errors

4 basically correct but with several minor errors

3 meaning somewhat obscured by errors

2 meaning frequently obscured by errors

1 meaning blocked by several major errors

RATING CHART

Rate your essay:	Essay 1	Essay 2	Essay 3
Overall Purpose/Main Idea	_____	_____	_____
Handling of the Prompt	_____	_____	_____
Organization and Development	_____	_____	_____
Sentence Structure	_____	_____	_____
Use of Language	_____	_____	_____
Grammar and Usage	_____	_____	_____
Composite Scores (Sum of each column)	_____	_____	_____

By using the following scale, in which composite scores are converted to the nine-point AP rating scale, you may determine the final score for each essay:

Composite Score	AP Essay Score
33–36	9
29–32	8
25–28	7
21–24	6
18–20	5
15–17	4
10–14	3
7–9	2
6 or below	1

AP Essay Scores Essay 1 _____ Essay 2 _____ Essay 3 _____

TEST SCORE WORKSHEET FOR PRACTICE TEST D

The scores you have earned on the multiple-choice and essay sections of the exam may now be converted to the AP five-point scale by performing the following calculations:

I. Determine your score for Section I (Multiple Choice)

Step A: Number of correct answers _____

Step B: Number of wrong answers _____ (Note: Do not count unanswered questions.)

Step C: Multiply the number of wrong answers by .250 and enter the figure here _____ .

Step D: Subtract the figure in Step C from the figure in Step A _____ .

Step E: Multiply the figure in Step D by 1.2500 to find your Multiple-Choice Score _____ (If less than zero, enter zero.)

II. Determine your score for Section II (Essays)

Step A: Enter your score for Essay 1 (out of 9) _____

Step B: Enter your score for Essay 2 (out of 9) _____

Step C: Enter your score for Essay 3 (out of 9) _____

Step D: Add the figures in Steps A, B, and C _____

Step E: Multiply the figure in Step D by 3.0556 _____ (Do not round.) This is your Essay Score.

III. Determine Your Total Score

Add the scores for I and II to find your composite score _____ .

To convert your composite score to the AP five-point scale, use the chart below. The range of scores only approximates what you would earn on the actual test because the exact figures may vary from test to test. Be aware, therefore, that your score on this test, as well as on other tests in this book, may differ slightly from your score on an actual AP exam.

Composite Score	AP Grade
108–150	5
93–107	4
72–92	3
43–71	2
0–42	1

AP essays are ordinarily judged in relation to other essays written on the same topic at the same time. Therefore, the scores you assign yourself for these essays may not be the same as the scores you would earn on an actual exam.

Glossary

The list that follows is made up of words and phrases used by scholars, critics, writers—in fact, all literate people—to exchange ideas and information about language. Most of the words and phrases have appeared in recent years in the multiple-choice or essay sections of AP Language and Composition exams.

abstract (*n.*) An abbreviated synopsis of a longer work of scholarship or research. (*adj.*) Dealing with or tending to deal with a subject apart from a particular or specific instance.

ad hominem Directed to or appealing to feelings or prejudices instead of to intellect or reason.

adage A saying or proverb containing a truth based on experience and often couched in metaphorical language. Example: "There is more than one way to skin a cat."

allegory A story in which a second meaning is to be read beneath the surface.

alliteration The repetition of one or more initial consonants in a group of words or lines in a poem.

allusion A reference to a person, place, or event meant to create an effect or enhance the meaning of an idea.

ambiguity A vagueness of meaning; a conscious lack of clarity meant to evoke multiple meanings or interpretations.

anachronism A person, scene, event, or other element that fails to correspond with the appropriate time or era. Example: Columbus sailing to the United States.

analogy A comparison that points out similarities between two dissimilar things; a passage that points out several similarities between two unlike things is called an *extended analogy*.

anecdote A brief narrative often used to illustrate an idea or make a point.

annotation A brief explanation, summary, or evaluation of a text or work of literature.

antagonist A character or force in a work of literature that, by opposing the *protagonist*, produces tension or conflict.

antecedent A word to which a pronoun refers.

antithesis A rhetorical opposition or contrast of ideas by means of a grammatical arrangement of words, clauses, or sentences, as in the following: "They promised freedom but provided slavery." "Ask not what your country can do for you, but what you can do for your country."

aphorism A short, pithy statement of a generally accepted truth or sentiment. Also see *adage* and *maxim*.

Apollonian In contrast to *Dionysian*, it refers to the most noble, godlike qualities of human nature and behavior.

apostrophe A locution that addresses a person or personified thing not present. Example: "Oh, you cruel streets of Manhattan, how I detest you!"

arch (*adj.*) Characterized by clever or sly humor, often saucy, playful, and somewhat irreverent.

archetype An abstract or ideal conception of a type; a perfectly typical example; an original model or form.

assonance The repetition of two or more vowel sounds in a group of words in prose or poetry.

bard A poet; in olden times, a performer who told heroic stories to musical accompaniment.

bathos Insincere or overdone sentimentality.

belle-lettres A French term for the world of books, criticism, and literature in general.

bibliography A list of works cited or otherwise relevant to a particular subject.

bombast Inflated, pretentious language.

burlesque A work of literature meant to ridicule a subject; a grotesque imitation.

cacophony Grating, inharmonious sounds.

canon The works considered most important in a national literature or period; works widely read and studied.

caricature A grotesque or exaggerated likeness of striking qualities in persons and things.

carpe diem Literally, "seize the day"; "enjoy life while you can," a common theme in life and literature.

circumlocution Literally, "talking around" a subject; i.e., discourse that avoids direct reference to a subject.

classic A highly regarded work of literature or other art form that has withstood the test of time.

classical, classicism Deriving from the orderly qualities of ancient Greek and Roman culture; implies formality, objectivity, simplicity, and restraint.

clause A structural element of a sentence, consisting of a grammatical subject and a predicate. *Independent clauses,* sometimes called *main clauses,* may stand on their own as complete sentences; *dependent clauses,* which are used as nouns or modifiers, are incomplete sentences and cannot stand alone grammatically. Dependent clauses are sometimes called *subordinate clauses.* Dependent clauses that function as adjectives, nouns, or adverbs are known, respectively, as *adjective, noun,* and *adverbial clauses.*

climax The high point, or turning point, of a story or play.

comparison and contrast A mode of discourse in which two or more things are compared and contrasted. Comparison often refers to similarities, contrast to differences.

conceit A witty or ingenious thought; a diverting or highly fanciful idea, often stated in figurative language.

concrete detail A highly specific, particular, often real, actual, or tangible detail; the opposite of abstract.

connotation The suggested or implied meaning of a word or phrase. Contrast with *denotation.*

consonance The repetition of two or more consonant sounds in a group of words or a unit of speech or writing.

critique An analysis or assessment of a thing or situation for the purpose of determining its nature, limitations, and conformity to a set of standards.

cynic One who expects and observes nothing but the worst of human conduct.

deductive reasoning A method of reasoning by which specific definitions, conclusions, and theorems are drawn from general principles. Its opposite is *inductive reasoning.*

denotation The dictionary definition of a word. Contrast with *connotation.*

dénouement The resolution that occurs at the end of a narrative or drama, real or imagined.

descriptive detail Graphic, exact, and accurate presentation of the characteristics of a person, place, or thing.

deus ex machina In literature, the use of an artificial device or gimmick to solve a problem.

diction The choice of words in oral and written discourse.

didactic Having an instructive purpose; intending to convey information or teach a lesson, usually in a dry, pompous manner.

digression That portion of discourse that wanders or departs from the main subject or topic.

Dionysian As distinguished from *Apollonian*, the word refers to sensual, pleasure-seeking impulses.

dramatic irony A circumstance in which the audience or reader knows more about a situation than a character.

elegy A poem or prose selection that laments or meditates on the passing or death of someone or something of value. The adjective describing an elegy is *elegiac*.

ellipsis Three periods (. . .) indicating the omission of words in a thought or quotation.

elliptical construction A sentence containing a deliberate omission of words. In the sentence "May was hot and June the same," the verb *was* is omitted from the second clause.

empathy A feeling of association or identification with an object or person.

epic A narrative poem that tells of the adventures and exploits of a hero.

epigram A concise but ingenious, witty, and thoughtful statement.

euphony Pleasing, harmonious sounds.

epithet An adjective or phrase that expresses a striking quality of a person or thing; *sun-bright topaz, sun-lit lake,* and *sun-bright lake* are examples. Can also be used to apply to vulgar or profane exclamations.

eponymous A term for the title character of a work of literature.

euphemism A mild or less negative usage for a harsh or blunt term. Example: *pass away* is a euphemism for *die*.

exegesis A detailed analysis or interpretation of a work of prose or poetry.

exposé A factual piece of writing that reveals weaknesses, faults, frailties, or other shortcomings.

exposition The background and events that lead to the presentation of the main idea or purpose of an essay or other work; setting forth the meaning or purpose of a piece of writing or discourse.

explication The interpretation or analysis of a text.

extended metaphor A series of comparisons between two unlike objects.

fable A short tale, often with nonhuman characters, from which a useful lesson or moral may be drawn.

fallacy, fallacious reasoning An incorrect belief or supposition based on faulty data, defective evidence, false information, or flawed logic.

fantasy A story containing unreal, imaginary features.

farce A comedy that contains an extravagant and nonsensical disregard of seriousness, although it may have a serious, scornful purpose.

figure of speech, figurative language In contrast to literal language, figurative language implies meanings. Figures of speech include, among many others, *metaphor, simile,* and *personification*.

frame A structure that provides a premise or setting for a narrative or other discourse. Example: a group of pilgrims exchanging stories while on the road is the frame for Chaucer's *Canterbury Tales*.

genre A term used to describe literary forms, such as novel, play, and essay.

harangue A forceful sermon, lecture, or tirade.

homily A lecture or sermon on a religious or moral theme meant to guide human behavior.

hubris Excessive pride that often affects tone.

humanism A belief that emphasizes faith and optimism in human potential and creativity.

hyperbole Overstatement; gross exaggeration for rhetorical effect.

idyll A lyric poem or passage that describes a kind of ideal life or place.

image A word or phrase representing that which can be seen, touched, tasted, smelled, or felt; *imagery* is the use of images in speech and writing.

indirect quotation A rendering of a quotation in which actual words are not stated but only approximated or paraphrased.

inductive reasoning A method of reasoning in which a number of specific facts or examples are used to make a generalization. Its opposite is *deductive reasoning*.

inference A conclusion or proposition arrived at by considering facts, observations, or some other specific data.

invective A direct verbal assault; a denunciation; casting blame on someone or something.

irony A mode of expression in which the intended meaning is the opposite of what is stated, often implying ridicule or light sarcasm; a state of affairs or events that is the reverse of what might have been expected.

kenning A device employed in Anglo-Saxon poetry in which the name of a thing is replaced by one of its functions or qualities, as in "ring-giver" for king and "whale-road" for ocean.

lampoon A mocking, satirical assault on a person or situation.

litotes A form of understatement in which the negative of the contrary is used to achieve emphasis or intensity. Example: *He is not a bad dancer.*

loose sentence A sentence that follows the customary word order of English sentences, i.e., subject-verb-object. The main idea of the sentence is presented first and is then followed by one or more subordinate clauses. See also *periodic sentence.*

lyrical prose Personal, reflective prose that reveals the speaker's thoughts and feelings about the subject.

malapropism A confused use of words in which the appropriate word is replaced by one with a similar sound but inappropriate meaning.

maxim A saying or proverb expressing common wisdom or truth. See also *adage* and *aphorism.*

melodrama A literary form in which events are exaggerated in order to create an extreme emotional response.

metaphor A figure of speech that compares unlike objects. When several characteristics of the same objects are compared, the device is called an *extended metaphor*. A metaphor referring to a particular person, place, or thing is called a *metaphorical allusion*; for example, referring to someone as "a Hercules."

metaphysical A term describing poetry that uses elaborate conceits, expresses the complexities of love and life, and is highly intellectual. More generally, *metaphysical* refers to ideas that are neither analytical nor subject to empirical verification; that is, ideas that express an attitude about which rational argument is impossible.

metonymy A figure of speech that uses the name of one thing to represent something else with which it is associated. Example: *"The White House says . . ."*

Middle English The language spoken in England roughly between 1150 and 1500 A.D.

mock epic A parody of traditional epic form.

mock solemnity Feigned or deliberately artificial seriousness, often for satirical purposes.

mode The general form, pattern, and manner of expression of a piece of discourse.

montage A quick succession of images or impressions used to express an idea.

mood The emotional tone or prevailing atmosphere in a work of literature or other discourse. In grammar, mood refers to the intent of a particular sentence. The *indicative mood* is used for statements of fact; *subjunctive mood* is used to express doubt or a conditional attitude; sentences in the *imperative mood* give commands.

moral A brief and often simplistic lesson that a reader may infer from a work of literature.

motif A phrase, idea, or event that through repetition serves to unify or convey a theme in an essay or other discourse.

muse (*n.*) One of the ancient Greek goddesses presiding over the arts; the imaginary source of inspiration for an artist or writer. (*v.*) To reflect deeply; to ponder.

myth An imaginary story that has become an accepted part of the cultural or religious tradition of a group or society.

narrative A form of verse or prose (both fiction *and* nonfiction) that tells a story. A storyteller may use any number of *narrative devices*, such as skipping back and forth in time, ordering events chronologically, and ordering events to lead up to a suspenseful climax. Also see *frame*.

naturalism A term often used as a synonym for *realism*; also a view of experience that is generally characterized as bleak and pessimistic.

non sequitur A statement or idea that fails to follow logically from the one before.

objective (*adj.*) Of or relating to facts and reality, as opposed to private and personal feelings and attitudes. Its opposite is *subjective*.

ode A lyric poem usually marked by serious, respectful, and exalted feelings toward the subject.

Old English The Anglo-Saxon language spoken from approximately 450 to 1150 A.D. in what is now Great Britain.

omniscient narrator A narrator with unlimited awareness, understanding, and insight of characters, setting, background, and all other elements of the story.

onomatopoeia The use of words whose sounds suggest their meaning. Example: *bubbling, murmuring brooks.*

oxymoron A term consisting of contradictory elements juxtaposed to create a paradoxical effect. Examples: *loud silence, jumbo shrimp.*

parable A story consisting of events from which a moral or spiritual truth may be derived.

paradox A statement that seems self-contradictory but is nevertheless true.

parallel structure The structure required for expressing two or more grammatical elements of equal rank. Coordinate ideas, compared and contrasted ideas, and correlative constructions call for parallel construction. For example: Colleges favor applicants with *good academic records, varied interests,* and they should earn a high score on the AP exam. The underlined section of the sentence lacks the same grammatical form as the italicized phrases. To be correct, it should read *high scores.*

parody An imitation of a work meant to ridicule its style and subject.

paraphrase A version of a text put into simpler, everyday words or summarized for brevity.

pastoral A work of literature dealing with rural life.

pathetic fallacy Faulty reasoning that inappropriately ascribes human feelings to nature or nonhuman objects.

pathos That element in literature that stimulates pity or sorrow.

pedantic Narrowly academic instead of broad and humane; excessively petty and meticulous.

periodic sentence A sentence that departs from the usual word order of English sentences by expressing its main thought only at the end. In other words, the particulars in the sentence are presented before the idea they support. See also *loose sentence*.

persona The role or facade that a character assumes or depicts to a reader or other audience.

personification A figure of speech in which objects and animals are given human characteristics.

plot The interrelationship among the events in a story; the *plot line* is the pattern of events, including exposition, rising action, climax, falling action, and resolution.

point of view The relation in which a narrator or speaker stands to a subject of discourse. A matter discussed in the first person has an *internal* point of view; an observer uses an *external* point of view.

predicate The part of a sentence that is not the grammatical subject. It often says something about the subject. A noun that provides another name for the subject is called a *predicate nominative*, as in:

> *Lynn* (subject) is the *president* (predicate nominative) of the company.

An adjective that describes the subject is called *a predicate adjective*, as in:

> *Harold* (subject) is *courageous* (predicate adjective).

prose Any discourse that is not poetry. A *prose poem* is a selection of prose that, because of its language or content, is poetic in nature.

proverb A short pithy statement of a general truth that condenses common experience into memorable form. See also *adage* and *maxim*.

pseudonym A false name or alias used by writers.

pulp fiction Novels written for mass consumption, often emphasizing exciting and titillating plots.

pun A humorous play on words, using similar-sounding or identical words to suggest different meanings.

realism The depiction of people, things, and events as they really are without idealization or exaggeration for effect. See also *naturalism*.

rebuttal or **refutation** The part of discourse wherein opposing arguments are anticipated and answered.

reiteration Repetition of an idea using different words, often for emphasis or other effect.

repetition Reuse of the same words, phrases, or ideas for rhetorical effect, usually to emphasize a point.

retraction The withdrawal of a previously stated idea or opinion.

rhetoric The language of a work and its style; words, often highly emotional, used to convince or sway an audience.

rhetorical mode A general term that identifies discourse according to its chief purpose. Modes include *exposition* (to explain, analyze, or discuss an idea), *argumentation* (to prove a point or to persuade), *description* (to recreate or present with details), and *narration* (to relate an anecdote or story).

rhetorical question A question to which the audience already knows the answer; a question asked merely for effect with no answer expected.

rhetorical stance Language that conveys a speaker's attitude or opinion with regard to a particular subject.

rhyme The repetition of similar sounds at regular intervals, used mostly in poetry but not unheard of in prose.

rhythm The pattern of stressed and unstressed syllables that make up speech and writing.

romance An extended narrative about improbable events and extraordinary people in exotic places.

sarcasm A sharp, caustic attitude conveyed in words through jibes, taunts, or other remarks; sarcasm differs from *irony*, which is more subtle.

satire A literary style used to poke fun at, attack, or ridicule an idea, vice, or foible, often for the purpose of inducing change.

sentence structure The arrangement of the parts of a sentence. A sentence may be *simple* (one subject and one verb), *compound* (two or more independent clauses joined by a conjunction), or *complex* (an independent clause plus one or more dependent clauses). Sentences may also contain any of these structures in combination with each other. Each variation leaves a different impression on the reader, and along with other rhetorical devices, may create a countless array of effects.

sentiment A synonym for *view* or *feeling*; also a refined and tender emotion in literature.

sentimental A term that describes characters' excessive emotional response to experience; also nauseatingly nostalgic and mawkish.

setting An environment that consists of time, place, historical milieu, and social, political, and even spiritual circumstances.

simile A figurative comparison using the words *like* or *as*. Example: She sings *like a canary*.

stream of consciousness A style of writing in which the author tries to reproduce the random flow of thoughts in the human mind.

style The manner in which an author uses and arranges words, shapes ideas, forms sentences, and creates a structure to convey ideas.

stylistic devices A general term referring to diction, syntax, tone, figurative language, and all other elements that contribute to the "style" or manner of a given piece of discourse.

subject complement The name of a grammatical unit that is comprised of *predicate nominatives* and *predicate adjectives*.

subjective (*adj.*) Of or relating to private and personal feelings and attitudes as opposed to facts and reality. Its opposite is *objective*.

subtext The implied meaning that underlies the main meaning of an essay or other work.

syllogism A form of deductive reasoning in which given certain ideas or facts, other ideas or facts must follow, as in *All men are mortal; Mike is a man; therefore, Mike is mortal*.

symbolism The use of one object to evoke ideas and associations not literally part of the original object. Example: The American flag may symbolize freedom, the 50 states, and the American way of life, among many other things.

synecdoche A figure of speech in which a part signifies the whole (*fifty masts* for *fifty ships*) or the whole signifies the part (*days* for *life*, as in *He lived his days under African skies*). When the name of a material stands for the thing itself, as in *pigskin* for *football*, that, too, is synecdoche.

syntax The organization of language into meaningful structure; every sentence has a particular syntax, or pattern of words.

theme The main idea or meaning, often an abstract idea upon which an essay or other form of discourse is built.

thesis The main idea of a piece of discourse; the statement or proposition that a speaker or writer wishes to advance, illustrate, prove, or defend.

tone The author's attitude toward the subject being written about. The tone is the characteristic emotion that pervades a work or part of a work—the spirit or quality that is the work's emotional essence.

tragedy A form of literature in which the hero is destroyed by some character flaw or by a set of forces that cause the hero considerable anguish.

transition A stylistic device used to create a link between ideas. Transitions often endow discourse with continuity and coherence.

trope The generic name for a figure of speech such as image, symbol, simile, and metaphor.

understatement A restrained statement that departs from what could be said; a studied avoidance of emphasis or exaggeration, often to create a particular effect.

verbal irony A discrepancy between the true meaning of a situation and the literal meaning of the written or spoken words.

verse A synonym for poetry; also a group of lines in a song or poem; also a single line of poetry.

verisimilitude Similar to the truth; the quality of realism in a work that persuades readers that they are getting a vision of life as it is or could have been.

voice The real or assumed personality used by a writer or speaker. In grammar, *active voice* and *passive voice* refer to the use of verbs. A verb is in the active voice when it expresses an action performed by its subject. A verb is in the passive voice when it expresses an action performed upon its subject or when the subject is the result of the action.

> ACTIVE: The crew raked the leaves.
> PASSIVE: The leaves were raked by the crew.

Stylistically, the active voice leads to more economical and vigorous writing.

whimsy An object, device, or creation that is fanciful or rooted in unreality.

wit The quickness of intellect and the power and talent for saying brilliant things that surprise and delight by their unexpectedness; the power to comment subtly and pointedly on the foibles of the passing scene.

Index

Success on Advanced Placement Tests Starts with Help from Barron's

Each May, thousands of college-bound students take one or more Advanced Placement Exams to earn college credits—and for many years, they've looked to Barron's, the leader in Advanced Placement test preparation. You can get Barron's user-friendly manuals for 22 different AP subjects, most with optional CD-ROMs. Every Barron's AP manual gives you—

- **Diagnostic tests**
- **Extensive subject review**
- **Full-length model AP exams**
- **Study help and test-taking advice**

Model exams are designed to reflect the actual AP exams in question types, subject matter, length, and degree of difficulty. All questions come with answers and explanations. All books are paperback.

AP: Art History, w/optional CD-ROM
Book: ISBN 978-0-7641-3737-2, 448 pp.
Book w/CD-ROM: ISBN 978-0-7641-9463-4

AP: Biology, 2nd Ed., w/optional CD-ROM
Book: ISBN 978-0-7641-3677-1, 496 pp.
Book w/CD-ROM: ISBN 978-0-7641-9327-9

AP: Biology Flash Cards
ISBN 978-0-7641-7868-9, 504 cards

AP: Calculus, 9th Ed., w/optional CD-ROM
Book: ISBN 978-0-7641-3679-5, 672 pp.
Book w/CD-ROM: ISBN 978-0-7641-9328-6

AP: Calculus Flash Cards
ISBN 978-0-7641-9421-4, 300 cards

AP: Chemistry, 4th Ed., w/optional CD-ROM
Book: ISBN 978-0-7641-3685-6, 688 pp.
Book w/CD-ROM: ISBN 978-0-7641-9329-3

AP: Chemistry Flash Cards
ISBN 978-0-7641-6116-2, 500 cards

AP: Chinese Language and Culture, w/Audio CD
ISBN 978-0-7641-9400-9, 592 pp.

AP: Computer Science Levels A and AB, 4th Ed., w/optional CD-ROM
Book: ISBN 978-0-7641-3709-9, 736 pp.
Book w/CD-ROM: ISBN 978-0-7641-9350-7

AP: English Language and Composition, 2nd Ed., w/optional CD-ROM
Book: ISBN 978-0-7641-3690-0, 224 pp.
Book w/CD-ROM: ISBN 978-0-7641-9330-9

AP: English Literature and Composition, 2nd Ed., w/optional CD-ROM
Book: ISBN 978-0-7641-3682-5, 416 pp.
Book w/CD-ROM: ISBN 978-0-7641-9331-6

AP: Environmental Science, 3rd Ed.
ISBN 978-0-7641-4052-5, 504 pp.
Book w/CD-ROM: ISBN 978-0-7641-9565-5

AP: Environmental Science Flash Cards
ISBN 978-0-7641-9599-0, 500 cards

AP: European History, 4th Ed., w/optional CD-ROM
Book: ISBN 978-0-7641-3680-1, 336 pp.
Book w/CD-ROM: ISBN 978-0-7641-9332-3

AP: French w/Audio CDs, 3rd Ed., w/optional CD-ROM
Book w/3 audio CDs: ISBN 978-0-7641-9337-8, 464 pp.
Book w/3 audio CDs and CD-ROM:
ISBN 978-0-7641-9336-1

AP: Human Geography, 2nd Ed.
ISBN 978-0-7641-3817-1, 336 pp.

AP: Human Geography Flash Cards
ISBN 978-0-7641-9598-3, 500 cards

AP: Italian Language and Culture, w/Audio CDs, 2nd Ed.
ISBN 978-0-7641-9368-2, 448 pp.

AP: Microeconomics/Macroeconomics, 3rd Ed.
ISBN 978-0-7641-3930-7, 360 pp.

AP: Physics B, 4th Ed., w/optional CD-ROM
Book: ISBN 978-0-7641-3706-8, 476 pp.
Book w/CD-ROM: ISBN 978-0-7641-9351-4

AP: Physics C, 2nd Ed.
ISBN 978-0-7641-3710-5, 768 pp.

AP: Psychology, 3rd Ed., w/optional CD-ROM
Book: ISBN 978-0-7641-3665-8, 320 pp.
Book w/CD-ROM: ISBN 978-0-7641-9324-8, 320 pp.

AP: Psychology Flash Cards
ISBN 978-0-7641-9613-3, 400 cards

AP: Spanish w/Audio CDs, 6th Ed., and w/optional CD-ROM
Book w/3 audio CDs: ISBN 978-0-7641-9406-1, 448 pp.
Book w/3 audio CDs and CD-ROM:
ISBN 978-0-7641-9405-4

AP: Statistics, 4th Ed., w/optional CD-ROM
Book: ISBN 978-0-7641-3683-2, 560 pp.
Book w/CD-ROM: ISBN 978-0-7641-9333-0

AP: Statistics Flash Cards
ISBN 978-0-7641-9410-8, 500 cards

AP: U.S. Government and Politics, 8th Ed., w/optional CD-ROM
Book: ISBN 978-0-7641-3820-1, 510 pp.
Book w/CD-ROM: ISBN 978-0-7641-9404-7

AP: U.S. Government and Politics Flash Cards
ISBN 978-0-7641-6121-6, 400 cards

AP: U.S. History Flash Cards
ISBN 978-0-7641-7837-5, 500 cards

AP: U.S. History, 8th Ed., w/optional CD-ROM
Book: ISBN 978-0-7641-3684-9, 496 pp.
Book w/CD-ROM: ISBN 978-0-7641-9334-7

AP: World History, 8th Ed., w/optional CD-ROM
Book: ISBN 978-0-7641-3822-5, 512 pp.
Book w/CD-ROM: ISBN 978-0-7641-9403-0

AP: World History Flash Cards
ISBN 978-0-7641-7906-8, 400 cards

Please visit **www.barronseduc.com** to view current prices and to order books

The following documentation applies if you purchased
AP English Language and Composition, 2nd Edition with CD-ROM.
Please disregard this information if your version does not contain the CD-ROM.

SYSTEM REQUIREMENTS

This program will run on a PC with:
Windows® Intel® Pentium II 450 MHz
or faster processor, 128MB of RAM
1024 × 768 display resolution
Windows 2000, XP, Vista
CD ROM Player

This program will run on a Macintosh® with:
PowerPC® G3 500MHz or faster
128MB of RAM
1024 × 768 display resolution
Mac OS X v.10.1 through 10.4
CD ROM Player

INSTALLATION INSTRUCTIONS

The product is not installed on the end-user's computer; it is run directly from the CD Rom. Barron's CD-ROM includes an "autorun" feature that automatically launches the application when the CD is inserted into the CD drive. In the unlikely event that the autorun features are disabled, alternate launching instructions are provided below.

Windows®:
Insert the CD-ROM. The program will launch automatically. If it doesn't launch automatically:
1. Click on the Start button and choose "Run."
2. Browse to the CD-ROM drive. Select the file **AP_English_Language_and_Composition.exe** and click "Open."

Macintosh®:
1. Insert the CD-ROM.
2. Double-click the CD Rom icon.
3. Double-click the file **AP_English_Language_and_Composition** to start the program.